ALSO BY JOSEPH D. COLLEA, JR.

The First Vermont Cavalry in the Civil War, A History

New York and The Lincoln Specials: President Lincoln's Pre-Inaugural and
Funeral Trains Cross the Empire State

OUR TOWN—ILION, NEW YORK:

A Selective Look at 300 Years of History

JOSEPH D. COLLEA, JR

DEDICATION

The late Ron Jensen, Joe Short, Alan Staring, and Dave Whalen were not all acquainted. Though contemporaries, to my knowledge the four were never together...save in two instances. For a time, they were once inhabitants of Ilion, and now the four collectively remain forever in my heart and mind. In addition to their community residence, they shared two other commonalities—all four were close friends of mine who left us way too soon; and the quartet were Ilionites to the core, having spent their youth on its streets and ballfields, graduated from IHS, shopped in its stores, and lived large parts...if not all...of their adult lives in the village.

Affable, hard-working, and unassuming, they were the kind of people whom we often reference as being "nice guys" and "the salt of the earth." In conducting my research for this book, they would have served as valuable resources about our town as each one knew it. Hopefully, they would have been pleased with the outcome.

For those of us in the winters of our lives, one of the downsides we must cope with daily is the growing absence of people and places that were once so much a part of our existences. Like many of you, I too miss "old Ilion." Like all of you, I lament the loss of family, neighbors, and friends who have gone on ahead. To your memories of that village and all those individuals whom you too count among the dearly departed—like Ron, Joe, Alan, and Dave— this book is dedicated.

CONTENTS

PREFACE

In sorting through three-hundred years of village history, a mix of deliberate triaging and personal preferences of necessity came into play. In a sense, these two perspectives offered conflicting outcomes. Should the author sift through centuries of people, places, and events and then write only about those deemed the most important? Or should he focus on topics which were of the greatest interest to him? In both instances, important mitigating factors that impacted the final choices were available time and resources.

By virtue of yours truly growing older by the day, finishing this book turned into a race against my biological clock. Not knowing when its final tick would sound imparted a sense of urgency to my research and writing. An all-consuming project, the book's completion took on the personal quest the likes of climbing Mt. Everest or searching for the *Titanic* has held for others. In the back of my mind every day was the observation made by Luther Whitney—Clint Eastwood's character in the movie *Absolute Power*—that "tomorrow is promised to no one." But in the end, the news was good. For, if you are reading these words, then you know that my time lasted long enough to complete the project.

After maintaining my longevity, the other crucial matter was that of finding useful material. Regardless of how interesting a given topic might seem in theory, locating sufficient information to flesh-out a chapter was not always possible. Local libraries and historical societies are certainly key places in which to conduct searches; however, though their holdings are often quite extensive, a certain degree of randomness and chance unfortunately pervades what materials wound up in their collections.

For researchers, no matter how earnest and thorough their efforts are, an element of luck nevertheless is needed. First, the information sought must have existed at some point in time, be it in a letter, a newspaper, magazine, or book. Then, a repository must have gained possession of these relevant materials, and finally the researcher/writer must discover them.

Working within these parameters guided me in selecting the chapters which appear in this book. But a disclaimer is in order here: by no means is this intended as an all-inclusive volume. Other authors, tackling the same goal, could produce works comprised of entirely dissimilar subject matter. Still a history of Ilion, their focus might chronicle much different aspects of the village's past, such as detailed profiles of its industrial, commercial, or social development. If someone chose to mirror the format of this book, more than enough material exists to fill several additional volumes.

One important understanding about the topics chosen and the way they were framed was my desire to not write disparagingly of fellow Ilionites and the decisions which they made either in the distant past or in more recent years with respect to village matters. Revisionist history has never been my cup of tea. Therefore, this book is neither meant to be a hard-hitting exposé nor a critique of mistakes our forefathers made. If anything, this volume is generally intended as a collection of pleasant reflections, one awash with nostalgia and compiled as a scrapbook of fascinating and informative stories of the village's past.

In the pursuit of these goals, no discussion of our town's history would be complete without a tip of the hat the late Harold Whittemore and H. Paul Draheim. Over the course of many years,

these two individuals—writing for various area newspapers—
religiously produced detailed columns chock-full of stories about
people, events, and places in not only Ilion but the surrounding area.
As such, they have provided excellent sources of historical anecdotes
that are invaluable to writers who have followed them.

Our Town—Ilion, New York: A Selective Look at 300 Years of
History represents the culmination of my research into topics that
interested me and in turn hopefully proved likewise to you. My desires
for the outcome were three-fold. The first was to present a gift to the
people who spent some or all their lives in this community,
individuals to whom the village holds a special place in their hearts.
The next objective was for the book to serve as a memorial to those
who over the years helped the town to prosper and grow. Finally,
above all else, my intent was not simply to produce a history of the
village, but also to create an incarnation that preserves a treasure, one
personally more valuable and much dearer to us than the riches that
King Solomon's mines ever yielded—a book of our memories.

INTRODUCTION

"Where we love is home—home that our feet may leave, but not our hearts."[1]

— OLIVER WENDELL HOLMES, SR.

Among the words in the English language heavy with sentimentality, "home" is one with connotations that evokes thoughts and feelings carried with us for a lifetime. The same applies to "hometown." For some, the two terms are often seen as synonymous and interchangeable in context. In a sense, we all have two designations for our residences—one denoted by a street address and the other by a zip code. Understandably, each of our respective home lives—the one unfolded at the street address—are quite unique and varied, and more than any single element goes a long way in defining who we are. Still, another factor influences the development of each one of us.

This existential contributor is the place where we grew up—as identified by a zip code. Living in one of the boroughs of New York City, a rural village in the Southern Tier, or in a small upstate town in central New York also factors heavily into shaping who we are. Individual beliefs and values are often profoundly influenced by the setting that nurtured them—outside forces beyond the home and family that can have an impact all their own. Comprised of people, places, events, and experiences, the local environments surrounding our houses help to shape our lives in ways that our families could not. Each succeeding generation—in a sense passing through town like its predecessors--is exposed to that communal milieu, one that leaves an indelible imprint on the personal growth of its inhabitants.

Nevertheless, even with that common ground, no two of us possess precisely the same set of mental images about our hometowns. Since none of us have had the same experiences, we all have individual histories. Depending upon the years in which we may have lived in the same town, our memories are shaped by the circumstances at the time. Some of us attended the pre-fire high school in Ilion, while our grandchildren are now taught in a third expansion and refurbishing of the building and grounds first reconstructed since that terrible night over fifty years ago. Some can recall seeing movies at the Capitol Theater, while the current generation watches Netflix at home. Some of us played Little League baseball, whereas today youth football and soccer are popular options. Like our own images in a mirror, the face of a village also changes over time.

But, for all the differences that may occur from one generation to the next, whenever old friends meet at class reunions, perhaps the most-spoken phrase crossing over the decades begins: "Do you remember...?" Bring together graduates from different years at a mega-reunion, and the discussion can become a local history lesson. Spontaneous exchanges that follow often lead to comparisons of what once was likened to that which now is. Probably, the most compelling breakpoint for appraisals of Ilion is often that between the pre-and post-urban renewal village. Almost five decades ago now, in one fell swoop wholesale changes were wrought on a key portion of the community. Yet, considering its physical impact, the area involved was relatively small, perhaps less than a half-square mile in total.

While the outcome of this multi-year project represented a profound transformation, the fact remains that the larger part of the village did not undergo any radical alterations when the central core did. This does not, however, preclude other areas of the community from undergoing changes that have occurred over the passage of time. For example, in the last sixty or so years, West Hill, East Frankfort, North Street, and Annunciation Schools have all closed. Remington Arms has both outsourced and downsized its local operation. The Moose Club has ceased to exist. The public library now offers its patrons online access, dvd's, and books on cd's. The Sugarbowl sliding venue in Russell Park is overgrown with trees and underbrush. Each of these changes, modifications, or eliminations has affected various members of the community in different ways.

In some instances overtly, while at other times with subtlety, the lives of residents were nevertheless summarily altered. Not everyone always agreed with or wanted these changes, but they came by way of various means such as governmental fiat, lack of interest, fiscal necessity, or technological innovation being motivators. But with or without unanimous support in all cases, the reality has been that any one of these and other changes could have impacted people. In the end, these alterations to the community have served to impart a different generational experience to the concept of what it means to have grown up in Ilion.

Collectively, all these permutations represent figurative pages in the history of the village. Whether they become literal pages depends upon a writer's interest in setting them to paper. Since the first settlers came in 1725, almost 300 years can be chronicled in telling the story from Ilion's earliest years down to its present status. Unfortunately, for all the books written by historians over the almost 250 years of our country's existence, certain genres—such as our Presidents, the American Revolution, and the Civil War for example— have received far more than their fair share of attention, generally to the exclusion of other interesting and worthy subjects. Local histories are one of those content areas that have often gotten the short end of the scholarly stick.

Ilion is a case point of this abject neglect. Written in 1977, only a single volume about this historic village exists—Warren Schulz's Ilion

—The Town That Remington Made. A couple of informative, oversized booklets were also produced, one celebrating the village's centennial in 1952 and the other its sesquicentennial in 2002. But sadly, these few editions represent the extent of any formal publications of an overarching, historical nature. Granted the public library contains an impressive wealth of primary source material, but, regardless of how interesting and fruitful a visit might be, most people are not inclined to spend hours cherry-picking through the mound of information on its shelves to learn about the village's past triumphs and tragedies.

The book which you hold in your hands is my attempt to share various aspects of Ilion's bygone days. Some topics are of a more recent vintage than others, and by no means is this compilation meant to be all-encompassing. For every topic that was chosen for inclusion, another had to be left out. This volume really amounts to nothing more than a first step—Volume I if you will.

The history of Ilion is rich, one of which we can all feel justifiably proud. There is a myriad of anecdotes to be told. As time goes by, many of these stories will fall deeper into the past, making them harder to trace and validate. As those who remember them first-hand pass on, vivid eye-witness accounts go with them. Without doubt, the urgency of compiling a local history in written form increases with every passing day. The alternative is to have it blurred or lost forever. While carrying fond memories in our hearts may buoy our personal spirits, committing our recollections to paper preserves them for posterity. Among the last of their many accomplishments and legacies that "baby-boomers" can leave for future generations is a record of life in Ilion during the 1950s and 1960s—a pivotal time in both the life of the village as well their own.

In writing this book, one of my intentions was to offer selected stories about the community's unique and interesting past. If reading its pages increases your knowledge about Ilion and in the process bolsters your civic pride, then a second of my aims has been accomplished. Finally, if others among you are motivated to join in on the preservation process in some way too, another objective will also be met. For without doubt, as most of you would hopefully agree with

Oliver Wendell Holmes and me, our hometown, regardless of the era in which we lived there, remains a very special place to us. As you revisit Ilion in the following pages, let the memories they evoke drift through your mind once more and hear in your head the words that Bruce Springsteen sang to his son: "...take a good look around, this is your hometown."[2]

I

EARLY SETTLEMENT:

BRAVING THE DANGERS OF THE FRONTIER

In the great timeline of urban settlement, three hundred years is not a long time—for instance, Athens, Greece was founded over 7,000 years ago, Luxor in Egypt 5,200, and Rome, Italy about 2,700. As for towns and cities in the Empire State, three hundred years is at about the mid-point of their ages—with New York over four hundred years old and Buffalo almost two hundred. Generally, places west of Ilion in the state are less than three centuries old and those farther to the east and south along the Hudson River have existed for more than three centuries Not surprisingly, Ilion occupies an important historical niche in the history of New York State.

Over the first sixty-plus years of European inroads into the Mohawk Valley, living in the vicinity of our present-day village meant that settlers resided on the frontier, daring to live at the extreme outpost of civilization in first the colony and later the state of New York. A hardy lot were these people. Imbued with independent stripes, they fended for themselves with little governmental support, braving the trials and tribulations with which Mother Nature and their fellow man often confronted them. Though dangers existed, living in central New York did have its selling points.

Being in the Mohawk Valley offered some degree of climatic

protection for those who chose to settle there, with extreme weather
vagilities such as hurricanes and tornadoes being anomalies that rarely beset the region. Winter conditions, while capable of producing an occasional blizzard, did not experience deep and prolonged cold spells.

The Mohawk Valley of central New York drew those brave and hardy enough to venture forth and establish new lives on the frontier. (Source: Library of Congress)

By virtue of the river running through its heart and the many streams that comprised its tributaries, the land was blessed with abundant, life-sustaining water for consumption and agriculture, even though the Mohawk River was known to flood the land along its banks. When springtime arrived, the thaws caused a valuable trade-off to occur, for its waters in receding left behind rich topsoil. Ownership of plots in this highly-desirable stretch of fertile lowland came legally into the hands of the area's first white settlers—known as Palatine Germans—in 1725.

Located in the southwest corner of what was then known as Albany County and later subdivided under the auspices of a royal grant into a parcel called the "Burnetsfield Patent," sections were earmarked for settlement. Ninety-four adventurous pioneers stepped forward and took advantage of the opportunity afforded them. What each head of a household or single individual received was a one-hundred-acre tract. Some parcels started at the Mohawk River and went south, while others lay to the north from the opposite bank. Most properties appeared on the map as long, narrow strips. Seizing this opportunity, members of this first generation of inhabitants cleared land in the vicinity of where some of their descendants a century-and-a-quarter later would incorporate a village named "Ilion."

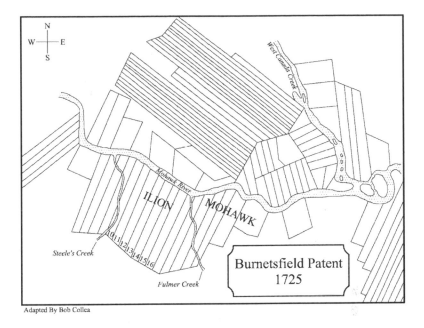

Adapted By Bob Collea

The motive that drove the Palatines to accept propositions offered first by the English crown and then later by the colonial government of New York was simple and pure. After decades of displacement and wandering unwanted across western Europe, they desired to own land of their own, places where they could live in peace and prosperity. After serving a period of indenture in return for passage to America, the Palatines next acceded to moving into the western end of the Mohawk Valley. While the Burnetsfield Patent came with no stated *quid pro quo*, the British authorities did have an ulterior motive. "The purpose of establishing settlements in the Mohawk Valley," wrote H. Paul Draheim, "was to create a barrier against sudden incursions by the French who had made this their road when they last attacked and burned the frontier town of Schenectady."[1] In effect, these innocent settlers were purposefully being placed in harm's way. While the danger was ever-present, their day of reckoning would not come for several decades.

While these Palatine Germans represented the initial band of permanent settlers in the vicinity of what became Ilion, they were in fact not the original people who had trod upon the flats, drank from the waters of its streams, walked the nearby forest pathways, and hunted for game up and down its hills and glens. This distinction belonged to Native Americans. The most recent among those indigenous people who preceded the influx of Europeans were members of the mighty Iroquois Confederacy. While no archeological discoveries have ever been made to indicate any villages or castles from the Pre-Columbia era in or near Ilion, evidence found in the 1920's indicated that native groups were undeniably once here.

Confirmation of their presence—most likely established as they passed through the area seeking food or scouting for enemies—came to light when an old tree was taken down during the third decade of the 20th century. Located at about the mid-point of what is now Arlington Avenue, even if the venerable old elm had not yielded some historically-significant artifacts, this arboreal growth of the *Ulmus Americans* species was memorable. For no mere sapling was this tree, but rather instead it was a sterling example of the extreme size which this species could attain—in this instance measuring a circumference of sixty-eight feet at its base with a branch spread said to be close to two-hundred feet across. Factoring-in its over one-hundred-foot height, and this tree presented one very imposing sight. The word "goliath" comes readily to mind.

When this long-time village landmark finally reached the end of its days and had to be taken down, the tree had one last gift to give the community. Though its legacy in being a giant among giants of its kind would live for several generations among those who had seen it, its bark revealed historical treasures that created a mystery. The presence of several hundred arrowheads imbedded deeply in the outer layers of its rough covering gave rise to the conclusion among many residents "...that the old elm witnessed a great deal of history-in-the-making."[2] Exactly why these hand-hewn pieces of flint happened to be there is unknown. Perhaps, in camping nearby for the night, Mohawk or Oneida warriors used the elm as either a target for marksmanship contests or possibly warm-ups prior to a raid.

While the Iroquois were known to build their villages on higher, more easily defended ground—in the proximity of water—the Ilion area was not a chosen site. Though upland terrain of West and Armory Hills would seem to offer good spots for a settlement, Native-American conclaves existed to the east and west below Little Falls in the former direction and near Oneida in the latter...but none have been found in the immediate vicinity of Ilion. The area around German Flatts apparently served as an undisturbed hunting preserve, as well as a buffer zone between the Mohawks and Oneidas, who even though allied as members of the Iroquois Nation nevertheless maintained separate tribal identities and turf.

According to Nelson Greene in his epic, four-volume History of the Mohawk Valley: Gateway to the West, "the Palatine setters of the German Flatts section had a period of peace for the greater part of thirty-five years ..."[3] Largely through the efforts of colonial officials in Albany and especially the work of British crown's lead agent, Sir William Johnson, the Iroquois had been kept mollified through various treaties, thus permitting the inroads of white settlement into the upper Mohawk Valley to be made without opposition.

Where life experienced trepidations for the residents of the region came most prominently for the first time during the French and Indian War. Fought between 1757 and 1763, this conflict was the fourth and last between England and France for control of North America. While the previous three wars had inflicted pain and suffering on the settlements to the east and west, the Palatines of German Flatts had been spared. However, in this final struggle, their luck ran out.

Anticipating that the shoe could drop at any moment, pioneer families on New York's frontier had prepared to defend themselves. "With the knowledge that they were in the wilderness and on the extreme edge of white man's habitation," columnist H. Paul Draheim noted, "the Palatines deemed it necessary and wise to establish defenses against hostile attacks, and so they set about building stockades or forts."[4] On November 12 of 1757, their worst fears materialized when a war party consisting of 300 French marines, Canadians, and Indians swept down into the upper valley. While their main target was the settlement at the site of present-day Herkimer, the wave of terror and destruction which these raiders perpetrated also encompassed the homes and farms that lay to the west along the river, which included in the devastation those outliers in the area that became latter-day Ilion.

The results of the surprise attack were that it "...killed 40, captured 150, and burned 60 houses, barns, and other buildings."[5] In Greene's appraisal of the aftermath, "the destruction wrought that day equaled that of any of the sectional raids of the Revolution."[6] The area west of Little Falls had been devastated. Fort Herkimer now marked the westernmost bastion of defense in the Mohawk Valley. Most of those settlers who had survived reluctantly, but wisely, relocated to east, as far as Albany in some cases where they remained until peace was restored six years later. Then, "with the war ending, at Burnetsfield," wrote historian Jane Bellinger, "the survivors returned and the many who had left their burned out homesteads returned to start anew....with hope, prayer, and hard work, they rebuilt their homes and barns, replenished their stock and prepared their fields for seed. Life was worth living again."[7]

The losses incurred because of the raid had been a severe blow to an area that had but a limited population and ended the prospects of any influx of new settlers for the immediate future; however, for those who survived, persevered, and came back, the Treaty of Fort Stanwix in 1763 provided the Palatines with another temporary interregnum of peace and prosperity. According to this benchmark agreement between the Iroquois and crown, lands east of the treaty line—which ran from present-day Rome south to and then along the Unadilla River to the Susquehanna in the southern portion of the colony of New York—the land to the east of the demarcation was available for exploitation by the colonists, while the expanse of wilderness to the west was reserved for Native American habitation.

Unfortunately, the period of tranquility was short-lived, for the year 1775 witnessed the return of political unrest. This time the combatants were the British pitted against an unruly faction of their disgruntled subjects in the thirteen colonies. Once again, residents of the upper Mohawk found themselves in an exposed, forward position. With the Iroquois, though possessing divided loyalties, situated to the west, substantial British forces based in Canada, and cadres of Tory or Loyalist forces recruited locally, enemy commanders had the necessary manpower to unleash raids against the rebels.

Given the chance to develop the land unmolested for twelve years, the population of the entire Mohawk Valley had ballooned to over 20,000 people at the start of the Revolution. With the heaviest concentration to the eastern or lower end of the valley, settlement by the war's outbreak stretched all the way to an outpost of thirty log cabins and a blockhouse at New Petersburg. Located on the north side of the Mohawk River, the little enclave lay only five miles west of the smattering of homes at German Flatts. In times of peace, these bold forays into the wilderness served as the tip of the spear for western settlement in New York and marked the frontier, circa 1775. Even though the Mohawk passageway offered a strategic water-level route to Albany, no army of British regulars was ever able to take advantage of this inviting corridor. As a part of the grandiose "Three-Point Plan" of 1777, a substantial force led by Colonel Barry St. Ledger tried, but its advance was stopped by American militiamen in the Battle of Oriskany.

Avoiding occupation by St. Leger's troops, however, did not spare the Mohawk Valley's patriots from living an edgy, tenuous existence during the remaining war years. As author Peter Silver described the situation for those living on the frontier, "they felt, with reason, that a horrible death could come at almost any time and from any direction."[8] Even if the British were unable to conquer the region, the means still existed within their power to sow terror and destruction. The method employed would be same as the French and Indians had used against the valley's settlers—hit-and-run raids. The results would be similar, the only difference being the composition of the attacking forces. This time around French troops were no longer involved, but their place alongside Indian allies was taken by Loyalists, many who had once been neighbors, friends, and in some instances even relatives of the very people whom they would be attacking.

Over the years of the Revolution, raids were conducted against various targets in the Mohawk Valley, mostly to the east of German Flatts. But the locals' run of good luck could not last forever. The feared hammer blow finally fell on September 17, 1778, when word was received that an enemy force was headed their way from the south. For immediate protection, the area around present-day Ilion had a blockhouse—like

Living in the Mohawk Valley made patriotic settlers vulnerable to attacks by enemy forces, necessitating the construction of protective sites where safety could be sought in the event of raids by Tory and Indian forces. (Source: Library of Congress)

other two-story structures located around the valley—in the vicinity of Catherine and East Clark Streets: however the log build was small and capable of withstanding assault only by a small war party. But given any advanced warning, the settlers had, as their best chance for survival against a sizable force, the hope of gaining Fort Dayton, located three miles to the east on the north side of the Mohawk River in the heart of what is now the village of Herkimer or heading eastward for ten miles where they could enter the protective stockade of Fort Herkimer on the Mohawk River's southern bank.

Before engaging in their depredations, the raiders camped for the night on the grounds of Shoemaker Tavern, an inn once located just within what are now the western village limits of present-day Mohawk, behind the spot along Route 5S where a dairy isle is now situated. Since its proprietor was a known Tory, the structure was one of the very few in the area that were spared the raiders' fiery torches and ultimately survived the war. But little else did. By the time the attackers were finished, they had "...burned 63 dwellings, 57 barns, 3 gristmills, 2 sawmills and killed or took off 235 horses, 220 horned cattle, 269 sheep, and 93 oxen."[9] The only gratifying outcome to these devastating results was that neither Fort Dayton nor Fort Herkimer was attacked, and the loss of life was limited to a pair of settlers.

These furtive, random, and wanton attacks, directed at farmers and their crops and livestock, were indicative of another motive by the

British. Since the Mohawk Valley had seen a substantial output of agricultural products to feed the Continental Army—long ago having earned the region the nickname of "Breadbasket of the Colonies"—it behooved King George's troops to disrupt this flow of sustenance. In this regard, where the upper Mohawk Valley was concerned, their sanguinary efforts were successful. Faced with prospect of continued raids, other than the garrisons of the two forts, most survivors had fled farther down the valley toward the more heavily populated and safer parts of the new state.

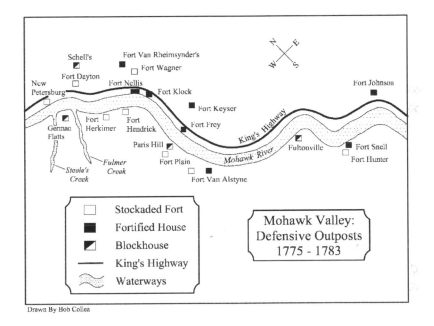

Drawn By Bob Collea

To protect vulnerable civilians from the devastating attacks of enemy forces, a chain of defensive sanctuaries were maintained along the valley. (Source: Ilion Free Public Library)

There, in locations to the east, these refugees would bide their time until the war ended. Then, after 1783, many of these settlers would return to the former homesteads to start over, though sadly not all were able to do so. According to one historian, "…one third of the population of the Mohawk Valley had been killed and that among those who remained were 2,000 orphaned children and 300 widows."[10]

Nevertheless, despite these substantial losses and accompanying heartache, the pioneering spirit residing in these former residents gave them the resolve to start anew. Along with a large infusion of new immigrants from Europe, the pre-war life in the upper valley not only picked up where it had left off, but in time also blossomed into a thriving portion of the state. The rest is history—the coming of the Erie Canal, the founding of new industries like Remington Arms, and the incorporation of communities such as the village of Ilion.

These advancements occurred over a relatively short time-frame, only sixty-nine years from the end of the Revolutionary War, and all were made possible by the pioneering spirit and Yankee ingenuity of those first generations of hardy settlers who persevered through the hardships of multiple wars to establish a life that was prosperous, enduring, and fulfilling. For those of us who call Ilion their hometown, we have our forefathers to thank for firmly planting the roots of our heritage almost 300 years ago and then their descendants for conscientiously sustaining them ever since.

2

PRESENT AT THE CREATION:

ELIPHALET REMINGTON FOUNDS A COMPANY

T he story of Remington Arms in Ilion is that of a personal project which evolved over time into an international business. One that can now—over 200 years later—proudly lay claim to the title of being "America's oldest gunmaker." However, the company's heritage is much broader than that limited assertion, for in fact Remington is one of America's longest-lived producers of any manufactured item.

Given the era in which the enterprise began, offering firearms for sale was certainly very much in line with the needs of the people. In 1816, when Eliphalet Remington fashioned his first rifle, the Revolutionary War and the devastating raids by Tories and Indians had ended but two generation ago. The War of 1812 was still quite fresh in everyone's mind, having only concluded the previous year. Few families in the vicinity had been free from the loss of a relative in these years of turmoil. In addition, wild animals still roamed the forests of New York. People were by nature ever-vigilant and wary, making gun ownership a key element in their sense of personal security and home defense.

The Remington's, however, had been spared the fear and anxiety that so many pioneer families in New York had endured in those turbulent years of the 18th century, for they had lived in the comparative safety of Connecticut. Then, in 1800 the elder Remington, Eliphalet I, brought his wife and children to the Empire State and settled them in the upper Barringer Road area, three miles to the south in the hills above what is now Ilion. From locally quarried rock, he raised a substantial stone house, so solidly-constructed that the building remains standing and inhabited to this very day. In addition, part of Mr. Remington's holdings encompassed 300 acres of land that extended east, all the way to the western rim of the Ilion gorge and then downslope to the banks of Steele Creek. It was on the lower location, at the easternmost tip of his property, that a blacksmith's shop—the humble precursor to a sprawling factory complex that would come later and become the dominating of the village of Ilion—was eventually located. But for the time being in 1816, the placement of a waterwheel in the stream provided Remington with a source of power to operate some of the machinery in his forge...and give birth to an industry.

The area in which Remington had chosen to settle was situated on the southern rim at the western end of the Mohawk Valley. Though still a frontier setting, the region was becoming less so with each passing day. As the barriers to settlement beyond Fort Stanwix—sited at would in time become the city of Rome—were removed by treaties with the Iroquois Nation, settlers began heading west. However, even if the dangers of war were over, the surrounding woods were still full of both game and predatory animals. A rifle was of necessity one of the primary possessions for most people. Furthermore, the newly enacted United States Constitution, along with its Bill of Rights, protected the ownership of firearms, primarily with the intent of allowing people to defend themselves against any future attempt at a hostile takeover by a foreign power or the evil machinations of their own government gone astray.

While the situation never got to the extreme of the Wild West, an often precarious environment wherein folks strode about with six-shooters strapped to their hips in open-carry fashion, a rifle standing beside the farmhouse door or hanging above the fireplace represented a commonplace piece of 18th and 19th century interior furnishing for American pioneers. Farmers working in their fields usually had a weapon propped against a nearby stump. Probably not needed on any given day, but always kept handy if the unexpected should arise.

Nor did the matter stop with simply owning a weapon. A fair degree of prowess in its use was also desirable. In a time before men could display their masculinity on a football field or baseball diamond, physical attributes were manifested in such ways as footraces, wrestling matches, and target-shooting. Occasions like "Independence Day" celebrations, "Militia Day" gatherings, and local harvest fairs provided excellent venues at which such friendly competitions were staged.

It was at one these get-togethers that twenty-three-year-old Eliphalet Remington II made an unforgettable impression. He arrived with a new flintlock rifle cradled in his arm. The firing mechanism of his weapon duplicated the standard method of the times: a chiseled piece of flint, approximately one-inch square with its front edge beveled and held in place by a screw-tightened locking device on the component commonly called a "hammer." Pulling the trigger released this hammer, causing it to strike an upright metal piece known as the "frizzen." Amidst a shower of sparks produced from the flint striking against its surface, the frizzen snapped backwards, simultaneously exposing a small pan of fine black powder. At this point, chance took over.

A gunmaker who came to have a worldwide market, Remington's first "factory" consisted of a simple stone building on the banks of Steele Creek. (Source: Ilion Free Public Library)

The expectation was for one of the sparks to ignite the powder in the pan, hopefully causing the resulting flame to flash through a hole bored into the adjacent barrel. If all went well, a secondary explosion occurred when a larger measure of gunpowder placed at the back end of the long metal tube—the barrel—ignited. In those occasional instances that the first ignition did not set off the second, the disappointing misfire gave rise to the adage "a flash in the pan." But when the dual discharges successfully occurred, the second, larger explosion then propelled a lead ball seated in the front of the charge. While the procedure was relatively rapid, a slight time lag did exist between the pan flash and the expulsion of the lead ball. For those not steeled to expect and ignore the initial explosion occurring virtually in their faces, shooters sometimes twitched or jumped—producing the "flintlock flinch"—and wasting a shot that usually proved far less than erring and ended up anywhere but on target.

From the beginning, Remington had the necessary blacksmithing facilities and acquired skills to make all of the metal and wooden pieces needed to fashion a rifle; however, one step that he was at the time unable to do for himself was to bore out and then rifle or groove the inside of the future gun's barrel. The first process created the hollow tube that was the barrel of the gun, while the latter process was the key to imparting greater accuracy to the flight of the soft lead bullet, that of cutting a spiraling groove along the inside of the barrel. To achieve these very important stages in the gun-making process required Remington to travel all the way to Utica to have his rifle barrels bored. This entailed a one-way journey which amounted to fifteen miles, carrying as many of the heavy metal bars on his shoulder as he could and returning with any that he might have previously dropped off.

At this juncture in his life, the young man could not possibly have anticipated what the future held in store for him. His immediate goal was to win a shooting contest. But the downside of that quest was a second-place finish and short-term disappointment; however, the upside that ultimately became a lifelong benefit was the attention that accrued to his homemade longarm. After many of his fellow competitors had asked to examine and heft his creation, their collective judgment held that the young man was indeed the maker of a quality weapon.

As other contestants soon learned, Remington's rifle was not just an old family relic that he had brought to the shoot. His flintlock was instead a beautiful piece of craftsmanship which the young man had painstakingly fashioned for himself at the family homestead. So much so did others admire his work that Remington soon received requests to fabricate one for them too. A blacksmith by trade, he began his gun-making business at a small forge on the Barringer Road farm.

Eliphalet II (Source: Ilion Sentinel)

In short order, this set-up proved insufficient to handle his growing list of orders. He subsequently relocated his enterprise to his father's new forge, one which was in a stone building situated near the banks of Steele Creek in what was then called the "Ilion Gulph." In the manner of the times, each of the ensuing rifles was produced individually, one part at a time. While each completed weapon looked strikingly like its predecessor, the components were not intended to be interchangeable among his other rifles. As one reporter described the process, "... piece after piece was produced, each one a pattern unto itself."[1] The coming of standardized parts was on the horizon, revolutionizing whole industries, but for now the production process remained painstakingly slow and exacting. Consistent with what often occurs in any successful start-up endeavor, the original enterprise by the creek soon proved insufficient to handle the volume of orders that had been steadily growing, as word of Remington's expertise in weapons' production spread. As interesting to note as it is hard to believe—considering the widespread proliferation of gun- ownership in the young nation— there was not a single, privately-owned manufacturing company producing such a line of weaponry existing anywhere in American at the turn of the eighteenth century. The way Remington made his guns at the time was the same process used among smithies in all the existing fifteen states—one piece at a time, one weapon at a time. However, a significant difference did manifest itself in that Eliphalet Remington became recognized for the high-quality of his workmanship, as compared that of competitors.

Over time, as orders increased, the budding businessman had important assessments to make about the future direction of his enterprise. This led to a pair of his early decisions aimed at enhancing production. One was the acquisition of a boring machine. With this piece of equipment, he could complete the process of making barrels on the premises, thus eliminating the time-consuming treks to and from Utica. The other was the relocation of his whole operation in 1828 from the creek bank in the gorge to a canal-side location that would in time place the new factory within the village limits of a town destined to be called "Ilion"...and fortuitously on the banks of the recently opened Erie Canal.

Pictures of his original flintlock and the forge he used to make the gun flank a portrait of Eliphalet II on a souvenir postcard sold at time of the 1916 centennial observance of the Remington Arms Company. (Source: Terrance J. Sweeney Collection)

Though Eliphalet Remington II would pass away in 1861, the company which he left behind—by then bearing the proud name of "E. Remington & Sons, Ilion, NY"—was about to enter a golden age of prosperity and overall manufacturing and sales acuity that would carry the company on into the next century and beyond. During the week of May 13, 1957, Remington Arms quietly celebrated a highlight in its manufacturing history: the production of a ten millionth gun...a notable milestone spotlighting a legacy for the company that had existed up to that time for one-hundred-and-forty-one years, after having started out with one man, one goal, and one rifle.

3

THE ERIE CANAL:

A LIFELINE FOR THE COMMUNITY

T o lie directly in the path of history, seeing its approach in what over time would become recognized as a life-changing event, and then be caught up in and borne along in the tidal wave of good fortune it created is not an opportunity most people are often afforded. However, just such an experience was introduced to thousands of New Yorkers between 1817 and 1825. Continuing its influence on for another half-century, the face of the central and western regions of their state were so significantly altered that its imprint can still be seen today.

The event in question was the opening of the Erie Canal. Once disparagingly called "Clinton's Ditch" and "Clinton's Folly" by its detractors, the brainchild of Governor DeWitt Clinton ultimately proved itself to be the complete antithesis of a failure, becoming known in the process as the "Grand Canal." That what amounted to a simple, unpretentious channel forty feet wide, four feet deep, and three-hundred-sixty-three miles long could have such a profound impact as to help solidify New York's claim as the "Empire State" would have seemed a highly improbable outcome when the project was first proposed. But, in the decades that followed the canal's opening, shining examples of the growth and prosperity wrought by this transportation artery abounded across the state.

Governor Dewitt Clinton (Source: New York Public Library)

Since the Mohawk Valley represented the only water-level gap in the Appalachian Mountain chain, the route had long been recognized as a viable corridor to the interior of New York. However, prior to the Revolutionary War, the ceding of lands beyond the valley to Native Americans for their exclusive use negated any need for a conduit into the western part of the growing colony. Much to the disappointment of the Iroquois Nation, however, the ground rules were changed once the conflict ended. White settlement was now allowed by treaty onto lands that were previously off-limits. Still, progress in moving out into what was the uninhabited part of the state was slow.

With horses, oxcarts, wagons, and stagecoaches being the primary means of transportation available, the size of the loads or number of passengers that could be carried was limited. While turnpike companies did get into the business of constructing improved roads, land travel was nevertheless slow and expensive. The Mohawk River was useful for transporting smaller loads, but by turning north and eventually terminating in the lower Adirondacks its value to shippers and travelers was limited to the valley corridor. Though settlers were able to slowly make their way westward—with many passing through our area long before it was officially named "Ilion"— their long trek took time. Regarding the development of an east-west, two-way trade conduit, cost proved an inhibiting factor.

But all of this was to change virtually overnight once the Erie Canal came into existence. As the two termini of the waterway—Albany in the east and Buffalo in the west—benefitted immensely from its opening, so also did countless communities in-between. Many hamlets became villages; some villages became cities. As the term "boom town" later came to describe places west of the Mississippi River, whose overnight growth came directly from their fortuitous location on the route of the Transcontinental Railroad or near a site where gold or silver was discovered, so also could such explosive development categorize the similar effect that the canal had on New York's heartland.

A microcosmic example of the Erie Canal's profound impact, one that changed the demography of a sizable portion of the state forever, can be observed in the metamorphosis of the village of Ilion from a small collection of scattered buildings to a sizable community with a substantial population and a diverse industrial base. Three years after the canal's construction was completed in 1825, the town consisted of a cluster of "seven dwellings, two storehouses, and a schoolhouse," a population of approximately fifty residents, and the name "Morgan's Landing."[1]

By 1870, the population had mushroomed to 2876 inhabitants—an increase fifty-seven times greater than it was forty-five years earlier. Many interrelated factors also helped the town's growth, such as the expansion of Remington's production capabilities and merchandizing line. Like the former Morgan's Landing—by then officially known as Ilion—many other communities in the post-canal-construction era grew in leaps and bounds, suggesting that the Erie was a contributing factor many times over. Interestingly, though the canal has long since been abandoned, "nearly 80% of upstate New York's population lives within 25 miles of the Erie Canal."[2]

To have lived in Morgan's Landing and witnessed the gradual insertion of the canal into the landscape and subsequently witnessed the rapid development of the village that followed must have been an exciting experience. For our forefathers who lived in the Age of Homespun, change was customarily a slow, gradual, and deliberate process. In an agrarian economy, the lifestyle of the people did not vary much from year-to-year beyond what the cycle of seasons annually brought. While occasional social activities such as going to church, attending local fairs, participating in militia days, engaging in turkey shoots, and celebrating the holidays helped relieve some of the boredom, the fact remained that the repetitive, taxing nature of the limited callings in which people lived out their working lives back then brought little deviation day-in and day-out, for however many decades might constitute an individual's earthly existence.

Then came the news that a state-wide canal was going to be built. Learning that the projected route called for the big dig to pass through German Flatts, about a half-mile to the south of the Mohawk River, had to have been an exhilarating revelation. As construction plans were drawn up and released, anticipation must have grown proportionately, especially once details about the exact nature of the route were made public. Though at the time Morgan's Landing had no "downtown," the pathway laid out did in fact run the waterway in the immediate vicinity of the settlement's few existing structures. Of those already built, several were farmhouses down near the flatlands closer to the river, and others were mills along Steele Creek near the tributary's junction with the Mohawk.

Once surveyors came through, delineating what was to be the canal bed, the few existing, manmade structures at Morgan's Landing did not pose any impediments to the desired route. But once the canal opened, all types of business and residential establishments sprang up along the channel. On one side, facilities were often situated right up to the water's edge, while on the opposite bank structures were set back twenty feet to allow a right-of-way for the towpath.

For the residents of Morgan's Landing proper and those living on the flats along the river, the long-awaited excavation for their section of the canal did not begin until late in 1820. By this time, the stretch between Utica and Rome to the immediate west had been operating for two years, giving area residents a sneak preview of what the completed system would look like. Since the channel east from Utica through the valley to Little Falls was over level terrain, the digging progressed quickly. With no need for locks or extensive aqueducts, this section was finished and opened in 1821. The only unusual canal-related feature was a drydock, necessary for boat repairs, which was constructed in the just beyond the western boundary of present-day Ilion.

Also in evidence was the piecemeal approach to construction which was practiced in building the waterway. Rather than have one large army of workers digging their way across the state in a single continuous advance like an army of ants, the procedure in place was to offer different portions of the excavation to local contractors and then link up these adjoining subsections as they were completed, relying on the skills of surveyors to keep the differing portions aligned. Depending upon their availability in each sector, every effort was made to hire laborers who lived in the area where a construction phase was in progress. If the numbers coming forth were insufficient, then Irish immigrants were readily obtainable from a virtually limitless supply.

For the people living along the newly completed excavation, the eagerly-anticipated news eventually came: the grand opening of the waterway was set for October 26, 1825! After eight years under construction, the expenditure of seven million dollars, and the ridicule of the nay-sayers, Governor DeWitt Clinton—the canal's unwavering supporter—could be excused the indulgence of orchestrating a grandiose celebration to inaugurate the opening of the canal. In a specially assembled flotilla, he intended to lead a procession from one end of the engineering marvel to the other and beyond. The starting point was designated as Buffalo, and, eight days later, the harbor of New York City would bear witness to its conclusion. Even the master showman of a later era, P. T. Barnum—a man to whom hoopla was second nature—would have marveled at the extravaganza that His Excellency put together.

The festivities commenced on the shores of Lake Erie at 9:00 o'clock on Wednesday morning, the 26 of October. After a brief waterfront ceremony, the *Seneca Chief*, serving as the royal barge for the governor, entered the canal. This simple act, one that commenced a triumphal journey, triggered a series of unique announcements. Since this was still the pre-telegraph era, communicating the kickoff of the voyage in timely fashion to the rest of the state posed a problem. However, this conundrum was eventually resolved in a novel way.

Artillery pieces were placed at ten-mile intervals from Buffalo east to Albany and then south to New York City. Once the report of the first cannon reached the waiting ears of the next gun crew, they fired their piece. In a chain reaction, the sounds of cannon fire reverberated across the Great Lakes Plain, through the Mohawk Valley, and then down the Hudson to the shores of the Atlantic Ocean. Eighty minutes after the first shot was touched off, the last cannon was belching flame. As Morgan's Landing was 213 miles from Buffalo, twenty-one of the big guns had to sound forth before the news of the canal's opening reached the ears of residents. With respect to Morgan's Landing, the nearest cannon to the west was placed on Frankfort Hill, while to the east the next piece of artillery was positioned near Fort Herkimer church. Then, to acknowledge that the glad tidings had been received, all the artillery pieces subsequently repeated the consecutive-firings process in reverse order north than west back to Buffalo.

Once opened, the Erie Canal soon became a reliable thoroughfare, north and south of which Ilion grew. Main Street and its intersection with West Street were on the opposite or south side of this row of buildings. In the foreground is towpath. (Source: Ilion Free Public Library)

Once the governor's road show—or more correctly "canal show"—

left Buffalo, he and his entourage were treated to a series of spectacular welcomes in the various villages and cities along their waterborne parade's route. Bands, fireworks, speeches, and banquets all contributed to the festive air surrounding the arrival of the dignitaries in Rochester, Syracuse, and Utica, as well as the smaller communities in-between. It was not until Monday, October 31, that the convoy of packet boats left Utica and started down the Mohawk Valley. Up ahead, folks began gathering along the canal, excitedly awaiting the flotilla's passage.

Then, after a couple of hours—for canal boats traveled at the slumber-inducing rate of four miles per hour—the boats passed through the enclave that would become Ilion. First came the vessel bearing the canal's proudest benefactor—DeWitt Clinton. With his packet pulled by four gray horses, the chief executive of the state smiled and waved at his constituents. In addition to the governor and the splendor of his floating chariot, spectators could also see the two, highly-publicized wooden kegs sitting conspicuously on the deck. Richly decorated with colorful eagles, this pair of small casks contained water drawn from Lake Erie. When the *Seneca Chief* reached New York City, the plan was to open the barrels and pour their contents into the Atlantic Ocean. This dramatic gesture was intended to represent the union of the lake and the sea at opposite ends of the state—a symbolic "wedding of the waters" compliments of the Erie Canal.

While not visible to spectators, the *Seneca Chief* carried not only the governor's entourage, but also a relevant cargo. To symbolize the trade that was now possible, stowed in her hold were products assembled from the western hinterlands made accessible by the canal. Included in the variety of goods with which she was laden were found: "...pot ashes, from Detroit, Sandusky, Erie, and Buffalo; white fish, from Lake Erie; flour and butter, from Michigan, Ohio, and Buffalo; and some bird's eye maple, and cedar wood..."[3] The point of carrying these regional products was to tout the trade possibilities the Erie Canal was going to engender. Before long, vessels would pass through the future Morgan's Landing in both directions, indicative of the lucrative two-way trade that the canal had fostered.

Following in the wake of the governor's ride came many other boats. Among these were vessels bearing names tied in some way to the history of the newly-accessed region: *Superior, Commodore Perry, Buffalo, Niagara,* and *Young Lion of the West.* On board, as honored guests, were a gaggle of dignitaries, various people who had played roles in bringing the canal from the drawing board to fruition.

Next to the packet bearing the governor, the boat that drew a large share of attention was a vessel called *Noah's Ark.* Amounting to a traveling zoo, the boat "...held a motley cargo of fauna from the west, consisting of birds, beasts, 'creeping things,' a bear, two eagles, two fawns, several fish, and two Indian boys in the dress of their nation."[4]

For the people of the future of Morgan's Landing as well as those multitudes in countless other communities across the state—individuals whose life cycles held little more than daily expectations of unending hard work—their constant striving to keep the wolf from the door made for an existence with few distractions and deviations from their normal routines. So, for them, the opening of the canal and the accompanying falderal were welcomed events. The arrival of the governor's packet was a thrilling sight. Seeing DeWitt Clinton in the flesh was far from an everyday occurrence for folks living in rural New York. Cadwallader Colden, a New York politician and friend of Governor Clinton's, was aboard one of the boats and observed first-hand the passing scene: "From Utica to Little Falls, a distance of 23 miles, the country is rich and populous...hundreds of yeomen flocked to the banks of the canal, and where groups were collected did not fail to send forth a cordial and loud huzza..."[5]

Yet, for all the pageantry that attended this memorable occasion, it amounted to little more than a momentary observance, one so long anticipated that passed like the snap of a finger. But even if fleeting, this once-in-a-lifetime event gave folks all along the canal a topic to discuss and relive for weeks and months to come—and preserve forever in their minds as one of those special stories to share with generations yet unborn.

What no one could not have known in Morgan's Landing, Utica, Syracuse, Rochester and all the other places through which the Erie Canal wound wind its way was the immediate and lasting impact that this engineering marvel was going to have on their lives and the future of their communities, state, and nation. Assuredly the governor had a vision, but only time would give his dream validation. When that day came, no longer would the 4' by 40' channel be derisively called "Clinton's Folly" by doubting Thomas's. Instead, people would look at the growth and prosperity around them and speak with reverence of what the "Grand Canal" had wrought.

Virtually overnight, the long ribbon of water had opened a window on the world for people who would otherwise have spent their earthly days in a state of semi-isolation, possessing but a limited knowledge of distant events and far-away places. In just "the second year of its existence," observed the late Warren Schulz in his book Ilion—The Town Remington Made, "...the average number of canal boats passing the site of Ilion was seventy per day."[6] On board the passenger packets were a variety of individuals, most of them traveling in an outbound direction. Some were immigrants from Europe, heading into western New York and beyond to start new lives; others were businessmen from eastern cities seeking to set up a profitable trade by establishing connections with local entrepreneurs located in the interior of the state, places where none was all that feasible before the opening of the canal.

For the freighters, on the other hand, who also came to ply this inland waterway, the canal represented a two-way proposition. From the upstate region, crops grown by yeomen farmers and product's manufactured by fledgling industries like that of the Remington's found their way to Albany, New York City,

"The Wedding of the Waters"
(Source: New York City Public Library)

and beyond, while in return came finished goods from American cities and foreign markets alike. "The Erie Canal was in fact the key that opened the Mohawk Valley to industrialization," was the conclusion drawn by Alden Hatch in his Remington Arms: An American History, "and changed its little mills and hand-work foundries into big business with a national distribution."[7] For Ilion, physical growth in its size became an immediate result of the presence of the waterway. New businesses were established to service the canal such as taverns, hostelries, trading posts, and a drydock. One of the larger supporting enterprises spawned was the coal company of A. A. Morgan, which had a series of sheds located between the southern bank of the Erie and Main Street. From this facility's bunkers, fuel was transported to meet the increasingly voracious needs of Remington Arms.

Of all the businesses which profited from the new mode of transportation available in Ilion, no better example existed than that of Ilion's soon-to-be world famous gunmaker. Realizing the advantage that the canal would come to offer in terms of bringing in raw materials and shipping out his finished product, Eliphalet Remington II moved his operation from the Ilion gorge to the banks of the Erie. While the canal is gone, Remington remains in the same location to which it was moved over two hundred years ago.

Most of the accolades that the Erie Canal earned attested to the wide-spread economic benefits which it brought, though its social/cultural impacts should not be overlooked. Being the heartline and highway that it was, people gravitated toward its banks. Sometimes the pursuit was just to watch the passing panoply of boats. Others liked to fish the handy waters. Despite the health hazards potentially lurking in its untreated waters, Ilion boys were known to swim in the canal, as well as hitch rides on the towlines which amounted to an early form of what later became a dangerous 20th century practice of skitching on car bumpers in the winter. Public swimming races as part of local summer celebrations were frequently held on the canal too.

When colder weather arrived, a separate slate of activities became possible, for purposely undrained portions of the channel were ideal for skating and horse racing. These opportunities came about in Ilion on the stretch of canal between the lift bridge (then on Railroad

Street, now Central Avenue) and the Typewriter Bridge (now Clark Street to Main Street). Late in the shipping season, before the canal froze over, the channel "...was drained by tilting planks in the bottom of the aqueduct over Steele's Creek and allowing the water to run out..." in the ¼ mile or so between the two bridges.[8] Wooden slats were then used as small dams to keep the canal in that section filled.

Along with the two-mile stretch where the canal sliced through Ilion, two additional features stood out as a part of the local infrastructure of the waterway. First, there were the bridges that had to be built, serving as connectors for the parts of town to the south that had been artificially separated from those to the north of the Erie. While not given much thought, the canal served as a shallow moat, splitting the village by its watery presence for almost a hundred years. In time, seven overpasses would come to link the two sections with one another: at its extreme western end, near DeJohn's convenience store today, were the "Trolley Bridge," a span which got the electrically-driven coaches of a later era over the canal, another for the road, and a smaller footbridge for pedestrians; "London Bridge" was just east of Sixth Avenue's juncture with Main Street; the "Railroad Street Bridge" or "Lift Bridge," located in front of the now Central Fire Station's driveway, connected Railroad Street with Main Street at what came to be known as "Bridge Square" in the heart of downtown; the "Typewriter Bridge" or "Rasbach Bridge" connected Clark Street to East Main Street; and the "Gas House Bridge" brought East Street into East Main Street.

Of these spans, the Gas House, London, and the west-end's trolley, road, and foot bridge were of flat construction, the kind referenced in the words of the famous song about the Erie Canal: "Low bridge, everybody down." The Typewriter Bridge was higher and slightly arched, built as it was on tall piers at each end, so no ducking was required. The Lift Bridge, first operated manually and later by means of electricity, was called by some "the bridge to be remembered."[9] Due to its location in the center of town, a considerable amount of pedestrian and vehicular traffic passed across this span, more so than its counterparts in Ilion. When the bridge was in its "up" position, pedestrians could still cross by ascending sets of stairs on either side, passing over the bridge, and then going down either of a pair of fights at the opposite end.

Old-timers recalled how Ilion youngsters planned "their walk across the [lift] bridge so that they might ride up with it and watch boats go underneath."[10] Since the mechanism was not that of a drawbridge, breaking apart in the center, but rather one wherein the whole bridge went up in one section, the tactic of staying on and going up as if taking an elevator ride was not as dangerous as it might sound. Adding to the unique appearance and operation of this span was the presence of a bridge tender, a man who "had his shanty on the northwest side and sold candy and cigars on the side."[11]

In addition to the bridges, several other places along the Erie in Ilion were scenes of great activity. One of these was about a hundred feet west of the lift bridge behind the row of buildings which in time would be the location of Powers News. At this spot could be found the Ilion dock, where travelers would board packets for trips east and west. In its first year of operation, it was estimated that "40,000 people passed up the valley on the canal."[12] For those who boarded in Ilion and wished to go to Utica, a packet left at 8:30 a.m., bringing its passengers to their destination at 11:30 a.m. For day-trippers, a returning vessel left Utica at 3:30 p.m., with its arrival back in Ilion at 6:30 p.m.—at a one-way "toll of fifteen cents."[13]

Another busy place on the Ilion canal scene was near what was known as the "Junction." Here the highway out of town to the west, trolley tracks connecting with Utica, and the Erie Canal crossed each other. This confluence of different forms of transportation had necessitated the construction of three separate bridges over the Erie Canal in the late 1800s, the first for the roadway, another for the streetcars' right-of-way, and finally a span for the pedestrians. Long after the bridges were removed due to the abandonment of the canal and rerouting of the trolleys, a tribute to their historic location and legacy remains in the name "'Bridge Street'," which is situated at the westernmost end of Ilion near where the Junction used to be.

Slightly to the west of the junction was an operation known as the

"Frankfort Dry Dock Company." Constructed just outside Ilion, enough folks from the town were employed there and its function sufficiently supported the community's canal interests to make it worth noting. Located on the southern side of the waterway, the dry dock was used as a repair shop for canal boats. The facility had a pair of gates, very similar to the large wooden panels found at each end of a canal lock. With the gates opened, boats could easily be towed into an enclosure. Once a packet or freighter was completely within the slip, the gates were closed, and the water was drained out. The dock was now "dry," with the craft resting on a wooden framework of supports. Workmen could now make repairs as needed on any part of the vessel, including its underside. Once the work was completed, water was allowed in to flood the dry dock. When the boat was afloat, the gates were opened, and the refurbished canal boat resumed its journey.

The slow, unhurried ride on a packet boat gave travelers the opportunity to take in the natural beauty of the Empire State. (Source: New York State Library)

While boat repairs were the primary purpose for the dry dock, an allied service was also available. This important benefit was that of a blacksmith shop. Here mules and horses could be brought to have their shoes replaced. The enterprising manager of the dry dock, a man named Milo Brown, also operated the smithy.

In addition to the entertainment value for locals that came with sitting along the canal and watching the daily cavalcade of shipping pass by, the people whose livelihood depended upon plying its waters introduced an often colorful, transient subculture to the local scene. Foremost in this mix were the captains and crewmen who manned the boats—the "canawlers" as they were called. While not all vessels stopped at Morgan's Landing, those so doing brought news and views about the world beyond the valley. Frequently informative and sometimes even eye-popping, the tales which they told of the world beyond the valley gave the locals a window onto the world to the extent that they had never called. As a result, for many their previously isolated homespun lives would never seem quite the same again.

Often, the captain's family lived and traveled on the vessel too. If winter came early, shutting down operations on the canal, boats in transit were stranded until spring. When that happened, "whole colonies of boaters would tie up at the nearest village and settle down for the four or five months of cold weather and schooling."[14] To some extent, those onboard assimilated themselves into their temporary surroundings. Crew members often took temporary jobs, some at the Arms. Women shopped at nearby stores, and available services were accessed. Local deliverymen included stops at the boats on their daily rounds. Children, enrolled in the local school system, made new friends, even if the relationships were only of a limited duration.

From its inception until the end of the nineteenth century, the Erie Canal was an undeniable force, reshaping the economic, demographic, and social outlook of both New York State and the Ohio Valley. However, in time, the very same winds of progress that brought the canal led to its demise. Railroads, coming into their own as a common carrier for both passengers and freight, eventually posed a formidable threat and finally fatal challenge to the canal for transportation supremacy.

Attempting to reestablish the Erie Canal's relevancy, its channel was deepened and widened in 1882, so that larger, steam-driven boats could navigate its waters. But with so many towns having grown up alongside its banks—one of which was Ilion—the channel could only be widened just so much. Given such restrictions, the state then elected to build a new and deeper waterway. From 1903 to 1918, construction crews worked on what was a 96.7-million-dollar project, finally supplanting the now the original Erie Canal bed with what became known as the New York State Barge Canal System.

The end for the old "Grand Canal" finally came in 1915, when the state closed its last open stretch of the water, a section running from Ilion and Mohawk that served local traffic only. The heralded lifeline of yesteryear—a passageway that had once meant so much to so many—was now relegated to the pages of history.

The wagons are standing in Steele's Creek. Ilion's aqueduct is visible rising behind them, running parallel to Main Street. The buildings situated off to the right were located on the south side of the street. Where Little Falls needed a multi-arched structure with which to transport the canal over the Mohawk River, Ilion needed only one span to cross above the stream. (Source: Ilion Free Public Library)

As time passed, substantial portions of the now empty channel were filled-in to provide usable space to allow other opportunities to flourish. But the imprint left on the face of the land by the canal did not disappear overnight. Emily Denton, a long-time reporter for the *Herkimer Evening Telegram*, recalled seeing in her youth vestiges of the canal along the north side of Ilion's Main Street at the east and west ends of town. She described "how houses perched high on the opposite hillside looked down on the street and across the street on remnant ponds and swampy areas that had been the canal."[15]

Eventually the state, which had originally owned the canal's right of way, gladly peddled what was now an unneeded strip of property to the communities through which the waterway had passed. "For a while …the canal…was a haven for dumpers, auto graveyard men, and just about anybody who had something to discard simply through it or dumped it in the canal," Ms. Denton noted.[16] Finally, in February of 1934, a forty-man work crew was assigned to commence filling in the old canal bed on the east and west ends of the village. The cost of was estimated to be $12,500.[17]

The project was authorized through the New Deal's Civil Works Administration (CWA). From its creation on November 3, 1933, through to March 31, 1934, over four million men nationwide obtained temporary, short-term jobs that were primarily those requiring manual labor. Hauling dirt to both ends of Main Street clearly met the with the intent of the CWA's designers. Along with eliminating the festering eyesore that was the old canal bed, workers in an allied endeavor installed "...storm water sewers along the northern border of West Main Street."[18] According to a published report, "dirt to be used for filling material will be obtained from the hill near Spring Street."[19]

Dirt, however, did not provide the only material for hard fill, as all sorts of trash including automobile chassises were used. In a rather ignominious end for one of the canal's most identifiable features in Ilion, "the Typewriter Bridge...was cut loose by acetylene torches and allowed to drop into the canal bed."[20] The southern end of Catherine Street now covers the final resting place of this once well-traveled landmark.

With the distribution of more dirt to level off the final appearance, the land was all prepped for drawing up plans regarding how the community parks that many people in later years came to so highly prize might appear. For a time, the state toyed with the notion of reacquiring the canal land, not for another channel, but rather as an already-cleared route for a revamped NYS 5S. But significant howls of protest by the affected municipalities, many of whom had invested significant tax dollars on improvements to the property in question, cooled the state's ardor. While most of the land today belies little of its history from two hundred years ago, a few places along the old route have been well-preserved, four of these being sites at Schoharie Crossing, Canastota, Syracuse, and Jordan.

But what became of the waterway that once threaded through Morgan's Landing? Though it has long-since been covered over, tracing its route through Ilion is quite easy. When surveyors plotted the original pathway, few if any manmade obstructions existed, for the simple reason that Morgan's Landing was little more than a random sprinkling of buildings. Perhaps a barn here or a shed there had to be removed, but obstacles such as these were few and far between.

With so much open space in existence, the channel laid out followed for the most part a straight line. The only naturally-occurring impediment with the village limits was Steele Creek, which was broached with a short, one-arch aqueduct. Today, following the same pathway for a canal would present an entirely different story. Much like a repeat of the urban renewal project of the late 60's and early 70's, many structures would first have to be removed, clearing the lengthy site before any digging of a ditch could ever start.

The last remaining section of the Erie Canal in Ilion was the stretch behind Plant 3. On the opposite side of the building is old Main Street. To its right is now the Arms' Clark Street parking lot. As the picture runs east to west, Central Avenue would be in the distance near the lower righthand edge of the picture. (Source: Author's Collection)

In superimposing a mental image of the Erie's route on top of what is the layout of the town as it currently exists, the early, continuous evolution of the community to the north and south of along the former east/west axis of the canal is easily ascertained. Starting at the westernmost village limit, the canal entered Ilion by crossing Route 5S in front of the convenient store now situated on the north side of the road, just west of the large welcome sign. From this crossing point, the waterway swung east and passed down what is now an attractive green stretch of parkland. Continuing along, the buildings of the small bank, the workers' monument, the Challenger Memorial, an empty lot, the Salvation Army Store, the Ilion Lumber Yard, another empty lot, the creek bed, the London Towers property, and the Mobil Station are all located upon the old canal route parallel to Route 5S or West Main Street.

Traversing West Street east of the Mobil Station and just north of the stoplight on the Elks Lodge corner, the canal's route would have passed through the large parking lot later built on the opposite side of the street. Continuing eastward, the Central Fire Station now rests astride what was once the bustling water route for travelers heading west and farm products and manufactured goods heading east. Crossing Central Avenue in front the fire house, canal boats passed alongside the rear of what in time became the Remington Typewriter's buildings. Today, this area is identifiable as the vast expanse of the Arms' parking lot just north of the factory complex adjacent to old Main Street.

After passing under the Typewriter Bridge, which is now part of Catherine Street, the canal's route took it through the current properties of an abandon gas station and a former car dealership, and another former gas station's property. Crossing another expanse of green parkland, then under the Gas Works Bridge that is now East Street with present-day East Main Street on its south side, the canal would then have exited Ilion as we now know it, passing through a second long, green strip and then what are now a community garden, car wash, and a motel before exiting town.

With the wisdom that hindsight has the power to instill, it is unfortunate that no existing vestige of the Erie Canal remains anywhere in the town. Considering the lasting contribution which this singular achievement made to the growth of the community, it seems fitting that some sort of plaque or monument ought to have been erected. Yet, in a larger sense, one could argue that a fitting tribute does exist—one called the "Village of Ilion."

Looking west, the Erie Canal is seen as it cuts through Ilion. The lift bridge is clearly visible. The canal above the bridge was filled in as park land, while in the foreground the canal now lies beneath the Arms' Clark Street parking lot. (Source: Ilion Free Public Library)

❧ 4 ❧

LET US CALL OUR VILLAGE
ILION:

A NAME FROM THE PAST TO LAST FOR
THE AGES

Whether the entity under consideration is a newborn, a boat, a business, or a town, a fair amount of thought, discussion, and negotiation usually precedes the selection of its name. Part of the serious nature surrounding such debates stems from the fact that the parties involved in the decision-making process want to get it right the first time, for in most instances whatever appellation is finally chosen becomes a life-long designation. The other significant consideration of equal import is the defining nature of a name. The right one—particularly to the extent that it matches the individual, place, product, or service—has the inherent power to not only make a good first impression, but also imbed a lasting, positive reaction when others hear it.

Given this awesome responsibility, it is not surprising that prospective parents can wrestle for months before agreeing on just the right name for a child about to arrive. Perhaps not as obvious—with the rationale behind its origin sometimes lost in the mists of time—is that of the christening a community with the label by which all posterity will know it and under which heading its history recorded. In the case of New York, place names are as many and varied as was the heritage of the people who were the founders of communities across the Empire State.

English, Dutch, Native American, French, German, and Hispanic influences have all left their indelible marks across the Empire State's sovereign territory. Geographic features and political subdivisions all abound with names of different origins, combing to create a rich tapestry that readily highlights the long history of the state and the diversity of its settlers.

However, regarding the historical legacies of many communities in central and western New York, another major bank of names also exists—those of classical origin. Interestingly, the motto of New York State— "Excelsior"—is itself of Latin derivation. Found prominently emblazoned on its flag, this phrase first appeared on the state's military standard adopted in 1777, with that same banner being only slightly modified eventually becoming New York's official ensign in 1901. As a result, it now proudly waves as one of the oldest such emblems in the country. Translated as "Ever Upward," the use of this classical term reflects our forefathers hope that New Yorkers would always strive for the best outcomes in their endeavors, seeking to achieve heights of continued success that earlier civilizations, such as the Roman Empire, had also sought to attain. In the process, these American dreamers were quite wary of falling prey to the mistakes that brought an end to past realms, hoping instead by their industry, caution, and enthusiasm to each build a thriving community—a contributing domain within the greater nation-state—that would endure for time immemorial.

The need for a trove of new names came about in New York mainly due the distribution of land acquired by the state government after the Revolutionary War. Prior to end of the conflict, settlement in the western portion of the state, once the colony of New York, had been prohibited by the Treaty of Fort Stanwix. Signed in 1763, this pact established a line running south from the fort—now where Rome, New York lies—to the Unadilla River—whose headwaters rise just below present-day Route 20, a little beyond West Winfield, in what is now Unadilla Flats—and then followed the waterway south to the

Susquehanna River. Land east of the superimposed boundary line was open to white settlement, while the territory to the west was reserved for Native American use. Unfortunately for the Iroquois, who for the most part sided with the British, the outcome of the Revolutionary War not only placed several of its allied tribes on the losing side, but also nullified the treaty previously negotiated with the crown's agents. Since the state had pledged to reward its veterans with land for their service, the pre-war status quo about western lands in New York clearly had to change.

With the first pioneers living in cabins scattered across the landscape of German Flatts, no need existed yet as to name towns, for none existed along the frontier of which the western end of the Mohawk Valley marked the furthest reach of white settlement in pre-Revolutionary New York. (Source: Library of Congress)

The solution that finally resolved the matter was contained in a pair of treaties, one in 1788 and the other in 1789. Negotiated between the state and representatives of the Senecas and Cayugas, these agreements called for the purchase of almost two million acres of what had formerly been set aside as tribal property. This massive expanse, thereafter known as the Military Tract, "...extended from Lake Ontario southward to Seneca Lake, and from what is now Onondaga County westward to Seneca Lake."[1] Though anxious to receive their promised allotments, for the war had ended in 1783, the fulfillment of the former soldiers' expectations were put on hold until a thorough survey was completed, and the land subdivided into lots for distribution.

With the concept imbued in the term "Excelsior" already waving over their heads on their state's flag, logical thinking dictated that choosing a classical designation for the numerous locales sprouting up in the Military Tract made perfect sense. Hoping to associate their communities with the glory and majesty evoked by the Old World, many town fathers opted to select a Greek or Latin term once used by the ancients. The choices most frequently adopted were those of historic places and famous people. On occasion, a name was one drawn from mythology. Among the scores born out of this prevailing philosophy came Utica, Rome, Syracuse, Homer, Lysander, Ithaca, Ovid, Greece, Fabius, Cincinnatus, Pompey, Carthage, Aurora...and Ilion.

While the townships' names in the Military Tract were assigned by two of the men who first surveyed the region—both lovers of the classics—the settlers who came between 1790 and 1850 had the opportunity to choose designations for the smaller political entities like villages and hamlets that sprang up over the years. In many instances, they continued the trend of adopting classical names.

It was within the context of this milieu that the village of Ilion got its current name. Settlers had lived on scattered plots of land along the south side of the Mohawk River since the first quarter of the eighteenth century. However, the impetus that sparked the growth of an actual community did not gain any traction until the completion of the Erie Canal one hundred years later. That momentous event, followed soon after by Eliphalet Remington's relocation of his gun business, were key factors that saw a town began to sprout. Soon the burgeoning burg needed a name. Unofficially, several came and went.

First, German Flatts—derived from a combination of the ethnic heritage of the early Palatine German inhabitants along the Mohawk River with the contour of the land—was in vogue to describe the general location which we now know as Ilion. Using level land as a reference point is not without precedent, for it appears today in the names of two places in New York: Big Flats in Chemung County and Burlington Flats in Chenango County. Another topographical feature, "Steele's or Steele Creek," was later commonly used, taking note of the tributary of the Mohawk that flowed nearby. North Creek in the Adirondacks and Silver Creek on Lake Ontario have both derived their names from local waterways, so to be referenced as "Steele's Creek" was not an outlandish idea. But that name did not stick either.

For a time around 1830, the name "London" was used to identify what was a growing settlement. Among the establishments that comprised the hamlet then were "two hotels, a hat factory, two cooper shops, a blacksmith shop, a paint shop, the county house, and about a dozen dwellings."[2] Also, on the western side of town was the Remington's newly constructed factory. In addition, a one-room schoolhouse was built nearby. Once again, the use of nomenclature derived from Old-World places like "London" was not unique in New York's toponymography, for Amsterdam and Berlin already existed and Copenhagen, Paris, Vienna, and Warsaw would follow.

Source: Village of Ilion

Not satisfied with "London," folks began calling their hamlet "Morgan's Landing." The derivation here was due to the proprietorship of a store by one Solomon L. Morgan in partnership with Eliphalet Remington. With the business located on the banks of the Erie Canal for convenience in off-loading wares, using "Morgan's Landing" to identify that spot was an easy, obvious association readily recognized, particularly to boatmen. Bolton Landing on Lake Champlain and Schodack Landing on the Hudson bear witness that using the sobriquet of a mooring site as a community identifier was an appealing approach to some New Yorkers. Though the use of his name for the town was relatively short-lived in Ilion's village's history, Mr. Morgan's legacy still appears today in the street bearing his name.

Given the growing importance of Remington Arms to the local economy, as well as the national prominence that the company was achieving, it was not long before people started calling the village "Remington Corners." For the most part, residents seemed quite comfortable with that designation; however the one individual whose opinion mattered the most, Eliphalet Remington II, was not.

The decision was then made to poll village townsmen, and suggestions were sought at a general meeting of the citizenry held in a local store. From a list of some thirty proposals, "Fountain" and "Vulcan" emerged as the top two choices, with the former far outstripping the latter in the first round of voting. However, even when the time to submit a petition to the post office department for official registry of the new name drew near, some residents were still not sold on "Fountain."

Then, at the eleventh hour, a small group of men—charged to complete and turn in the requisite paperwork—staged a silent coup and tendered the name of "Remington" instead of "Fountain." When the folks back home were finally apprised of the change, no backlash was forthcoming, the simple reason being that people found it hard to divest themselves of the relevance and suitability of using Remington's name. For whom was there that could deny the strong association between the gun-maker and town? Warren Schultz—valedictorian for the IHS Class 0f '40—in his 1977 book about the community even titled his work with that relationship in mind: <u>Ilion: The Town That Remington Built</u>.

Once the growing community at long last had an official name, a post office could be established. With David Devoe in charge, the location of this important addition to the village scene was sited at the corner of what is now Main and Otsego Streets. Unfortunately, there was still one person to whom the use of the name—even shortened from "Remington Corners"—remained unacceptable: the ever-obstinate Eliphalet Remington. Adamant about the issue, he stubbornly stood his ground, emphatically displaying his displeasure by taking his mail to be postmarked at the German Flatts post office in Paines Hollow, nine miles away. Though this necessitated frequent, time-consuming rides, the inconvenience in Remington's mind was an acceptable trade-off for avoiding the personal displeasure and aggravation of seeing his name affixed to incoming correspondence addressed with a destination that read "Remington, New York."

Compounding his dissatisfaction even further were the mix-ups in deliveries and resulting delays in receiving mail that sometimes occurred. Letters intended for Remington, New York, were on occasion routed to similar sounding but incorrect designations such as: Bennington, Vermont; Bennington, New York; and Perrington, New Jersey. The reverse also happened when postings for those locales wound up instead at the Remington post office.

The whole matter finally came to a head in 1843, when Messers Remington and Devoe, acting on their own initiative, decided that a change had to be made. This basically unilateral decision and usurption of power was effected by these two gentlemen for one simple, compelling reason: Eliphalet Remington did not want his name used to identify the village. According to the *Utica Daily Press*, "considerable time was spent by them in searching for an Indian name for some point in close proximity to Remington, but without effect."[3] At that point, Postmaster Devoe, a passionate devotee of classical literature, suggested "Ilion," the Greek name for Troy. Remington blessed it, and the people accepted it. The deal was done. With the selection of this designation, the village joined an extensive list of New York's communities that had classical names. The name selected was that of an ancient city on the Mediterranean coast. Famous as the objective of a Greek army that crossed by the city's walls aided by the Trojan Horse, nine different Troys have occupied the site. Given its long history, Ilionites had chosen a truly storied namesake.

Welcoming visitors to the village at the southern Route 51 and western Route 5S entrances to the community, these attractive signs have the added touch of including the name of the incumbent mayor as a part of the display. (Source: Village of Ilion)

Yet, in being so chosen, Ilion represented an anomaly for several reasons. First, the decision came in 1843. After a fifty-year run of communities opting for classical names, that craze was ebbing by 1852. Second, Ilion was in central New York, quite a distance from the western region of the state which had been the hotbed of reviving names from antiquity. Finally, Ilion had been in existence for a long time before receiving a name that endured.

The good news was that a quest spanning almost one hundred-and-twenty years and seven fruitless tries before a name finally stuck was at last over. The latest choice became even more firmly set in stone in 1852, when the village was legally incorporated as "Ilion." Henceforth, whatever its destiny was going to be, history would record its story under that name.

Once mounted atop the village's incinerator, the warm red and white neon
glow emanated by this one-of-a-kind sign resurrected from the scrap heap,
provides an attractive greeting for visitors who approach the town by way of
the canal and the marina or as travelers looking down from the Thruway.
(Source: Village of Ilion)

THE OCTAGON HOUSE:

A UNIQUE STRUCTURE FROM ANOTHER ERA

D uring his storied lifetime, the famous 19th century phrenologist, writer, and lecturer Orson Fowler never visited Ilion, but he did nevertheless leave his imprint on the village at the northwest corner of Third and John Streets. For it was on the lot there that Harvey Hakes built a novel residence unlike any other in town. Hakes' unusual choice for his family's domicile was an eight-sided house. While many people came to gawk and marvel at this unique living space, in the end it was the only one of its kind in Ilion, though a few such buildings from that era are found across the length and breadth of the United States. As near to our village as Newport and as far away as San Francisco, the urge to build octagonally-shaped residences was a part of a national phenomenon that captivated the imagination of some folks around the country, primarily in the years before the Civil War.

The impetus that drove Mr. Hakes' decision to opt for such an unconventional design in building a home was a philosophy espoused by Fowler. Writing in his 1848 book A House for All, this out of-the-box thinker contended that adherence to the octagonal plan made for a structure that promoted the presence of improved ventilation and extra sunlight. Since this unorthodox design created more angles than a traditionally-styled house normally had, the twin benefits that resulted led Fowler to suggest that its inhabitants enjoyed a healthier living environment .

Orson Fowler - (Source: Library of Congress)

In retrospect, Orson Fowler would have preferred a house whose exterior contour was round, as he believed that a circle represented the ideal shape. However, the lack of suitable building materials in the first half of the nineteenth century to achieve such a configuration precluded the construction of a novel building conforming to this shape. As a result, his fallback position was to adopt the octagon as the next acceptable style.

For a decade or so after the release of his book, house construction adhering to his principles were built to the tune of several thousand. But by the end of the decade of the 1850's, the tide of public taste had ebbed precipitously, manifesting itself in the unflattering epithet of "Fowler's Folly" to describe a home built using his experimental design.

But it was at a time when this unique construction format's popularity was in its ascendency that Hakes made a very momentous decision—he would have an octagonal house constructed for his family. Public records indicate that Dennis Dygert and Harvey Hakes, both employees of Remington Arms at the time, "...purchased a large tract of land located west of Steele Creek from a John Ingersoll, Jr."[1] Both men set about building their respective residences. Mr. Dygert's, while a comfortable brick house, was decidedly the more conventional of the two in its appearance.

Mr. Hakes, however, opted for the much more radical plan of an eight-sided house. The edifice which he constructed in 1853—though now somewhat altered from its original look by additions such as a garage connected to the main building—still clearly projects its distinctive style one-hundred-and-sixty-five years later. In standing before the house today, some of its beauty and elegance are impaired by encroachments around it. For example, to its immediate north and east homes have been added, thereby seriously constricting the size of Hakes' original lot and crowding the sight lines when viewing the house.

Based on the description from an 1857 real estate ad—for apparently being somewhat given to impulsiveness, Mr. Hakes now wanted to sell and move west—the parcel of land upon which the house once sat extended further to the east than it presently does along Third Street and quite likely back toward Second Street via John Street. This is borne out by the advertisement referencing the lot size of as being a "2 ½ acre plot"—an acre being a 55' by 88' thus making Hakes' property slightly larger than two football fields side-by-side —"well-stocked with fruit trees of the choicest kinds; also, raspberries, gooseberries, currants, and grapes."[2]

Seeing that Mr. Hakes was a florist by trade, it was likely that these plantings were expertly tended and pruned. In addition, further adding to the attractiveness of the property was the knowledge that "a never-failing stream runs across the lot."[3] Here the reference is to Steele Creek, perhaps a hundred or so feet east of the Hakes' home.

That a much more spacious chunk of acreage might once have accompanied the house than presently exists was further hinted at on an 1857 map of the village. At the time this rendering was executed, John Street was not yet laid out. Only two houses were depicted from Second Street to Third Street. One was Hakes', while Dygert's was the other laying directly across Third Street from its octagonal neighbor. Both homes would eventually find themselves located on the opposite corners of John and Third Streets.

Twenty-two years later, the octagonal house stood out on the well-known "Bird's Eye View of Ilion Map—Circa 1881," which was a pictorial/geographical rendering with the Hakes' house clearly identifiable by its distinctive shape. (See map on page 144). However, several changes in the lot size and the village in general are clearly in evidence at this later date.

Now, only a single empty building lot existed between the Hakes' house and the next residence north on John Street, and then instead of the nearest neighbors to the east being a row of houses situated along West Street, well-beyond the eastern bank of Steele Creek which was the "never failing stream" previously referenced in the newspaper listing announcing Hakes' desire to sell his parcel, two new houses existed east on Third Street. The upshot of all the alterations that occurred to the property's configuration and the neighborhood in a little over two decades was striking.

But as noticeable as the constriction of the Hakes' property dimensions were, the opposite was true for the parameters of the village. That Ilion had experienced a changing geopolitical face was most dramatically portrayed by its increase in population. From 1,000 souls at the time of the Civil War, the little community had seen an increase of 450% to 4500 people in a mere twenty-eight year span! Needing to provide accommodations and services for this influx of residents, the town grew. On the 1857 map, Harvey Hakes' home had been on what was then the extreme southern edge of a small village; however, by 1881, building construction had proliferated, so the town's outer limit to the south was now slightly beyond Frederick Street, thereby placing the octagon house more toward the center of Ilion than it had previously been. All around it—on both sides of John Street, east down Third Street, and around the corner on West Street —other homes had sprung up. From being an outlier of sorts when first built, the octagon house was now clearly ensconced in a neighborhood.

As shown on the following 1857 map of the village, a structure existed on the southern side of Third Street across from the Hakes' home. This was the residence of Dennis Dygert. While lacking the architectural uniqueness of its octagonal neighbor, this building nevertheless deserves recognition for its longevity. While its exterior covering of yellow paint somewhat masks its brick surface, Dygert's house was as solidly built as was Hakes'. Together they have faced each other for almost 180 years, making them among the oldest existing domiciles now found in Ilion.

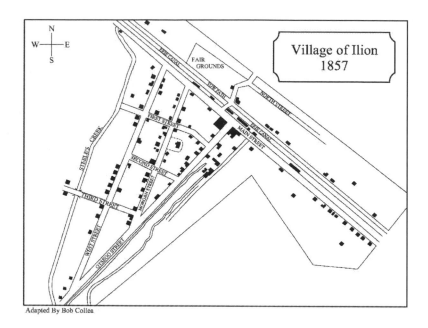

The Third Street house on the northwest side of Steele's Creek is the octagonal house of the Henry Hakes' family. Ilion in 1857 boasted a population of nearly 1000 residents, most located on the flats below the hills and within a triangle created by West and Otsego Streets. (Source: Ilion Free Public Library)

Though the size of the Hakes' property was gradually reduced over a relatively short period of time, the structural integrity of the unique house itself largely was retained. Resting on a limestone cellar's foundation of blocks twenty-four inches thick, the first and second floors had brick exterior walls twelve inches deep, rendering them impermeable to frost. To a viewer from the street, the house exudes the solid, substantial look that this type of construction material imparts. Centered most conspicuously atop the roof is a cupola, also octagon-shaped, which serves as an adornment, since its purpose was more decorative than functional. In the words of a local tour book, "the front doors and porch are enhanced with Italianate carpentry."[4] As for outbuildings—attachments which Fowler frowned upon because they interrupted the symmetry of the octagon—greenhouses once existed, very much in keeping with Harvey Hakes' chosen occupation in horticulture.

Unusual among housing designs today, at one time in the mid-nineteenth century this unique style of residential architecture—though not built in profusion—was still constructed in various locales across the country. Some are still in existence, like the former Hakes' home, now found on the corner of Third and John Streets. Another local version, called the "Yale House," is located in Newport, New York. (Source: Ilion Free Public Library)

Among its interior accommodations, the house once boasted a well and a cistern. In addition to having interior plumbing that permitted a bathroom, it also contained a hot air furnace instead of fireplaces to provide a source of heat. To move from the cellar to the first floor and then on to the second floor, a pair of staircases were available. What was unusual about their positioning was that they were set along the outside walls of the house, rather than as circular sets of stairs located in the center of the building. Also unique, several rooms contained closets, features which were not common in homes of that era. The kitchen was placed in the basement, with a dumbwaiter used to deliver food to the dining area upstairs. A vegetable or root cellar and fuel storage area were also located at the lower level.

Another attractive feature of the house was that the spacious area below ground level often served as a makeshift ballroom. In later times under different ownership, parties were held there and, at one time or another, hosted the famous silent film actress Doris Kenyon and the family of the renowned soldier/statesman/politician Theodore Roosevelt, though the great man himself had remained in Washington during their visit.

Though the vintage residence now stands on a severely contracted piece of real estate, is crowded in by neighboring homes, rests on a more squared-off lot, and is framed by a picket fence—all of which to some extent detract from gaining a full appreciation of this distinctive architectural rendering—the octagon house's exterior appearance has been well-maintained by its various owners down through the years. By so doing, they have given the community "a village jewel," a window into its historic past, and a living link that harkens of bygone times to take forward into the future.[5]

6

THE PASSING OF LINCOLN'S FUNERAL TRAIN:

THE COMMUNITY BIDS A SAD FAREWELL

T he news of President Lincoln's assassination spread rapidly, hitting the citizens of the northern part of the country particularly hard. No small wonder, for that was the region which had committed itself to the preservation of the Union by twice electing him as their leader and answering his subsequent calls to enlist in the Union's armed forces. Positive feelings about the late president in central New York had been clearly manifested when he made his mid-February of 1861, pre-inaugural excursion from Springfield, Illinois to Washington, D.C. In brief stops at Utica and Little Falls, the president-elect was greeted by large, enthusiastic crowds.

As the son of a prairie state far to the west, Lincoln was not a well-known political commodity to easterners such as the residents of the Mohawk Valley. Unlike today, when candidates receive virtually unlimited coverage by the media, those seeking national office during the middle years of the nineteen-century in some ways remained somewhat of a nebulous lot to many voters.

Certainly, candidates' views were covered in newspapers, and those who could read gleaned a given office seekers' positions on various issues of import through these publications. Then there were the inns and taverns, the political clubs, and the back fences were the merits of respective candidates were frequently discussed. But for the most part, as was the case with Lincoln's candidacy, comparatively few voters ever actually saw or directly heard him speak before casting their ballots. Since the newspapers of his era were technologically incapable of printing photographs, line drawings or sketches were the best sources for people living far removed from Illinois to gain some idea of the Republican candidate's appearance.

For people who were not likely to buy a horse sight unseen, the idea of choosing a president in this manner seems a bit inconsistent, especially when the comparative importance of both choices are weighed side-by-side. Yet the idea of a whistle-stop campaign to get the office seeker out among the people was not a practice that had caught on in 1860. Perhaps the extreme example of how limited politicking in those times often was, the non-campaign practiced by Lincoln's predecessor, James Buchanan, serves as an excellent example to the point of absurdity. During his successful run for the presidency in 1856, the Democratic Party's candidate gave but two speeches— both from the front porch of his Pennsylvania home! One was delivered when he accepted his nomination, and the other given in acknowledgement of his victory. So it was, in a backwards way, that Lincoln decided to gain a modicum of public exposure in a novel manner. By embarking on a thirteen-day train trip to the nation's capital in February of 1861, the president-elect's goal was to appear before as many of his new constituents as possible.

While the primary objective was to arrive in Washington for his March 4 inauguration, Lincoln used the trip and lead-in time as an opportunity to meet and greet as many of his new constituents as possible. Instead of availing himself of regular passenger service and reducing the journey to less than a week, he chose to ride what was known as the "Lincoln Special." Counting layovers in Buffalo, Albany, and New York City, this two-coach express allowed him to spend five days in the Empire State alone. Stopping briefly in numerous small stations located between the larger metropolitan areas permitted

Lincoln to collectively be seen and heard by a decent cross-section of his countrymen.

Except for the leg from Baltimore to Washington--one which resulted in his foregoing public exposure in favor of a hurried, clandestine night-time passage to avoid a possible assassination attempt—the long excursion went as Lincoln and his advisors had hoped. Nowhere along the way was the benefit which he accrued more prevalent than it was along the portion funneling through the Mohawk Valley. In addition to the gatherings at planned stopping points, the train was seen by countless other New Yorkers as it chugged through several cities and many small villages, rolled past countless farms, and rumbled over numerous road crossings.

While Lincoln had already carried the Empire State and garnered all its electoral votes in the fall balloting, the tour de force offered by his highly-visible journey across New York not only served to confirm for his supporters that he indeed was the right man for the job of President of the United States, but also made many converts among skeptics and opponents who were now at least willing to give him a chance.

Over the next four years, President Lincoln guided the nation through the most difficult and challenging times in its history. The peoples' faith in him was manifested by his re-election to office in the fall of 1864. But high hopes that Lincoln's steady hand would be able to reunite the post-war nation were cruelly dashed by his assassination. Coming as it did on April 15, 1865—so close to his second inauguration barely a month before on March 4 and then Lee's surrender April 9—his sudden and unexpected death hit the nation hard. At a time when the country should have been amidst great rejoicing over the end of the war, people were instead abruptly plunged into an abyss of sorrow. Allowing for the fact that the deceased was the chief executive of his country, some type of national mourning was very much in order. Since Victorian cultural mores were very much in vogue at the time, the observance of powerful protocols heavily influenced many aspects of American life. Not the least of these conventions were the expectations that governed mourning rituals.

In the instance of Lincoln's death, the fact that he was a figure of national prominence meant that his wake and funeral was not going to be simple, low-key ceremonies. His widow's desire to have her late husband's remains interred in Springfield, Illinois, 800 miles away, added another contingency in planning an appropriate farewell. However, another problem, one that further compounded any decisions with respect to the making the necessary arrangements in a timely manner, was that Mary Lincoln's ability to focus and make meaningful contributions to the planning was very limited. After issuing a few edicts, such as no photographs of the deceased and that the burial would be in Springfield, the distraught widow took her bed chamber for several weeks of private mourning.

With Mary's abdication from the responsibility for making most of the funeral arrangements, the enormous task fell on the shoulders of Edwin Stanton, her husband's capable secretary of war. One important concession that the secretary had managed to extract from Mrs. Lincoln was a change in her preferred route in returning the late president's remains back home. Instead of going directly via a non-stop express, he convinced her that a slower, more circuitous pathway was a consideration owed the nation. Its grieving populace, to whom her husband had come to mean so much, also deserved an opportunity to say farewell.

In making the return trip with the President's remains to Illinois, a funeral train would follow virtually the same route the first "Lincoln Special" had taken in the spring of 1861, when the newly-elected Chief Executive was making his way to Washington for his inauguration. Most of the very same people who had turned out to welcome him and cheer on his passage then would now be waiting in the same stations to offer their mournful respects as another train, heading in the opposite direction this time and noticeably dressed in black crepe, as it slowly chugged westward. For the country lawyer who had once drawn a portion of his income from representing railroad interests, it seemed only fitting that trains, once so much a part of some of the greatest moments in his life were now to play a significant role in what amounted to his last public appearances in death.

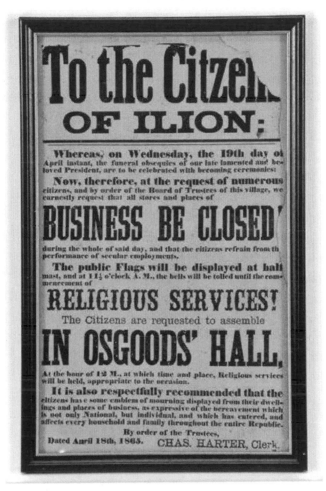

In the possession of the Ilion library, this handbill announcing local memorial services for the late President is a rare artifact.
(Source: Ilion Free Public Library)

WHILE WAITING for word to come from Washington on the details of the final plan, cities and villages across the North were preparing local ceremonies, known at the time as "obsequies," to be held concurrently with the services scheduled to occur in the East Room of the White House. The date for these nation-wide observances was Wednesday, April 19, 1865. Their starting time was designated as 12:00 p.m. As noted by contemporary author John Carrol Power, in addition to the heavily attended services "...the people of hundreds of thousands of towns and cities turned out in solemn processions, bearing emblems, mottoes, and other devices expressive of their love for the memory of Abraham Lincoln, and of their sorrow for his death."[1]

In Ilion, the village board requested that all places of business be closed on the designated day. Flags were to be flown at half-mast, and at 11 o'clock church bells were to begin tolling until religious services commenced at noon. Given its enhanced size compared to other possible venues around the community, including local churches, Osgood's Hotel was chosen to house a gathering that was most likely to be quite substantial. Folks were also encouraged to dress appropriately and wear emblems of mourning. In another custom of the times, people were asked to adorn their homes and businesses with appropriate displays of bereavement. These expressions usually took the form of hanging black-hued wreaths on doors and draping similarly colored crepe around window and door frames.

❧

AT THE CLOSE of this emotionally draining day, most folks thought their participation in any further public tributes to the deceased president were over. They were now left to grieve in their own private ways for as long as it might take. For many, the process could involve purchasing one of the readily available photographs of Mr. Lincoln in a *carte de visite* format to display in their homes. Others would write letters to friends and relatives, trying to achieve closure by conveying their feelings and striving to make sense about what had just happened. However, the situation quickly changed for tens of thousands of mourners following a decision made in Washington on April 19: the route of the funeral train to Springfield was finally selected. The train bearing the late president's remains was going to follow, in reverse, the same lengthy pathway that the pre-inaugural tour had taken.

With this second "Lincoln Special" scheduled to depart from the national capital on April 21, the rail borne cortege would arrive in New York City on the 24th and depart north up the Hudson Valley for Albany the next day. After a brief, overnight stop there for Lincoln's casket to lay in state at the capitol building, the train would turn west toward Buffalo. The passage of the "Lincoln Special" through the Mohawk Valley would then occur during the afternoon and early evening of April 26. All along the projected route, citizens were galvanized into action, putting their heads together in order that their community might offer some sort of appropriate show of respect, regardless of whether the train was stopping to allow for brief vigil or only slowing down upon its arrival at stations along the way.

For Ilionites, standing respectfully along the New York Central's tracks in the early evening of April 26, 1865, the last unit in the funeral train—the coach on the far left containing the President's coffin—was the car which they patiently waited to view. (Source: Library of Congress)

Given the late notice on the decision regarding the route, communities along the right-of-way of the New York Central Railroad had to scramble to produce suitable trackside tributes. Much to their civic credit, having but a week or less to pull a plan together, a suitable variety of differing local homages were devised by the hastily convened committees. Word was disseminated through newspapers and handbills, and, per a published schedule of the funeral train's itinerary, mourners then gathered at designated times and places as the cortege slowly passed through and, in some instances, stopped for a few minutes. Only in New York City, Albany, and Buffalo would the casket be removed from the train and opened for several hours of public viewing.

For the residents of Ilion, the appointed hour to meet was slated for seven p.m., on Wednesday, April 26, 1865. Beyond getting the word out, the only real glitch to take into consideration was that the railroad did not pass through the village, as it did in so many other places. Instead, the tracks and station were situated just north of the Mohawk River and over a half-mile from the center of the village proper. Taking this into account, the plan that was decided upon called for mourners to gather at the Osgood Hotel, which was at the northwest corner of Otsego and Main Streets. From there, a procession would go west on Main for a half-block to Bridge Square. Turning right onto Railroad Street (now Central Avenue), the bereaved would walk to the rail crossing, which lay due north of downtown. The trek, moving at a slow but measured pace, probably took at least a half-hour, given that cavalcade was comprised of people of all ages. After crossing the lift bridge over the Erie Canal just north of Main Street, the marchers proceeded on down a noticeable incline until the grade flattened out at River Street. Then a slight upslope brought them along a wooden causeway over the marshy wetlands south of the river. This corduroy-styled roadway of split logs then brought the procession to the bridge over the Mohawk, with the railroad tracks laying perhaps a hundred feet beyond the span's northern portal. It was in this open space between the river and the rails where most of the people would gather, spreading out to the east and west along the tracks. Others crossed the two sets of tracks, turned to face south, and stood between the Mohawk Turnpike and the train tracks.

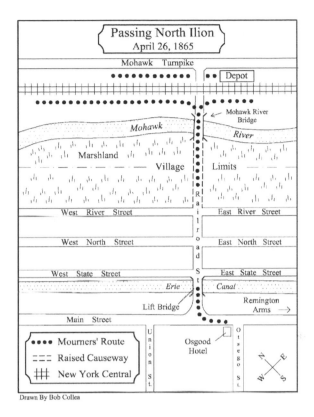

Drawn By Bob Collea

Source: Author's collection

Before the mourners had reached the trackside locations in order to view the slowly passing train, night had fallen. Prepared for this eventuality, many of the participants lit the lanterns or firebrands which they carried. In the chill air of the mid-April evening, the flickering flames burned brightly, serving to light the way as well as casting the townspeople as shadowy figures. As they stood along the tracks, the torches which were not the only source of illumination that pierced the darkness. Behind them, on the eastern side of the village, the Remington Arms factory complex was all aglow, offering a stunning tribute to the man whose cause its weaponry had supported on the battlefields of the war.

Against this backdrop, members of the waiting crowd conversed in low murmurs. Frequently, individuals in the waiting delegation peered down the tracks to the east, their eyes straining into the darkness, as they looked for an indication that the "Lincoln Special" was approaching. Then, through the gloom, the dim, crepe-shrouded headlight of the engine materialized. The rhythmic chug of the pistons moving the drive wheels of the *Edwin Jones* soon became audible, accompanied by the muffled sound of the locomotive's bell. The slow cadence of its tolling was a sound that came to be indelibly imbedded in the minds of those who heard it.

Taken looking south from Oak Hill, this post-Civil War photograph shows North Ilion. Just over the bridge, north of the river and south of the tracks is an open patch where many mourners gathered. Today the area lies beneath the ramp leading from Route 5 onto the overpass heading to Ilion. (Source: Ilion Free Public Library)

Even though slowed to five miles per hour to facilitate viewing by trackside mourners, the ten-unit consist passed between the two lines of bereaved townspeople altogether too quickly. While the mourners took in the decorated engine and the crepe-draped cars following behind, the last car was the one to which everyone's attention was drawn. Easy to identify by the golden eagles centered below the windows on each side, this was the coach known as the "hearse car." Inside, resting on a wooden frame, was the ornate, silver-trimmed casket bearing the body of the deceased president. Also, in same the car was a smaller, less pretentious coffin that contained the remains of Lincoln's son Willie. The boy had passed away from a case of typhoid fever in 1862, and now his corpse was being transported home to be buried alongside that of his father.

As the train passed, the crowd stood in quiet reverence, save for the sobs of those for whom the enormity of what they were witnessing proved too difficult to bear silently. Some stood with bowed heads, while others knelt with hands clasped in supplication. Men removed their hats. Heads turned slowly as the train rolled past.

In a line up-front, standing at attention, was a row of young boys dressed in Zouave uniforms. A gaudy style of dress worn by some regiments on both sides early in the war, this clothing evoked the memory of the late Colonel Elmer Ellsworth. Founder of a famous Zouave regiment and dear friend of Abraham Lincoln, Ellsworth had ridden the pre-inaugural train as a protector of the president-elect.

A native of Malta, New York, he made the acquaintance of Lincoln when clerking in the future-President's law office in Springfield before the war. When the conflict began, Ellsworth immediately answered the President's call for troops by raising the 11th New York Infantry. So close had the bond between Lincoln and Ellsworth grown that the President thought of his young protege as almost a son. He would have been on the funeral train too, but for his death in the very early stages of the war—in Alexandria, Virginia., when he was killed after removing a Confederate flag from a local hotel's roof serving as a sad harbinger for not only the president, but the entire nation as well, that many loved ones were likely to perish before the hostilities were over.

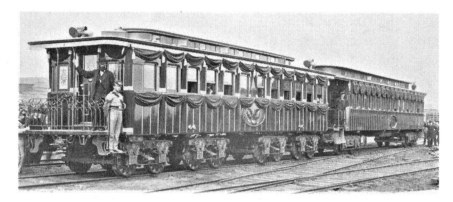

The last coach in the consist of the second "Lincoln Special" was the hearse car, charged with the sad duty of bearing the remains of the late President and his deceased son Willie home to Springfield, Illinois. (Source: Library of Congress)

Once the train had rolled on down the line—having spent approximately eighty-two seconds passing before them—the mourners began their slow walk back to Ilion and their homes. Buoyed by the consoling thought that they had been able to pay their respects, however fleetingly, to their fallen leader, the townsfolk nevertheless trod with heavy hearts. For a man whom few if any had ever seen or heard in person, his election to a second term had been their thanks for a job well-done. Their presence at the North Ilion crossing this night had been to say farewell to this remarkable leader and unique friend to all—an individual whom most had never met, yet none would never forget. While the train carried his mortal remains to a place far from the valley, the memory of the man and his deeds would linger in their hearts and minds for as long as they live.

7

MANSION ON THE HILL:

SPENDING MONEY TO MAKE MONEY

The Victorian Age in America was a time of excess and ostentation. Whether it was in clothes, furnishings, or homes, those who had the wherewithal spared no expense when it came to lavishing on themselves the best that money could buy. Among the well-known examples of this overindulgence in housing that remain today is the artist Frederic Edwin Church's Hudson Valley residence "Olana." With its soaring ceilings, ornate woodwork, and exquisite chandeliers, this estate epitomized what the extravagant lifestyles of the rich and famous were like in the last quarter of the nineteenth century.

Armory Hill, Ilion, NY Circa 1880
(Source: Ilion Public Library)

While not reaching the same level of opulence manifested by the residences of such affluent contemporaries as Frederic Church, Cornelius Vanderbilt, or John D. Rockefeller, one member of the Remington family of Ilion nevertheless constructed a monument to his wealth and success that was none-too-shabby. Known simply as "the Remington Mansion," the home of Philo Remington—grandson of the company's founder—was located off what now is the corner of Remington Avenue and Armory Street. Situated on the grounds of what later became a parking lot for many years and then an Indeck power plant in 1987, Philo's home offered his family a breathtaking vista consisting not only of the nearby factory and village below, but also the Mohawk Valley.

The mansion is visible among the trees on the lower right. In this photograph, old Main Street starts from the upper right and runs west diagonally between the Arms' complex on its right and the Typewriter's on its left. In the lower left is the intersection of Main and Otsego Streets. (Source: Ilion Free Public Library)

The panorama afforded the Remington's was said to be nothing short of magnificent. For, from the upper reaches of the building's main turret, it was possible "to view the valley westward beyond Utica and eastward to Little Falls," impressive distances of over twelve and ten miles respectively.[1] In return, the house's commanding presence atop the high mid-town hillock made the mansion itself visible for miles around, making the edifice a landmark not only for Ilion but the region as well.

While the business fortunes of E. Remington and Sons had experienced cycles of prosperity and recession since the company was founded, the family was never prone to live a lavish lifestyle during the good times. In those years when they were financially comfortable, their accumulated bounty had not translated into any serious displays of wealth. However, in the late 1860's, a series of unplanned events ushered in a revised outlook with respect to how the windfall in earnings should be spent.

The first boon was the result of an ingenious breakthrough for the company that occurred in 1865. With research and development one of the hallmarks of its success in the highly-competitive gun-making business, a Remington inventor-employee—one Joseph Rider— devised an operating system that blew away those offered by contending firms. Called a "rolling block," this unique feature allowed a rifleman to experience a rapid transition from firing a round, to removing the spent cartridge, inserting a new shell, and then pulling the trigger again.

To begin the firing/reloading process, the curved, pronounced hammer of the weapon was pulled back into a cocked position. This repositioning of the hammer permitted the rifleman to then thumb or roll back the breech block, by means of another curved protrusion or lever not unlike that of the hammer. Initiating this two-step process ejected the empty casing out of the rear of the barrel. With the breech clear, a new shell could be inserted. The breech was then closed by rolling or flipping the block forward. The closing of the open breech by the rolling forward of the block rendered the weapon ready to be fired again. Pulling the trigger released the hammer which struck the firing pin located in the middle of the now closed block. Though still a single-shot rifle, this revolutionary process increased the speed at which the shooter could load and fire his gun. Furthermore, the mechanism was simple to operate and smooth in its functioning.

Due to its world-wide popularity, the rolling block was a rifle which made a
fortune for the Remington's. (Source: Author's Collection)

Once this advancement in firearms gave Remington an appealing piece of weaponry, another benefit that came their company's way was the build-up in interest on the part of the multiple international powers to engage in what amounted to an arms race—19th century style. The rolling block happened to hit the market at just the right time and became a desirable commodity for countries looking to supply their troops with a high-powered, accurate, and reliable model of military hardware. However, this international infatuation with the rolling block did not occur overnight. With domestic sales lagging due to the end of the Civil War, the Remington brothers began to think in terms of a world market, and by deliberate efforts they successful tapped into the coffers of Europe's monarchs. The wisdom of this decision was borne out by the economic bonanza for the local gunmakers that followed, ushering in what author Alden Hatch called "The Golden Age of Ilion" from 1870 to 1880."[2] According to another writer, K.D. Kirkland, the total production run of the rolling blocks "spanned a remarkably long period of gunmaker history, from 1867 until 1934."[3]

Three factors dovetailed to make this unprecedented prosperity possible. First, there was Samuel Remington—salesman *par excellence*. Though the youngest brother, he was promoted to the position of company president, with middle sibling Philo willingly stepping down into the role of vice-president. This flip-flop of responsibilities was predicated on the recognized talents of Samuel, whom author George Layman described as "the most quick-witted and fun-loving member of the family (who) had a line of persuasion that could effortlessly convince the most doubting soul."[4] Subsequently, this most outgoing of the Remington siblings was dispatched to Europe in the summer of 1866, where he established an office in Paris. Using his impressive business title as a door-opener, Samuel became a traveling salesman. The combination of his winning personality and a quality firearm began to open doors. With his attractive, vivacious wife Flora accompanying him, the winning couple was warmly welcomed in royal courts throughout Europe.

A second contributing element that helped light a fire under sales — the real coming-out party for Remington's rolling block rifle—was France's "Imperial Exposition of 1867." Upon seeing, handling, and testing the rifle, ordinance experts from several countries became convinced of the weapon's battlefield potential, deeming it a quality piece of workmanship that surpassed any other models then in existence.

Then the final contributing dynamic that served to further place the rolling block in the public's eye, the crowning glory, came when French president Francois Certain de Canrobert presented Samuel Remington with "the Silver Medal of the exposition, the highest award for military and sporting arms."[5] The foreign delegations present in turn reported back to their superiors that this was a "must-have" longarm with which to outfit their respective armies. Orders soon came pouring in from European nations. The Swedes purchased 30,000 rifles, while the Danes ordered 42,000.[6] But even these significant numbers paled next to the initial request for 85,000 rolling blocks which the Spanish wanted. But leave it to the French to outdo all competitors when they placed their stunning order for "the capacity of the factory."[7]

Though European governments signed contracts for these as well as additional purchases later, requisitions for the new rifle were not the sole propriety of Continental powers. Also thirsting for a potent killing machine was the Khedive, Ismael Pasha of Cairo, a ruler who eventually became one of the Remington's best customers. He invented Samuel to Cairo for a demonstration of his new weapon.

After seeing for himself how well the rolling block performed, he immediately placed an order. Once their country's contracts for this firearm were completed, Egyptian troops had over 250,000 of this stand of arms at their disposal.

Pleased with his purchases, the Egyptian potentate presented Samuel Remington with the gift of a prime piece of Cairo real estate. Protocol carried the expectation that its recipient would demonstrate his gratitude by building a suitable residence on the property. Though he adhered to expectations, the younger Remington brother never chanced to live in this exotic location. Egyptian authorities eventually repossessed the modest palace due to some unpaid bills and then sold it to the British government, which for decades used the building as an embassy.

As world-wide sales of various models of the rifle climbed to over a million pieces between 1867 and 1876, the domestic market also heated up and proved lucrative for the Remington's. While it became a weapon of choice among many buffalo hunters on the Great Plains, one larger-than-life personality of the post-Civil War West would become enamored with the rolling block, after he had purchased one of the rifles in its sporting model configuration directly from the company in 1872. Upon taking delivery in 1873, numerous photographs were eventually taken wherein he and his rolling block appeared together. Most notable among these were the ones made in camp while he was on his famous Yellowstone Expedition of the same year. Who was this giant of American history? He was none other than a well-known hero of the Civil War and soldier/hunter of the western plains—George Armstrong Custer.

So pleased was he with the weapon, that the general was motivated to write a letter to the company's headquarters in Ilion, extolling his satisfaction with his rifle's performance. After enumerating and identifying the many types of animals successfully brought down and the distances at which the kills were made, the general closed with glowing words of praise: "I am more than ever impressed with the many superior qualities possessed by the system of arms manufactured by your firm, and I believe I am safe in asserting that to a great extent this opinion is largely shared in by members of the Yellowstone expedition who had opportunities to make practical tests of the weapon in question."[8]

An avowed fancier of Remington products, among those that he was known to possess during his abbreviated lifetime in addition to the rolling block rifle was a Remington-Beals Navy Conversion revolver, manufactured during the 1860's. Today, of course, such a testimonial from a bona fide user of such stature as Custer possessed would result in an advertising bonanza. In the vein of Peyton Manning endorsing a certain brand of pizza or Shaquille O'Neal hawking insurance, the colorful, flamboyant, and nationally-known figure that was George Custer would have made an ideal spokesperson for Remington products. The fact that he carried their weapons literally to the end of his days in the Battle of Little Big Horn—potentially making it "the last gun that he fired"—only added poignancy to the otherwise marketer's dream of matching a famous persona with a remarkable rifle.

In the wake of the publicity generated and sales accrued by the success of the rolling block, Ilion became a popular destination for various foreign delegations and dignitaries. These representatives came to sign contracts, tour the facilities, and shepherd their country's orders home. While Ilion featured several hotels and among them the Remington brothers owned several fine homes about town, none matched the splendor of the accommodations which many of these upper-class visitors enjoyed in their homelands. The upshot of this luxury-gap was that Samuel and Eliphalet began urging Philo to construct a new, more pretentious house. They envisioned a residence suitably disposed to properly wine and dine their various international guests, though for the teetotaling Philo the liquid offerings would most likely and more accurately have been described as "lemonading and dining."

An impressive residence, its exterior presented a busy appearance with all of the differing treatments used in the color, shape, and design of its stonework, windows, and rooflines. (Source: Ilion Free Public Library)

Though reluctant to forego continued residency in his comfortable, though modest home on lower Otsego Street, Philo finally agreed to take one for the company, build a mansion, and entertain foreign emissaries. The site chosen was on existing company property, part of a 100-acre parcel of land acquired by Eliphalet Remington II in 1828. With 481 feet of street frontage and a set-back about 200 feet, the site chosen was located on the northwestern crest of Armory Hill, amounting in total to four-and-a-half acres of land near where Remington Avenue and Armory Street meet today, and the former Indeck co-generation plant now sits.

Designed by the highly-regarded Syracuse architect Horatio Nelson White, construction began in 1868, Within two years, the house was ready for occupancy. Built at the impressive cost of $65,000, which in its day was a hefty sum, that price tag may have amounted to a mere drop in the bucket for Philo Remington at the time, for older residents of Ilion estimated that its builder— after sharing with his brothers the profits from the sale of rifles to both sides in the Franco-Prussian War

—was left with a million dollars. In those days, this represented another unthinkable amount of money.

By virtue of its location and style, the edifice—known simply as the "Remington Mansion"—clearly was a structure like no other in town. Approaching the spacious grounds, visitors first passed along a four-foot high, hand-carved sandstone wall and then entered the property through double-wide, wrought-iron gates hung on two pillars, also of sandstone. The grounds were beautifully landscaped with well-tended flower beds, trimmed shrubbery, and a terraced fountain. Worthy of special note and admiration were the vast number of rare and beautiful trees that adorned the property—the nurturing of which was one of the passions of Philo's wife Caroline, who was especially proud of her well-tended mulberry tree.

The spacious grounds were well-landscaped with driveways to bring visitors to the front entrance or under a portico on the right if the weather was inclement. The stables in back are now all that remains of the estate. The street on the far right is Remington Avenue, and, in the foreground, the curving sidewalk served as a connection with the stairway leading down to Otsego and Second Streets. (Source: Green's History of the Mohawk Valley)

If arriving in a carriage, guests traveled up to the house at 21

Remington Avenue via a semi-circular gravel lane, passed along to the right side of the mansion where it stopped. Here "finely dressed ladies alit from victories under a porte-cochere, over colorful mosaics, past the baggage elevator, and into the great hall."[9] The carriage would then proceed forward, bear to the right, and eventually leave via a lower gateway. During the winter season, transportation suitable for navigating snow-covered roads might be seen when sleighs were pressed into service. Since the ownership of matching teams of horses drawing ornate conveyances were another means to publicly accentuate one's wealth, a variety of the best available transports were often seen parked in the driveway. Finally, for those who might be walking, they took the pathway to the left which led to the front of the mansion. Walking up a set of wide stairs onto an ornate, columned, wrap-around porch, visitors would have found themselves facing a set of tall, double-wide doors.

While most dinner guests would not likely have seen the area behind the mansion, several important auxiliary features existed that provided support services. One was a greenhouse where "black Hamburg grapes [grew] in clusters across from Marshall Nell roses..."[10] Here there were additional flower beds that provided cuttings to decorate the dinner table, gardens containing an impressive twenty-three varieties of vegetables from which the kitchen staff produced savory dishes, and a small pasture that accommodated a few cows which contributed fresh cream and milk. Dominating the rear area was a three-story brick and stone structure that served as the Remington's stables. Housed within the building were horses, cows, feed, the family's carriages, and the gardener and his family. With its turret and slate roof, this facility resembled a scaled-down version of the main house.

As beauty is often said to be "in the eye of the beholder," so it was with Philo's new abode. Unlike the stately, pleasing lines of a Mt. Vernon or Monticello, his mansion had the heavy look of a European castle. While this kind of architecture may have appealed to his guests from across the Atlantic, many of whom were used to such a style in accommodations, it was a domicile quite unique to Ilion. Adding to its imposing appearance was the choice for a primary building material, described by Alden Hatch as "a monstrosity of pink and gray sandstone which looked like strawberry ice cream."[11] While perhaps bordering on garish to some, its exterior look was softened by the dark gray of the steep slate roof and the cream-colored paint covering the wooden trim.

However, regardless of the mixed reviews on the tastefulness and appeal of its external appearance, the building was undeniably eye-catching. Architecturally, the most notable features of the mansion's asymmetrical configuration were its two turrets. The front tower was an impressive four stories high, while the smaller one in the rear rose for three. To the children of Ilion, these two imposing structures appeared not as medieval barbicans, standing tall and strong as if to thwart an enemy attack, but rather instead were playfully called "the owl tower and the cat tower...because at night their outline resembled a familiar picture of three owlets on a twig and a puss on a wall."[12]

Among the other features in vogue at the time and incorporated into the building's design were a large porch with ornate trim; double-wide entrance doors; pairs of tall windows; bay windows; hooded windows; dormers; bargeboarding; and corbels. The overall effect created by these Italianate treatments gave the mansion a look that was heavy, ornate, and busy. Then, once the front door was opened to admit them, callers found themselves ushered into a long, spacious center hallway, its marble floor glistening from the reflected light of a chandelier and newel post. All around them was a house adorned to the fullest with only the finest in Victorian furnishings.

Capturing their gaze immediately and drawing it upward was a grand, curved staircase set off by a rich black walnut banister, accented halfway up by full-sized suit of armor set into a wall niche. Both the lower and upper halls, along with the connecting stairway, were paneled with the same dark wood as the railing. Bathed in light from a large chandelier, the overall impression was stunning. On the first floor were a total of six large living spaces: a formal parlor, a family room, a dining area, a music room, a conservatory, and a large kitchen.[13] Complimenting these chambers were a variety of smaller service spaces that included coat closet, pantry, and housekeeper's room.

The sweeping curve of the elegant staircase made for a stunning first impression on guests. (Source: Ilion Free Public Library)

In keeping with the elegance that permeated the decor of the entire mansion, each of the main rooms on the entry level was furnished with a fireplace and mirror. However, it was under the feet and over the heads of visitors that the extra touches of elegance could be found. In the parlor, family room, and music room, the hardwood floors were appointed with plush, flowered carpets, most likely imported from abroad. While these rugs were elegant, the lofty ceilings were spectacular to behold, for Philo had commissioned a German artist to create "delicately colored frescoes."[14] The finishing touches in these rooms were supplied by satin curtains accenting the windows, various wall hangings, and many exotic curios—the latter pieces often being the gifts to their American hosts by foreign dignitaries entertained in the mansion.

For those who knew quality when they saw it, a casting of the eyes about any room provided sights that no other home in Ilion could match in terms of the splendor in its grandiose furnishings. The music room exemplified this proclivity in the selection of a grand piano as its focal point. The dining room had an exquisite inlaid floor, and the kitchen's woodwork was of the same carved walnut found throughout the living quarters. Where appropriate, ceilings were bordered with intricately fashioned molding.

But among the beautiful downstairs rooms, the formal parlor, highlighted in blue, was said to be the most attractive of all. Mary

Ellen Leonard, in a magazine article titled "Remington's Mansion," painted an eloquent word picture of this classy interior space: "Fringed draperies of soft blue satin lined with cream satin, chairs and love seats upholstered in satin damask in blue and rose, a mantel of Italian marble and imported tiles, and an imported carpet in tones of rose, cream, and blue made this room lovely, considered from the viewpoint of that day or even the present time."[15] Enhancing its stylish appearance to an even greater extent were the parlor's walls "were, which were sheathed in blue brocade."[16] For those being treated to the grand tour, ascending the grand staircase revealed yet another level of luxury.

Like the first floor, the second story was divided into six full-sized rooms and several smaller, ancillary areas. Four of the subdivisions were the sleeping quarters, with the master bedroom located on the northwest side of the front of the house. As in the parlor below, it too afforded a commanding view of the village and the valley to the west. Also, like the room beneath, the same dominant blue schema was repeated in the color of the material used in the drapes, carpet, chairs, and canopy of the four-poster.

In addition to the bedchambers, the second floor boasted a library and nursery to round out its compliment of six rooms. The library was well-stocked, with many of its volumes being coveted first editions. Inviting chairs upholstered in leather provided suitable comfort in which to while away the hours reading. As for the nursery, Philo and his wife, the former Caroline Lathrop, had two daughters, both young adults when the family first occupied the mansion. While Mr. and Mrs. Remington would themselves no longer need a dedicated room for a baby, the facility may have been included for the convenience of guests or in the hopes of future grandchildren. A dressing room and a pair of bathrooms filled the remaining space on the second floor.

Progressing up the next flight of steps, the third story presented still further wonders amidst the diverse uses for which the living spaces at this multi-purpose level were put. Its most impressive feature was a large ballroom. With crystal glass chandeliers and mirrored walls, it offered a spacious, attractive spot for entertaining party goers. From this area, another set of stairs led up to the front tower. Then, in the 19th century's version of the man-cave—Mark Twain 's home also had a similar masculine refuge on on an upper floor of his Hartford, Connecticut residence—a billiards room beckoned, as a sanctuary where Philo and his male guests could enjoy each other's company over one of the more popular games of that era. Two more bedrooms occupied the third floor to accommodate those occasions when a large party was staying overnight. A fifth room was reserved for storage, serving as an easily accessible location for trunks and suitcases. The remaining large space on the third level was one used to house rather novel pieces of equipment for their time: large water tanks.

High ceilings, plush drapes, polished woodwork, and sturdy chairs were features of the parlor in the foreground and music room the rear. (Source: Ilion Free Public Library)

These containers, while far from standard apparatus in most of Ilion's homes in 1870, were indicative of several innovations built into the inner workings of the mansion. Pumped up from artesian wells on the factory grounds, this water supply fed into the mansion's system of indoor plumbing. In turn, such amenities as fully functioning bathrooms, a kitchen, and a laundry room were available to inhabitants. More practical than flashy, this feature nevertheless added much to the quality of life experienced by the home's residents and guests.

But the modernized aspects of the building did not end with obviating the need for an outhouse. Just inside the front door was an elevator. Operated manually by a rope-and-pully system, this apparatus permitted heavy items, such as guest's trunks, to be hauled to the second and third floors with far less effort required than lugging them up the stairs. Another advancement in nineteenth century technology installed in the mansion was a simple intercom, consisting of speaking tubes between upstairs and downstairs rooms. Topping off the mechanical comforts contained in the house was its steam-heating system based on a pair of boilers located in the cellar and radiators positioned under floors.

No doubt exists that the Remington Mansion served its intended purpose. From 1870-1880, Ilion reigned as the hub of the gun-making universe, and, during this glorious decade, countless emissaries from abroad beat a path to this little upstate community. Here they spent delightful hours being entertained at the mansion on the hill, while the factory below filled their orders at a rate of 1,500 rifles a day. Many were the nights when the house could be seen aglow, it lights visible all over town and up and down the valley. A blazing testimony to a combination of Yankee ingenuity, business acumen, and successful merchandizing. But good times rarely last forever. Samuel—the accomplished salesman—passed away in 1882. The gracious host that was Philo resigned from his position with the family business in 1886, his failing health allotting him but three years of retirement before he too died in Florida. Then in 1889, after 173 years of plying its trade as gunmakers, the Remington family divested itself of its holdings in the company.

Though the mansion was not part of the deal, the purpose for which it was built had ceased to exist. Over the years that followed, most surviving members of the family left town. But regardless of how far their travels took them, the mansion remained. On one hand, it was an aging monument to past accomplishments, while on the other it was a financial albatross to the Remington heirs. Slowly the house began to deteriorate, and the once trim appearance of the grounds gave way to a wild, unkempt look. The younger of Philo's daughters passed away in the home in 1913. She was followed by her older sister, Ida Remington Squire, in 1918. Then, after Ida's son spent a few more years in his grandfather's old home, the great house remained unoccupied for the remainder of its existence.

The beginning of the end came when the decision was made to divest the house of its treasures. Set for Saturday, October 2, 1920, at 1 p.m.—following the passing of Mrs. Squire and the resulting need to settle of her estate—heirs authorized a public auction of the mansion's furnishings. For those looking to own a piece of village history or just find a bargain amongst many quality pieces, there was much from which to choose. A sampling of the items shows among the large assortment of articles for sale were the following: "1 Satin Seven-piece Parlor Suite...10 Rocking Chairs...2 Large Parlor Mirrors...1 Burled English Walnut Bedroom Suite including canopy top bed...pictures, art portfolios, statuary, and bric-a-brac...the Furniture of one Library Room..."[17] Most all of the fine furnishings which made the interior of the mansion as elegant as its exterior were going to fall to the highest bidder once the gavel of auctioneer Watts Bullock sounded, and he sealed the deal with his verbal conformation: "Sold!" Everyday people, never having been on a guest list for a gala party in the home, finally got to see its fabled interior and possibly even own some of the well-known furnishings of which they heard so much about. The billiards table, the marble-topped center tables, and the mahogany dressers—all could be had for cash-on-the-barrelhead. What could also be viewed, though regrettably not purchased, were the beautifully-frescoed ceilings, walnut woodwork, and inlaid floors.

However, the costs of taxes and upkeep kept mounting. The asking price of $100,000 for the mansion was beyond the means of most Ilionites. Rather than let the proud heritage of this historic house end with the place becoming an eyesore and blight on the skyline of the village, the decision was made to have the building torn down. Before the wrecking ball swung its first fatal arc, final offers were extended to deed the property over to the village or a local organization. Some harbored the hope of keeping what was once a show place of the valley intact, possibly as a tourist attraction. In one of last attempts that might have saved the home, the Ilion Chapter of the International Order of Odd Fellows considered purchasing the property, but "a proposition to buy the Remington Mansion for use as a temple...was defeated by a 5 to 1 vote" of its governing board.[18] Fearing that the house would become a financial boondoggle, the village fathers also declined to acquire the complex.

Still, there were those who harbored second thoughts about seeing the historic home razed. "It would seem to an outsider," mused the editor of the *Fort Plain Standard*, "that the home of a family which was virtually responsible for Ilion being on the map might have been saved from destruction by that same community."[19]

Overgrown and rundown, the mansion's final days belied its past magnificence. (Source: Author's Collection)

He went on to offer that "if preserved, it should be a real future asset to that important village."[20] Unfortunately, the value that the newsman foresaw would not be fully recognized and exploited around the state for several generations to come. But that to which he was alluding—historic preservation as a basis for tourism—would be one of the focal points of the "I Love NY" campaign, and a Remington Mansion in all its opulent glory could easily have been a nice drawing card for Ilion.

At the 11th hour, the Ilion Chamber of Commerce's board of directors stepped forward and called for any villagers who "may have suggestions for saving the mansion to submit such ideas to the chamber in the hope that some suitable plan may be discovered whereby the landmark can be saved."[21] This last-ditch appeal came about due to public protests over the impending removal of the edifice. But nothing materialized from the plea. No stay of execution for the venerable old estate was forthcoming.

That the house was clearly in a state of steady deterioration was obvious. With vandals having targeted the property for some time, it was truly becoming more of an eyesore with each passing day. That the final die had finally been cast for demolition was announced by the *Utica Daily Press*, indicating that the razing of the building was imminent by virtue of "the contract having been let to a Toronto, Canada firm which will start work on Tuesday, April 1, [1928]."[22] In the waning days of its existence, many souvenir hunters visited the unoccupied property. People came to lament the prospect that "its towers overlooking the city will top the skyline no more."[23]

Long-time residents of the community who remembered the mansion's heydays stopped by for one last look, as if paying their respects at the wake of an old friend. Many were the mourners when the village's historic legacy became all the poorer when the great house ceased to exist in 1928.

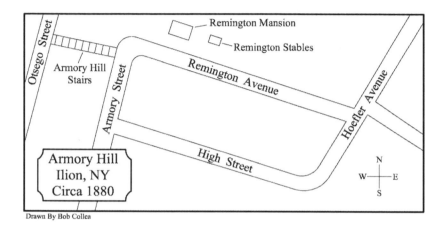

Drawn By Bob Collea

8

MABEN'S OPERA HOUSE
THE GREATEST SHOWS IN TOWN

John Zavinski, design director for *Life & Times* magazine once observed: "America's great cities wouldn't consider themselves great if they lacked proper venues for artistic performance and public assembly."[1] In this vein, Carnegie Hall was built in New York City in 1891. While most major cities would perforce have at least one dedicated site, if not multiple facilities, that housed the various musical and theatrical productions offered around within its metropolitan area, this same line of thinking also made its way to the hinterlands, where "civic pride and necessity led to the erections of many small-town opera houses, public halls, and fraternal lodge auditoriums in the era from the 1860s to 1890s"[2] In keeping with the national trend, Ilion's version entered upon the local scene in 1870. Following its construction, the building was called "Maben's Hall." After an enlargement occurred in 1874, it was rechristened "Maben's Opera House."

Unfortunately, ownership of the opera house proved somewhat of a money pit in those early years due to natural disasters. Early in the construction phase, strong winds blew down one of its unfinished walls, costing an additional $1000 to repair the damage. Then, a devastating fire in 1878 proved another set-back, though by no means a daunting one for the building's persistent, committed owner. "With characteristic enterprise," Dr. Hamblin Maben informed a reporter for the *Utica Daily Heralds* that he would "commence the work of reconstruction on his block and the opera house as quickly as the insurance was adjusted."[3] The loss this time was estimated by Dr. Maben at "$10,000 to $12,000," but the task of restoration was made somewhat easier and less costly because the outside walls had been saved and proved structurally sound.[4] Along with the repairs, Dr. Maben decided to enlarge the entranceway of the building.

His perseverance was rewarded by the erection of a first-class venue. Valley historian H. Paul Draheim—long-time columnist for the *Utica Daily Press*—praised its interior design as being one that made it "a plush and elegant showplace."[5] By comparison, its exterior was relatively pedestrian. Being a three-story brick building gave the opera house a heavy, ponderous look. By one floor, it was tallest structure on First Street. Possessing nothing like the soaring, airy lines of Sidney, Australia's world-famous opera house of current vintage, Maben's was for the most part a large box, devoid of architectural embellishments —functionality was the sole purpose of its exterior. Corbels or wooden brackets of two sizes under the roof's overhang provided the only noticeable outside adornments.

From the front at street level, the roof appeared flat. But from the side or looking down from West Hill, a peak with a modest slant was detectable that ran both north and south from the covering's mid-point. This little adaptation was actually a valuable if unseen feature of the opera house, for the slight gradiations facilitated the run-off off water. The opera house was located on the south side of First Street, between Otsego and Morgan. Since Dr. Maben had put up the $20,000 for its construction—amounting to a whopping $380,000+ in 2018 currency—he rightfully got to affix his name to the building. "Maben's Opera House" was duly christened!

A nice rendering of the façade of the opera house by a talented local artist named William Remmers. Note the storefronts along the ground floor that allowed Dr. Maben to generate some extra income through the rental of retail spaces. (Source: Bill Remmers' Family)

Like many similar structures of its era cross the country, the building was spacious and capable of serving multiple functions. The first-floor area was subdivided into three units. Two of its original tenants were the medical office of Dr. Maben and Ogden's Drug Store. In time, the basement was also rented out as a location for shops and offices. But it was the upper two floors that constituted the impressive venue which was the focal point of the facility, the place where large-group gatherings occurred. To reach these performance levels of the opera house, patrons of the arts climbed up a flight of stairs from the street, after first forking over the price of admission at a ticket booth situated just inside the front door.

Upon reaching the top of the stairway, spectators entered a

brilliantly-lighted lobby. Passing through this anteroom, they then found themselves inside the main hall consisting of 6000 square feet and capable of holding 1000 chairs for viewing plays, concerts, or speeches. If the evening's entertainment happened to feature a dance, then most of the seats would be removed.

Looking to the far end of the room, the all-important stage rose in an imposing manner. This platform was 54' deep and 80' wide, providing an ample setting of 4300 square feet upon which productions were held. Above the audience at the opposite end starting on stage left, a horseshoe-shaped gallery with gilt railings wrapped all the way around the hall to stage right. As was customary in any self-respecting theater, premium box seats had also been installed on both sides of the stage, projecting from the front curtain to its outer edge.

Known as the "proscenium," this was section of Ford's Theater in which President Lincoln was seated when assassinated.

Being the largest indoor facility of its kind in the entire village, Maben's was frequently in demand as a venue for many different uses. Pictured here may have been a temperance rally or a political speech. (Source: Ilion Free Public Library)

One of the oddities of Maben's Opera House was its name, for operas were far from the only art form to grace the floorboards of its stage. The reality was that the building functioned more like an all-purpose entertainment center, and not only for Ilion but also as "the social center for the Valley until the turn of the century."[6] With an eye toward sponsoring all kinds of performances, the facility was intentionally built to accommodate varied needs. Off-stage was a dressing room. The interior of the auditorium was at once expansive, functional, and decorative. Footlights and border lights surrounded the stage. Bracket lights framed the balcony, and a large metal reflector near the ceiling accentuated the glow of the gaslit chandeliers hung below. According to the Ilion Centennial booklet published in 1952, "different scenes were depicted on the bank of seven curtains" which could be used as befitted varied productions.[7]

Over the years, upkeep of the building was addressed on a regular basis. For example, the *Ilion Citizen* reported on August 25, 1882, that "the opera house has, during the summer, been put in good order for the season's work which will open next week. Dr. Maben has had the inside woodwork of the auditorium painted, the chairs varnished, and many other improvements and freshening's have been made."[8] While all these various embellishments aimed at the building's appearance and comfort made for more satisfied customers, the variety of the entertainment offered was still the bottom line that motivated the public to fill the venue's seats.

If what folks sought was quality entertainment, they were rewarded when top-rated stock companies began to include frequent stops in Ilion with productions such as the "Comical Countess" and "Uncle Tom's Cabin." So popular and enduring was the latter play, based on the Harriet Beecher Stowe's epic pre-Civil War novel of the same name, that performances were scheduled to kick-off the fall season of 1881 in back-to-back offerings by a pair of competing companies, one show scheduled for August 21 and the other on August 22!

General admission was set at twenty-five cents, while reserved seats went for a dime more. By way of comparison in 2021 dollars, a thirty-five cent ticket from 1881 would cost $8.98 today. While this may appear in hindsight to constitute a rather minimal charge, the cost was still one beyond the reach of many of that era.[9] Considering that that the average daily wage for a factory worker "...was approximately a $1.34 a day in 1880 which adds up to $345 annually for 257 days of work in a given year," it is amazing that Maben's shows played to packed houses on most occasions.[10]

Other traveling troupes offered their interpretations of other well-known shows such as "The Hidden Hand"—an action-comedy set in ante-bellum Virginia—and "Our American Cousin"—the sight and sounds of the latter comedy being the last that Abraham Lincoln ever witnessed—that provided can't miss opportunities for an enjoyable night out by Ilionites. Given favorable weather, most folks could easily enjoy a pleasant stroll to the opera house from almost anywhere in town without undue difficulty.

If the verbal prowess of a public speaker was more to an individual's taste, then Julia Ward Howe who composed the "Battle Hymn of the Republic," abolitionist preacher Henry Ward Beecher, nationally-acclaimed orator Edward Everett who spoke for two hours prior to Lincoln at Gettysburg, or controversial Civil War cavalryman General Judson Kilpatrick were among the notable lecturers that enticed patrons to Maben's.

For those whose tastes leaned more to the highbrow end of the performance spectrum, Maben's did remain to true to its name, for operatic productions were on occasion performed at the First Street hall. To wit, On October 11, 1881, "The Operetta of Laila, The Fairy Grotto" opened for a two-day run. The price of admission was "thirty-five cents to all parts of the house."[11] The following year, Pollard's world-renowned Lilliputian Opera Company—comprised of child actors between 7 and 16 years of age—presented its "novel and unique" interpretation of "Cinderella."[12]

From the more mainstream offerings of plays and speakers, the list of acts scheduled for Maben's often broadened to include quite a smorgasbord of performances. Minstrel shows were extremely popular, with a trio of these acts once being booked in less than a fortnight: Cal Wagner's troupe on August 19, 1881; followed on August 25, 1881 by "Happy Cal's Minstrels and Brass Band" comprised of "40 first-class artists"; and August 30 saw the "New Orleans Minstrels" sing, dance, and strum away above the footlights.[13] In the case of Wagner's company, the performers offered an enticing sneak preview of their talents when they paraded through the streets of town, prior to giving an evening show at Maben's.

Over the years of its existence, Maben's played host to a variety of events that catered to the differing tastes of its patrons. In addition to the more conventional plays, minstrel shows, operas, and guest speakers, there were concerts—one featuring the United States Marine Corps Band was especially memorable. But also among its range of offerings could be found temperance conventions, bazaars, political caucuses, speech contests, high school graduations, benefit shows, masquerade balls, magicians, occultists, fairs, vaudeville acts, walking marathons, and movies. With the seating removed, dances and roller skating parties were yet another type of activity sponsored by the hall's management.

Above and beyond Maben's regular playbill, several unforgettable events were held in its great hall that surpassed all others in the lasting impression which they made. One of these was the "Spanish Ball" in 1874, a western show in 1882, a performance by an internationally-known child star, and a boxing exhibition in 1891. The Spanish Ball was an extravaganza held in honor of the representatives from Spain who had come to Ilion to oversee their country's substantial purchase or weapons from Remington Arms. These gentlemen, some accompanied by their wives, spent a year living in the community. When the time for their departure arrived, a parting soirée was held. The event was so spectacular and well-attended that it was passed down for decades in the oral history of the village as the single greatest event of its kind ever held in the Mohawk Valley.

The western-themed performance featured none other than the traveling circus led by the world-famous showman William F. Cody. Popularly known as "Buffalo Bill," his exciting "Wild West Show" brought the color and thrills of America's last frontier to not only the east but also Europe. Given the limited confines of the second-floor hall, this particular production was a toned-down version of his more elaborate exhibitions that normally had buffalo, Indian warriors, stagecoaches, and US cavalrymen racing about an arena.

To drum up customers, Cody's entourage had strutted in grand style through the village before its evening performance, hoping to whet peoples' appetites to see the show. Native Americans dressed in their traditional regalia danced and chanted past wide-eyed boys, and real cowboys wearing six-shooters astride beautiful horses pranced up Railroad Street. Not to be missed, in his dashing goateed and mustachioed presence, was the living legend himself sitting astride a spirited white charger—the legendary figure of "Buffalo Bill" Cody! In addition to the story that would be acted out onstage, trick-shooting by the impresario himself was advertised as part of the evening's entertainment. In a town were gun-making was king, this portion of the show was eagerly anticipated, even more so because Cody had on previous occasions had visited Ilion to personally purchase a Remington firearm for use in his show.

The child star who graced the Maben's stage was the young Canadian prodigy Eva Tanguay, who in her maturity "became internationally known as the 'I Don't Care' girl [I.e.-after her hit song bearing the same name] of the Zeigfield Follies and other stage successes."[14] She thrilled audiences with her lively, unpredictable, zany, risqué, and bouncy performances. For twenty-five of her adult years, Miss Tanguay was a featured act on the vaudeville circuit. So popular was this star attraction, Maben's was motivated to announce in October of 1893 that "the Eva Tanguay Troupe appears every night this week at the opera house."[15] But when Eva first came to Ilion, she was just an ingénue in the early stages of her career. In addition to appearing at Maben's, the young girl forged a unique off-stage bond with Ilion, having attended one of the community's schools for several months when she and her parents were unexpectedly stranded, after the stock company that handled her bookings unexpectedly folded.

As for the boxing exhibition, the great John L. Sullivan—the last bare-knuckle champion who won the title in a 75-round marathon bout in 1889—came to Ilion in the 1890's. After spending the night at a local hotel, he sparred a few rounds at the opera house to the delight of local fight enthusiasts.

Unfortunately for the good Dr. Maben, his financial affairs were hard hit by the prolonged recession that stymied the country's economy from March of 1883 to May of 1885. Companies closed their doors, and approximately a million workers laid off. Tight money prompted many creditors to seek payment of debts. The latter predicament was the vice that put the squeeze on John Maben, for he lacked enough liquid assets to cover his debts which totaled "$18,616.95."[16] "His present embarrassment," offered the *Ilion Citizen*, "has been ascribed to unsuccessful speculation in oil."[17] On top of that drain on his capital resources, the doctor had also invested heavily in real estate around Ilion, a practice which further depleted his cash reserves. The result, as stated in the local paper, was that "out of the general wreck, nothing will be saved except the home furnishings of the doctor's wife." Thankfully, in perhaps his smartest business move, he had placed the Maben family's home in his wife's name in 1879, thereby shielding it from her husband's creditors.

Though a thoroughly humiliating experience, Dr. Maben had no choice but to put his holdings up for assignment. A man named Timothy Crisman was designated as the assignee. Mr. Crisman's role was to auction off all the doctor's worldly possessions—among these being "a fine team of horses, his gold watch and chain, his medical library, library desks, chairs, and many other articles with which it must be a great sacrifice to part."[18] Purchasers of any items received ownership of the article, but they did not incur any of Dr. Maben's debts. Those obligations remained his. At the end of the auction, any funds raised did not accrue to Dr. Maben, but instead they were dispersed, as far as they would go, to the outstanding creditors.

Perhaps of all his losses, the one that may have pained the doctor the most was that of his beloved theater: the opera house was sold for $15,000. "Notwithstanding hard times, this property is said to have paid two percent on the money invested in it. Expectation was that property would continue to be managed as before."[19]

After all was said and done, Dr. Maben moved to Kingston, New

York. But the change in residency did not improve the doctor's monetary woes, for in January of 1904 he filed for bankruptcy. Seventy-one years old at the time, it seems that he was still dogged by outstanding debts to the tune of $9325 from 1883. While in Kingston, he showed his affinity for the community he left behind by maintaining his subscription to the *Ilion Citizen* for the remainder of his life. Having been the attending physician to so many residents of the town, a member of the board of education, the village board, and at one time the German Flatts town supervisor, Dr. Maben had been an integral part of the community where he had made many friends over the years. As lauded in The History of Herkimer County, after "locating in Ilion in 1860, he gained a large practice and long occupied a foremost place in the profession."[20] Subscribing to the newspaper was a way for him to keep in touch the community that meant much to him.

Dr. Maben's earthly trials and tribulations ended on October 12, 1912, when he passed away at the age of seventy-nine from acute indigestion. For all his financial difficulties, his capabilities as a doctor were never in dispute. During his time in Ilion, he had enjoyed a highly successful practice, performing a variety of difficult surgeries successfully. Most noteworthy among his professional achievements, considering the relatively limited medical knowledge of the era in which he lived, was his work in the field of obstetrics, where he "attended over twenty-two hundred births, in no single instance of which did the mother die."[21]

To those who knew him personally, others who owed their lives to the man's medical prowess, and folks who spent many an enjoyable night at his opera house, Dr. Maben would be fondly remembered, not as a man who mismanaged his money but rather as a benevolent, engaging soul who gave much to the community. Fittingly, his remains were returned to Ilion, where he was buried in Armory Hill Cemetery. In an abbreviated eulogy, the *Herald* generously described him as "a good citizen, an excellent physician, and a level-headed, progressive businessman."[22]

In its post-Maben existence that outlived the doctor's ownership by forty years, the opera house continued to flourish well into the twentieth century. Under its new proprietor and manager, John F. Thomas, refinements were made almost immediately to the seating. In 1883, new folding seats were added. Two years later, specially designed opera chairs were installed, featuring "a wire hat-holder under each seat...a footrest...and an umbrella holder."[23]

Program from a Maben's Show. (Source: Author's Collection)

As had become the public's expectation, a variety of quality acts continued to find their way to the opera house's stage. In an era when most people worked a six-day, sixty-hour week, the building served as "an ornament to the village and a convenience to the public."[24] In the pre-radio, television, and movie era between the Civil War and the turn-of-the-century, live performances and events at the opera house provided one of the primary sources of public entertainment. In fact, a point of local pride came from the knowledge that "Ilion had the reputation of paying out more money for literary and dramatic entertainment than any other town between Utica and Albany."[25] On into the early years of the twentieth century, well-known touring companies continued to make Ilion a stop on their circuits.

After ten years in the theater business, Mr. Thomas sold the enterprise to a Charles Blum. Under Mr. Blum's stewardship, the opera house continued to offer the same varied line up of programs. In the fall of 1903, the musical "Man to Man" was on the playbill. A melodrama set in the Adirondacks, it had much local appeal. But as the years scrolled deeper into the 1900's, the days left for the opera house to serve as focal point of the arts as the community's unchallenged source of local entertainment dwindled. Other attractions, like movie theaters and sporting events, vied for the public's disposable income and leisure time. The radio hit the ground running, and, with its ability to bring plays, concerts, and ballgames inexpensively into the home, soon diminished the need for people to frequent civic gathering places for comparable types of performances.

As for other places that could accommodate large groups, the new Ilion Junior-Senior High School—opened in 1913—boasted both a spacious gym and an impressive auditorium with a stage, so events could be held at these sites as well. Then, in 1930, the depression made spending money on anything but the bare necessities out of the question for many people.

In its death throes, Maben's Opera House changed hands several times. With fewer paying customers, even minimal upkeep became too costly to afford. Improvements were out of the question. Among the last events at the venerable old building was a boxing card in 1931.

According to the *Utica Daily Press*, "matchmaker Anthony Merl announces that the boxing bouts under the auspices of the Elks will be in the future held in the Ilion Opera House, First Street, instead of the Temple Theater [i.e.-the Odd Fellows building on the northwest corner of First and Morgan Streets]." Then, in the mid-30s—due to continued deterioration—the auditorium was condemned. Instead of the thousands of patrons who once filled the seats of its spacious galleria, only a mere handful of the curious were now permitted upstairs at one time.

First Street—as it faced toward the Odd Fellows Temple looming in the background on the corner of Morgan and First Streets. Union Street enters to the right just past the long row of second floor windows. Maben's was the tall building on the left. First and Union Streets were both one-way at that time. Urban renewal took Union Street off the map of Ilion. The post office, seen behind the lamppost in the center, is all that remains in the photograph. (Source: Ilion Free Public Library)

The beginning of the end for the opera house came in 1946. Its owner at that time, a man named Charles Lawrence, decided to convert the idle upper floors to profitable uses once again, which meant that the facility would henceforth cease to exist in its original configuration as a performance hall. "When carpenters finish their remodeling," revealed the *Utica Observer-Dispatch*, "the stage will be used by local officials for a meeting site, the auditorium will become a billiards parlor, and the dressing rooms will become offices."[26] In its reconstituted format, the old opera house limped on into the 50s and 60s.

However, renovating the facility did not prove as lucrative as anticipated, and eventually the upper floors emptied out, leaving only the street level spaces with occupants. But the grand old dame was not fated to pass her final years with any modicum of grace or dignity. For one of the last times, Maben's made the pages of the local newspaper, which ironically was one of the businesses still located in the building. However, unlike the almost daily announcements once placed in the paper trumpeting an upcoming performance, this small blurb revealed the existence of one final embarrassment that had befallen the once vibrant and venerated theater. As is wont to happen with semi-abandon buildings, windows had been broken on the upper floors. To prevent water from getting inside, these openings were boarded over. Along with being an unsightly solution, this attempt at damage control created a worse problem, for "it accidentally bottled in some of the pigeons who had been residing in the opera house..."[27] The constant fluttering and cooing of the trapped birds proved distracting to the remaining tenants in the building, necessitating that some of the boards be removed until the feathered squatters found their way out.

But the opera house's long life finally came to an end in 1972. The village of Ilion was then amid a massive urban renewal project that was reshaping the appearance of the downtown area of the community. While most of the facelifting took place from the north side of First Street down to Clark, a strip of buildings on First Street's southside were also razed. One of these victims of progress was the now empty opera house. First Street had always had a dogleg to the left about one-half of the way between Otsego and Morgan Streets. This meant that a person standing on the southeast corner of Otsego and First Streets—opposite Freeman's—could not see the storefronts on the lower southwest end on the corner of First and Morgan Streets —Buckminster's Jewelers and Roach's Liquor being the last two establishments to occupy these spaces. Planners wanted the angle removed to allow for a straight edge to the parking lot being created from the northeast corner of Otsego and First Streets west to the post office. The Ilion Police Station now exists on part of the site where Maben's once ruled Ilion's entertainment world. Of all the former tenants on First Street, only the post office remains.

Preceded by DeWitt's Canal, Eliphalet's forge, Philo's mansion, and Osgood's Hotel, Maben's Opera House joined a growing list of former landmarks once intimately associated with the town's history —the unifying thread being that all were once vital, vibrant places that now no longer existed. Yet, the lack of a physical presence can never dim the glory of their past prominence. This is especially true of the opera house when the excited declaration that "We're going to Maben's tonight" heralded the prospects for an evening of first-class entertainment to generations of Ilionites.

9

THE SPANISH BALL:

HIGHLIGHT OF ILION'S SOCIAL SCENE

Following the end of the Civil War and the subsequent cancellation of its governmental contracts to supply rifles and revolvers, the fortunes of Remington Arms took an abrupt downturn. However, much to everyone's relief, the company's economic slump proved only short-lived. A reversal of fortune came about quickly due to the invention of the rolling block rifle with its superior breech-loading mechanism. Almost overnight, the military version of this exceptional longarm became the primary choice to outfit their troops among many nations around the world. In the opinion of gun-expert George Layman, "military sales of the Remington rolling block were the Remington brothers' most salable commodity, starting in the black powder era and ending well into the smokeless era of World War I..."[1]

With Samuel Remington operating out of a European office as the company's highly visible agent, orders came pouring into Ilion. Among the many buyers, one particularly substantial client was Spain. For almost a quarter-century, commencing in 1870, its army was supplied with the Remington product. As part of the promotional aspect of dealing with foreign governments, a frequent practice was for their representatives to visit Ilion. Since most of these delegations originated in countries which were monarchies, a certain level of protocol—a la the "red-carpet treatment"—greeted their excursions to the village and the plant. It was in keeping with this desire to put-on-the-dog that Philo Remington was convinced to build an elaborate mansion, so that a proper setting would exist in which to entertain guests from abroad.

While over the years many emissaries from different countries were feted by the Remington's, the epitome of not only the gunmakers' but the entire village's turn as gracious hosts occurred in the winter of 1874. For many months up to that time, agents for one of the company's best clients, collectively known as the Spanish Ordinance Commission—consisting of the Spain's New York counsel, fifteen army officers, three naval officers, and a dozen cadets—had stayed in town to oversee the crown's purchase of 140,000 rifles.[2] Once the last rifle was completed in December of 1874, the delegation was scheduled to leave, after maintaining almost a year-long vigil while they waited for their country's order to be filled.

Knowing that the day of departure was coming, plans had been in the works for some time to give these special guests a memorable send-off. With many willing hands among its population of 2,900, the community-wide endeavor was viewed as a fitting gesture to thank the foreign delegation not only for the lucrative contract bestowed upon the hometown business, but also for "contributing to the social entertainment of the ladies and gentlemen" of the village.[3] For during their lengthy stay, the Spaniards had hosted many elegant parties, and in turn they were frequently honored guests invited to equally lavish levees in homes about town. For a small industrial village set in a rural county of upstate New York, the introduction of these visitors from the Old World, with their gracious bearings and genteel manners, made "the summer and fall of 1874...[in] Ilion the scene of many social affairs..."[4]

The efforts of a planning committee called the "Gentlemen of Ilion," supported by the Remington's and other members of the town's business fraternity, culminated in a grand reception held on December 18, 1874. The whole affair was called the "Spanish Ball," and the venue chosen to host this extravaganza was the Maben Opera House. Built in 1871 by Dr. Hamblin Maben to provide villagers with a cultural center, the facility could seat 1000 people for performances. With its chairs being removable, sufficient room could be created to allow for a variety of diverse offerings. Over its lifetime, this interior flexibility gave Ilionites the opportunity to enjoy the likes of plays, concerts, recitals, orations, operettas, conventions, dances, movies, high school graduations, and minstrel shows. But without doubt, the most highly-acclaimed event in the building's long catalogue of performances and productions was the gala organized in honor of the guests from Europe's Iberian Peninsula.

Located in a building positioned on the south side of First Street, just around the corner from the main thoroughfare that was Otsego Street, the space for the opera house filled its second and third stories, stretching above several stores situated on the ground level. For the auspicious occasion of the "Spanish Ball," its cavernous auditorium was colorfully decorated with combinations of American and Spanish flags, fragrant sprigs of evergreen, exotic houseplants loaned by attendees, and lighted candles. The evening's activities were divided into three stages. First, a dinner was held at the Osgood Hotel, the village's premier hostelry located one block to the north on the corner of Main and Otsego Streets.

As for the backgrounds of the attendees, the majority of those who later made their way up the stairway of the opera house were Ilionites. Most families in town could boast of members who participated in the evening's gala activities. In addition to the Spanish military contingent, officers from the Egyptian Army—another big client of the Remington's—and the United States Army were also present. A local paper suggested that "nearly every city in the state and all counties were represented by ladies and gentlemen."[5]

One of the attendees, a young and vivacious woman at the time, was Miss Grace Howard. She had come into Ilion that night with a group of friends from West Winfield, attending the ball as a guest of her future husband Elvert Doty. Some seventy-four years later, that special evening remained a fond, glowing memory in her still-sharp mind. "I can almost see the hall decorated with massed Spanish and American flags," Mrs. Doty reminisced, "[and] the band on the stage in their striking uniforms, the vivid beauty of the Spanish ladies with the wife of Colonel Bermudez carrying a bouquet of pink and white camellias, a Mrs. Moore in red velvet with a red bustle and accompanied by her little son in a black velvet suit with a deep lace collar, Mrs. Seward Merry in a light blue satin dress with her hair piled high, and Mrs. Charles Crandall in black and white grenadine gown, with all of the gentlemen in full evening dress, some of the Spaniards wearing colorful decorations and others in uniforms loaded with gold braid."[6] Mrs. Doty also remembered that "each lady was presented with a beautiful favor, a dainty French box with colored flowers on the lid."[7] In socializing amidst a veritable who's who of prominent Ilionites, the event made a lasting impression on Miss Howard—indeed truly one of her life's most unforgettable moments.

While some folks decided to walk between the hotel and the opera house, carriages were lined up in proliferation on Otsego and Main Streets for those who either chose to forego strolling the block-and-a-half between venues along the dusty roads or simply preferred to arrive at the party in a style befitting the elegance of the occasion. Once the partygoers had settled into their seats at the opera house, they were in for special treat. The next part of the evening's program was a band concert. Anticipation for the performance was high and rightfully so, since this was not going to be just any concert. Given the special import of the occasion, planners had pulled out all the stops. That no expense was spared was best evidenced by the superior quality of the musicians engaged to perform, first in concert and then for the dance that followed. Not satisfied to engage the services of any local musicians, the planning committee cast a wide net in search of exemplary talent.

As gala events went, the Spanish Ball was a once-in-a-lifetime experience that gave those who attended a memory that they would carry with them forever. As one of the highlights in Ilion's "Golden Age," consensus has been that nothing like this extravaganza has graced the Mohawk Valley's social scene in the almost century-and-a-half that have passed since that dazzling Victorian era night. (Source: Ilion Free Public Library)

Scheduled to play that evening was no less than Patrick Sarsfield Gilmore's famous 22nd Regimental Band, featuring Matthew Arbuckle on the cornet. Based in New York City, both the musical group, its leader, and the showcased soloist enjoyed blue-ribbon, international reputations. In addition to his credentials as a renowned conductor before and after the Civil War, Gilmore had additional measures of acclaim attached to his resume, for he was an accomplished cornetist in his own right and a veteran of the Civil War.

In 1861, he and his musicians had enlisted in the Massachusetts 24th Infantry. However, instead of firearms, they carried instruments, performing their service as the regimental band. However, when the federal government deemed such accompaniment as an unnecessary financial and manpower drain, such bands were mustered out. Gilmore, however, continued to be of service to his country by offering benefit concerts, regrouping the Bay State's militia bands, and writing "When Johnny Comes Marching Home." Suffice to say, it was considered a real coup to have this esteemed musician and his entourage playing in Ilion.

So, how successful was this lavish event in the eyes of contemporary observers? For that grand evening, Ilion was clearly the place to be. In this one night, the extravaganza brought a level of glamor and glitz never previously witnessed in the Mohawk Valley. "The project caused quite a flutter in society throughout Central New York," reported the *Utica Observer Dispatch*.[8] The *Herkimer Democrat* inflated local pride when it called the event "a magnificent combination of pleasure, beauty, mirth, music, fashion, and rare social enjoyment."[9] The *New York Graphic* paid the ball its greatest homage by stating that "it is a question whether the famed Brussel's Ball, given on the eve of the Battle of Waterloo, excelled the Spanish Ball."[10] In the gushing estimation of the *Utica Morning Herald*, "Ilion leads the social column this season and deserves to be incorporated as a city for its liberality, enterprise, good citizens, genial gentlemen, and gloriously good and pleasing ladies."[11]

While over the next 150 years Ilion would go on to experience other celebratory highlights in commemoration of important centennial and bicentennial milestones in its history, the memory of the "Spanish Ball" as a unique occasion that was never duplicated lingered on into the twentieth century.

10

FRUIT OF THEIR LABORS:

THE "ILION STRAWBERRY"

Over the years, most of Ilion's acclaim has come from the durable goods made in its factories, with guns and typewriters being the foremost among the local industrial products that gained wide-spread national and international distribution. However, during an agricultural heyday that ran from 1885 through 1900, the name "Ilion" was also well-known for a perishable product grown on farms in the uplands south of the village. In fields located along Barringer and Old Forge Roads, what became recognized as "Ilion strawberries" were cultivated. In 1889, the *Utica Daily Observer* estimated that "there are between two and three hundred acres devoted to raising berries that are packed and shipped from Ilion."[1]

According to Katherine Osterhout Cameron, daughter of one of the early growers named Sanford Osterhout, "the season was at its height for a period of ten days to two weeks in June."[2] Mrs. Cameron added that "thousands of quarts of berries were shipped daily to the local market[s] east and west and in [a] refrigerator car to New York City."[3] Minus the aid of a reincarnated Paul Revere, the news that "the berries are coming" was a yearly phenomenon that spread rapidly to the markets throughout and even well-beyond the Mohawk Valley.

East and west across the region, newspapers for years provided abundant advertising, consistently informing their readers in timely announcements that the much-anticipated season was upon them. For example, *The Glens Falls Morning Star* on June 29, 1893 announced: "Ilion strawberries fresh today at J. S. Powers, 18 Warren Street."[4] The following year, a Utica paper alerted its readers that "Ilion strawberries are in their prime and plenty...hundreds of crates will find their way to eastern markets this week."[5] Nearing the end of the century, *The Canajoharie Courier* of June 30, 1899 reported: "Ilion strawberries are now on the market."[6] Even though the boom years had long since passed, a grocer in Richfield Springs ran an ad in 1932 that proclaimed "Ilion strawberries now available."[7]

The berry that grew so productively in the local fields was of a variety known as the "Wilson," a popular kind among the fruit's cultivated varieties. Described in such flattering terms as "large, luscious, and delicious," the berry was "a deep red, of medium size, and, while quite tart, still of a very pleasant flavor."[8] Many folks believed the Wilson was the closest domesticated berry possessing a flavor comparable to those found in the wild.

The familiarity of the public with the Wilson in the North, along with its accompanying popularity, grew out of a curious promotional offer from Horace Greeley in 1865. Desirous of increasing the circulation of his newspaper—*The New York Tribune*—the creative editor established a unique giveaway program: open a new subscription to his publication and receive a free strawberry plant!

In Ilion, the successful development of strawberry production had the Doty family to thank for introducing the fruit as a future cash crop in the mid-1860s. Abner Doty had purchased a farm, southwest of the village along Barringer road, in 1863. Shortly thereafter, "his first [strawberry] plants were obtained from the greenhouse of Harvey Hakes," a local florist whose shop was located on East Main Street.[9] "Rightfully considered the pioneer of the [strawberry] business in this section," Abner eventually took on his only boy as a partner. Henceforth their business became known as "Doty & Son. Abner Doty passed away in 1890, but "the going strawberry concern which he founded remained prosperous in the hands of Elvert."[10]

By the time young Doty assumed control of the family's strawberry fields—about twenty-five acres—years of trial and error had evolved into a very efficient system for harvesting the fruit. Given the delicate nature of the berries, they had to be hand-picked. With a relatively small window in which to gather in the ripened fruit, this process was of necessity very labor intensive. Since his operation was one of the largest, Mr. Doty usually hired anywhere from 100 to 150 hands of all ages, both sexes, and mixed nationalities. Some were long-time residents, while others were recent Italian immigrants. In the early years, "a packet on the Erie Canal brot (sic) pickers from Utica who alighted at the foot of Barringer Road and walked to the fields."[11] Since the expectation was that workers would begin their labors at the break of day, those who travelled over long distances were afforded accommodations on the premises in what amounted to a barracks-style facility.

Once out in the fields, the crews became integral parts of an efficient system that had evolved over the years to move the produce from farm-to-market as quickly as possible. Each picker was provided with a long, lightweight, foot-high stand that was set astride a row of plants. On the flat surface atop the little table were placed as many quart baskets as the platform could hold, which was usually around fifteen. As the worker moved along a row, the stand was brought along with him. Once all the baskets were full, an attendant quickly moved them to the edge of the field where they were transferred to waiting crates. A crate held thirty-six baskets. At one time, the crates and baskets were made right on the farm, but eventually they were purchased by the carload from an outside source and distributed among the berry farmers.

When the wagons were full, loads were slowly driven north down Barringer Road, east on Main Street until they eventually came to its intersection with Railroad Street, now known as Central Avenue. Turning left and immediately passing through what was once called "Bridge Square," the berry-laden wagons proceeded over the lift bridge and north toward their destination: the loading docks of the West Shore Railroad. These were located a half-block north of West River Street and then west off Railroad Avenue beside the train tracks. There the large wooden crates would be transferred to the warehouse's platform to await their eventually placement aboard an express train, destined to haul the precious perishables as rapidly as possible to New York and other cities along the eastern seaboard.

Once delivered to urban marketplaces, the well-known "Ilion Strawberries" flew off the grocers' shelves. The opening of the West Shore in the 1880s, followed by the introduction of refrigerated railcars, greatly expanded the distances to which the berries could be sent from Ilion. Boston, for example, eventually began receiving its own direct shipments of the coveted fruit.

In working the fields, pickers usually put in ten-to-twelve-hour days. The only respite until quitting time was a brief lunch break. An observer noted that "a field of pickers presents a curious sight, [for] they are all dressed in a variety of costumes."[12] Given the small window of opportunity to gather the ripening berries, staying focused on the job at hand was paramount. Yet, the workers were not driven mercilessly, for they were given sufficient leeway which allowed them to converse, sing, and joke. However, just as time was of the essence for the farmers, so also was putting their shifts to good use in the fields of equal importance to all the hired hands. Since their pay was not derived on an hourly basis, but rather instead by the number of quarts picked, it behooved them to keep moving up and down the long rows of bushes, filling as many baskets as possible. Each full basket meant that a picker got one ticket which indicated his running tally over the course of the work-day.

Strawberry pickers put in long days in the hot upland fields south of Ilion, where they helped harvest the local crop of this delicious fruit that gained a statewide reputation for its superior quality. (Source: Ilion Free Public Library)

As she later recalled, Katherine Cameron said numbers were the likes of "...1, 2, 3, 5, 7, 10, and 15, and payment was made at the close of the season. The price for picking was 1½ cts per qt. and later 2 cts."[13]

Of course, the bottom line in all of this for the farmers was not to provide jobs and an income for day laborers. Like any business, the whole enterprise was a venture intended to realize personal profits for the growers. Yearly sales' totals fluctuated, depending upon the size of the yield and going wholesale rate that buyers were willing to pay. However, some enlightening figures are available from the meticulous records that Mr. Doty kept beginning in 1875. Over the next twenty-nine years, his account book showed that through 1904, "1,200,163 quarts" were harvested, making the average per annuum about 40,000 baskets.[14] In the 1880s, the wholesale price per quart hovered in the range of 10 to 12 cents. Using Mr. Doty's cumulative quart tally and a low-ball ten-cent per basket wholesale price as an average, the strawberry entrepreneur would have realized a minimum of somewhere around $120,000. In today's dollars, the intake would be roughly about 3.4 million dollars.

Since Doty & Son was the largest producer in the Ilion area, a hefty return on their crop was to be expected. Other growers would have proportionately received profits commensurate with the lesser number of crates which they respectively had sent to market. Then, in 1885, several of the smaller growers banded together to form the "Ilion Strawberry Association." The idea behind the formation of this organization was "for the purpose of mutual helpfulness..."[15] Originally, fifteen members banded together. Though the Doty's never joined—perhaps seeing no benefit to their already flourishing business —those farmers who did watched their strawberry operations thrive too. By hiring an agent based in New York City and dealing directly and exclusively with him, association members realized the best possible prices for their strawberries.

While not every grower joined, enough did so to give the local association some clout in obtaining fair prices for its product in urban markets. (Source: Author's Collection)

By the time of the "Great Depression" in the 1930s, the strawberry business in Ilion had begun to wane. The decline occurred partly because the core of original strawberry farmers had passed away, and their heirs were not as inclined to stay with the venture. Another reason cited is that over the next ninety years change in the appearance of the area began to dramatically occur.

Many houses were built along Old Forge Road on what were once strawberry fields, while the Doty's extensive holdings on Barringer Road became a golf course. Outside competition from other parts of the country such as California increased too, as refrigeration permitted long-distance hauling. Frozen foods eventually added yet one more source of competition.

Today the acres of strawberry plants that once flourished just outside of Ilion are gone. No longer does the need exist for scores of pickers to arrive in June. Wagons, heavily laden with crates of fresh berries, do not ply their way slowly down to the railroad's freight house any more. But, for all that is gone, what does remain is everlasting...and that is the history of the land. Though the uses to which it is currently being put may change again in another ninety years, its past as the nurturer of a prosperous industry in Ilion will always give it a special niche in the rich and varied historical heritage of the village—telling of an era when June rolled around each year and New Yorkers kept an eye on their local papers, scanning their columns for one particular announcement especially guaranteed to please the palates of the entire family: "Ilion strawberries have arrived!"

II

CHRISTOPHER LATHAM SHOLES:

"FATHER OF THE TYPEWRITER"

Save for the large wooden box that he clutched tightly with his hands, the man's arrival was about as inauspicious as it could have been. Even if he had revealed to fellow travelers that what he carried was an invention, a crude model that he simply called a "writing machine," that disclosure would have meant nothing tomost, if any, of the nearby passengers. When he stepped down from the New York Central coach at the North Ilion station, no trumpets announced his appearance nor did a pathway strewn with rose petals lead him to the omnibus which waited to bring him across the river and into Ilion. Instead, considering the profound impact that the device carried by Christopher Latham Sholes was to have on the business world, his coming to the Mohawk Valley was indeed a very pedestrian and unheralded arrival.

The machine that Mr. Sholes brought with him was in a very real sense not solely his own contrivance. Over almost 150 years, other men with creative minds like his had experienced their own successes and failures as they in varying degrees tried to produce a device that could allow its operator to print words on paper by striking attached keys. While this mid-western tinkerer would be the one to finally bring a practical typewriter to fruition, his success had clearly come from building on the work of predecessors. Nevertheless, recognizing the originality of his efforts, Sholes was granted a patent by the government on June 23, 1868.

For Sholes, progress in developing his machine had been slow but deliberate. Working in increments that built upon each other—incorporating the knowledge gained from what worked and what did not—he moved steadily toward creating a device that fundamentally operated on the basic premise that all the typewriters that followed would function: the tapping of a key that caused a letter or symbol—a piece of "type" attached to a lever or arm—to pop up, strike a piece of carbon paper or an inked ribbon, and leave an imprint on blank paper placed underneath.

Christopher Sholes - (Source: Stromsburg Headlight)

An example of one of these early, incremental steps in developing a prototype for his invention saw Sholes produce a working model capable of printing one letter—a "W." With a telegraph office providing a temporary testing site and instrument, Sholes attached a brass rendering of the letter to the bottom of a transmission key. He placed a leaf of white paper, overlain with another of carbon, under the striking head of key. When the device was activated, the result was the imprint of a "W" on the paper. From that point forward, the challenge became that of adding more letters and symbols, synchronizing their rapid interactions, and providing a means for their manual operation.

In this sense, his brainchild would continue to be a work in progress, one for the most part continued by others. No sooner had he brought his machine to Ilion and turned it over to the Remingtons, than they immediately placed the project in the hands of W. K. Jenne, one of their ace mechanics and problem-solvers. As an example of the typewriter's continuous improvement, the device that Sholes handed over in 1873 now produced capital letters. By 1878, Jenne had introduced a shift key, allowing for the typing of both small and upper-case letters. The passing years and on-going research and development led to such upgrades as a reduction in the mechanism's overall size, automatic indentation, and greater portability. In an Australian newspaper advertisement run in 1924, the newest tweak was touted: "The Latest and Greatest Remington Contribution to Typewriter Progress is the New Quiet 34. This New Remington is Quiet in its Operation. The Natural Touch Makes it a Pleasure to Operate..."[1] The designation of number 34 is significant. For it meant since the introduction of the first Remington typewriter, identified as machine #1, there were 33 improved iterations over the intervening fifty years.

The inventor's journey from Milwaukee to Ilion covered 830 miles. A long trip to be sure, but one accomplished in a matter of hours, thanks to the then modern miracle of the train. However, his quest to perfect a working typewriter was a different story, a pursuit that had taken Sholes over six years of tinkering and the construction of what had comprised "over 25 model typewriters" to produce a working, saleable machine.[2] In addition to being a printer, journalist, politician, and publisher at various stages in his life, Sholes also liked to tinker with gadgets—making him a "Renaissance man" of sorts. In his spare moments, he often frequented a local Milwaukee machine shop, a place which served as hangout for amateurs like Sholes to share and test their ideas and innovations.

Once he got to the point where a breakthrough was imminent, Sholes knew that he needed far greater resources than those he had available to perfect, manufacture, and market a finished product. It was at this point in the saga that Remington family entered the picture. While gun-making was the company's bread-and-butter, the entrepreneurs' blood coursing through the three Remington brothers' veins made them interested in diversifying their product line. As luck would have it, Sholes' financial backer, James Densmore, had written a letter to Philo Remington, describing the new writing machine and inquiring as to whether the Ilion business man had any interest in the invention. Already engaged in the manufacture of sewing machines and farm products, the typewriter was envisioned as potentially offering a nice addition to the company's existing array of varied merchandise.

When Sholes and Densmore arrived in Ilion, they went straight to the Osgood Hotel, where the eldest Remington brother awaited them. After discussing the matter, a deal was tentatively hammered out. Remington bought out Sholes' half-share of the invention for $12,000. Densmore's rights to the patent were leased, in return for which he would receive royalties. By entering into this agreement with Philo Remington, Sholes and Densmore brought to bear on their machine the ingenuity and expertise found among the skilled craftsmen in the shops of Remington Arms. A fresh set of minds and willing hands would pick up where Sholes had left off.

Remington's First Typewriter
(Source: Ilion Free Public Library)

So it was that with the assistance of Remington personnel, the final kinks were worked out. The company moved quickly with the machine. Sholes had brought his prototype to them in February of 1873, and by September of the following year the first Remington typewriters were ready for market. In appearance, this progenitor of millions to come was a very bulky, crude-looking piece of equipment. Capable of only producing capital letters, it was mounted on a sewing machine table, using a foot-pedal to advance the paper. Given that it was somewhat functionally limited in operation and ungainly in appearance, the world did not immediately embrace the typewriter. In its coming out party at the 1876 Centennial celebration of the nation, Sholes' creation drew scant attention from a discerning world. While not a competing invention in terms of providing the same service, also making its debut was Alexander Graham Bell's telephone. While "the talking machine created a furor, the writing machine there neither dazzled nor convinced the public. "[3]

Part of problem was that "It was difficult to make the public believe that it would pay to invest $125 in a typewriter when a pen could be had for a cent or two."[4] However, the Remington's' ace-in-the-hole was that they had the resources and know-how to move their products. "Salesmen and advertisers were called in," the *Buffalo Evening News* reported, "and the typewriter was launched on its career of conquest."[5] Between 1874 and 1885, successive offices were open in England, France, Belgium, Italy, Holland, Denmark, Greece, Germany, and Russia.

In addition to the expansion of their marketing campaign accompanied by continued product improvement, the Remington brothers soon made another momentous decision—in 1886, they elected to sell their burgeoning typewriter business. The purchasers were a triumvirate of businessmen, all Remington employees: William Wycoff, Henry Benedict and Clarence Seamans. They initially named their new venture the " Standard Typewriter Manufacturing Co."

But in 1902, thanks to a stipulation originally included in the sale agreement, their business was henceforth rebranded as the "Remington Typewriter Company." This name tweak allowed them to trade on the highly-regarded reputation of the gunmaker, even though other than the proximity of their factories there was no longer any connection between the two enterprises.

Though trading on such an established, recognized name as "Remington" possessed was a wise business move, in hindsight some confusion was inadvertently created concerning the gunmakers continued involvement with the production of typewriters—which was none. In the years that followed, the wisdom of the original purchase and the subsequent name-change proved to be profitable decisions. By 1923, the 50th anniversary of Sholes' successful creation of a working machine, estimates placed the number of typewriters in the world at about 10,000,000! In addition to serving as a practical, useful machine in businesses and homes, the *Scientific American* also noted that the introduction of the typewriter "...has furnished profitable and pleasurable employment for thousands of men and women who might otherwise have been engaged in harder work at lower wages."[6]

In 1925, because of its ongoing quest for product improvement, the typewriter company introduced the first electric typewriter. Though it would not be until 1949 that all the bugs were worked out to the company's satisfaction, its engineers had kept tinkering until finally they created a device that "was not only faster and more practical, but it offered handsome, legible print work."[7]

A later model indicative of ongoing effort sat product improvement by the company. (Source: Ilion Free Public Library)

The next major step in the evolution of the typewriter business occurred in 1927, when a significant merger took place. The Remington Typewriter Company joined with a natural partner, the Rand Kardex Bureau, which made office equipment. The new enterprise would be called "Remington Rand," again trading on the established name of the respected gunmaker but still not having any direct affiliation with the Arms.

Over the years, the business continued turning a profit. Its machines became smaller until in time portable models were being built. Then quieter typewriters powered by electricity were added to the product line.

The heydays of lucrative sales did not let up until the 1960s, but then from that point forward typewriter purchases began to dwindle. By that time, the machines were no longer made in Ilion, with the company's location having been shifted to Elmira in 1935. The end came on April 1, 1972, when all production ceased.

It had been a good run for an innovative piece of equipment, one that had lasted a hundred years. Ultimately, typewriters weren't gradually phased out due to any shortcomings in their efficiency, usefulness, or design. Instead, a new kid showed up on the block: computers that possessed word-processing capabilities. By this time, Christopher Sholes and the tri-founders of the Standard Typewriter Manufacturing Company were all long gone, so they suffered no anguish from the demise of the device which they had carefully nurtured from an idea to a reality.

In their lifetimes, William Wycoff, Henry Benedict, and Clarence Seamans were rewarded two-fold: first, they were widely acclaimed as astute business men; and second, they each accumulated significant personal wealth that made for comfortable lives.

As for Christopher Sholes, he left the scene much too early, passing away in 1890. By contrast, he neither died a rich man like the entrepreneurs who produced, promoted, and sold his machine nor one who was overly lauded in his lifetime for the positive impact wrought by his innovation. With respect to his lack of financial gain from his invention, amidst the booming sales that came after he had sold his patent, Sholes wryly commented: "All my life I have been trying to escape being a millionaire, and at last I think I have finally succeeded."[8]

Unfortunately, along with the absence of personal profit, recognition for his accomplishment was not as forthcoming in his lifetime as it should have been. However, in the years since his passing, Sholes has posthumously received some of the respect for which he was long overdue. In 1923, for example, a monument was erected in Forest Home Cemetery where he was buried. Its simple inscription reads:

"The Father of the Typewriter
Dedicated By
The Young Men And Women of America
In Grateful Memory Of One Who
Materially Aided In The World's Progress"[9]

Commenting on the erection of this stone and bronze tableau, the *Newburyport Daily News* felt that this tribute was quite appropriate, since " he made a conspicuous gift to our modern society."[10] Then, two months later, a monument to Sholes was unveiled in Ilion, as a part of the 50th anniversary celebration of the founding of the Remington Typewriter Company. Perhaps the inventor's greatest public kudo did not come until long after his death, when he was voted into the "Inventors' Hall of Fame "located in North Canton, Ohio, in 2001.

However, Sholes did not leave this earth without some sense of satisfaction on what the value of his life's greatest accomplishment had meant to his fellow man...or more accurately woman. As he lay dying, he was tended by his daughter-in-law who tried to boost his flagging spirits by telling him: "You have done a great thing for the world."[11] To which he humbly replied, "I don't know about that."[12] Then the dying man added what he considered to be his most important bequest: "I feel that I have done something for women to help them earn a living more easily."[13]

With those words lingering over his deathbed, Christopher Sholes soon passed on into eternity. Having voiced his own epitaph, no other judgment really mattered to him. While his brainchild would join him fourscore or so years later when progress superseded the typewriter with new devices, the joint legacy of the man and his machine should never be denied, diminished, or forgotten. After almost 150 years since its introduction, the assessment made by *Scientific American* still stands as perhaps the definitive word on Sholes' accomplishment. In its December 15, 1888, issue, the magazine opined that "the typewriter takes rank as one of the principal inventions of the age."[14] Then, embellishing his endorsement, the editor noted how his magazine made "...use of these machines in its editorial work, in its correspondence, and in its patent business."[15] He closed by observing that "by its use, business has been greatly facilitated in these departments, and at the same time uniformity and accuracy have been secured."[16]

Christopher Sholes lived just long enough to possibly have read that *Scientific American* article. Combined with his own thoughts regarding his contributions to mankind, the final days and hours of his life must have been spent in relative contentment. Though he and his typewriter are now in their respective graves, the world of work became a better place thanks to the inventor and his invention.

12

BOBBING:

THE ULTIMATE DOWNHILL SLIDE

Every four years when the Winter Olympics make their much-ballyhooed reappearance, references to Lake Placid, New York and its Mt. VanHoevenberg bobsled course are likely to occur. For it is at this site that Americans train on that icy track, honing their skills for a shot at a coveted medal in that fast-paced, downhill event. As New Yorkers, the closest interaction most of us have with this storied facility is as tourists, making the drive of whatever the intervening distance between our homes and the northern Adirondacks happens to be. For the venturesome, the opportunity even exists to take an abbreviated ride down a portion of the bobsled run and get the feel of what this high-speed sport is like. Most assuredly, experience of "dashing through the snow in a one-horse open sleigh" pales by comparison!

Built in 1930 for use in the 1932 Winter Olympics, the venerable northland site is now listed on the National Registry of Historic Places. While it's almost one-hundred-year reign as America's premier bobsledding run is impressive, the history of the sport goes back another fifty-plus years to the mid-1870's in St. Moritz, Switzerland. There the activity was originally developed as a novelty form of entertainment to entice European and American vacationers to stay in the Swiss resort town for the winter. The sport became so popular that a dedicated run was introduced in 1884, ensuring that the speedy bobsleds would no longer go zipping down the mountain and through the nearby village, much to the peril of innocent pedestrians.

Taken from the center of Second Street, just past its intersection with West Street, this photograph shows the bobsled run down West Hill. While the slope loses some of its gradient in the picture, the incline was steep enough to propel the bobs downward with a high degree of speed, a rate sufficiently swift enough to satisfy any daredevil. (Source: Author's Collection)

Being that Ilion was such a progressive, vibrant, and sports-minded community in the last quarter of the nineteenth century, it is not surprising that this new pastime would eventually make its way to town, particularly since the village was already noted for having many clubs and organizations that appealed to the varied tastes and interests of its residents. Skating and horse-racing were already winter activities conducted on the portion of the Erie Canal that passed through downtown. John Street, the second right coming down Second Street hill, was the sight of cutter racing once enough snow had fallen, giving the long road its colorful nickname of "The Speedway."

Blessed with suitably steep hills and accommodating wintry weather, the introduction of bobsledding into the local scene was a natural fit. By the mid-1880's—quite early in the history of the sport —Ilionites had thrown themselves full-bore into the activity. While the gentleness of its name somewhat belied the speeds generated, the "Ilion Coasting Club" was born.

Looking downslope, this view is located very near the sleds' starting point at Prospect Ave. The two tall steeples pinpoint the churches on the corners, one at Second and West and the other at Second and Morgan. To the left of the right steeple is the turret of the Remington Mansion on Armory Hill. (Source: Ilion Free Public Library)

"One of the greatest thrills in Ilion during the old-time winters," mused a reporter for *The Ilion Sentinel* in 1950, "were the bobsled races down West Hill."[1] By current standards, the sleds of yesteryear were rather primitive machines. The smaller ones were about seven feet in length. Some of these devices—when two sleds were attached together—were called "double rippers" and attained lengths of fourteen feet or more. These contraptions amounted to a pair of runners, attached by a long board. Then a rope-and-pulley system, affixed to the front set of blades provided one way of piloting for the sled's drivers, while some of these machines were more stylishly crafted with the clever mounting of automobile-steering apparatus. While relatively simplistic in form and function, these snow machines of yesteryear were never built in loose or haphazard manner. Instead, bringing the sleds to life was "a calculated engineering project, noted *Observer-Dispatch* reporter Ernest Sitts, "figuring in the weight distribution, steering mechanism, and the quality of steel for the runners."[2]

The riders sat on a plank or planks two-inches thick. Ropes were strung along the top edges of the slat for passengers to grasp, and what amounted to narrow running boards protruded out along both sides of the plank and served as footrests. In the first position on the sled was the driver, charged with keeping the downhill plunge straight and safely negotiating the turns. He often had "a back rest to give him more pulling power on the steering mechanism."[3] Meanwhile, the rear seat was occupied by the brakeman, an individual who had to have a keen feel for speed as it related to the sled's location on the course. Going into turns, he had to be particularly aware of when and how much pressure to apply in slowing his sled's velocity, while at the same time not diminishing forward momentum more than was necessary. Though not part of any one team *per se*, men who were known as "starters" were ready at the top of the hill to assist the heavily laden bobs in making it up to and then giving them a push over the crest of the hill.

From an aesthetic standpoint, some sleds glammed it up with padded leather seats and nickel-plated metal parts. Most displayed a pennant on a small pole prominently affixed near the front end of the sled, proclaiming the name of their cherished chariot. Among these christenings were appellations such as "Red Cloud," "Tallyho," "Flyaway," "Comet," and "Nightmare." To further embellish their identity, some teams of sledders had a mascot, such as the hound "Major" who inspired the "Treadways."[4]

Unlike the sleek racing machines now used, the turn-of-the-century models at first glance looked a bit ungainly and rather top-heavy, with often upwards of twelve to sixteen riders crammed along the surface of the sled. However, in terms of generating speed, what these early sleds lacked in aerodynamics was to some extent compensated for by the excessive weight which they carried—the rationale being from a physics standpoint that the greater the weight, the faster the speed which the sled could attain. Among those on-board, the driver located in the front and the brakeman perched in the rear had important responsibilities that were key factors in determining the success or failure of a run.

For present-day Olympic competition, a bobsled with a four-man crew cannot exceed 1369 pounds. In a vintage picture, one Ilion bobsled is seen with sixteen riders on-board the plank. The individual in front was the driver. The crew were called "bobbers," due to the back-and-forth motion sometimes required to move the sled forward to its starting position and then heading down the hill. At an average of 150 pounds per rider, that would mean 2400 pounds of human ballast gathering momentum down the incline! Curiously, as a basis for emphasizing the swiftness at which modern bobsleds travel, the metaphor which we might use would be "like a rocket." Given that the gold standard for rapid transit in the 1880's was a train, one who witnessed the sledding, a John Hutchins, understandably described a bob's descent as being at "railroad speed."[5] Hats flying off riders at various intervals during the downward plunge were judged as a good indicator of a sled's having achieved an extremely desirable velocity.

With an interest in this high-speed coasting at a fever pitch among the younger adults in the village, the townsfolk seemed to have come together in one of those rare but delightful moments when the whole community puts its support behind a project. First, the village fathers graciously allowed for public sledding two nights a week. In being supportive, rather than seen as grinches squashing this exciting activity, officials knowingly turned a blind eye on an 1877 town ordinance that stated a penalty which could have made the participants guilty of being lawbreakers. The regulation in question clearly stated that "no person shall play ball, beat, knock or drive any ball or hoop or slide downhill on any street in the village. Fine. 50 cents to $1."[6] Apparently, the legislation was enacted in response to some youthful frolics, pastimes which most likely had posed a hazard to pedestrians living or walking in the vicinity of the hills around the community.

From among several possible inclines in Ilion, the slope chosen for the bobsled run was West or Second Street hill, a grade which provided a steep descent two-tenths of a mile long.[7] To prime the run, ruts or grooves to fit sled runners were made in the road's snow-covered surface, and water was then sprayed over the snow to provide a slick, frozen runway. The north side of the street was reserved for the bobsled track, while youngsters on sleds were allowed to use the remaining space to its left. At two corners—Second and Otsego Streets and Otsego and Main Streets—snow piles were banked and curved to allow the fast-moving sleds to turn ninety-degrees and switch from one street and direction to another. While shutting the hill down for four hours twice a week would constitute a major inconvenience today, around the turn of the century the problem was not nearly so acute. For at that time, relatively few people lived up in the West Hill area with most residing north of Second Street, and automobiles had not become a huge consideration with which to be dealt.

A heavily-laden sled, poised at the starting point of its run, affords a good look at the size of a machine, along with the density of bodies with which they were often packed. More riders translated into greater weight on the platform and in turn more speed. With the potential to attain rates of 50 mph or greater, rocketing downhill on-board one of these winter chariots was neither for the faint-of-heart nor the brittle-of-bones. (Source: Ilion Free Public Library)

Still, several side streets had to be closely monitored while the hill was in use for bobsledding. Therefore, to further assist this unique activity, the village made additional contributions beyond just reserving the hill and several streets as a dedicated course. Guards with lanterns were strategically placed on the corners of the three roadways crossed by the sleds coming off the base of the hill—West, Morgan, and Otsego. The established procedure called for the guard at the top of the hill to wave his lantern once a sled was ready to go. When he received return waves, indicating that all was clear from each of the corner watchmen, he would release a sled. Since the streets running perpendicular to the hill course were not closed off during the coasting hours, the precaution of stationing a sentinel was necessary to regulate cross traffic and pedestrians and thereby avoid potentially hazardous collisions.

Another measure of support, one that enhanced the festive mood, was the presence of various forms of outdoor lighting. In some spots, burning torches blazed away. In others, strings of colored Chinese lanterns contributed their cheerful glow. But, as much for the inventive marvel which they represented as for their radiance, a set of three electric lights along Second Street advertised the cutting-edge skills of the Ilion Light Company. From various locations around town, the sight of all the illumination, enhanced by the reflective backdrop of snowbanks that contrasted with a darkened sky, made for a spectacular, surreal, and stimulating scene. Add in the lively sounds of an occasional brass band that showed up to play, and the whole setting had the appearance of twice-weekly winter carnival. The sledding went on continuously through the evening until 11:30 when the lights were extinguished, a signal to the crowd that it was time to call it a night.

According to John Hutchins, "the citizens of the town…encourage the young people in their enjoyment, by giving of their money to aid in expenses, and their presence to witness them ride downhill at a fast rate of speed and are often seen riding with them."[8] The cost of a night's participation was sixteen dollars per sled and deemed well-worth the expenditure, one often borne both by the sledders and spectators alike. Some of the funding went toward ensuring that "the disagreeable duty of walking up hill and drawing up the bobs was done away with by nightly engaging livery horses to draw the coasters to the starting point."[9]

Crowds ranging in size from several hundred spectators into the thousands were known to line the course. They cheered and clapped with enthusiasm as the sleds came whooshing past. Blink and you might miss your favorite's run. Onlookers found it "amusing to stand on the street and see them pass...[for] some are bare-headed, [as] the momentum is so great at a certain place on the hill that they are quite often relieved of their hats."[10]

In-between runs, especially as the evening grew colder, folks could be seen stomping their feet and waving their arms to increase the circulation of their blood. Hailing from different backgrounds and representing a range of ages, those who came to watch melded into a very eclectic crowd. Among those who were observed gathered along the hill on one wintry night were "the greybeard grandfather and his ancient spouse, the portly businessman and his smiling wife, the robust fellow and his bright-eyed ladylove, fun-loving boys and rollicking school girls—all are there."[11] So exciting was the spectacle that on one occasion, "an elderly lady—who was homebound and had not been downtown all winter—"was drawn on a hand sled by her companions to witness the coasting."[12]

On some nights, forty to fifty sleds made multiple runs down the icy hill. If all went without mishap, the sleds moved rapidly eastward over lower Second Street, zooming past intersections with first West and then Morgan Streets. Given that the next intersection—with Otsego Street—was a T, successfully negotiating the abrupt left-turn was a must. To help reduce the speed of the hurtling bobs, cinders were spread on the roadway between Morgan and Otsego. While this did help lessen the chances of tipping-over or overshooting the bend, the trade-off was the reduction in speed took away some the ultimate distance the sleds could have otherwise achieved.

For those riders who leaned left and successfully rode along the banked curve, Otsego Street was the next straight stretch for two blocks. For those still going, another snow barrier awaited them at intersection of Main and Otsego Streets, redirecting the sleds eastward this time, with a few eventually reaching past the present-day Arms' buildings along Hoefler Avenue.

For some sledders, completing the entire course meant a trip of over a mile! Based on the clocking of one run that went from the starting point on West Hill to the corner of Otsego and Main Streets— opposite Osgood's Hotel—it was fifty seconds to that spot, so the longer ride over to Hoefler might have lasted a little over a minute. Covering a mile in 60 to 70 seconds, the rate of speed would have averaged out to a hair-raising fifty or so miles per hour! Anyone faint of heart was ill-advised to partake in one of these daring experiences.

So popular did these winter nights of sledding become that "neighboring villages sent delegations to compete with the home bobs," with some participants known to have even traveled from as far away as Schenectady and Albany.[13] It was also understood but unspoken that some gentlemen liked to place substantial wagers on the speed and distance various sleds might travel. Sports betting, if you will, right in the heart of town and in plain sight no less!

Given the tenor of the Victorian era when women in general were treated and protected as the fairer sex, opportunities outside of the home for recreational activities were somewhat limited and rather genteel in the earlier years of this age. In mild weather, croquet, badminton, archery, and walking were the norm for females, while winter saw skating and sleighing as perhaps the primary activities. At all times, propriety in dress was a paramount concern. However, by the 1880's, the winds of change had begun to blow. Ilionites, it would seem, in accepting women as participants in the sport of bobsledding, had subtly placed themselves at the head of the curve in an expanding social revolution.

In response to an early photograph of the crew of the famous bobsled "Red Cloud"—published in the January 26, 1950, edition of *The Ilion Sentinel*—then ninety-year old Marion Irlam Hakes wrote a letter to the editor, identifying those pictured.[14] Of the fourteen riders, seven were women, including Marion. She also noted that the sled had been built for her father, John Irlam, in 1875. As a graduate of Ilion High School in 1878, Marian Irlam would most likely have still been a young woman when she made her downhill forays aboard her father's sled. Since she was married to Seward Hakes in 1884, but referenced herself in the picture as "Marion Irlam," the group shot was most likely taken between 1875 and 1884, putting Marion in the sixteen to twenty-five age range.[15] Not only are her recollections important in confirming that women participated in this potentially perilous activity, but also that it was a sport best-suited for younger, more flexible bodies.

Clearly, given the speeds generated, concerns about safety were justifiable, for spills accompanied the thrills to varying degrees on a regular basis. Spinouts were possible at any time on the icy run. Sleds were known to tip over, dumping their riders all over the slope, with some continuing their downhill journey in all sorts of contorted positions other than seated on the sled. The bobs were also known on occasion to veer off course and head into the crowds of spectators lining the sides of the prepared route. These sudden, unexpected intrusions sent people scattering in all directions. Where turns were necessary, especially the one from Second onto Otsego Street, crashes sometimes happened. In these instances, the sled often became airborne. Tossed hither and yon, riders usually wound up in a snow bank or a nearby clearing.

Injuries in the form of bumps, bruises, and concussions were an accepted part of engaging in the sport, a price that the generally youthful, carefree riders were willing to pay. Sometimes the mishaps were of a more serious nature. During the winter season of 1882-83, a popular sledder named Russ Clark was hurt, severely injuring his leg. To help defray his substantial medical costs, the Coasting Club sponsored an amateur performance at Maben's Opera House the following April 27, 1883. The members produced a night of amateur acting, dancing, and singing with an all-volunteer cast and crew. Community spirit in support of a good cause was evident as "the opera house walls enclosed the largest audience of the season last Friday night," raising $150 "which will make the heart of Russ light and his pocket heavy."[16]

For the most part, the early years of the sledding frenzy passed without a major mishap. Contusions frequently occurred, but they were accepted as a trade-off for partaking in what was considered as a sporting event by participants and exhilarating entertainment for onlookers. Oh, yes, a cat ran out of lives one night when it darted into the path of an oncoming sled and was sadly sliced in two. On another occasion, a dog also met the same regrettable fate.

But by far the most lamentable incident occurred on Saturday night, February 16, 1884, during a gala coasting carnival. Even before the racing started, the signs of potential disaster were ominous, as a late winter "...thaw and freeze had put the hill in very treacherous condition."[17] The conditions were viewed as being so adverse that "many regular coasters contented themselves as spectators that evening."[18] Observers noted that any sleds that stayed in the center of the run found themselves safe in a depression, but if any bob turned out of the prepared track, there was no telling where it would stop, as on either side it was as smooth as glass and sloping to the deep gutters.

So, the stage was unintentionally set for a tragedy this winter's night. A sled named "West Shore" had almost reached the bottom of the hill, when, in the last twenty feet or so before the slope fattened out into the level stretch beyond, its inexperienced driver lost his ability to steer. The bob drifted to the left, out of the established tracks and onto the glare ice. At a point where the racer probably achieved a speed estimated more than sixty miles per hour, the "West Shore" was careening wildly out of control. Whereupon the sled "ran into the stone coping" of the bridge spanning Steele Creek just below the entrance to present-day St. Augustine's Church, smashed against a fence on its downside, and came to rest against a telephone pole.[19] The wooden craft broke up on impact, and its riders, numbering about a dozen, were flung in all directions or, as the newspaper described their plight, "...scattered to the four corners of the compass."[20]

Most of the displaced passengers were shaken and many bruised, but otherwise the majority sustained no serious injuries. Two of the individuals involved in the crash received more severe wounds from which in time they would recover. However, "John Holzer, a farm hand, aged nineteen was picked up insensible, having sustained internal injuries which may prove fatal."[21] Three days later, the poor boy succumbed to what his doctor diagnosed as "cerebro-spinal meningitis."[22] At the request of several citizens, an autopsy followed by an inquest ruled that the death was caused by "a transverse fracture of the fourth vertebrae of the neck."[23]

Though the young man had only been on the Ilion winter scene for six weeks, the camaraderie that existed among the bobsledders motivated members from the Coasting Club to attend their companion's funeral in Schuyler. Coming as the accident did near the end of the bobsledding season, the pall that it cast had time to dissipate over the summer and fall. But few could look at the bridge again and not recall the tragic event when all the mirth had ended in sorrow.

In the mishap's aftermath, interest in the sport waned. A brief revival occurred in the 1920's, but the introduction of automobiles into the village scene and the expansion of settlement up onto the West Hill plateau, made occasionally shutting down the hill and icing it over very impractical. In addition, a young girl broke her leg in a sledding accident around 1925, which was further motivation for the village fathers to put the kibosh on this exciting but dangerous sport.

"The fairyland created by colored lights, torches flaming to mark the course, the swing of the signalman's lantern, and enchanted crowds still remain in nostalgic memory" was the idyllic setting recalled in Ilion's centennial booklet. Perhaps once in a generation is it possible to catch such lightning in bottle. What must it have been like? When January comes again, you are invited to take a walk with me up West Hill and back in time on a snowy Saturday night. Picture the excited crowds lining both sides of the street ahead of and behind us. Smell the pine smoke from the burning course markers. See the glare of the electric lights reflecting off the icy run. Listen for the whoosh as a bobsled hurtles past us. Hear the shouts and laughter of the riders. Harken to the cheers from the excited onlookers. In few moments, the earnest call to "lean" rises into night air behind us, as a team tries to navigate the banked turn from Second Street to Otsego.

At the time bobsledding became popular, most village residents lived below the hills. This 1881 pictorial map of Ilion shows how much the community had grown since the since the Civil War, by then boasting over 5,000 inhabitants as compared to only 1000 in the pre-war village. The Erie Canal is in the lower righthand corner. Main Street lies parallel to the waterway, though on the other side of the buildings abutting the Canal. Otsego Street runs diagonally, just to the left of center. Third Street intersects with John Street in the center portion, and Second Street lies to the right, half of the way down from the top right. Note that the West Hill area is only just beginning to develop. (Source: Author's Collection)

The anguish of the Civil War has finally passed into history, and World War I is a catastrophe not yet on the horizon. Those were great times to be alive...in Ilion...on a winter's eve. But, alas, only H. G. Wells had a time machine, but fortunately you and I do have our imaginations. We are approaching the top of the incline now...the next sled teeters on the brink of the downslope, ready for a push off...so, make sure that you are bundled up...tighten your scarf...then close your eyes...engage your mind...and come on back with me to 1880. Are you ready to go bobbing?

13

DRILLING FOR OIL:

THE SEARCH FOR BLACK GOLD

S purred on by the discovery of oil in Titusville, Pennsylvania in 1859, efforts to find this valuable commodity spread rapidly to other parts of the country. The bug eventually made its way to Ilion in the 1880's. Two significant factors provided the impetus to search locally for a source of not only oil, but also natural gas: the first was the existence of shale, a sedimentary rock often known to contain the treasured substance, one which Native Americans had burned to provide heat; and the second was the need "for gas/electricity to run the local industrial plants and provide illumination."[1] Providing the weight of his considerable entrepreneurial stature, more so than any inherent geological expertise, was nevertheless the favorable opinion of Philo Remington. His belief that oil deposits quite likely existed somewhere in the vicinity of Ilion caught the ears of many of his fellow townsmen. To move the discussion from speculation to action, several local investors stepped forward and provided the requisite investment funding necessary to underwrite exploration.

Initially capitalized with $10,000, the Ilion Gas Company sought the services of someone who possessed the needed expertise to do the job. Eventually, after putting sufficient cash on barrelhead to attract a bona fide driller, these stockholders were able to engage the services of a Pennsylvania contractor.

The location chosen for the first test well was just outside of the village near the mouth of the gorge, south of the turn-off for the Elizabethtown Road. Similar in appearance to the modern-day apparatus used in drilling, the centerpiece of the site was a tall derrick—one made of wood in that era—which provided the housing which supported the steam-driven drill.

As part of a national trend in seeking oil and gas deposits, wells were drilled in the Ilion Gulph. (Source: Ilion Free Public Library)

Accompanied by the high hopes of not only the investment group, but also the great interest and enthusiasm on the part of villagers as well, the metal bit began boring into the soil. Located about two miles from the center of the village, the site was readily easily accessible to curious townsfolk. Given the novelty of the endeavor...and the potential for an exciting denouement if oil gushed forth...rubberneckers gathered at a safe distance to monitor progress, as the drill ate its way deeper and deeper into the antediluvian depths of the earth.

An arrangement had already been made with the Arms to announce any success. If a strike was made, then the fire whistle would sound. But with futility accompanying each passing foot, the hopes of both investors and spectators alike sagged a little more. "Finally, at 1,900 feet below the surface of the ground with no oil in sight, and no prospect of seeing any, the project was given up."[2] Much to everyone's disappointment, the Arms' whistle remained silent.

While wildcat drilling accompanied by a frequent fleecing of investors occurred far too frequently in America in those days of rampant speculation, the Ilion company was not about being saddled with such a sordid reputation. Though money was indeed lost when the well in the gorge came up dry, to prove the company's good intentions "...the amount of money left was paid back to the investors, which was returned in the form of a dividend of 25 dollars."[3]

While sorely disheartened that no gusher was forthcoming, not everyone immediately gave up hope that somewhere beneath the soil in the vicinity of Ilion lay valuable deposits of a useful resource. This time, the geological experts were sponsored by Remington Typewriter. Initially, the scene of exploration shifted to the area north of the Erie Canal. Instead of oil, the search was now on for a pocket of natural gas.

Eventually, after several failed attempts, the decision was made to try drilling on a section of property located within the factory grounds. This time the search proved fruitful, and a pocket of natural gas was found. Proper piping was laid to bring the fuel into the factories, where it was utilized for illumination. Eventually, the flow of the free resource began to diminish to the point that the well was abandoned and capped. The factory than switched to commercially available gas, which had by then become cheaper, plentiful, and more readily available.

As late as 1921, the possibility of discovering oil deposits in the gorge was a quest that some people would not relinquish. "There is oil in the Ilion Gulf [i.e.-gorge] according to G. F. Champney the most recent purchaser of the twenty-five-acre tract of land in that location."[4] Since that proclamation was almost a century ago and proved unfulfilled, no further attempts have occurred in the interim to locate gas or oil in the gorge. Though such exploration met with only limited local success, it was not surprising that the attempt was made, for Ilion in the latter years of the 19th and on into early 20th century was known as an industrial laboratory of sorts, a place where experimentation and innovation were welcomed and supported. Together with the sponsorship of such endeavors is the understanding that all will not succeed. But, as T. S. Eliot—a 20th century American poet—once said, "only those who will risk going too far can possibly find out how far it is possible to go."[5]

14

THE SILENT SENTINEL:

ILION'S SALUTE TO ITS WAR HEROES

In the decades following the War Between the States, communities of all sizes in both the North and South wished to honor the men who had put their lives on the line for the cause of their choice. Some places with enough means built extravagant tributes. In this vein, the "Soldiers and Sailors Monument" in Indianapolis—though originally intended as a Civil War commemorative—recognized the sacrifices of the city's sons in the five conflicts from the Revolution through the Spanish-American War. Dedicated in 1902, its colossal size and detailed statuary created an impressive memorial. In Boston, a stunning bronze bas relief was unveiled across from the state capitol in 1897, depicting Colonel Robert Gould Shaw as he accompanied a marching column of the 54th Massachusetts Infantry. To the south, the city of Richmond once erected a bevy of statues along Monument Avenue in memory of several Confederate leaders. In Georgia, Stone Mountain depicts Robert E. Lee, "Stonewall" Jackson, and Jefferson Davis carved in high relief, making it the largest in this genre of outsized sculpture in the world.

While these represent some of the more ambitious projects, smaller communities of far lesser means also joined in the wave of monument construction that swept the country in the late nineteenth and early twentieth centuries. Fortunately for such places, a means existed for them to reasonably acquire a suitable memorial of their own also. Since the cost of commissioning an original work was usually too prohibitive, well-intended townsfolk frequently had to seek a design that fell within the constraints of their municipal budgets or donors' wallets.

At this point, opportunity met need. For those seeking a proper but affordable memorial, a Connecticut-based firm known as the "Monumental Bronze Company" came to the rescue. For a period of thirty-five years, beginning in 1879, agents for what blossomed into a going concern enjoyed a thriving business in the sales of what amounted to pre-fabricated sculptures. The memorials which were being merchandised became overnight successes. However, by choosing this option, originality went out the window as communities essentially selected the crowning piece for their own project from the same catalogue of limited offerings that their neighbors were doing. This amounted to what author Cara Giamo described as producing "cookie cutter" statuary.[1]

Not surprisingly, comparing the end-products in village parks across New York alone illustrates the high degree of replication that occurred. Patchogue, Cortland, Liberty, Hudson Falls, Olcott, Huntington, Saratoga Springs, Warsaw...and Ilion... are among the host of New York villages that boast memorials topped with a likeness of the same soldier. In form, they depict an infantryman with a kepi-styled cap perched on his head and a caped greatcoat draped over his shoulders, hands clasped on his rifle's barrel, and posed in a posture of "parade rest." Art historian Sarah Beetham "estimates that there are 2,500 of them [monuments] across the Northern states, with the Silent Sentinel version believed to account for perhaps as many as half of them. "[2]

Most communities did not dedicate their memorial to any one individual, but instead, like Ilion, they made the monument a tribute to all their citizens who fought in the war. In that sense, he is John Q. Soldier. A stone shield one-third of the way up on the pillar's face proclaimed this all-encompassing gratitude: "In memory of our heroes who served in defense of the Union." As Ms. Beetham pointed out, the depiction of the soldier as everyman allowed people to "... go and see in them their sons or fathers who had fought in the war."[3]

Intentionally left nameless, the statue thus became a tribute to all of the men from the community who fought in the the Civil War. (Source: Author's Collection)

Driven as communal decisions often are by expediency and finances, the intent to honor the men who fought for the Union was in no way diminished by the uniformity in the memorials erected. In Ilion's case, the method of funding the monument was the brainchild of Mrs. Rose Watson, who at the time was the president of the Women's Relief Corps—a ladies' auxiliary originally an arm of the local Grand Army of the Republic veterans' post. After launching the drive, the ladies' fund-raising progressed slowly. The opening contribution of the corps to the memorial fund was thirty dollars, realized from a sale of rubbers for shoes. Next came five hundred dollars amassed through a co-sponsored fair. When the women were done, they had raised a pot of $3500 towards the monument.

At that point, the project was handed over to Alexander Jarvis. Mr. Jarvis was an accomplished local sculptor who ran a monument business in the center of town on West Main Street along the Erie Canal bed. According to an article in the *Herkimer Citizen*, this talented resident had the entire project placed in his capable hands, for the paper noted that "he is not only its designer, but will also carve the statue and pedestal from marble and will erect the same."[4] A tip of the hat and three cheers were due to the local sculptor. As reporter Chris Carola pointed out in a recent newspaper article titled "Silent Sentinels Still on Guard North, South," the "... commissioning of a monument made of Italian marble or New England granite could cost tens of thousands of dollars, much too expensive for most small towns."[5] Yet Mr. Jarvis was going create his for $3500. For his medium, he did not chintz, selecting as he did granite purchased from a quarry in Barre, Vermont.

Perhaps he gave the village a hometown discount. Maybe he saw the gesture as free advertising...or could he have simply been a very patriotic and civic-minded individual? As if he was not motivated enough already, the pressure to give the project his best effort was squarely placed upon his shoulders by the press, when a contemporary article noted that "Mr. Jarvis has been entrusted with most of the more expensive and artistic pieces of marble cutting done for Ilion's people since he came to this place and his work is recognized by all as the work of an artist..."[6] That he succeeded in his commission was borne out by a plaudit in the *Ilion Citizen*, one which saluted the monument as "a thing of beauty in its graceful proportions and expert workmanship, which reflected great credit upon its designer and maker, Mr. Alexander Jarvis, to whom this handsome piece of work will be a lifelong honor. We know of no soldier's monument of equal cost which can equal this in point of beauty, design, appropriateness, and workmanship."[7]

In viewing Ilion's monument today, several little touches stand out as unique and different from those erected in other communities. First, on the lower segment of the pedestal is a palm frond, a Christian symbol of both victory and peace. Above it is a shield, emblematic of protection. Near the top of the shaft, just below the soldier, is a square block with a star cut on each face. Up the side of the middle portion of the main pedestal and underneath the last platform a delicate filigree adorns the edges. Only in its being topped off with the statue of a soldier does this work of art mirror memorials of countless other shrines.

But this representation is perhaps the least unique aspect of Mr. Jarvis' creation. For the proud warrior does not just look like his brethren held aloft on other pedestals in other places, he appears identical. Could the local sculptor have purchased a ready-made statue? According to the firm's catalogue, "in 1890, a 'life-size' soldier from Monumental Bronze Company would set you back $450."[8] In spite of being called "white bronze,", the statues were made of zinc and not bronze. Cast in a mold and then sand-blasted to give them a rough, stone-like surface, these renditions were deemed capable of being able to "...last as long as the Pyramids of Egypt."[9]

Still, while Mr. Jarvis' soldier looks indistinguishable from the mass-produced variety, one telltale sign is missing. The white bronze versions, over time, have acquired a bluish-green patina. Ilion's capstone soldier displays no such weathering. With no records to disclaim otherwise, Mr. Jarvis—apparently unhindered by any patent violations—just may have fashioned his entire sculpture out of granite, which included copying the "Silent Sentinel" marketed by the Connecticut company. In support of this possibility, a newspaper article—taped into a binder labeled "Philo Scrapbook" in the Ilion library's possession—states that "the soldier was carved out of a solid piece of granite."[10]

IF THIS ASSERTION IS TRUE, then the only conclusion that can be drawn is that Mr. Jarvis did in fact sculpt the entire statue, making the whole piece a creation rendered by his own hand. However, the one caveat exists about the originality of his work: what was the inspiration for the soldier's likeness? Given that in its appearance Ilion's sentinel seems identical to a standardized pattern used to top-off scores of prefabricated Civil War tributes throughout the North, the reality may be that the local sculptor simply replicated the same design for the culminating piece on his monument. After 115 years, other than for purposes of historical accuracy, the point is moot. No lawsuit was ever filed by the Connecticut Monumental Bronze Company, so either they never knew or did not care, and, unless someone is inclined to climb up and give the statue a rap with his knuckles—listening for a telltale sound that would indicate metal—

the jury will probably forever remain out on the true composition of the "Silent Sentinel."

ONCE THE LAST SECTION—THE seven-foot, six-inch warrior—was lifted into place using chain hoists and a derrick, the monument was complete, just in time to serve as the centerpiece for Memorial Day services on Wednesday, May 30, 1906.[11] With the foresight that not every community had, the thirty-ton stone shrine was placed upon a concrete pad to ensure that it stayed upright and plumb.

Originally, the plot of land on what one reporter dubbed the soldier's "campgrounds" was much larger.[12] The small, oblong park, in what came to be called "Monument Square," was surrounded by dirt roadways, for it was located at the confluence of Benedict Avenue and Otsego, Morgan, and Third Streets. Eventually, the local chapter of the Women's Relief Corps came to the fore once again and this time funded the installation of granite curbing, which served to frame the little park and at the same time offer the statue some protection from the horseless carriages that were beginning to appear. Until the park was later downsized to accommodate the need for a widening of the roads, the grounds of the monument were accented with a few benches, some shrubbery, and a couple of large flower urns. Three vintage cannons also shared the tight space, but they were later moved to Russell Park, eventually joining several others which were also relocated there from the West Hill park.

That first Memorial Day with the monument in place was an emotional experience for the estimated 3,000 individuals who witnessed the lengthy parade and accompanying ceremonies under a cloudless sky. Participating were fifty veterans of the Civil War, a substantial but nevertheless slowly decreasing number, as the ravages of old age reduced their ranks in ways that Confederate bullets had not. By the time of the 1927 observance, only four of those venerable Yankee soldiers remained, though the parade by then included veterans of the Spanish-American War and World War I.

At the turn-of-the-century and with the erection of the monument as a focal point a few years later, the observance of Memorial Day—which many older folks still referenced by its former name of "Decoration Day"—was a much bigger, more community-wide event than it has become in recent years. Virtually all places of business were closed. As a reporter for the *Ilion Citizen* observed, the occasion was also marked by a "generous display of stars and stripes throughout the village."[13]

The 1927 observance was typical of the programs held in the early years of the 20th century preceding the parade. Alongside the monument, a raised platform was temporarily constructed and suitably bedecked with flags and bunting. Crowded onto its limited dimensions were several dignitaries, along with the Armory Glee Club. Ceremonies commenced that morning at 10 o'clock. After various local notables had spoken, Reverend Samuel Greenfield, pastor of the First Methodist Church, stepped forward. As the main speaker for the day's observance, he discoursed on the topic of "A Patriot's Duty in Time of Peace."[14]

Most notable by today's standards was the extended route of the parade, which once went from the monument on Otsego Street, up Benedict Avenue to the cemetery for a brief service and decoration of veterans' graves, then down Armory, Highland, and Hoefler to Main Street, west on Main to Otsego, up Otsego to First Street. After this lengthy tour, everyone was hungry. In keeping with the spirit of a village-wide observance, at least up until the depression era strained available resources, a dinner was sponsored in honor of all comrades and guests. In support of this public celebration, the Women's Relief Corps asked that "the citizens to contribute as they may feel inclined; it will be a hungry occasion, and the board should be bountifully spread."[15] The repast was originally held at the Grand Army of the Republic's hall located at the southwest corner of First and Morgan Streets, the same spot where the Ilion Police Station now stands.

In its overview of the day's events, the *Ilion Citizen* offered a glowing summation: "...And thus closed the most perfect Decoration Day that Ilion has ever seen. The weather was the finest. The attendance the largest, [making] the occasion the most notable on record. It was a pleasure to see the thousands gathered such an observance of this day of patriotic purpose cannot but be largely to the welfare of both old and young."[16]

Monument Park as it first appeared—with cannons, a bench, and urns—in a much larger setting bounded by numerous shade trees. (Source: Author's Collection)

But times change. Advances in technology and transportation altered lifestyles. Needs, perceptions, and values shift. Generations come and go, as the years roll by. The village has seen well over one-hundred Memorial Day observances since the monument was erected. In more recent history, the parade had fewer participants. Its route became shorter, and the dinners ceased long ago. The last Civil War veteran—Alonzo Rivers—passed away in 1941, and he has since been joined by all the men who fought in the Spanish-American War and World War I.

But international politics being what they have been since 1918, many other veterans from more recent conflicts have taken their places on battlefields and in parades, reminding us of the other wars and more sacrifices on behalf of their country that have occurred since

World War I. Sadly, Ilion no longer hosts a Memorial Day parade. Yet, through the years, the one constant that has appropriately been present for every Memorial Day in Ilion since 1906—parade or no parade—has been Mr. Jarvis' monument, at whose base a wreath was traditionally placed. Like the many soldiers whom he represents, the "Silent Sentinel" has faithfully done his duty and resolutely stood at his post for over a century, facing toward the cemetery on the hill above him and keeping watch over the final resting places of not only all his old comrades, but also the more recent generations of warriors who have since joined them. As a *Telegram* reporter wrote in his Memorial Day article sixty years ago: "And 'Private Smith' on top of his pedestal, will nod understandingly at this observance for the veterans of all wars, although he honestly thought his war would be last one."[17]

15

HATS-OFF TO REMINGTON ARMS:

THE KICK-OFF FOR A GRAND 100TH ANNIVERSARY PARTY

F or those who may not have arisen in time to take in its unfolding, a reporter for the *Ilion Citizen* eloquently painted a picture of the centurial moment for his paper's readers: "With Old Glory streaming from hundreds of homes and business places, and with the gentle rays of a fading summer sun shining down upon the city that has grown in leaps and bounds in a hundred years, the Remington Centennial was ushered in Tuesday morning."[1] The whole event would be a memorable occasion in the history of the community, an extravaganza that extending over three days in a joyous, village-wide observance. A later headline in the same newspaper unabashedly proclaimed the festivities as the "Greatest Celebration Ever Held in the Mohawk Valley."[2] Tuesday, Wednesday, and Thursday —August 29 thru August 31, 1916—had been declared holidays in the village. Given the importance of honoring contracts signed with European combatants in the war raging on the continent at that very moment, Arms' employees were not originally scheduled to have the days off; however, as an accommodation of sorts, many activities were thoughtfully set to be held during all three evenings, so the working men could still participate in at least parts of the celebration. But the irony of the situation was not lost on many discerning Ilionites: those who had contributed to the success of the company being recognized could not attend a large part of the celebration in its honor, since business was booming and the need to fill urgently-needed orders required uninterrupted production at their jobs.

FOR SOME RESIDENTS of the village, the "Great War" in Europe presented a moral dilemma of deep and unsettling proportions on many levels. Of immediate concern, many families still had either direct familial ties or at least ethnic roots on both sides of the battle lines, since many Ilionites were of both German and British heritages. Then, the looming possibility existed that the United States could someday become embroiled in the conflict, putting the lives of local boys in harm's way in what many viewed at the time as strictly a foreign conflict. Perhaps most disconcerting of all, if one allowed his mind to go down that road, was the reality that guns made in Ilion would wind up as killing machines in the hands of soldiers fighting in that war.

Much of this situation however, remained fraught with speculation and uncertainty in the spring of 1916. Certainly, America's inclination to stay disengaged, beyond being a purveyor of the weapons of war, was not necessarily a status quo guaranteed to last for the conflict's duration. Though Americans were reassured by President Woodrow Wilson's campaign slogan—"He Kept Us Out of War"—the reality was that a precautionary movement toward preparedness on a nationwide scale was already underway.

For a hometown manifestation of this readiness, Ilionites had to look no farther than the Remington Arms complex. "All around the factory buildings a fence seven-feet high has been built," the *Ilion Citizen* reported, "...[with] steel ribs, spear-pointed on top."[3] Supporting this first line of protection, a series of sentry boxes had been constructed at intervals along the fence line. Twelve-feet high, these lofty perches "jutted over the fence, giving the guard within a view up and down the sidewalk."[4]

PLANS for the 100th anniversary celebration had been in the works for some time, with a committee appointed by the Ilion Board of Trade in 1914 to get the ball rolling. Herbert House was appointed chairman of a blue-ribbon committee to oversee the many, varied aspects of the preparations that would evolve into a three-day affair. Early on, it had been decided that two overarching themes would be melded: a nostalgia-driven welcome to past residents interwoven with special events directed at recognizing Remington Arms' accomplishments and contributions over its long existence. The committee felt that "the old home week part would appeal to all, for no village the size of Ilion has more of its sons scattered throughout the country and the world holding prominent positions than this village, and an occasion of this kind would serve as an excellent reason for them to return and renew the friendships of the past."[5]

Between the yards of bunting and the hundreds of flags, the village was completely festooned in red, white, and blue. Otsego Street intersects with Main just beyond the building on the left edge of this photo. The two white columns on each side of the street are demarking "Bridge Square." Overhead is hung a portrait of Eliphalet Remington II, and a string of novel electric lights descends from the pole on the left. (Source: Ilion Free Public Library)

Giving further credence to the cordial, symbiotic relationship that existed between the town and the company, the Ilion Board of Trade had readily collaborated with the Remington Arms' Advertising Department in laying out a magnificent summer festival. In addition, "the gunmaker, to help ensure the success of the celebration, has subscribed many thousands of dollars, and the Remington Typewriter Company, the Library Bureau, and other manufacturers have promised additional financial help."[6] Due to the importance of the company to Ilion, a local paper was of the opinion that "businessmen and citizens in general are sure to put their shoulders to the wheel to make the affair a success."[7]

When the big week finally arrived, a quick tour of the village dramatically revealed the extent to which everyone had pitched in to give the whole community a festive appearance. As one newspaper headlined an article, the "Town Was in Holiday Dress."[8] Flags proliferated on homes and businesses. Red, white, and blue bunting was hung in profusion. A week-long "clean-up, paint-up" campaign had resulted in spruced up lawns, streets, and homes. Tall, white ornamental columns had been placed in key locations. Strands of electric lights were generously strung over many of the downtown streets. Store windows contained "numerous exhibits of guns and ammunition, mementoes of war, and articles of local historical interest."[9] Still another paper was equally effusive with its praise, commenting that "the village has put on gala attire, is beautifully decorated, inviting everyone to come and assured all the visitors a warm welcome."[10]

Once the influx of out-of-towners began to fill the streets, restaurants, and hotels of the village, locals would take note from time to time that all the faces did not belong to strangers. The reason was that many former Ilionites, folks who had gone off to seek their fortunes elsewhere, had—just as the planning committee had hoped—made a special effort to return home during the centennial week. Part of their interest in coming back was certainly to experience the gala celebration, but for many a driving motivation was to reconnect with their roots and enjoy the company of family and friends once again.

In its lengthy column called "News of the Week," the *Ilion Citizen* usually offered tidbits of what local folks were doing. Part of its socially-oriented, chatty coverage included the comings and goings of village residents. In the days preceding and during the centennial, much movement was chronicled about former townspeople who had come back. Some came from nearby communities around central New York, such as "Mrs. James Lyman of Booneville" who visited relatives during the celebration and "Mrs. Monica Carrol of Port Leyden [who] spent the centennial with her sister Leona Murray of Morgan Street."[11] Others traveled greater distances to visit their hometown, like "Frank Goldman of San Antonio, Texas"..."Charles R. Redway, of Lowell, Mass., Thomas Van Alstyne of Florida, and Dr. John R. Schmidt of Brooklyn."[12] Along with its gossipy column, the *Ilion Citizen* made a another small, subtle contribution in an effort to at the bottom of a page: "Don't You Wish That You Were Back Home Again? Come to the Remington Centennial August 29, 30, 31 – Ilion, NY."[13]

Among the returnees, one of the more heralded individuals was Hiram Green, an elderly gentleman who had traveled to Ilion all the way from Tacoma, Washington, and would stay with his brother on John Street. What made him so noteworthy was due to his personal recollections of Eliphalet Remington III, for they had been "staunch friends and as such had often been together."[14] Thanks to that former relationship, Mr. Green brought to the grand observance an oral history of one of the key figures in the company's annals. Unfortunately, Mr. Remington himself was unable to attend. Now eighty-eight years old, the last of the three brothers who had once owned and operated the company, Eliphalet now lived in Philadelphia and was deemed much too feeble to make the trip to Ilion for the observance.

In the run-up to the big week scheduled for the end of the summer, Ilion was not the only place where people were hard at work on behalf of the Remington centennial. Artists on several fronts were busy in their studios, striving to add their imaginative contributions to the celebration. Acting under the auspices of the Centennial Commission of the Village of Ilion, which had secured the blessing of the War Department, New York City-based sculptor Albin Polasek was in the process of creating a twenty-seven-inch tall clay statue. Resting on its nine-inch ebony base, the figure depicted Eliphalet Remington at work forging his first rifle. In the final step of an ambitious plan, the finished carving would be cast in bronze, with one figure to be delivered to the adjutant general of each state as a gift from the citizens of Ilion.

Sculptor Polasek and his competition trophy. (Source: Ilion Free Public Library)

Inscribed on the base of the statue were its source and intent: "Presented by Citizens of Ilion, New York to Organized Militia of the U.S. for Perpetual Competition."[15] The goal was that the various militia or National Guard units in each of the then 48 states would compete in yearly marksmanship contests—to be known as "The Remington Centennial Trophy Match"—all vying for the right to retain and display the 40 pound statue at their unit's headquarters until the next year's contest. With the obvious intent of promoting the shooting skills of America's modern-day minutemen, the trophy also served as a subtle promotional tool for Remington Arms.

Evidence exists that the gift was well-received by several states at the time of its donation. In North Dakota, the *Bismarck Daily Tribune* informed its readers that "there is great interest on the part of the general public, as well as in military circles, in the coming of this beautiful statue—a work of art, not an ordinary shooting trophy—to our state."[16]

Similarly, the Adjutant General of Connecticut acknowledged his receipt of the statue; however, 3000 of the Nutmeg State's guardsmen were currently down on the Mexican border in the expedition against Poncho Villa. Uncertain as to when these troops might be returning home, it was deemed improbable "...that the first contest for the statue will be held before next year."[17] Until such time as a competition could be arranged, the gift was displayed at Hartford's armory.

Meanwhile, in Maryland, the wishes of the trophy's benefactors were fully implemented and continued for almost two decades. In a 1933 article titled "Company G Expects to Take Rifle Trophy" at the First Maryland Regiment of the state guard's summer training session, two rifle teams were entered ..."by the Cumberland outfit in the Remington Centennial Match..."[18]

While some of the desired competitions may have been held early on, little evidence exists that any are still conducted today. For many years, the whereabouts of only five of the original forty-eight were accounted for after a century had passed. Up until 2017, of the five statues known to be in existence, only in Kentucky—where its 100-year old gift is displayed at its National Guard headquarters—is the original state militia connection still maintained.

However, in a very recent development, the Wyoming State Shooters Association is reinstituting a competition for once what was called the "Remington Centennial Trophy." Known historically in the "Equality State" as the "Iron Mike" trophy, not only is there once again going to be an annual competition—though civilian and not military in nature— but the original Polasek casting sent to the state in 1916 has been found. According the WSSA's vice-president David Urasky in one of the

Source: Author's Collection

organization's recent newsletters, the trophy "was in the Pioneer Museum in Douglas. It will soon be prominently displayed in the capital building in Cheyenne."[19] Certainly this represents a turn-of-events that would warm the hearts of the Commission's members who authorized and dispersed the original trophies a century ago.

In addition to Mr. Polasek's striking, three-dimensional rendering, the art world was encouraged to lend its talents in support of the Arms' anniversary in another medium, this one by means of a Remington Centennial Poster Contest. Competing for a generous purse of $1000 in gold, five of the foremost designers in the United States working in that style of graphic art submitted entries. The basic themes to be pictured were two-fold: one commemorating the making of the first Remington gun and the other announcing the upcoming celebration. An old art form of western European origin, these colorful broadsides were once again in vogue. *The New York Telegram* recognized this phenomena's resurgence in taking note of several current poster revivals, "…as evidenced by the great public interest in the Newark competition and the prize-winning poster in the Remington contest that will be reproduced in full-color and sent to individual sportsmen and dealers throughout the world."[20]

From the original printing, the first 2,000 were distributed to residents of the village. Unfortunately, in spite of its widespread dissemination, "the poster in the [Remington] museum is the only surviving poster known to Remington historians."[21] With the award being made based upon the criteria of "historical accuracy, general artistic treatment, and commercial value," the prize went to Louis Fancher. While some today question whether the winning entry brought $100 or $1000 in gold to its artist, an August 24, 1916, edition of the *Ilion Citizen* quotes the higher amount, and the poster itself has the $1000 figure included among its graphics. Rendered in six bold colors, the main feature of the print shows Eliphalet Remington, flintlock held in his left hand, shaking hands with a circa 1916 sportsman carrying in his other hand a Remington rifle of the day. Fancher's work was praised as "a splendid interpretation of this momentous event in the history of arms' making in the United States."[22]

Even when the celebration was long since over, interest in the poster remained high, and not only for the winning entry, but also the quartet not selected. This curiosity resulted in a public showing of all five posters, along with a collection contributed by members of the Bridgeport Art League, at Watkin's Art Store in Connecticut. "Because of the situation of the Great Remington factories in this city," *The Bridgeport Evening Farmer* speculated, "the exhibition of posters commemorating the making of the first Remington rifle in 1816 and announcing the centennial occasion, should be of particular interest to Bridgeporters."[23]

Along with the promotional boosts that the statues and posters provided on both local, state, and national levels, other opportunities to advertise and profit at home were not overlooked. In the case of a celebration toasting the hundredth anniversary of a successful entrepreneurial venture, it seemed appropriate that the event would spawn money-making projects to capitalize on the vast influx of people attending the various functions. One enterprising group quick to take advantage of this golden opportunity were the Boy Scouts, who were given the exclusive right to sell the official Remington Centennial button.

The village itself also got into the souvenir business, purveying what in that era were popular men's accessories: watch fob medallions. Before the advent of the wristwatch in the next decade, a pocket watch was a basic item carried by many men. To facilitate its retrieval, a fob was attached to the ring at the top of the time piece and dangled out from a pants or vest pocket, thereby expediting its removal without its owner having to fish around among other items that he might also be carrying. Fobs could be fabricated out of any type of material. It could be as simple as ribbon, as personal as entwined hair, or as costly as leather. Frequently, the upper end of the fob was adorned with a decorative piece, one which also served to add a counterbalancing weight to that of the watch. In keeping with the centennial theme, the Ilion version had a bronze pendant adorned with two scenes rendered in low relief, one being that of the original forge and the other depicting the current factory. Other incised details included a banner inscribed "Ilion Forge 1816" and "Ilion 1916." The Erie Canal, a rifle and a typewriter were also pictured. From sales of this memento, the village realized a profit of $188, the equivalent of which today would be $4300.

Other popular items that were available during the celebration were postcards portraying Eliphalet and his three sons, pennants with "Remington" or "1916 Ilion NY Remington Centennial" emblazoned on them, and programs outlining the events over the three days. Restaurants and hotels also fared well, as an appreciable number of visitors came from other parts of the state and country to partake in the festivities.

While not selling a product *per se*, an enterprising army recruiter was quick to take advantage of the potential manpower inherent in the large crowds that would be present in Ilion. To facilitate his efforts, Captain J. E. Parish of the 1st Infantry Regiment of the New York State National Guard moved his station temporarily to Ilion. Since an air of some urgency existed due the ongoing border war with Mexican revolutionaries, Captain Parish hoped that he might find willing enlistees caught up in the inspiring aura created by the patriotic red, white, and blue decorations, the stirring airs from marching bands, and the crisp trod of uniformed troops in the parades.

With the mindset of being thorough in the scope of its preparations, the Centennial Committee was lauded by the press for "...leaving nothing undone that will make the affair the biggest ever."[24] For instance, even garbage collection in the village did not miss its scrutiny. Regularly handled Monday through Wednesday, the task was still scheduled for those same days, but all routes were to be covered between the hours of 1:00 a.m. and 10:00 a.m., so as not to interfere will any of the day's events. Since available hotel space was already at a minimum due to the increased, war-related employment at the Arms', arrangements were made with willing village residents to temporarily rent out spare rooms to visitors. The New York Central and West Shore Railroads showed their support by agreeing to add additional excursions to help accommodate the influx of out-of-towners expected to attend.

Along with the nuts and bolts of scheduling the events, designating parade routes, and identifying venue sites, the planners were also on the lookout for spectacular, unique opportunities to generate greater interest and propel excitement to a whole new level. They struck gold when a contract was let for an extensive electrical display covering several blocks. At a then princely sum of $1700, Hoefler Avenue, Remington Avenue, Armory Street, Benedict Avenue, and Otsego Street all the way to Main Street were to be illuminated at the commission's expense. The portion of East Main from Otsego to Hoefler would also be lit with the Arms' picking up the tab.

Set eighteen inches apart, the lights were attached to wire arches strung above and across the streets. For those walking along the illuminated lanes, night was turned into day. Looking down from the heights of West Hill, the eastern side of town appeared all-aglow with a surreal nocturnal brightness, the likes of which no one had ever before seen.

The reason for all of this neighboring hoopla was nicely captured by Cooperstown's hometown paper *The Otsego Farmer*: "Thousands of people from all parts of the country are in Ilion this week, attending the celebration of the 100th anniversary of the making of the first Remington gun at that place—an act which has grown into a splendid industry for which our sister village is noted."[25] Though the ups-and-downs of the business cycle had brought both flush times and lean years to the company, its employees, and the community, no one disputed the importance of Remington Arms to the fortunes of the town. As one reporter assessed the relationship, "Ilion can look more like a factory with a village than a village with a factory."[26] Further defining the connection between the town and its major employer, *The New York Evening Post* postulated that "the making of guns, weapons, and military devices has represented work, bread, and comfort to its people; and the industry has grown from a country crossroads settlement to a flourishing town of 10,000 in population grouped around the mammoth brick buildings which now turn out the successors to the rifle that Eliphalet Remington made in the old wooden 'armory'."[27]

⛥

BUT THE BEST laid plans can sometimes be unexpectedly jeopardized. Just prior to the arrival of the celebratory week, an ugly rumor began to circulate which threatened to seriously diminish the success of the program or possibly, in a worst-case scenario, put the kibosh on the whole affair. The negative buzz that got into peoples' heads was the very real fear of infantile paralysis, a dreaded disease that was most prevalent in the summer months. Before the arrival of Jonas Salk's polio vaccine in 1954, parents lived in dread of their offspring contracting this crippling and sometimes fatal malady. Since one of the common contact points for its spread were large crowds, the upcoming Remington centenary was being suggested as a potential breeding ground that possibly should be avoided at all costs. These local rumblings were heavily reinforced by the knowledge that Brooklyn was at that very moment in the throes of a serious polio epidemic, one that would witness several thousand deaths in the New York City metropolitan area alone that summer.

Realizing that this was not a matter with which to trifle, the Ilion Board of Health firmly tackled the issue on the morning of August 14, 1916. The outcome of its special meeting were regulations that effectively banned children under the age of 16 from participating in any centennial-related events. While certainly disappointing, discretion was the better part of valor when dealing with this very honest and emotionally charged concern on the part of parents. The Ilion Free Public Library supported the precautions by extending them to include its facility, thereby not admitting children under 16 into the building until further notice as of August 17.

As proactive as these precautions were, however, to many alarmed and in some instances hysterical parents they were not viewed as enough. At what amounted to the eleventh hour, some residents began circulating a petition around the village, seeking for the postponement of the festivities until October, when the cooler weather would eliminate the threat of the disease until the next summer. Letters to the editors of local papers were also used to make the case for a delay. One such impassioned plea came from the pen of a Mr. William J. Ross of Sixth Avenue in Ilion, a father of two, who wrote: "...Do we fully realize Ilion is surrounded by the "dreaded disease? Nearby cities, towns, and farms in all directions are afflicted.

Are we to be next? Who knows? Are we to wait until our own loved daughter, son, or mother is stricken down? Think!"[28]

In a response and rebuttal to quiet lingering fears, the *Ilion Citizen* addressed the matter in a reasoned column. The paper's editor argued that the thousands of men from places outside the community entered the town every day to work in the factories around town. In so doing, they mingled with numerous residents of Ilion, employees who returned home to sit at supper tables with their families. The implication was of course that ample opportunity for the spread of the disease already existed daily. "If thousands of persons coming here from infected districts has not caused the least apprehension," argued the paper, "why should a three-day event cause it?"[29] The article went on to assure residents that Ilion's health authorities would remain alert to the best interests of their children.

Furthermore, with so much time, energy, and money having already been invested in planning, scheduling, and advertising the celebration, moving the whole program back to a later date could seriously jeopardize its chances for success. For example, many of the dignitaries expected to attend, some as speakers, might not be able to rearrange their personal calendars to still come to Ilion at the new time. Finally, after much deliberation by the Ilion Village Board, Ilion's Board of Health, the planning committee, and Remington officials, the decision was made to leave the centennial's dates as they were.

In a last bit of sound advice, one that was not limited to polio but rather applied to a myriad of ailments, readers were advised to pay attention to the hygiene surrounding their hands. "If the human race would learn to keep the unwashed hand away from the mouth," the paper submitted, "many human diseases would be greatly diminished."[30] Giving a recommendation that still soundly resonates one-hundred years later, the United States Public Health Service in 1916 listed five instances either before or after which people should "Wash Their Hands Immediately!"

WITH THE PUBLIC'S fears sufficiently allayed by the restrictions, final preparations were made. However, because of the board of health's decree, some of the original plans had to be scrapped. No youths under 16 could participate in what had been intended as the "Children's Parade," and these same adolescents would not be able to greet and meet Governor Whitman on the celebration's second day. As reported by the press, though, the impact on the parade was deemed minimal, for "with the exception of one float planned for small children only, every float will appear as originally planned."[31]

Forging ahead, in spite of lingering fears, the festivities began as scheduled at 10:30 in morning of Tuesday, August 29, 1916. This was designated as "Ilion Day," to be followed on Wednesday by "New York State Day" and "Military Day" on Thursday. Moments before the first speaker stepped forward to address the crowd, the headquarters for the centennial observance had been officially opened in the Masonic Temple, a facility located fifty feet behind the "Silent Sentinel" in Monument Square.

With a bright summer sun already bathing the town in what would unfold as a picture-perfect day, Ilion was prepared. Red, white, and blue bunting was copiously festooned all over the business district on buildings and above the streets on wires. Banners dotted the downtown area, with one especially huge creation featuring a picture of Eliphalet Remington II hung over the intersection of Main and Otsego Streets. A large electric sign—spelling out "Remington"—was conspicuously suspended across the front of the Central Avenue lift bridge over the Erie Canal. Attractive white, classically-styled columns were erected in selected locations, such as Bridge Square. Most homes prominently displayed flags, with the granddaddy of them all being a spectacular 50' by 30' foot version of "Old Glory" unfurled above the Remington factory complex.

For the opening ceremonies, a "Court of Honor" had been constructed in a place of special significance to Ilionites: immediately on the north side of the venerated Civil War statue. The focal point of the setting was a raised wooden platform, perhaps 15' x 10' square, six-feet high, and decorated with red, white, and blue bunting and star-covered cloth. Adding a touch of imperial majesty to the scene were eight pedestal-mounted columns some 15' tall with ornate gold-painted capitals. Spotted around the square, they provided an element of elegance to the setting.

A sizable turnout assembled to witness these opening events of the Arms' celebration. However, with thousands of Remington employees hard at work in the factories, a host of potential attendees were unfortunately absent. Typical of an era devoid of electronic communications, public oratory was very much in vogue, to wit a series of speakers had been lined up to kick-off centennial tribute. The president or mayor of the village, Philip Ward, opened the proceedings with the village's official welcome.

"Monument Square" was selected as the site for the opening-day ceremonies. A raised platform was constructed and temporary pillars added to impart an aura of stateliness to the site. With the Civil War monument located to the left just out of the picture and the façade of the Masonic Temple in the background, the setting was very attractive and offered an appropriate spot that suited the grand occasion. (Source: Ilion Free Public Library)

After his brief remarks, Orange B. Rudd, an Ilion businessman of long-standing, assumed his duties as master of ceremonies. Before relinquishing the podium to the first speaker, Mr. Rudd offered a few brief remarks of his own. After presenting a brief history Remington Arms' development from its inception with one gun to a diversified manufacturer of impressive proportions one hundred years later, he concluded by observing that "the name Remington has always been a guarantee for quality and all goods having that name have a world-wide reputation for being of superior excellence. Within the past 30 years, under the management of men of large means, the business has become so large that the crack of a Remington rifle and the click of a Remington typewriter are heard in all parts of the civilized world."[32]

He then introduced the first speaker. This gentleman was a highly-respected Ilion attorney named Frank Schmidt, who chose as his topic "The Industries of Ilion."[33] Of noteworthiness in Mr. Schmidt's presentation were some of the striking facts which he offered. One was that the various manufacturing facilities in Ilion collectively employed "10,000" workers, a statistic made all the more impressive because that figure was double the indigenous population of the host community.[34] The second data point was the "$190,000" total weekly payroll received by all factory laborers in Ilion—an amount that would convert to the absolutely astounding sum of almost 4.4 million in 2019 dollars, after adjustment for inflation.[35] Based on these numbers, the Ilion of 1916 was a thriving community, with Remington Arms unequivocally recognized as being the driving force behind that prosperity.

Next up in the program was Captain Thomas A. Marshall. Billed as "the Western Representative of the Remington Arms Union Metallic Cartridge Company," the officer's address was titled "Remington."[36] Having only just returned from the West on Saturday, Captain Marshall was immediately dispatched to Ilion to represent his employer as an opening day speaker. With his focus being on the company, he began by first lauding the more recent owner, Marcellus Hartley Dodge, while also paying tribute to the local managers currently running the operation. Next, the captain flashed back to the founding role of Eliphalet Remington, giving appropriate kudos to his successes in the fledgling years of the business, as he already had to its more recent accomplishments. Finally, with his concluding thought, the captain brought a smile to many faces when he said that he "hoped that he would be able to meet his audience again at the next 100th anniversary."[37]

The remainder of the program was filled with congratulatory tidings brought forth by representatives from neighboring communities. Frankfort, Mohawk, Herkimer, Little Falls, and Utica had all sent delegates. While none of these four valley towns hosted a Remington factory, members of those communities certainly worked for the Ilion-based business and in turn brought their paychecks home to spend in local stores. Each man had his own special message to deliver, the common denominators among them was their praise for Remington's success and best wishes for Ilion's continued prosperity. The last speaker, George Dunham from Utica, spoke for everyone when he said: "It can be your boast that Remington is a word familiar all over the globe, synonymous with honesty and excellence. That fixed and firm reputation is well worth this hundred years of sturdy, faithful toil which has been a wonderful century of growth and progress."[38]

Upon the conclusion of this introductory segment of the day's scheduled activities, folks had choices to make. It was now almost noon. The next big event was scheduled for 2:30 p. m., three miles south on the gorge road. If they so chose, people could start for the next venue in a leisurely manner, or they could go home or downtown to get lunch. Some of the better planners may have packed a food basket, allowing them to stop for a picnic somewhere on the picturesque route up along Steele Creek.

For those who liked multiple options, another rather odd possibility existed. At noon, a local boy named Albert Van Arnem was going to put on the performance of his young life in the downtown business area. His specialty was high diving. His stunt this day was to jump off the multi-storied Morgan building into the Erie Canal, which at that time was seven feet deep. In an era of daredevils who walked on the wings of airplanes and braved Niagara Falls in barrels, Van

Arnem's feat was relatively tame, though not without an obvious element of danger to life and limb. Why this carnivalesque act was included in the program is uncertain. Perhaps the planning committee just wanted a lighter bit of entertainment to offset the two serious presentations on either side of it. A mindless diversion, over quickly, that did not require deep concentration and prolonged attention by spectators. Assuredly, the performance would be brief by comparison to some of the speakers who could be quite long-winded at times. Of course, the possibility that Mr. Van Arnem might have broken his neck loomed as an ever-present possibility; however, the dampening effect that such an adverse outcome might have had by putting a chill on the upbeat atmosphere was apparently considered worth the risk.

Assisted by what amounted to a sideshow barker—an energetic man with megaphone in hand calling on passers-by to stop and watch the performance—the youngster poised dramatically on the edge of the building's roof. Its ranks swelled by factory workers on their lunch break, a crowd numbering in the thousands stood below him with necks craned upward. Uttering a gasp of awe, they watched him dive into the air, rapidly descend 90-feet, and disappear into the murky waters of the canal. Given that no headline appeared in the paper the next day announcing his demise, Mr. Van Arnem apparently performed his daring plunge without incident. He would repeat his intrepid performance again at noon on each of the festival's last two days, emerging no worse for the plunge each time.

In addition to the officially published schedule, listing the times and places for the main events on each of the three days, other attractions were offered for those who sought alternative venues. One of the more popular choices was that of listening to quality band music. Six bands were hired and eager to perform: the Municipal Band of Utica, the Little Falls Band, the Fort Plain Band, the Remington Typewriter Band, the Fort Dayton Band of Herkimer, and the Ilion Military Band. The plan was for these musical groups to play at various intervals throughout the course of the celebration, providing lively entertainment between the major activities. Given the popularity of outdoor concerts in that era, including these relatively inexpensive performances added a simple but appreciated addition to the overall festivities.

The 2:30 event listed on the program was the most significant and lasting of all the tributes that occurred during the three-day festival. The location selected was not a random choice, but rather done very purposefully. It could even be said that Eliphalet Remington I had chosen the spot himself. For it was there, three miles south up the winding dirt road from Ilion above the western bank of Steele's Creek, that his son's skill and industriousness spawned the company being celebrated. In the grand design of the three-day schedule of events, this one was special. One newspaper even framed the journey to the site as "a pilgrimage up the gorge road."[39]

Unfortunately, the location did not offer a lot of room for spectators, horses, and carriages, owing to the creek and the road being squeezed in side-by-side and then up against a bank and a hill. On the opposite side of the stream were the crumbling remains of an old blacksmith shop. But not just any building had this gray-stoned cabin once been. For it owned the distinction of being both the original home and first epicenter of the Remington business world, the very place where a century before Eliphalet II had established as his first "factory." All that remained of this revered site was the now empty and dilapidated building.

One other equally important relic related to the observance was also still in existence and made its appearance during the festivities too. Taken from the family farm, the anvil upon which the budding young gunsmith had fashioned his first rifle had been saved. The free-standing, t-shaped iron pedestal was then in the possession of an area resident, a gentleman who had generously loaned this treasure for display in the downtown Board of Trade room. But unfortunately, for the sake of history and posterity, no one considered the old forge worthy of any similar consideration for long-term preservation. Before long, any semblance of a building would be gone, leaving nothing more but a jumbled pile of rocks.

To at least commemorate this historic site, a bronze tablet was affixed to a six-foot tall, ten-ton boulder resting on a concrete slab.

The memorial had been placed between the road (i.e.- Route 51) on its east side and the streambank to its west. Compliments of the then local chapter of the United Daughters of the War of 1812, the metal plaque reads as follows: "On the farther bank of the stream stood the forge where Eliphalet Remington 2nd made the first Remington gun. This tablet erected by Commodore Oliver Hazard Perry Chapter United States Daughters of 1812 of Ilion New York."[40]

Mirroring the format of the morning's ceremonies, the schedule for the afternoon's program also had several components. This time a blend of songs and speeches were offered, with the music being a mix of vocal and instrumental pieces. Mrs. Frank Callan, regent of the local chapter of the Daughters of the War of 1812, had the distinction of giving the main address, one in which the *Utica Herald-Dispatch* acknowledged that she "eloquently eulogized" Eliphalet Remington II.[41] Among her many well-chosen words, she declared: "We often hear it said of a man that everything he touches succeeds or everything he touches turns to gold. So it was with Eliphalet Remington. By the force of his character and the creative power of his thoughts, he could wring success from the most adverse circumstances..."[42]

Upon the conclusion of her address, the plaque was unveiled. Giving this moment special import, by providing a connection from the present to the past, was the presence of Ida Remington Jones, granddaughter of Eliphalet II. She was afforded the honor of unveiling of the tablet. Accepting the plaque was the Hon. Watson S. Squire, a former United States Senator and Governor of the state of Washington. Though not an Ilionite himself, he had ties to the community through the late Philo Remington, who had been his father-in-law.

Three more speakers followed, interspersed with an equal number of musical selections. The last song was a stirring rendition of the "Star-Spangled Banner," one in which the audience was encouraged to join in and sing along with the featured quartette. The Rev. Calvin French then brought the proceedings to a close with a benediction.

For those attending this function, they were now faced with a three-mile trek back to Ilion. But these folks had plenty of time to return, eat supper, and rest up a bit before the final event of the day—a parade not scheduled to shove off until 8:30 p.m. The first of several such processions over the three days, the evening's spectacle included women and adolescents over sixteen. Conspicuously absent of course, as both participants and attendees, were all children and younger teens, due to the lingering fear of their contracting infantile paralysis. While the upshot was that only one float was compromised by their absence, the reality was that youngsters who would have thrilled at the pageantry were for their own protection denied the opportunity of being a part of this once in a lifetime extravaganza.

Credit was due the event's planners who had worked diligently to overcome setbacks such as this to put together a memorable program. With respect to the parades, their pathways were varied from the traditionally followed route of past years' processions, so that residents living in different parts of the village could enjoy the exciting experience of a long cavalcade passing directly through their neighborhoods. These reconfigured approaches resulted in the route of march for Tuesday's parade starting at Benedict Avenue, moving north along Otsego Street to Main, and then heading west as far as West Street. From there, it proceeded south to Third Street, across Third to John Street, and south to its intersection with Otsego at Ingersoll Park. Turning sharply left, marchers then returned to their starting point by going north down Otsego Street. Comprised of a variety floats, Tuesday's parade featured the women and older teens of the village as its principal performers. In length and route, it would be the shortest of all the processions over the course of the three-day celebration.

As had become the custom In Ilion to set parades in motion, the Arms' steam whistle sounded twice. The order of march began with a contingent of police, followed by Grand Marshall Colonel James Palmer. Next were officials of the village. Then came the main body of the parade, a mix of bands and floats. The music, so essential a component of such pageantry was provided by three units: the Ilion Military Band, the Herkimer Band, and the Typewriter Band. Marchers included members of the Child Welfare Station, Red Cross Nurses, New England women, the Daughters of the American Revolution, and the Daughters of the War of 1812. Interspersed with the bands were floats depicting a rather eclectic array of historical themes, among them being those titled "The Old Forge," a "Grecian Scene," a "Venetian Street Scene," "Spring Leading Summer," "Indian Life," a "Japanese Tea Garden, and "Coaching in 1861." As these creations passed, an observer commented that "the spectators reacted with… exclamations of admiration and wonder, and the applause was frequent."[43] The critique was also offered that the floats displayed "… a surprising degree of ingenuity and artistic skill, and this spectacle will never be forgotten by those who witnessed it."[44]

By the time the entire parade had covered the route of march, it was close to ten o'clock in the evening. After twelve hours of festivities, the first day of the celebration was in the books. The consensus among the event's organizers, participants, and spectators was that the day had been an overwhelming success, whetting everyone's appetite for what the next two would bring.

Saluting Remington Arms. (Source: Author's Collection)

16

THE CENTENARY CONTINUES:
NOTABLE FIGURES JOIN THE FESTIVITIES

A ugust 30 dawned with another beautiful sunrise, the precursor to a second day that Mother Nature would bless with excellent late-summer weather, one that was warm yet tempered by the coming autumn that was felt in the air. The next two-days of the centennial would feature star-power as their central attractions. On Wednesday, Ilion would be graced by the presence of Governor Charles Whiteman. Thursday would have as its guest of honor Warren G. Harding, then a United States Senator from Ohio and six years later the President of the United States. In keeping with the thematic approach to each day's rotation of festivities, August 30 had been designated as "New York State Day" and August 31 titled "Military Day." The former title made good sense, but the inspiration for the latter one, viewed today out of context by over 100 years, is not as clear as to its origin. Quite likely, the intent for "Military Day" was a nod to past contracts which the Arms had been awarded by the army and undoubtedly seeded with the hopes that future purchases were still to come.

In keeping with the format established on August 29, the second day's main events were also divided into morning, mid-afternoon, and evening segments. Kicking off the schedule on Wednesday was an address given by the Governor Whitman from the platform in Monument Square. Though scheduled for ten o'clock, His Excellency did not arrive until 12:30. The breakdown of his car, as he and his driver motored westward from Albany, was the culprit, causing much of the delay while roadside repairs were made. However, even when at long last the governor's vehicle arrived in Ilion, a second interruption was incurred when his car had to pull over as fire engines raced past to reach a home in distress—one located opposite Monument Square and very near to the site of the upcoming ceremonies!

Finally, preceded by the Ilion Military Band, the governor was ceremoniously conveyed up Otsego Street to the square, where a rough estimate identified between 500 and 1,000 spectators anxiously waiting. In an interesting turn of events, some members of the audience who had been expecting the governor to arrive since 10 o'clock had gotten restless and started to leave around 12 o'clock. However, his appearance at half-past noon happened to fortuitously coincide with the mid-point of the lunch hour for Remington employees. As a result, many of the workers returning to the factory stopped by just as he began to speak. So, while the composition of crowd had changed, the number of onlookers by chance remained about the same.

On the platform to greet Governor Whitman was a veritable who's who among the movers and shakers of the village, men bearing such prominent surnames as Brill, Rasbach, Rudd, Heacock, and Russell. Also seated with the local dignitaries was "…young Marcellus Hartley Dodge, the millionaire owner of the gun works, who had come to Ilion to attend the celebration"[1]

Given a rousing welcome by the waiting crowd, the governor did not disappoint those who had come to hear what he had to say. "In a speech ringing with the enthusiasm and spirit of the occasion," wrote a local reporter, "and one which extolled in fitting manner the record of achievement which the Remington industries have maintained for a century, Governor Charles Seymour Whitman addressed an immense throng in Monument Park Wednesday noon."[2] Memorable among the governor's well-chosen remarks was his observation that "Remington,

Governor Charles Whitman -
(Source: Library of Congress)

along with Whitney and Fulton, sounded a bugle call that wakened the inventive genius of America, that released the creative energies, and that set America to the great task of mastering materials."[3]

After the speakers had finished their presentations, they were feted with an elaborate luncheon at the 47 West Street home of Chairman Herbert A. House and his wife. To add a touch of class to this special occasion, a vocal quartet crooned in the background as the guests dined. In anticipation of hosting the dignitaries visiting Ilion during the centennial celebration, the Houses' had seen to the installation of the latest style of bathroom fixtures in their residence.

While the governor and forty-nine other guests were enjoying the hospitality of the House family, the next big event on the schedule was forming on the east side of town. This was the pageant known as the "Industrial Parade." If only by virtue of numbers alone, it presented a spectacle not witnessed in the Mohawk Valley before or since. All-totaled, approximately 8,000 men and women would participate in the parade. Its First Division consisted of 5,000 employees of the Remington Arms and Ammunition Company with four area bands spaced at intervals among the marchers. The next division was comprised of 2,000 workers from the Remington Typewriter Works, accompanied by two bands. The third and last contingent of 1000 featured the combined work forces of the Library Bureau, A. N. Russell and Sons, the Ilion Lumber Company, Klippel Lumber Company, Dyett Manufacturing Company, and the Ilion Concrete Company.

While scheduled to jump off at 2:30 p.m., getting such a large group lined up and ready to go was understandably a difficult task, so the first marchers did not in fact step out until 3:30. As the ranks passed by in files aligned four abreast, few if any of the thousands watching curbside could lament that they did not recognize at least one relative, friend, or neighbor in the parade. The men and women "marched in close, heavy columns, distinguished from their fellows by some emblem, some special cane, or parasol, uniformly in their shirtsleeves, and all having a tremendously good time on their day off."[4]

Initially, Governor Whitman watched from the front steps of his host's home; however, he was soon apprised that the marchers were unable to determine his whereabouts. To accommodate his constituents, His Excellency moved down closer to the road where he stood upon a rectangular granite slab known as a "horse block," once used to assist riders in mounting their steeds. However, amidst a crowd of people also wearing straw boaters and their Sunday best, this attempt at enhancing the governor's visibility fell short of being a satisfactory solution but had to nevertheless suffice until a more effective remedy was determined.

Eventually, someone came up with the perfect answer. By placing an American flag on a standard next to the governor, his exact location was pinpointed for the parade's participants. The problem was finally solved! The fact that he had to remain in the blazing sun an hour was of no mind to the governor, for 1916 was an election year. By standing where he did, waving grandly at the marchers, he was seen by thousands of voters. In turn, when they found him, those in parade cheered enthusiastically, a salute that constituted well-received recognition by the politician. "We're with you another term, Charley, old boy," shouted one young man in the ranks, "and the Governor laughed outright."[5]

One of the most popular attractions in the "Industrial Day" parade was the oversized American flag carried by marchers, shown as it had just been borne through "Bridge Square" and passes in front of Powers News Store. (Source: Ilion Free Public Library)

The young lad's remark was indicative of the fact that governor's presence in Ilion was not by happenstance. The truth was that his willingness to participate was driven by two motives. One was certainly to honor the 100th anniversary of one of his state's thriving industries. The other was to promote Charles Whitman. Running as he was for-election, his campaign staff had been encouraging him to get out and mingle with the voters in every way possible. The invitation to partake in the celebration in Ilion afforded him just the kind of exposure which they had sought.

With the thousands of constituents pouring into the village, the opportunity to make two addresses, view the parade, and tour the factory put the candidate smack dab in the public's eye in several instances. Later, newsreel coverage of the celebration—screened in movie houses across the state—would provide him with additional time in the spotlight, for some of the footage was devoted to his Monument Square oration.

Ultimately, on November 7, 1916, Republican Charles Seymour

"Industrial Day" Float (Source: Ilion Free Public)

Whitman would defeat the Democratic candidate Samuel Seabury by about 150,000 votes, giving his supporters in Ilion a degree of satisfaction in thinking that his August visit might well have contributed to his margin of victory in winning his second term of office.

Along with viewing an awe-inspiring display of the collective manpower employed in Ilion's factories, the crowd lining the streets—fifteen spectators deep in many places—was especially taken by the sight of an American flag as it passed. While everyone had certainly seen our national banner on countless previous occasions, the rendition of "Old Glory" to which the crowd had reacted so demonstratively was one that presented a most unusual and exhilarating sight, for it was "...75 feet long and 60 feet wide carried by 78 men of the Remington Arms Company."[6] When this oversized display passed by them, spectators all along the way were given to cheering wildly. Following essentially the same route as the day before —with only the starting point moved from Monument Square to East Main Street to provide a more adequate staging area for the extraordinarily large number of participants—the "Industrial Parade" was the main feature on the afternoon's agenda.

As for overall composition of the gala march, in addition to jubilant workers striding proudly along, bands were again judiciously slotted into the procession. Decorated automobiles were also interspersed in the column, each one carrying dignitaries of one stripe or another. Lastly, there was a collection of the ever-popular floats, many depicting scenes reflecting the various departments involved in the gun-making process.

The only glitch that occurred during the afternoon to mar the spectacle was neither foreseen nor preventable. About halfway into the march, Mother Nature literally rained on the parade. Immediately, onlookers scrambled for any available cover that included awnings, hallways, and stores, seeking protection from the sudden, late summer deluge. Meanwhile, the irrepressible participants continued their forward progress, undaunted and nonplussed. Though the gusting wind, torrents of rain, and spot flooding made managing the large flag and holding to an orderly line of march challenging tasks, the amateurs in the procession carried on like seasoned troupers.

At the conclusion of the parade, the governor joined hundreds of others in taking advantage of an "open house" at the Remington plant, where tours were being offered to the public. At the age of forty-eight, Whitman must have possessed an admirable stamina quotient, for he had been on the go since leaving Albany early that morning and still had two events to attend following his visit to the Arms' factory.

For those who wished to take in as many of the activities as possible during the three-day celebration, a late afternoon baseball game offered a second option. This contest and another game on the docket for the next day were indicative of the passion that Ilionites of that era had for what became known as the "National Pastime." Wednesday's contest between the Remington Arms' nine and a squad representing the Corona Typewrite Company of Groton, New York, was assured of being a spirited affair, for the highly regarded local team had already been defeated during the current season by the out-of-towners. This occurred when the opposing lineups had twice met on Groton's home field on July 14. Each team had captured one game. This meant that bragging rights were up for grabs in this the rubber match of the three-game series. Since the sport was as popular in Groton as it was in Ilion, a large contingent of fans from that town located just southwest of Cortland and slightly more than 100 miles from Ilion made the long trip to hopefully root on their hometown nine to another victory. As an added attraction in keeping with the festive air that abounded all over the village during the centennial celebration, Groton's company band also made the drive and entertained spectators by performing between innings of the game.

Moving to the evening portion of Wednesday's activities, two special events had been scheduled. The first was a dinner, attended by Governor Whitman, that had a built-in element of exclusivity to it.

Since the Masonic Temple could accommodate only 176 attendees, all who wished to dine with the state's Chief Executive had to purchase tickets in advance at the local establishment of McGowan and Richardson. In addition to being served a fine meal, those present were afforded the opportunity to hear the governor's second set of remarks for the day. It was reported that the chief executive was "… vociferously greeted and made a most pleasing address."[7] This time he focused first on the role which Ilion's industrial capacity had played over the years on behalf of the nation. Then, referring to a feeling of "regret that arms and munition plants are made necessary by the most horrible occupations of man," the Governor went on to say that in the aftermath of the war currently raging he "nevertheless felt good might come of evil and that from it a better civilization and better government might result."[8]

The second attraction which concluded the program for August 30 was a grand display put on by the highly-regarded Payne Fireworks Company. The launching site for the pyrotechnics was the strip between the New York Central's tracks and the Mohawk River, placing the staging area on the north side of the waterway just east of the bridge and well away from the nearest spectators and the village. The show was open to all and visible from a variety of viewing spots around town. Some people stood and watched from higher elevations, such as the northeastern end of West Hill. Others positioned themselves in their cars on the flats at Morgan Park, located at the west end of East Street. Here ample space offered enough room to accommodate 1,000 automobiles.

Folks, opting for this comfortable viewing venue, also had at their fingertips a unique way of registering their approval of a particularly impressive display: honking their vehicles' horns. "A night of fire" was how one reporter described the spectacle, as he witnessed "…star bombs, sheaves of fire, and snaky fire-trailing rockets painted on the skies above the Remington's rifle's home a mighty picture of light and fire."[9] Among the more impressive of the blazing presentations that dazzled onlookers was the one that opened the show, wherein the blackness above the northern horizon was illuminated by the words

"Ilion Welcomes Her Guests."[10] This surprise introduction was later followed by several more displays that were equally well-received. One was "...a fountain springing into life and dripping dazzling drops," while a flaming likeness of Eliphalet Remington burning in red and another depicting Niagara Falls in stars of blue, red, and green thoroughly wowed spectators, as judged by the crescendo of beeps that were received.[11]

After the success of the first two days of the celebration, the third and final date—August 31—was highly expected to at least provide their equal, if not outshine them, in bringing the whole extravaganza to a rousing, entertaining, and memorable conclusion.

As pictured by the *Utica Daily Herald*, August 31 was staged in dramatic fashion, "the tramp of marching feet, the reflection of the sun on hundreds of gun barrels, and the presence of Gen. Hugh Scott, chief of staff of the United States Army, combined to give a proper martial air to military day..."[12] The kick-off event for Thursday was to be at noon and featured speeches by General Scott, Senator Warren Harding of Ohio, and Congressman Homer Snyder of Little Falls at the Court of Honor in Monument Square. The presence of a large crowd was guaranteed by the closing of the Arms' plant at 11:30 a.m., thereby affording ample opportunity for the workers to hear the orations. The crowd, estimated at several thousand, was so large that many attendees could not find standing room around the podium and side streets. As a result, many watched and listened from the banks of the slope fronting on the speakers' platform, which placed them above the cement retaining wall now located north from the corner of Benedict Avenue and Otsego Street.

General Scott, who had arrived in Herkimer from Washington early in the morning, spoke first. Resplendent in his gold-laced uniform, he cut an impressive figure. Coming from the perspective of an Army officer, the general shared his belief that "the role of a soldier is to keep in the background, on civil occasions, to be seen and not heard, until that day when he is called to speak for his country and speak in tones of thunder."[13] He then went on to laud Remington Arms and its long history of quality production, particularly as it related to the preservation of American independence. General Scott then intoned appropriate words of praise for the focus of the centennial celebration: "…We are gathered here to do honor…to its illustrious founder and to those men who have had the foresight, courage, and patriotism to carry it forward to its present high conditions. I say patriotism because the manufacture of munitions of war is one of the most important branches of industrial preparations for the defense of the nation, without which the efforts of armies are of no avail."[14] After speaking for several minutes, the general concluded his remarks with a final tribute to the company whose centennial had brought everyone together: "Let us then, each do his part today, to honor to a very high degree, those men who have done so much for industrial preparedness of the nation, who had the foresight, courage, and patriotism to build up the plant that came to the aid of the National Government in the Mexican and Civil Wars, and is ready to do it again…for the salvation of the Republic."[15]

Following General Scott, the Hon. Homer Snyder, congressman from Little Falls, was next up. Sandwiched between the warrior and the statesman whom the people had come to hear, he obligingly kept his remarks brief. But, even in his short oration, he offered an intriguing concept that at the time seemed wholly possible. Referencing the large number of industries located in the immediate vicinity, Representative Snyder suggested that in time "they will continue to extend and expand until the territory lying between the boundaries to the west of Frankfort to the east of Herkimer becomes one vast city. While the megapolitan eutopia that Snyder envisioned never materialized—due largely to unforeseen changing national demographics and economic priorities that adversely affected the Mohawk Valley—he nevertheless left his audience with food for thought.

He then turned the dais over to Senator Warren G. Harding, whom he introduced as the "speaker of the day."[16] As he took his place, the crowd could easily note how natty Harding appeared on this late summer day. Very much in keeping with the fashion of the times, he wore white pants, shoes, and shirt, set off with a contrasting dark jacket and tie, and kept one of the popular straw boaters handy to adorn his head when needed. Being that he was an up-and-coming figure on the national stage, people were very interested he what he had to say. According to a reporter who was present, "Senator Harding commented on the fact that 100 years of Remington history coincided with the country's progress at the time and said that while he did not wish to spread the eagle's wings, he was sure that America had done more in one and one-third centuries than any other nation of the world in five centuries."[17]

Warren G. Harding - (Source: Library of Congress)

In a kudo to Eliphalet Remington, Harding emphatically stated: "Men, all of you, we ought to everlastingly take off our hats to honorable success...If there is one man I admire more than another in this world, it is he who can honorably succeed."[18] He closed that thought "by expressing the belief that every man should strive for the best that there is in him."[19] Four years later, when Harding was in the midst of his campaign for the presidency, the *Utica Herald-Dispatch* recalled his visit to Ilion in most favorable terms: "On that date he made an eloquent address at Monument Square and his remarks as well as his personality made him highly thought of by Ilionites."[20]

In keeping with many villagers' interest in sporting events, several concurrent competitions were being held on August 31. One was a day-long event involving exhibitions of prowess with long guns. Slated for the premises of the Arms Athletic Club located on the flats by the river and sponsored by the Remington Gun Club, those choosing to attend were treated to demonstrations of shooting skills. The first was the unique opportunity to see two world famous marksmen—William Hill and Thomas Marshall—who conducted shooting exhibitions which demonstrated their prowess with a variety of Remington rifles and shotguns that afforded folks a unique opportunity that no gun owner or outdoor sportsmen wanted to miss.

Cited by the *Ilion Citizen* as "one of the best attractions of the centennial celebration," the shooting feats performed by Captain Marshall included the use of a Remington .22 Repeating rifle, a .35 HP Autoloading rifle, a pump gun., and a high-powered slide action rifle.[21] Among the targets which he would knock out of the air using the different guns were five oranges, four eggs, a bean, a pea, and no. 4 & 5 shot. Some feats of accuracy were also going to be performed holding the rifle or shotgun upside down, while others increased the difficulty level using mirrors. Above and beyond the precision shooting demonstrated, those in attendance had to be equally impressed with the amazing eyesight required to even see, much less hit, some of these minuscule targets.

The second exhibition of proficiency, conducted throughout the day, was a trap-shooting tournament. Open to all comers, the event was sponsored by the Remington Gun Club and sanctioned by the Interstate Association. The contest drew competitors not only from across New York, but also the country and even foreign lands—"crack shots" as the *Ilion Citizen* called them.[22] Though several Ilionites participated, the eventual winner was H. J. Pendergrast, a contestant who hailed from Phoenix, New York. After taking 150 shots spaced over ten rounds of fifteen, in taking the top prize the winner missed but a mere four clay pigeons. At one point on his way to victory, Mr. Pendergrast hit a run of 100 consecutive targets. His reward was the three-foot "Remington Trophy," a casting of the same statue of Eliphalet Remington previously sent to the National Guard units of each state. Additionally, a sterling silver trophy was presented to winners in each of twelve class categories.

For track and field enthusiasts, spirited competitions were scheduled at Recreation Park, where "starting pistols barked, bare legs flew, and faces strained to a grimace at the white finish tape."[23] Held under AAU sanctions, gold, silver, and bronze medals were awarded for 1st, 2nd, and 3rd place finishes. A variety of events made up the meet, including such popular attractions as the 100-yard dash, 440-yard run, the one-half mile relay, and the high jump.

For those who liked a touch of the unusual, a pie-eating contest was also included for levity's sake, one in which the ultimate winner downed his pastry in two-minutes flat. Another novelty event featured Ted Meredith, the University of Pennsylvania's well-known intercollegiate sprint champion. The young runner challenged all comers in a 440-yard dash. Even after spotting his competitors an eight-yard handicap, Meredith won going away.

Finally, catering to those interested in partaking of yet another experience, a baseball game was played at Recreation Park, starting at 4:30. Since Ilionites of that era dearly loved their baseball, scheduling a tilt as a featured part of Thursday's program made perfect sense. This contest featured a team comprised of workers from Remington Arms against one from employees of the Remington Typewriter Company, inherently guaranteeing a spirited contest by pitting squads from the neighboring businesses against each other. The two teams had already met twice that summer, with each squad having won a game. The rivalry between the two teams was described as "intense," so much so that a local paper's editor with tongue in cheek warned that "persons subject to heart trouble had better take precautions," if they intended to take in the big game.[24]

With a roster of players who worked for the gunmaker, the Arms' nine was by no means a pick-up squad or a bunch of beer-ballers. To the contrary, a Utica paper revealed that "records…show that the Arms' team is composed of ex-college and professional players whose past performances are creditable and prove the team entitled to the prominent place in amateur athletics it already occupies."[25] Further praise was heaped on the Remington boys when it was opined that "it is doubtful if there is a faster aggregation of ballplayers representing any industrial corporation than the team playing under the colors of the Remington Arms & Ammunition Company of Ilion."[26]

Having lost but three games to date that summer—all in extra innings—this highly competitive team was often requested to play at county fairs, taking on a local entry which they usually vanquished, though drawing sizable crowds in the process. But despite its proven ability, the Remington entry did not administer a drubbing to their in-town rivals in that Wednesday afternoon contest, winning by only the slim margin of 4-2. Even at that, several spectacular plays were needed late in the game to seal the victory. Among these was a diving stop by the home team's shortstop in the top of the ninth, dramatically preserving both the lead and win coming as it did with two on and two out. Contributing to the festive air that accompanied the game, spectators were serenaded between innings by a company band playing popular renditions of the times.

With the last day of the celebration jam-packed with interesting events in the morning and afternoon, the culminating activity on Thursday evening needed to go some for the festivities to end on a more spectacular note than what attendees had already experienced. Knowing this, event planners had in fact saved what many would agree was truly the best until last. What was designated to be the grand finale? None other than Ilion's ever-popular "Booster Parade!" This pageant was not new, for it had already been established as a yearly occurrence held in conjunction with the fire department's annual inspection. With the firemen and their vehicles again guaranteed participants, anticipation ran high for what other components would be included in the 1916 edition of the spectacle. As prophesied by the *Richfield Springs Mercury*, "in past years, the boosters' parade has been the talk of the valley, but this year's event will be the biggest yet."[27]

While the cavalcade was beginning to form in staging areas at the east end of town, the various dignitaries who had been involved in the celebration gathered once again at the Masonic Temple for one last dinner. On this occasion, the guests of honor were General Scott and Senator Harding. Three of the attendees spoke: H. A. House, in his capacity as general chairman for the centennial celebration; Charles Wickwire, noted Waterville attorney; and then General Scott, commander of the United States Army. Once their meal was finished and the speeches concluded, everyone moved over to the reviewing stand located by the Remington offices to await the passing of the much ballyhooed "Boosters' Parade."

The route which this pageant was to follow covered what was much of Ilion that was not located on one of the hills: "W. Main Street, to Railroad Street, to Clark Street, to Cottage Street, to North Street, to E. Main Street, to West Street, to Third Street, to John Street, to Fourth Street, to Otsego Street, to Main Street, to the point of counter march..."[28]

The make-up of the procession coming the spectators' way amounted to an all-encompassing extravaganza—twenty-five floats of elaborate design, typifying the participating organizations, merchants, and societies of the village intermixed in with ten thousand marchers drawn from "all of the fraternal and social lodges and clubs and businessmen's organizations" comprised a colossal line of march.[29] Adding in decorated automobiles, fire engines, multiple bands, and ubiquitous clowns made for an exciting spectacle that appealed to onlookers of all ages. Also taking part were National Guard Companies A and B from Utica and M from Mohawk.

Just as the participants in the parade did their did best to provide onlookers with an energetic and entertaining spectacle, so also in turn were those in the crowds packing both sides of the route of march equally inspired to respond with appreciative cheers and applause, as the various contingents passed by them.

The third day's parade, or pageant as it was called, featured two companies of National Guard troops, local units who would be called up in 1917 when the United States ultimately entered the "Great War" raging in Europe. (Source: Ilion Free Public Library)

Many described the scene as having a carnivalesque atmosphere. First, the overhead lighting across the main downtown streets created alternating patterns of light and shadow. Then there was the smoke and glow from the flares—called "redfire" in that era— that were placed along the route and combined to give off a murky, hazy light. Between the flares and overhead lighting, the whole scene had a surreal aura about it.

People were packed so deeply that many were unintentionally forced off the curb by the crush of bodies and into the street. Then, when the parade finally came through, it was able to do so only by navigating a narrow channel through a sea of humanity. With bands blaring, car horns honking, and onlookers cheering, the sound was deafening.

As an incentive to get creative juices flowing, the Centennial Committee had offered prizes of $50, $35, and $25 for floats deemed worthy of 1st, 2nd, and 3rd place recognition. "The Pythian Sisters were awarded the first prize of $50 for their float in the boosters' parade Thursday evening. The Odd Fellows were second and received $35, and Deaner's Meat Market received $15 for being third."[30]

Apparently, the 1916 edition of the traditional "Boosters' Parade" proved in keeping with the high standards for which much-heralded event had achieved and maintained over the years. According to the *Little Falls Journal and Courier,* "in the evening the three-day celebration was ended with a riot of fun and hilarity as the Boosters put on their famous parade. It was a marvel and filled with novelties from start to finish."[31]

In the afterglow of the centennial celebration, few, if any, among villagers, visitors, planners, and the Arms' family would fail to praise the gala as an unqualified success. Like so many highly anticipated events in life, the three days seemed to pass altogether too quickly. Given its staying power in an ever-changing world, Remington Arms has continued to survive and prosper, remaining in business long enough to hold both sesquicentennial and bicentennial observances of its founding. However, compared to 100th year's celebration, the latter two milestones passed with noticeably diminished enthusiasm from the Arms as well as the village, even though the longevity of the company's existence was perhaps worthy of more rather than less recognition.

But times change. Remington Arms has been sold and resold several times. From the village that gratefully participated in the centennial celebration for a business that provided so much of its lifeblood, the relationship over the years had become more distant and less cordial as labor unions, absentee ownership, relocation of departments, and gun-control concerns all made their intrusions on and impacts into the company's operations and community relations. Though the village still desperately needs the jobs provided by the Arms, the relationship between the town and the company will never again be the seen as it once was—that of a deeply proud and appreciative community thankful for the employment opportunities offered by a benevolent hometown industry.

While the future of the Arms very existence continues on shaky grounds, threatened as it is through lawsuits by anti-gun forces who wish to hold the company accountable for damage done to the public by its products—specifically the AR-15— and most recently bankruptcy proceedings followed by still another sale of the business, one of the beauties of studying history is that a story is often well-known and not subject to much alteration over time. Wherever its destiny takes Remington Arms in the years to come, those special three days of the company's centennial observance can neither be denied or erased. With America's entry into World War I on April 6, 1917—a conflict that was already being fought with rifles made in Ilion but would soon include the blood of soldiers from the village too —the exciting days of the centennial would mark the last carefree occasions for some time to come.

At the conclusion of the festivities, the *Utica Daily Press* offered a well-deserved tip of its hat to what had been a wonderful experience for all: "When the real history of Ilion's centennial is written with the perspective that time and distance alone can give, the word 'balance' will characterize the events of the three days that ended with the final wink of street-adorning electrics early this morning. From beginning to end it was a success. Like all great celebrations it had its interruptions, its mistakes, and its delays, but viewed from the standpoint of the historian it glows in shining tribute to the name of the man whom it honored and to the men whose energy, enterprise, and ambition made it possible."[32]

17

SAMUEL RUSSELL'S LEGACY:
THE GIFT THAT KEEPS ON GIVING

W hat became the crown jewel was added to Ilion's growing array of park lands in 1924. That spring, Samuel T. Russell donated 162 acres of woodland to the village. Dedicated in memory of his late father Albert, the park was located along the town's northeastern boundary, this tract proved to be a very versatile piece of real estate that has served the village well for almost a hundred years. In offering the property as a park, Mr. Russell wrote: " I make no restrictions except that it be forever used for park and recreational uses."[1] In addition to his donation of the land, for the remaining five years of his life Mr. Russell also footed the bill for developing an athletic field, putting in a roadway, and a picnic pavilion. Initially, upon receiving title to the land, the village had appropriated $2000 annually for its upkeep; however, without Mr. Russell's continued generosity, many of the enhancements that he funded might have gone years before being realized.

Samuel Russell donated the land in 1923 as a memorial to his father. The sign is one of the many Eagle Scout projects that grace the village. (Source: Village of Ilion)

Shortly after being deeded the property, the village board established an unpaid, appointed "Park Commission" to oversee the care and maintenance of this important addition to the town's outdoor facilities. Originally a three-member board, the committee was increased to five in later years. In keeping with the vision which its donor had prescribed for the park's use, a variety of pursuits were developed within its confines for the enjoyment of village residents and their guests.

Today what is known as the "Parks and Recreation Commission" handles the oversight of not only Russell Park but other similar venues around the community. Appointed by the village board, is volunteer members serve without pay.

This and other similar commissions provide valuable recommendations to the board about the status and management of their domains.

Old-fashioned outdoor hockey was once played in the park. (Source: Ilion Free Public Library)

In essence, the main features of Russell Park have existed on both its upper and lower levels almost since its founding, with several offshoots adding additional activities over the years. After driving past the turn to the high school on its north side, a winding, rising roadway brings visitors to the park's lower recreational area.

At this site can be found the location of playground equipment, picnic tables, and barbecuing facilities. On the slightly higher, opposite side of the only road that traverses the entire park, various structures have existed. At one time, the spot contained a cabin that was used by a park caretaker.

In the sixties, a hockey rink was built in support of the high school's team. Villagers also used the facility for free skating at other times. Given that the overall space available on this site was limited, a fair-sized, all-purpose building was wedged in at the north end of the rink, serving as a setting for rest rooms, a locker room for the teams, and storage. A covered picnic pavilion is now located on what was the space dedicated to the hockey rink.

Moving north along the road, which features a rather steep incline, the upper end of the park can be accessed. More so than the lower section, this portion of the park has been the scene of changing uses. Since this area features a spacious plateau, its surface has been home to several different sporting activities. Originally, it was laid out as a baseball field. Football games were played there in the '20s, '30s, '40s, and, at least once in the '60s, when a game was held there due to the high school's regularly-used gridiron being in unplayable condition. This upper field continued to see use as a practice area for high school teams, until in more recent times when a youth soccer league has played games on its surface. If a drawback exists to utilizing this picturesque setting for any event drawing spectators in large numbers, the lack of sufficient space for parking constitutes its most prohibitive limitation.

In keeping with its multi-purpose uses, for many years at its southern end this upper park featured a bandshell. As late as the 1950's, summer concerts were held on its wooden stage under a large, half-domed roof. Here the Remington Rand and Ilion Firemen's bands were frequent performers. In an era of simpler pleasures, long before cable television and the internet became attractive options, these concerts were extremely well-attended. During the 1949 season, it was approximated that "13,000" music aficionados collectively attended the six concerts, almost doubling the number of attendees from the previous year.[2] At a total cost to the village of $625, this outlay amounted to about a nickel per head—surely one of best expenditures of taxpayers' funds that any board ever approved.

Then the following year—on the second Wednesday evening of the month, July 12, 1950—the first of 6 summer programs was a huge success, one that drew "an audience estimated at more than 3000 persons by Eugene Mosseau, head of the detail of volunteer police on traffic duty."[3] At times, more than 500 automobiles were wedged onto the

The bandshell in Russell Park all aglow in the twilight. (Source: Ilion Free Public Library)

field and later driven out of the narrow confines of the park without incident, which was a definite feather in the cap of Chief Mosseau and his men. The sponsoring parks commission attributed some of this noticeable increase in attendance to the inclusion of more novelty numbers on the bands' playlists, along with the featuring of popular guest soloists from the area.

As a child, two quaint aspects of attending these concerts that always fascinated me were the procedures for "seating" and "applauding." When we arrived in front of the bandstand, we were directed by the special officers on duty to park grandpa's Ford coupe in one of the horizontal rows facing the performance venue. The significance of this parking alignment was that it allowed us to stay in the car, watch, and listen to the concert like people did the features at a drive-in movie. Then, as if that was not a unique enough experience, the method of rewarding the bandsmen for their efforts surely was. Once a musical offering was completed, attendees seated in their cars would send up an approving cacophony of sound by the honking of car horns! To a kid, this aspect of the show was looked forward to with greater anticipation and enthusiasm than most of the music.

The uses and attractions which other parts of Russell Park have offered has likewise ebbed and flowed over the years, as park goers' interests have changed with the passage of time. For a while, a beach volleyball-style court was a popular site opposite the main playing field atop the hill. The same was true of the deep depression to the immediate right once the upper level was gained. Known as the "Sugarbowl," its steep sides were excellent for sledding, tubing, and tobogganing, but only to the extent that underbrush and small trees were kept clear of its sides and far end at the bottom. For several years in the early '70s, the high school's student council utilized this slope for some of its "Winter Carnival" festivities. But in recent years, nature has reclaimed the sides and lower area, with the tangle of young trees and underbrush now rendering both the approaches and the destination completely unsafe for sliding.

Just before reaching the western edge of the "Sugarbowl," a right turn exists, leading to one of the more recent additions to the facilities offered. Set a quarter-of-a-mile down the road is a small, auxiliary park. With a pavilion, tables, grills, and rest rooms, the spot offers an alternative to the oft-crowded amenities in the lower area. With several pieces of playground equipment, the site is self-contained. Unfortunately, by being somewhat out-of-the-way and visually isolated, vandals have made it a prime target for their destructive urgings.

Moving behind this modest recreational area leads to a wonderful, circuitous pathway through the woods that winds downhill, levels out for a short stretch, and then returns uphill along the western side of the bowl in the vicinity of where the bandshell used to be located. In the winter, the byway offers a serviceable cross-country ski trail, while during the rest of the year the route beckons hikers with a chance to pass along a sylvan lane and commune with the local flora and fauna.

While most of the previously described portions of the park are largely still in use, some sections have fallen into disrepair or abandonment down through the years. One of these was a spot located up on the left hand, northern rim of the lower park entrance. Known as "Camp Kiwanis," access was gained by means of trail that went up through the woods on the school-side of the fork, where the road now diverges to allow entrance to the park on the right or access the high school's property on the left. Built by members of the Ilion civic organization for which it was named, the cabin was utilized by Brownies and Gil Scouts as a day site in the summer and on occasion for an overnight stay during other times of the year. Outfitted with a rest room and later a kitchen, the building served its campers for years. As pointed out in the local paper, the cabin "provides our girls with an ideal location and gives them an excellent opportunity for outdoor living at small effort and little cost."[4] Eventually, use of the facility tapered off, until vandals sealed its fate when they wantonly burned the building to the ground.

Moving on up the road to the main area on the lower level, along with the complete removal of all vestiges of the hockey/skating rink, a secondary playground that used to exist a short trek through the woods to the right beyond the west end of the rink is no longer maintained. A metal gate now discourages any wandering off in that direction.

In the main playground area to the left in the lower park, all the old-style equipment—the overhead monkey bars, the swings, slides, teeter-totters, and what we called the "merry-go-round"—have been long-since been phased out. While their absence may be lamented by some of the more nostalgic baby boomers among us, the truth of the matter was that spinning wheel was for sure responsible for the loss of many a picnic lunch, while a freefall from the monkey bars probably caused more than a few concussions, including a good rattling of yours truly's noggin. Today, all that equipment is gone, replaced with a far smaller collection of colorful apparatus that overall is quite visually attractive and probably deemed less hazardous, yet may come up a bit short in its thrill factor.

But it is the upper section of the park that has experienced the most significant changes over the years. The airplane spotter post has come and gone from the knoll at the north west end of the park. Also, missing from that same location is the 95-foot high flagpole made from an Oregon fir tree, donated in 1924 by the grandchildren of Albert Russell. Dominating the landscape, its unfurled flag could be seen for miles up and down the valley. In later years, a metal pole replaced the wooden shaft, but its lifespan has far outlived its usefulness. So the tall pole now stands slowing rusting away, surrounded by trees that would block any view of a flag if one were flown.

Another former attraction now absent from the park is a collection of vintage military hardware, gone from the park scene since 1942. Five in number, these relics came from past eras, one dating to the Civil War and another to World War I. The oldest weapon was a piece of ordinance taken during the War of 1812. A 23-pounder, this naval gun was captured from the British by American Captain Thomas Mcdonough in the Battle of Lake Champlain, an engagement fought on waters off Plattsburgh, New York.

Among several vintage pieces of weaponry that once were displayed in Russell Park was this rapid-fire gun taken in the Spanish-American War by the naval forces of Admiral Dewey during the Battle of Manilla Bay. (Source: Ilion Free Public Library)

A second cannon in the group that also possessed a noteworthy pedigree was a 9-inch Rodman gun from the War Between the States. Mounted on the USS *"Minnesota"* when the vessel was launched in 1855, this armament had belched forth iron shot in several Civil War battles. Its most famous engagement came on March 8, 1862, when it dueled with the Confederate ironclad *"Merrimac"* at Hampton Roads, Virginia.

The other three pieces, though historically lesser lights by comparison, were still impressive and intriguing to gaze upon. Two of them were far less prodigious on appearance than the third. One was a small Spanish rapid-fire gun taken in the Battle of Manila Bay by Admiral George Dewey's victorious feet, and the other, an even more diminutive saluting cannon, was not a weapon of war, but rather a ceremonial model named "James Garfield" and used at political rallies.

But the fifth piece was the one that immediately caught everyone's eye. This behemoth was a long-range German artillery piece. Mounted on a four-wheeled carriage, the cannon's size was as impressive as its apparent potential for destruction was frightening. While next-to-nothing is known of its history, it was established that the big gun was manufactured by the famous arms' maker Krupp in the last year of World War I. Though it may never have seen field service, by virtue of its sheer dimensions alone an ominous quality was imparted to its appearance, conjuring thoughts of the damage this monster could have unleashed on distant targets.

A captured German artillery piece.
(Source: Ilion Free Public Library)

Once the guns were placed in Russell Park in 1924, most people, if asked, would have concluded that these former weapons of war had reached their final destination. Here they would stand in perpetuity, daily reminders of past glories and sacrifices that Americans had made in defense of freedom. Little did anyone anticipate that this collection of artillery was destined to make one last mark on the pages of history, serving once again in a time of need.

Though none would ever be fired in anger at an its enemy or in support of a patriotic cause again, these historic artifacts still had one last contribution to make on behalf of maintaining the security of the United States. Though these old veterans were going off to war for one last time, it would only be in an altered state. With the United States finally drawn into World War II, urgent requests for support of the war effort came from a variety of sources.

Early in 1942, the mayor of Ilion received a letter from Governor Herbert Lehman, asking if the village had any trophies that could be donated to the War Department for salvage purposes. One idea that the parks commission settled on to contribute scrap metal was to offer the cannons from Russell Park. Even though the governor had suggested that he did not want objects of historic interest destroyed, a local decision was nevertheless made to the contrary. Given the tenor of the times which saw enemy forces making headway in both the European and Pacific Theaters, any contribution to assist the Allied cause could not in good conscience be held back. Ilion's military showpieces would be going off to war again. But this time, after being melted down and recast, they would take the field of combat in the reconstituted form as parts of tanks, planes, bombs, and artillery shells. The chairman of the Park Board estimated that "between 30,000 and 36,000 pounds of metal would be salvaged..."[5]

Perhaps as way a to provide an honorable farewell to these potent reminders of wars past, the village decided to have a ceremony, just before the cannons were cut-up for shipment by rail. The artillery was moved from Russell Park and deposited on a section of the green strip of land near the west end of town. Appropriate words were spoken regarding the sacrifice of these historic relics, and then acetylene torches were used to cut them up into manageable sections for transportation to a smelter.

In the seventy-seven years since the cannons were removed, Russell Park has remained intact and functional. With certainty, changes have occurred over the years. Caretakers have been employed from time-to-time, men who have taken an interest in the maintenance of the park as if it were their own. A large water tank was added at the north end of the upper playing fields. Soccer began flourishing on those same fields where baseball and football once held sway. The high school's cross-country team has used the park for training, league meets, and invitationals. Wooden flower lower boxes and entrance signs were installed at both the eastern and western approaches to the park by Boy Scouts and tended by members of the Garden Club. New pieces of playground equipment were erected. Park facilities were utilized by the village's Recreation Department for summer youth activities. The popularity of snowshoeing and cross-country skiing in recent years has made the back trails a destination for winter outdoor enthusiasts. In one of its more non-traditional endeavors, the park board on multiple occasions has contracted out for logging to take place in the park, partly to properly thin the stands of trees as well as to take in a few extra dollars that were reinvested into the park.

Regardless of the changes which have occurred over the years, one aspect of Russell Park that has remained constant and appreciated by generations of residents has been the quiet solitude it has offered. Likened by some as a welcome oasis set amidst the hurried, hurly-burly world that is modern day America, residents have been drawn to its easily accessed acres for relaxation, recreation, and repasts. Whether alone, with a pet, or accompanied by family and friends, the park continues to be sought out by residents as a desirable venue, just as Samuel Russell had envisioned it would be when he made his generous gift of the property almost a century ago.

18

THE REMINGTON TYPEWRITER COMPANY:

ITS FIRST FIFTY YEARS

I lion has had the distinction of its name being tied to a pair of historically significant, world-renowned manufactured products. The first—the Remington line of firearms—has had its praises sung for over 200 years. The other—the typewriter—has not been locally acclaimed to the same degree. Part of the disparity in recognition stems from the reality that the gun company has remained in Ilion and is still producing sporting rifles to this day. In glaring contrast, the typewriting company moved out of town many years ago and has long since discontinued making its signature product.

Remington Typewriter's extensive works as they appeared in the early 1900s. (Source: Terry Sweeney Collection)

However, in the first quarter of the 20th century, the Remington Typewriter was quite a going concern in Ilion, a thriving hometown industry that was as much appreciated by its employees and townsfolk as was the Arms. The year 1923 represented a 50-year benchmark in the history of the company, for it was in 1873 that the Remington's, after embellishing Christopher Sholes' original invention, produced the first practical typing machine. Being visionaries, the Remington brothers had seen the commercial possibilities for this groundbreaking device. After buying out Sholes' share of the invention and agreeing to royalties with his partner, they turned their new acquisition over to their research and development staff. These ingenious employees ironed out the last kinks in Sholes' brainchild amidst an industrial laboratory setting that provided the wherewithal in terms of equipment, tools, financing, time, and expertise.

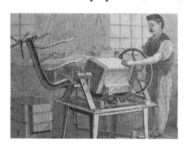

A worker in the typewriter factory. (Source: Scientific American)

Shortly thereafter, a deal was made: the Remington's sold the patent to a trio of former employees who incorporated as the "Remington Typewriter Company." Though no longer manufactured by or affiliated with the gun makers in any way, the new owners had the business acumen to include the use of the former owners' name as a part of the transaction. Once on the market, sales of the new product started slowly. "But by the 1880s things were moving," Richard Snow wrote in *American Heritage* magazine, "[and] five thousand Remington typewriters were sold in 1886, twice that number two years later, and then something on the order of a hundred thousand by the turn of the century."[1] Sales were absolutely smoking! Though they had divested themselves of their holdings in the company in 1887, the Remington's intuition about the marketability of the typewriter was ultimately proven correct. Not only was the newfangled contrivance selling briskly, but the machine was fast becoming an indispensable piece of equipment in offices across the country and eventually the globe. As a local newspaper summed up the machine's status in 1923, "it would be impossible to compute the value of the typewriter to the business world of today..."[2]

Unfortunately, the key player in all of this, Christopher Sholes, did not live long enough to reap either the long-term benefits or accompanying acclaim from his groundbreaking invention, for he passed away just three days after his birthday on February 17, 1890, at the age of seventy-one. The fruits of his creative genius did not result in a lucrative estate, for one estimate calculated that he "...probably made about twenty-thousand dollars all told."[3]

However, when the 50th anniversary of the typewriter's birth rolled around in 1923, Sholes was destined to be posthumously recognized for his contribution to mankind. Having hosted three-days of festivities in honor of Remington Arms' 100-year existence only seven years ago, the people of Ilion were no strangers to putting together large-scale celebrations. Called a "semi-centennial," this event was set for September 12, 1923. Though compressed into a single day, a variety of activities were planned that made for a fitting and fulfilling tribute, one that did justice in honoring the memory of Christopher Sholes and praising the functionality of his invention.

Preparations for the big event had begun in 1921, when Colonel John Vrooman, President of the Herkimer County Historical Society, suggested that some type of observation should be considered. Due to his expressed interest, Colonel Vrooman was appointed acting general chairman for the preparations. In carrying out the charge, he was ably assisted by two committees: one composed of an *ad hoc* group of semi-centennial supporters; and the other drawn from the Ilion Chamber of Commerce. While very supportive of proper recognition for Christopher Sholes, the Remington Typewriter Company was not directly involved in the planning. In addition to putting together a full day of activities scheduled for September 12, the architects of the celebration had also included a couple of preliminary exhibitions to provide some advanced hype in the days before the main events.

The first was hiring the Kosier Decorating Company of New York City, whose crew arrived on the 10th of the month to hang bunting, streamers, and flags on public buildings and over the streets along which a parade was going to pass. The second was the extensive installation of what were called "ornamental street lights" along Wednesday evening's route of march. This meant that the special illumination "extended on Main Street from West Street to Hoefler Avenue, Railroad Street from Clark to Main, Otsego Street from Main to Second, First Street from Otsego to Morgan, and the entire length of Union Street."[4]

With expectations optimistically high for a large turnout, part of the committee's responsibility was to ensure the safety of both residents and visitors. Toward this end, steps were taken bolster the Ilion Police Department with support drawn from state troopers, officers loaned by neighboring towns, and plain clothes detectives. Ilion's police chief also "cautioned residents against leaving their homes unlocked, leaving valuables around, and carrying large sums of money."[5] Looking ahead to the influx of humanity that would be in town on September 23, Chief Hyuck requested Ilionites to leave their locked cars at home, hoping to relieve traffic congestion as much as possible.

⚜

AS ANOTHER PART of the run-up to the day of the festivities, promoters of the event did their best to keep the upcoming celebration in the news, hoping that advanced publicity would generate enthusiasm and in turn help to draw as large a crowd as possible. One of their more successful attempts at grabbing people's attention was the release of a congratulatory letter received from then Vice-President Calvin Coolidge in early August, shortly before the untimely death of President Warren Harding later that same month and "Silent Cal's" elevation to the presidency. Through his correspondence, the man of few words nevertheless managed to substantively share his thoughts on the typewriter's invention with John Vrooman. In his letter, Coolidge wrote that "it is difficult to comprehend how the business of the present day could be transacted without the use of this machine." Then, after praising the invention, he went on to laud its creator, saying that "Christopher Sholes is entitled to be remembered as a man who made a remarkable contribution to the welfare of his fellow men. He is entitled to rank along with Whitney, Morse, and Howe."[6]

৶৵৶

FOR THE MOST PART, the observance was confined to a relatively small portion of town. The three featured venues encompassed an area less than a quarter-mile square: one was the "Remington Park" bleachers/baseball field complex on East Clark Street opposite the Typewriter Plant; the second was the auditorium inside of the Remington Cash Register building also on Clark Street; and the third consisted of a second, newly-constructed "Sholes Park," this one set back from the corner of the Catherine and East Main Street intersection and a block north of East Clark Street. A brief walk, perhaps the equivalent of two or three blocks, was all that separated the trio of facilities featured in some aspect of the day's ceremonies.

In what was a tightly-packed schedule that began at nine o'clock in the morning and continued well-past sundown, a preliminary event took place in the central part of town, slightly outside of the core area where the other activities were planned. This kick-off was a band concert given at the corner of Main and Railroad Streets. Once identified as "Bridge Square," this location in the heart of Ilion had traditionally been the site for similar musical performances down through the years. In all probability, the concert by a 55-piece band lasted perhaps forty-minutes tops, for any spectators so inclined had to move on to the next venue and be seated for a 10:00 a. m. start to the ceremonies there.

The setting for the next event on the schedule was a spacious auditorium. As observed by a newsman who was present, "elaborate decorations abounded everywhere and especially in the big cash register building of the Remington company where the speaking exercises were going to be held..."[7] Even though its large hall had a seating capacity of 2,500, the place soon overflowed to the extent that the doors had to be closed, and people denied entrance. However, anticipating just such a huge turnout, the event's planners allowed for the excess crowd to be accommodated on temporary bleachers set up at the new Sholes Park and the permanent ones located at Typewriter Park, both situated nearby. Taking advantage of available technology, a public address system was used that broadcast through amplifiers placed both inside and outside of the building, so that the proceedings could be better heard not only by those seated in the hall, but also brought to those relegated to the exterior benches as well.

Given the relatively early hour at which the program commenced, the size of the crowd was indeed impressive. Part of the turnout— which would swell to over 25,000 by the end of the day—was attributed to the fact that "all industrial and mercantile houses were idle, as a general holiday had been declared."[8] For our ancestors living in an era without a multitude of diversions the likes of television or the internet, such public galas were welcomed diversions from the demands of long working days and the humdrum existence of everyday life.

As an observer noted, a cross-section of people streamed into the auditorium: "Governors, industrial leaders, factory hands—and stenographers perhaps even more particularly—today paid unusual tribute to the memory of Christopher Latham Sholes, who, fifty years ago, perfected the first commercial typewriter."[9] 9:45 saw the arrival of the guests invited to take part in the semi-centennial, two-hundred of whom had just arrived in town at 7 a. m. that morning by way of a special fourteen-car train, an express which had departed from New York City at midnight on the tracks of the West Shore Railroad.

At 10 o'clock, the day's program began with an invocation, followed by the Remington Typewriter Band playing "America." Colonel Vrooman, welcomed the honored guests and members of the audience, saying that "we rejoice to have you participate in these interesting and historic ceremonies and feel both proud and grateful that thousands have kindly responded to the invitation."[10] He then turned the podium over to Congressman Homer P. Snyder, the gentleman acting as the chairman for the day's program. Mr. Snyder had the pleasure of introducing four distinguished individuals who came from varied backgrounds and would deliver addresses.

First up was Henry Harper Benedict, an Ilion native and the only surviving member of the entrepreneurial triumvirate who had founded the typewriter company. From his unique historical perspective, he offered reminiscences about Christopher Sholes' persistent efforts and ultimate success in producing a working machine.

Mr. Benedict was followed by Frank Lowden, the former Governor of Illinois. Having also been a member of the US House of Representatives for six years, Mr. Lowden had gained a measure of national recognition as a candidate for the Republican presidential nomination in 1920. He had words of praise for Christopher Sholes, who like Lowden was a mid-westerner, only from Wisconsin rather than the "Land of Lincoln."

When it came to name recognition, the third speaker was an individual well-known in state, national, and international circles. A native of VanHornesville, Owen D. Young was a lawyer by education. He rose to prominence and fame as the CEO of General Electric Corporation, a position which he first held from 1922 to 1933. With his sharp financial acuity, he had amassed great personal wealth. In time, Young became known for his philanthropy, particularly with regard to his hometown. For his oration, he chose a topic most relevant to the times, his background, and the invention which brought everyone together that day. "Speaking upon 'The Age of Communications,' [Young] made clear the typewriter's part in modern facilities for exchange of thought."[11]

The last individual who stood before the crowd was a man who needed no introduction. In his second term of four as governor of New York, Alfred E. Smith—the popular Happy Warrior" to legions of the Empire State's voters—had gained a well-deserved reputation as a social reformer. Taking time from his executive responsibilities in Albany, Governor Smith came to the semi-centennial for two reasons. One was to join in celebrating the life of a man who had a far-reaching impact on the history of both Ilion and the state. The other was for the recently-elected Democratic politician to gain some positive exposure in one of the Republican strongholds of his 62-county constituency. Foreign to the ears of upstaters, he spoke with a heavy accent, the legacy of being born and brought up in New York City. But ever-engaging and affable, Al Smith was a man hard not to like when met in-person.

One if the more memorable moments of the morning's speeches came in a bit of extemporaneous repartee which occurred between the two politicians of differing parties on the dais, both known to harbor aspirations for higher office. The light-hearted exchange was a by-product of Chairman Snyder's acknowledgement of the unusual circumstances that existed when he presented two of the guests accompanying him on the platform to the audience: "In introducing ex-governor Lowden and referring to Governor Smith, [Snyder] remarked that it was a hard task to properly introduce both as a possible Republican and a possible Democratic candidate for President and give each his proper credit."[12]

When the time arrived for him to speak, the ex-governor from Illinois immediately followed up on Mr. Snyder's professed dilemma. "I will wave all my ambitions today in order to relieve the Chairman of the day of embarrassment," said Mr. Lowden, in opening his address, "and leave the field open to the Governor of the finest State in the Union."[13] He then went on to laud the accomplishment of Christopher Sholes, arguing that "whoever invents any machine or any method which saves human labor, whether he intends it or not, becomes a benefactor of the human race."[14]

When Governor Smith's turn to talk came a few minutes later, he returned the compliment. "It is my advice to you, Governor," he said, addressing Mr. Lowden, "to accept the nomination in Ilion today. You seldom have the opportunity to receive it in New York State, while I have the honor thrust upon me at least twice a day in all parts of the state."[15] After this brief aside, New York's chief executive focused his address on a comparison of how the state functioned as compared to the operational approach of the Remington's. Noting that the state was using organizational methods a half-century old, "...stumbling along doing the best we can by making just a little progress every year," he expressed the hope and trust that someday "we will be able to carry on the business of the state at least in something like a business-like manner."[16]

After each of the distinguished guests had said his piece, the morning's program concluded with a stirring rendition of the "Star-Spangled Banner" by the band. At this point, everyone broke for lunch. Most of the local attendees went home to eat, while out-of-towners headed for one of the various dining establishments around town. At the same time, the platform guests and distinguished visitors were treated to a luncheon on the premises, for the cash register building had a cafeteria on its first floor. To add a touch of class to the dignitaries dining pleasure, a troupe of well-regarded area troubadours, Ralph Perry and his orchestra, were engaged to provide music.

After the successful morning program held in the Remington Cash Register factory's auditorium had kicked-off the celebration, the rest of the day's activities were all scheduled to take place at outdoor venues. The first of these, set for 2 o'clock in the afternoon, represented the focal point of the day. The site was the newly created "Sholes Park" on the eastern side of the corner where Catherine and Main Streets intersected. Here several tiers of temporary bleachers and a speakers' platform had been set up.

Seven guests were seated up-front. Two were locals, while the others had traveled some distance to be a part of the ceremonies. Congressman Snyder was again the master of ceremonies. Joining him were: John Lowden, James Vrooman, Mrs. Lena Lake Forest, Mrs. Elizabeth Sears, Elizabeth Latham Sholes, and Christopher Lathan Sholes IV. A look at the program revealed that three of these individuals were slated to speak. In recognition of the new career fields opened for women by the development of the typewriter, the key orations were appropriately going to be delivered by females. The *Buffalo Evening News* praised the origin and effect of what Sholes had wrought when it affirmed how "the typewriter brought women into the business world in large numbers and did more, perhaps, than any other one thing to set them on the road to economic independence, and that is held to be responsible for at least two-thirds of the changes in the social order."[17]

Speaking on behalf of their working sisters across America were first Mrs. Lena Lake Forrest, honorary president of the National Federation of Professional and Business Women's Clubs who spoke on "The Advent of Women in the Business World." During her address, Mrs. Forrest offered her thoughts on how the menace to America was not the vote of the foreign-born population, but the absent vote of the American men and women.

The 1909 Model # 10: (Source: Remington Centennial Souvenir Program)

Sandwiched between the presentations by the Mrs. Forrest and Mrs. Elizabeth Sears, Congressman Snyder read aloud a variety of laudatory communications to the audience. Interestingly, the congratulations from the President of the United States presented in the morning session was far from the only tribute making its way to Ilion, but rather one of over 1000 greetings sent by several nationally-known figures. From several senators came words of praise: Albert Capper of Kansas wrote how he felt that "it is fitting that the semi-centennial anniversary of this wonderful machine should be celebrated and that appropriate recognition should be extended to its inventor. It is impossible to overestimate the service that has been rendered to mankind through the invention and development of the typewriter. It has revolutionized intercommunication and so universal has become its use that it may well be considered a necessity in modern business and social activity."[18]

In New York's Senator James Wadsworth's opinion, "there may be some inventions—the cotton gin, and the reaper and binder for example—that have had a more profound effect upon our daily lives than the typewriter. They may be counted upon the fingers of the hands, however, and in any estimate of the relative value of inventions the typewriter must stand very high indeed."[19] Other letters written in similar vein were received from Senator Seldon Spencer of Missouri, Senator Bert Fernald of Maine, and Congressman Walter Magee of New York.

But the list of well-wishers did not stop at the federal level, for another bevy of communications was received from correspondents in state positions, as well a number of governors who contributed their thoughts on the worthiness of the golden jubilee being held in Ilion. "The typewriter is one of the instruments which makes our present civilization possible," wrote Governor George Hunt of Arizona, who went on to add that "it is impossible to imagine present-day business being conducted without its aid."[20] Governor Channing Cox of Massachusetts suggested that "undoubtedly Christopher Latham Sholes accomplished in the invention of the first practical typewriter one of the greatest single steps in commercial enterprise and progress."[21] Acclaim was also forthcoming from other state leaders, like Governor William Flynn of Rhode Island, Governor John Blaine of Wisconsin, and Governor John Parker from Louisiana, with the latter offering that "the business world would be at a loss without the typewriter, and a monument should certainly be erected to its inventor."[22]

Also numbered among the pieces of positive correspondence received by the committee were telegrams sent by several individuals of note such as Theodore Roosevelt, Thomas Edison, and Chinese ambassador to the United States Alfred Sao-ke Sze.

But the one missive that was read in its entirety came from Mrs. Douglas Roosevelt Robinson—vice-president of the Herkimer Historical Society and sister to Theodore Roosevelt. In her correspondence, Mrs. Robinson continued the theme of what a godsend the typewriter was in furthering the cause of women's liberation by providing a whole new genre of job possibilities. She took the opportunity to praise three men who played key roles in advancing women's causes: Christopher Sholes for his inventive genius that produced the wonderful machine; General Francis Spinner of nearby Mohawk—Lincoln's appointee as Treasurer of the United States—who hired the first women to work as federal clerks; and her brother who throughout his political life had "raised his voice for the enfranchisement of women...and he assisted them to become what they have now become, a force in the councils of those who wield the destinies of America..."[23]

To conclude the oratorical offerings for the afternoon, Mrs. Elizabeth Sears, President of the New York League of Business and Professional Women chose "The Keys to Success" for her topic, an oration which she delivered quite forcefully: "We women of the business word needed no emancipation," she declared, "for the typewriter did not free women for they had never been slaves, but it did widen the limits of our possibilities and show us how to broaden our scope of accomplishments."[24]

Once Mrs. Sears had returned to her seat amidst a round of applause, Chairman Snyder directed all eyes to focus on a huge boulder sitting in the forefront of the park. Covered with a large American flag, it awaited the youthful hands of Elizabeth Latham Sholes and Christopher Latham Sholes IV, the great-grandchildren of the inventor, to be drawn aside and expose for public viewing a heartfelt tribute to the late inventor. With a tug on the strings, the veil of secrecy fell away, disclosing a bronze tablet mounted on the face of a huge stone. The tablet was large and square, measuring perhaps 2' x 2' in dimensions.

In a format identical to a rock and plaque combination that had been dedicated in 1916 to honor Eliphalet Remington II and mark the location where his forge was located in the Ilion gorge, the raised lettering on the tablet read:

In Memory of
CHRISTOPHER LATHAM SHOLES
1819 – 1890
One of the World's Greatest Benefactors
Inventor of the
First Practical Typewriter
The product of his genius
revolutionized business
And brought economic independence
To millions of women.
The manufacture of this first
Typewriter began at the works of
E. Remington & Sons, Ilion, N.Y.
September 1873
This monument erected September 12,
1923, the 50th anniversary of the
Birth of the typewriter.[25]

Following the much-anticipated unveiling of this tribute, 100 typewriter girls stood behind the monument. Dressed in in white with blue sashes inscribed "Remington," each one held up a flag representing one of the different nations of the world in which the Remington typewriter was marketed. "Set off in their midst was a banner inscribed: 'Women of the world honor the man who opened to them the doors of business'."[26] Following the presentation by these

young ladies, the band brought the afternoon's gathering to an end
with a rendition of "Auld Land Sine."

WHILE NOT PART of the program, three special individuals were
also present in Ilion that afternoon, people who by now were on in
years, but in their respective heydays played important roles in the
advancement of the typewriter as valuable tool in the business. One of
these folks was Charles Weller, an octogenarian who had come all the
way from LaPorte, Indiana. His claim to fame was two-fold: he was a
long-time friend of Christopher Sholes and recognized as the "first
typist."[27] While Sholes was still developing his machine, the story
goes that he had invited Wells down to his shop to see and try out an
experimental model. Then, in 1868, Weller received from Sholes "…
five years before it was manufactured for sale, the first complete
model of the machine."[28] Weller went on to practice his skills as a
court stenographer.

Possessing a similar historical pedigree was a lady named Lillian
Sholes Fortier. The daughter of Christopher Sholes, she was
recognized as the first female typist. As a sixteen-year old teen, she
was summoned to her father's workshop where she came face-to-face
with the future—"a huge basket-like machine" that was both "heavy
and awkward."[29] At her father's behest, she typed out a piece of
correspondence. In time, Lillian became a competent typist, though
she never was professionally employed to utilize this skill. Her
pioneering contribution to the field, however, was recognized in 1939
at a celebratory dinner commemorating her father's transcendent
invention, where she was honored by the National Federation of
Business and Professional Women's Clubs of New York.

While Mr. Wells and Mrs. Fortier were strangers to the spectators,
the third guest was a local man who needed no introduction to those
who caught a glimpse of him. "One of the proudest figures in Ilion
today," a reporter respectfully observed, "was that grand old man of
the upper Mohawk Valley, Eliphalet Remington."[30] Ninety-four years

old by then and a resident of a sanatorium in Herkimer, the scion of the fabled gunsmith had made the short trip between towns in an enclosed automobile. In failing health, he remained seated in the car, while being driven around the streets of the town which meant so much him. Unable to stay for long, he did grant a brief interview in which he offered a few words about Christopher Sholes: "Yes, indeed, to him great honor is due. He was a great genius. His invention has meant so much to the commercial world."[31] After his brief, nostalgic visit, Mr. Remington returned to his convalescent quarters. That little public appearance in his beloved village would be one of great businessman's last, for he passed away in the spring of the following year at the age of ninety-five.

WITH THE COMPLETION of the afternoon's formal program, attendees had several immediate options available to them, while awaiting the evening's activities scheduled to begin at 7 p. m. One possibility was attending an open house at the West Street home of the Catholic Daughters of America, where some of the day's guests of honor—including Mrs. Al Smith and Mrs. Frank Lowden—would be present to meet them. Before the doors closed to end the reception, 500 women had accepted the invitation. Another opportunity of which out-of-towners could take advantage were tours of Ilion and scenic spots in the immediate area. Some people decided to watch as members of the fire department gave a demonstration of their new equipment and a life-saving net. At the nearby Remington Park, a 3:45 baseball game between two local teams was scheduled—the Typewriter nine would take on a squad known as the "Little Falls Independents." Prior to the contest, the Typewriter girls were in the spotlight again, this time performing a drill. Unfortunately, a late afternoon shower interrupted this part of the day's activities.

(l to r) Elizabeth and Christopher Sholes IV, the great-grandchildren of the inventor; Henry Harper Benedict, one of the founders of the Remington Typewriter Company Charles Weller, the first typist; Mrs. Charles Fortier, inventor's daughter and the first female typist; and Mrs. Christopher Sholes, daughter-in-law of the inventor. (Source: Herkimer County Historical Society)

However, by evening and the start of the final third of the day's observances, the skies had fortuitously cleared. Precisely at 7 o'clock the fire whistle blew, a signal that was used for decades to follow in announcing the start of parades. While on other occasions these might be for Memorial Day, the Fourth of July, or Armistice Day, in this instance the event was called the "Booster Parade," a highly anticipated annual event of long-standing in the village. For purposes of organization and management, the procession was divided into the three divisions. Each grouping contained similar components consisting of bands, floats, automobiles, and marchers. Each of the floats was to be preceded by an individual on foot and carrying a numbered sign, so the judges at the Monument Square band stand could properly assign their ratings to the correct entry. In addition to the 1st, 2nd, and 3rd place monetary prizes for the floats, recognition was given to the "finest decorated auto," the "organization having the largest turnout," and the "organization having the most unique and best appearance."[32] In all, the parade featured 3,000 marchers, five bands, 20 floats, and assorted vehicles.

The line of march was east across Main to Otsego Street, starting from West Street, south up Otsego to the junction with John Street.

Then back down to Main via John and Third Streets, west to Railroad Street, and north on Railroad to its conclusion at East River Street. Normally, evening parades were a rarity, for by seven p. m. on a fall night darkness would have begun to envelop the town. However, the new twist this night was the recently-installed lights that would brilliantly illuminate much of the route, turning night into day and in the process creating a phantasmagoric setting along many of the village's streets.

Following this unique entertainment, a block party was held on East Clark Street, between the Typewriter factory and the park. Music was provided by the company's band. The dancing continued until 8:30, when the grand finale of the day arched overhead. With spectators filling Typewriter Park and lining the nearby streets, a magnificent fireworks display flashed in an array of colorful bursts against the night sky to the north. It was a spectacular end to what had been a memorable day, accomplishing all that the planning committee had hoped to achieve.

While in 1923 no one could have foretold what the next fifty years would bring for the business being celebrated, the good news in hindsight was that there would be another half-century's worth of typewriter production, leading eventually to a modest centennial celebration in 1973. Once again, the oft-overlooked name of Christopher Sholes would be spoken with appreciation and reverence that was due to the "Father of the Typewriter."

19

GINKGO TREES:

A PREHISTORIC GIFT OF NATURE

One of the fall's time-honored artistic activities in which many first graders participated at West Hill School in the 1950s was that of pressing leaves between two pieces of waxed paper. With the arrival of autumn, trees began to shed their lustrous mantles. This annual defoliation signaled the onset of the traditional October school activity. In a quest to fulfill our "homework" assignment, we all would vie for the prestige of who could find the most colorful, the most gargantuan, or the most perfect representation of a species. Oaks, maples, and elms ranked as the prevalent species found around Ilion. Sometimes examples from chestnut, birch, catalpa, butternut, hickory, and ash trees made an appearance in the classroom too.

Prior to the 1960s, finding a variety of leaves to bring into class was easy. Most streets were tree-lined with tall, stately elms and full, luxurious maples. Back yards flourished with varieties of fruit trees. Lilacs were in ample abundance, while magnolias could be found, though not in profusion. A walk through a nearby woodlot would expand the selection many-fold. For a zealous student, varied samples abounded from which a substantial collection of diverse leaves could be put together. However, when it came to the rarest of the rare, I was luckier than others, simply by virtue of where I lived. In this instance, location, location, location was the difference maker. For me, the treasured tree grew across the street from my parents' house on South Third Ave. There, more bushy than tall, stood a unique species that had taken root, sprouted, and grown to maturity: a ginkgo!

How many of these flourished about town at their peak is now undeterminable. Though adaptable to both northern and southern climes in the United States, the answer is probably not too many, as the one on Third Avenue and another on John Street were the only two in my local frame of reference. Both are gone now, and, in a recent drive around Ilion, no others were observed. That is until my sister, on one of her early-evening walks about town, discovered a stand of seven ginkgoes growing along one of the lanes in Armory Hill Cemetery. In a 1953 article run by the *Utica Observer-Dispatch*, these exact trees were referenced, noting that they had been planted by Mrs. Elizabeth Hoefler when she had been a member of the Cemetery Board earlier in the century.

Ginkgo Trees in the Cemetery.
(Source: Author's Collection)

From a distance, the ginkgo's full, leaf-laden branches could be mistaken for those of a maple; however, a closer inspection would quickly dispel such a misidentification. Once able to see the individual leaves, the notable feature that sets a ginkgo's foliage apart from its other deciduous neighbors is very evident. With surfaces ribbed by subtle vertical striations, the leaves distinctive shapes are unmistakably like no other, for they resemble small fans. These telltale markers measure on-average approximately three inches at their widest point. In autumn, the ginkgo's summer greenery takes on an attractive golden yellow hue.

Also referenced as the "maidenhair" tree—for its foliage looks like the leaves of the maidenhair fern—ginkgoes are native to the Orient, originally found in China, Korea, and Japan. Existing in but one species with several varieties, the tree possesses an enviable heritage, tracing its roots back two-hundred-and-fifty million years to the Permian Period of the Paleozoic Era. Looking at it another way, the ginkgo is a living fossil whose existence on our planet pre-dates the dinosaurs!

Sprouts of this venerable plant made their way to Europe in the early eighteenth century on the ships of Dutch traders. Then, in 1784, ginkgoes were introduced to America. Their reputation was that of a tough tree, resistant to disease and insects. In addition, this species is impervious to salt, chemicals, and carbon monoxide, thus making them a highly desirable choice for urban areas. A deep root system also affords protection from damaging winds and heavy snows. Given its reputation for hardiness, New York City became a thriving location for these newcomers, offering shade coupled with minimal maintenance.

In a tree census last conducted by the city in 2007, the ginkgo ranked as the tenth most common tree found within the boundaries of the "Big Apple." Another attractive feature of the ginkgo is its reputation for longevity, with a lifespan that is known to range between one and two hundred years. In its original habitat of the Far East, "the survival power of the ginkgo is legendary in China, Japan, and Korea, where there are many trees close to a thousand years old."[1]

As a tree noted for its long-term survival, it seems appropriate that the species has made a contribution aiding in mankind's existence too: gingko biloba as an extract. Used as a supplement derived from the tree's leaves, many people believe that taking it in leaf or pill form aids in blood circulation and combats memory loss among other benefits.

The distinctive, fan-shaped ginkgo leaf. (Source: Author's Collection)

If there is a downside to this unique gift of nature, it manifests itself in the fall. This is the time when the life cycle of the ginkgo's verdure takes on its gilded hue and then falls to the ground. Especially noteworthy is the way this deciduous tree divests itself of its foliage. "The ginkgo loses its leaves in a half hour," readers of the *Observer-Dispatch* were informed, "and, as soon as the first frost arrives, the leaves fall like snowflakes."[2]

Along with the leaves, a soft, fruit-like ball also descends at the same time. A product of only the female version of the tree, this fleshy orb emits a foul-smelling stench that has been characterized by several unflattering descriptors—the odor of vomit, gym socks, and rancid butter being among them. When squashed, the resulting smell is further accompanied by a safety hazard, as the cement or asphalt surface underneath becomes extremely slippery. However, if an epicurean could get past the odor and was so inclined, this plum-like fruit has "an inner oval nut containing a sweet, oily, edible seed."[3]

If you have not chanced to see a ginkgo, do yourself a favor. Track one down and make its acquaintance. Its heritage of survival over eons, singularity in appearance, and scarcity of numbers make it a worthwhile addition to any bucket list—just be sure that your pilgrimage does not coincide with defoliation day!

20

THE DEMISE OF THE AMERICAN ELM:

SLOW DEATH IN THE STREETS

A mong the vintage postcards depicting the village of Ilion in the early 1900's, one of the most striking juxtapositions between street scenes as they appeared then and the same locales now, is the current absence of trees. In truth, the reality is more than just an absence—it is instead a dearth, and most notable among the missing from the scene are elms.

Once virtually all of Ilion's streets were graced by stately elms, creating leafy tunnels both pleasing to the eye and appealing to the psyche like these two converging thoroughfares—Morgan and Otsego Streets. (Source: Joe Smith Collection)

Before their devastating disappearance from the village's forestation occurred, interlocking branches of elm trees along each side of many streets frequently met over the roadway, creating a leafy canopy that was welcoming, soothing, and pleasing both to the eyes and psyches of pedestrians and drivers alike.

Not that those elms were the only trees in town, for many species abounded around Ilion on residential properties, public lands, and in small woodlots. Among these competing varieties were maples, oaks, magnolias, beeches, evergreens, catalpas, chestnuts, willows, apples, cherries, birches, gingkoes, lilacs, and ashes. Generally, this differing assortment of timbers was to be found set back from the roads and adorning the front, side, and back yards of residential lots. The prestigious spots holding the highest visibility—those situated between the sidewalks and the curbs—were virtually the exclusive domain of the elm. Known scientifically as the *Ulmus Americana*, the elm was a prodigious denizen found populating both urban and rural landscapes. As such, these majestic trees were virtually impossible to overlook, for individual specimens could "...reach a height of 160 feet, a girth of 25, and a spread of 147."[1] Growing straight and tall with long lives, the elm was an excellent species for planting in these prime locations.

Such tree-lined vistas were most prevalent in the older parts of communities. In Ilion, this pattern would have been found north from the South Fifth Avenue ballfield, east to the village limit, and west to Barringer Road. The newer parts of town, such as the grid south of George Street to Brook Street for example, were laid out devoid of sidewalks and curbing. Subsequently, rows of arborescent plantings could not be seen on the green strip between the road and walkways... simply because none existed.

Furthermore, in these last sections of the village to be developed, elm trees by then were not even an option for landscaping purposes any longer, thanks to the ravages of the Dutch elm disease.

Idyllic setting along Morgan Street that was just beginning to see the growth of
over a dozen elms that would eventually soar high above above the roadway.
(Source: Author's Collection)

Unfortunately, these blissful settings which our forbearers enjoyed are for the most part gone. Some streets in Ilion are now virtually bereft of any trees lining the roadways, much less elms. The preceding postcard from 1909 shows the stretch above First Street south along Morgan to Second Street and beyond. In the near block alone, nine trees are visible—sadly, not even one still exists in that same location today.

While many reasons can be offered as rationales for the gradual disappearance of elms as shade trees along the village's streets—such as the widening of the roadway, the erection of light poles, and the accommodations for electric, telephone, and cable tv lines—none of these hallmarks of progress were the biggest single offender in the demise of Ilion's impressive, in-town rows of elms. Instead, the culprits that caused the most destruction were neither axes nor saws in the hands of public works' or utilities' employees, but rather instead the devastation was wrought by a widespread infestation of insects!

The culprits were European elm bark beetles, *Scolytus multistriatus,* which was a minuscule greenish-yellow bug whose one-tenth-of-an-inch-long size belied its massive powers for creating havoc. How was the disease transmitted by this uninvited arthropodal immigrant? As described for the patrons of the *Richfield Springs Mercury*, "the Dutch elm disease is spread by the spores of fungus carried on the bodies of the elm bark beetles as they move from dead and dying Elmwood to feed on healthy trees."[2]

First discovered in The Netherlands in 1919, the malady spread quickly over western and southern Europe. Then, "in 1930," it was accidentally introduced into the United States through a load of tainted European elm logs destined to be made into furniture.[3] Initially, the infestation was found in only a finite area, with the first instance of unhealthy elms being observed in Cleveland in the early 1930's. But by 1934, the *Schenectady Gazette* was reporting that the destructive disease was "already discovered in five states."[4] Four years later, one of these heavily contaminated landscapes was identified by the United States Department of Labor as being "an area radiating out about 50 miles from New York City into Connecticut, New York, and New Jersey."[5] From these limited beginnings, the Dutch elm disease spread like the plague that it was.

Unfortunately, the damage to come was not an experience completely foreign to Americans living in the early years of the 20th century, for they had just recently weathered attacks against two native species by invasions from other foreign-born afflictions. The first began in 1904 and ran unfettered for two decades. Called the "chestnut blight," before this infestation had run its course the disease had killed several billion trees, decimating forests of a common variety and in the process impacting the nut and lumbering industries. Then, around 1915, Japanese beetles made their uninvited appearance on the scene. Attacking the leaves of a wide variety of plants, these insects wreaked havoc on crops in fields and gardens.

With these two recent legacies still fresh in the public's mind, federal authorities quickly stepped in and devised a three-step eradication campaign to combat the new threat: (1) the discovery and removal of every diseased elm as soon as possible after the first symptoms of infection were noticed; (2) the burning of all dead and dying trees; and (3) the destruction in the swamps and woods of dead and dying wild elms that had no value and might harbor the Dutch elm disease spores.

As the primary line of defense, individuals known as "scouts" were recruited to patrol the streets of villages and cities, as well as forested areas outside the communities. Their mission was to eyeball all the elms in their assigned tracts, looking for telltale signs of the disease: yellowing and wilted leaves and dying branches. Most infected trees died within twelve months, though some were known to take several years for their decline to fully run its fatal course.

As time went by, the outbreak began its irrepressible march across the northeastern and northcentral parts of the country, basically the belt from New England to the Great Lakes. Then came World War II. The four-year conflict was blamed by some as being a major factor in the advancement of the disease, for most of our country's resources, manpower, and focus were allocated to fight much more dangerous political enemies abroad than bark beetles at home. Due to this wartime neglect, it was "estimated that in [1946] elms died at five to ten times the previous rate."[6]

However, in 1947, Ilionites' spirits were temporary buoyed by an ill-advised article that appeared in the hometown newspaper. Under the reassuring headline "Ilion Unhampered by Elm Disease," a local official was quoted as stating that "no problem existed in Ilion because the trees were sprayed every spring, keeping them free from the disease."[7] The choice of pesticide chosen to attack the beetles was a chemical compound known as lead arsenate. If the authorities knew then what is now known about this insecticide, it may never have been used or at least might have been applied in a more careful, judicious manner.

Late May through early June was the optimum window for the spraying to kill the larvae before they burst forth as young beetles, unwitting but obliging carriers capable of spreading the disease. After wintering in attics, unused chimneys, under eaves, and in barns, the beetles unlimbered their black-striped wings and headed for a nearby host elm. In selecting lead arsenate as the instrument of death, the existing medical and scientific knowledge of the time was aware of what the concoction would do to the insect, but no one apparently gave any thought to its potential effect on humans or the environment in general. Since a community like Ilion had elms along virtually every street—not to mention those also flourishing in front, side, and back yards—the spraying would of necessity have to take place near private homes and their inhabitants.

Growing up in Ilion in the 1950's, my recollections of the spraying routine are still quite vivid. The truck used was a flatbed. Mounted on its back platform was a "cannon." It looked something like the portable cement mixers that contractors would employ when laying sidewalks or the stubby mortars used in Civil War-era sieges. As the vehicle moved slowly down the street, the equipment operator would swing the cannon from side-to-side and up-and-down as needed, according to the height of the targeted trees. While he may have had on some sort of limited protective gear, it was nowhere near as impressive as the HAZMAT suit in which he should have been encased, as perhaps we all should have been for that matter.

With the hindsight that continued advancements in scientific research often gives us, we are now armed with the information that exposure to arsenic can cause cancer, while contact with lead can adversely affect the developing brains and nervous systems of babies and the kidneys of adults and children too. Where this all gets scary is that no special precautions were taken to safeguard residents. As the truck came down our street at different times over the years, announced by the whooshing sound of the spray being propelled skyward, I can distinctly recall occasions when we were eating supper and heard the truck coming. Though windows and doors were immediately closed, our food still sat on the table. Eventually, though a chemical smell and metallic taste became noticeable, we blithely continued with what was now our invisibly tainted meal.

The blast emitted by the spray gun or cannon was powerful, able to reach the all-important leafy tops of elms that sometimes stood fifty-feet tall. When the discharge hit the leaves, they were whipped up and around, as if caught in the winds of a violent thunder storm. Droplets misted the air and fell to the ground, landed on houses, streets, sidewalks, bicycles, and cars. Other species of trees caught in the line of fire were also doused with an unintended shower. Some were fruit trees. One now wonders what happened to the birds, bees, squirrels, and pets caught in the open, as a chemical dew floated down upon them.

This annual ritual of late spring/early summer spraying in my recollection was conducted for several years in the '50s. In the end result, the "save-the elms" campaign proved to be an expensive, frustrating, and losing proposition. Part of the problem was the lack of a complete understanding with respect as to how the disease was spread. While the beetles remained identified as enemy number one, continued research uncovered another avenue regarding the transmission of spores.

Far less obvious than the insects operating above ground was the insidious, unseen spread of the disease beneath the surface of the earth. Pathologists studying the problem eventually discovered that the root systems of adjacent trees were passing the infection by way of intertwined and self-grafted roots. What this revelation meant was that one of the most common and admired practices—that of lining the streets with neat rows of elms planted in relatively close proximity to each other—was unknowingly contributing to their deaths. While everyone was gazing upward and marveling at the wonderous canopy of sheltering branches and leaves overhead, these same trees were committing a form of communal suicide beneath the onlookers' feet.

Places both large and small kept up the good fight to save their cherished trees. As late in the battle as the sixties, spraying continued in Utica, Richfield Springs, and Ilion to name but a few of the stricken communities that doggedly continued the fight. The cost of the airborne treatments and the cutting down and incineration of dead and dying trees both placed an added burden on already tight municipal budgets. In the little village of Richfield Springs, the local government picked up the tab for applying pesticides to elms on public property and charged one dollar per tree to spray those on private land. The fallacy with this plan, however, was that unless the whole community got on-board in unison, gaps existed in the protective coating. Otherwise, as pointed out in the hometown newspaper, "technically one owner can destroy the beetles on his own trees—but the insects will return the next year, spreading from nearby trees that were not sprayed."[8]

Once Ilion discontinued its spraying, efforts shifted to cutting down the diseased trees. However, the number of infected elms requiring removal began to mount, necessitating an ever-increasing cost to the village. To guard against its budget being swamped by too many trees being taken down at the owner's request but on the local government's tab, the village board in 1949 had to address the issue of the status of elms located between the curb and the sidewalk. The decision finally arrived at was one wherein "no trees may be removed from properties between the curb and the sidewalk in the village until they have been inspected by the village engineer, street superintendent, and the fire chief."[9] This committee would then report their findings to the board, which would then make the final determination on how to proceed.

Mom and me...but look at all of those beautiful elms circa 1947 on South Third Avenue! (Source: Author's Collection)

But in time, eventually even this guarded practice began to take its toll on the village's financial resources triggered by a pair of simple realities —too many trees, too little money. At a board meeting in August of 1969, "Trustee Harold Riddell estimated that it would cost about $40,000 for the village to cut down 220 bad trees."[10] Much to the chagrin of residents, the board decided to "revert to a 1961 ordinance that makes property owners responsible for removing trees on the right-of-way."[11] Following up on this policy, the village codes enforcer, William

Thomas, apprised the mayor and trustees that to date he had already sent out 100 notices to homeowners on whose property were found dead trees, which were those with no greenery and therefore posing a hazard from falling limbs. Thus far, fifty people had seen to the recommended elimination, but unfortunately the remaining fifty trees, if their removal was not forthcoming, would still imperil pedestrians as well as serve as hosts for the beetles.

In addition to the obvious upfront costs of removing and burning diseased trees, other hidden expenditures remained. The matter of the unsightly stump was one. For those who could afford its extraction, money solved that problem. Our family did not have such means, so for several years my dad worked on the stubborn remnant in the backyard, alternately dousing it with kerosene, setting it afire, and then chopping away the charred wood. Over time, only a small, round patch of dirt remained where a mighty elm had once stood. It then became a spot where my father planted flowers, almost as if it was a memorial to a now-departed, old family friend.

As a further illustration of both the rampant nature of the Dutch elm epidemic's along with its economic impact on middle-class families, a look fifty miles slightly to the northeast of Ilion was the community of Gloversville that provided another example. There lived Ed Kuehner, his wife, and two children. Like the Colleas of Ilion, they too had an enormous elm in their backyard, and, just like its counterpart to the west, the Kuehner's elm became diseased. Mr. Kuehner now faced the same decision as my dad. As his daughter Carol Lincoln years later defined his dilemma, "to leave the elm standing was to invite an accident from a falling limb, but to take down the ailing tree involved expending funds from an already tight family budget."[12] In the end, safety concerns won out. In addition to the food budget getting a little tighter for a few weeks, a long-time landmark on the family's property was gone.

The second expense, existing in the wake of many of those trees that had once grown next to the road, was generated by the upheaval that roots caused to the nearby sidewalks, often necessitating the replacement of one or more concrete blocks.

All these measures were collectively costly, for small communities and large cities alike, where portions of precious budgets had to be diverted to the Dutch elm fight. But, after the spraying, cutting, and burning had run its course, still another potential drain on limited fiscal resources remained. What to do about replacement trees? Huge gaps existed in urban landscapes which some local governments addressed by bulk purchases of saplings, while other municipal authorities did little or nothing. The result at best was the sporadic, inconsistent introduction of a new species—most often maples—along the streets...and at worst significant gaps between unaffected kinds of trees or stretches where none were left at all, leaving a stark, uninviting, and almost post-Apocalyptic look to countless neighborhoods that exists in some places to this day.

With respect to Utica, which for years had proudly worn its title as "City of the Elms," the fight to save its beloved trees fared no better than those engaged in by its neighbors. A brief ray of hope surfaced in the mid-sixties when the development of a chemical called "Bidrin" was announced. This new pesticide was "heralded as a deadly killer of the disease-bearing elm bark beetle..."[13] Introduced directly into the bark by injection, the arrival of Bidrin on the scene wound up being more of a fleeting, panacean hope than a bona fide savior because the serum was more expensive than spraying, had a limited shelf life, and had to be applied by an expert or risk killing the tree. In addition, Bidrin was not yet available in any meaningful amounts, for as Utica mayor Frank Dulan pointed out: "We would need 300,000 capsules in Utica alone to inoculate our trees, (but) I understand that only 100,000 capsules are currently available for the whole country."[14]

Eventually, despite man's best efforts, nature ran its course. Where hundreds of thousands of elms once proliferated, yawning gaps came to exist in urban landscapes, as well as in the surrounding farmlands and forests. No place was safe from the ravages of the disease. Even the venerable grounds of the White House were not spared, when it was announced in 1969 that "Dutch elm disease had claimed two stately trees on the White House lawn...dating from the 1880's or 1890's..."[15] Though the lead horticulturist for the Chief Executive's estate indicated the new trees would be immediately planted, nothing could be done to replace a witness to almost 100 years of American history.

Nor was sentimentality limited to the grounds of the Executive Mansion. Granted that every living thing has a finite existence, yet knowing this does not necessarily lessen the emotions that come with its passing. Be it people, pets, and, yes, even with trees, a sense of loss in varying levels of intensity can accompany their demise. Closer to home, reporter William Witt, writing for the *Herkimer Evening Telegram*, observed in mid-1967 that "many more residents during the summer have been saddened by the removal of trees from their property... some of the trees were seedlings when the property owners were born."[16] Also regrettable to note was the fact that "it takes about 100 to 125 years for an elm tree to grow to maturity, but it takes tree contractors only about a day to chop it down and carry it away."[17]

The tall elm in our back yard had grown to maturity perhaps all of fifteen feet from the house. The tree was a monster in height and girth. The old boy had been present for many joyous family events, such as my mother's first birthday party in 1921 and then twenty-six years later when my parents held mine. Its leafy crown had shielded our back porch and kitchen from the heat of the setting summer sun. It stood still, watching patiently when dad mowed the grass in a circular path around its trunk. As adolescents, my sister and I played in our wading pool, shading by this sturdy elm. While as children, we did not realize the implication, occasional bugs from the tree dropped down and joined our watery frolic. But right there, bathing with us, was the telltale sign that our tree was sick. Eventually, somewhere in the mid-fifties, was when Dad had to have it cut down. Insects in the pool may have given us the skeevies, but they were tolerable. However, the proximity of such a huge growth of timber so close to the house—with its diseased branches already starting to fall—made its removal a necessity.

The loss of the tree was not seen as a particularly moving event by either my sister or me. But for my mother, that rather straightforward process held deeper meaning. For thirty-seven years, mom had seen that elm standing outside two of her homes, heard the wind rustle through its leaves, or watched snowflakes decorate its branches. She once commented in later years that how much she missed seeing it, "like an old friend who had passed away."

Just as municipal governments had for years felt the impact of the financial burden thrust on them while trying to save the elms, individual homeowners like my dad had to shoulder the burden of taking down diseased trees on their own property. Since he was already working three jobs, incurring this unplanned cost was no small decision to make, even if the removal was warranted. The danger that a weaken, diseased tree could inflict was emphatically driven home with a devastating visual effect when a neighbor's tree landed on his house.

This heightened awareness happened in the mid-1950s when a near tragedy had taken place only five doors north from us on South Third Avenue. The incident involved the home of an elderly couple, a Mr. and Mrs. Louis Beebe. One sultry summer night, Alma Beebe decided that it was too hot to sleep upstairs and relocated herself to a cooler first floor living room couch. Sometime in the wee hours before dawn, a violent thunderstorm passed through town. During the downpour, a bolt of lightning hit the gigantic elm that stood near the side of the Bebee's house, sending a sizable portion of the tree crashing through its roof. The point of impact caved in the attic and a bedroom, the one previously vacated by Mrs. Bebee. The next morning, the neighborhood flocked to see the damage. Given that the tree was diseased, the fact not lost on all of us was the amount of damage and risk to life that a falling elm could inflict.

Ultimately, the realization came that a war lasting almost a half-century was a lost cause. One by one, communities simply gave up. The bugs had won. The August 3, 1974, edition of the *Utica Daily Press* banner headline that morning told the sad story: "Replacement Called Only Solution: Fight Against Elm Disease Appears Lost."[18] For safety reasons, the dead and dying trees would of necessity continue to be removed, but any hope of saving the elms was now nothing more than a forlorn hope. The loss was staggering. Over 77 million trees had perished. Many urban landscapes would never appear quite the same again. Future generations would be denied the impressive sight and towering majesty created by this giant of the American woodlands. Columnist Emily Denton, writing for the *Herkimer Telegram*, summed up this loss in a brief but poignant eulogy: "No other tree has the same arching grace, and village streets are the poorer for their disappearance."[19]

Leaf of the American Elm. (Source: Author's Collection)

❧ 21 ❧

A CAPITOL DESTINATION:

GOING TO THE MOVIES

L iving in Ilion in the 1950's, most folks who owned televisions had but a single choice every night when it came to satisfying their home viewing pleasure—turn on the tv and watch the one channel offered. However, another form of entertainment was readily available and located within walking distance for families who lived in town. This alternative diversion existed in the form of the Capitol Theater.

Thanks to its distinctive marquee, the Capitol Theater was easy to locate—especially at night with its colored lights ablaze. Otsego Street ended at the row of buildings in the background which are on the northern side of Main. The road now curves to the left and joins Central Avenue, the buildings are gone, and Ye Olde Medicine Shoppe is located in their place. Kinney's Drugs occupies the space where the white-sided wall appears beyond the theater. The turn onto First Street is between the fourth and fifth cars on the left. (Source: Author's Collection)

Located just a few doors south from the corner of Otsego and First Streets, the building's distinctive appearance had been welcoming devotees of the silver screen since 1927.[1] Unlike the comparatively bland façades of today's cinematic houses, the Capitol Theater beckoned movie-goers with its captivating entranceway, one typical of most movie houses of that era. Compared to the far less-gaudy frontages of businesses around it, the theater immediately grabbed your attention with its array of lights that blazed around the three sides of its protruding marquee. With these sign boards framed by the glowing bulbs, large letters proclaimed the title of the film being shown, along with the names of the feature's star or stars. The whole effect was to create an atmosphere akin to that of a carnival: glitzy, exciting, and enticing.

Note the awning to the right of the theater. Prior to urban renewal, the another storefront and building occupied the southwest corner of First and Otsego, but that row was pared back to straighten out First Street and by so doing gave the Capitol Theater a corner spot. (Source: Author's Collection)

Looking at the front of the theater as it exists today, the building's facade has a three-part definition. On its right and left are what look to be two towers that extend from the ground level to perhaps five feet above the roofline. Everything about them appears purely decorative from the outside. At the base of each were niches, their recesses housed display cases in which attractive movie stills were hung. Adding to the mystery and intrigue of what awaited patrons inside, a "grotesque or gargoyle" was perched high up on each tower.[2] Below them were two extremely narrow windows which had semi-circular, wrought-iron balustrades that created small balconies—even though no one could have ever slipped through the constricted portals.

Moving to the central core, this portion of the building—located between the two towers, but five-feet lower—offers a different, though compatible, look. Across its top, between the towers and below the roof were three windows of conventional size. The impression is that the space behind them could have been an office. Under each of the left and right fenestrations was a lion's head, carved in high-relief. The triple set of windows were framed with columns, capitals, and arches —all rendered in low-relief. The fascia above the arches at the roofline appeared as a carved stone filigree.

Unlike the two towers, however, the center portion of the structure clearly served as the functional section of the theater. There, beneath the overhang of the marquee, was a well-lit entranceway. Heavy glass doors allowed access to a lobby. The all-important ticket window was located just to the left. Along the walls on both sides of this spacious foyer were hung colorful posters of coming attractions.

After purchasing a ticket, the theatergoer walked perhaps forty feet or so up a slight incline to another set of doors. Here was posted an usher who tore your ticket in half, handing you the stub and encouraging you to "enjoy the movie." Since only one screen existed, the route to a seat was easy. No need existed to direct patrons to Screen 3 or screen 12. Most likely for purposes of muffling footfalls along with adding a touch of elegance, crossing the threshold from the bright front lobby to the darker inner sanctum meant stepping from a hard, slick flooring onto a soft, carpeted surface.

Before taking a seat in the viewing area, located about twenty feet ahead on the left, was a brightly lit counter comprised of metal and glass. Willpower, finances, and appetite were all put to the test by an alluring display of sugary delights—all purveyed at what was known as "the concession stand." To a teenager, the caloric content of Snowcaps, M & M's, Jujubes, or Sugar Daddies was never a consideration. On the other hand, though, buying popcorn meant having to purchase a companion soft drink, and, in so doing, for an extra coin or two get to use one of the electronic marvels of the time: the self-service soda-dispensing machine. This amazing contraption was refrigerator-sized, brightly illuminated, and easy to operate. Put your money in the slot, push the selector button for one of a half-dozen flavors, and then step back to watch in fascination the workings of a wonder of the teen-aged world circa 1959—a veritable show in its own right!

First, into a six-inch-by-six-inch-by-six-inch chrome-lined opening a Dixie cup dropped down, resting on a grate after being lowered into place by a metal, funnel-like guide. This preliminary stage was followed by the appearance of two separate streams of fluid, one being the syrup and the other carbonated water. Presto! In a matter of seconds, a cup of soda was ready to join a bag of popcorn down a gullet ride to a waiting stomach. Except...on that rare occasion...when Murphy's Law manifested itself. In this case, the snafu was as simple an occurrence as it was horrifying to watch—sometimes no cup was downloaded to start the dispensing process. With no override switch or escape button to use, all that the erstwhile buyer got was an education, as he watched the precious streams disappear down the drain. Oh, so maybe that's why a grating was installed in the receptacle?! The good news, whenever this little tragedy chanced to happen, was that the management was sympathetic and fair about refunding the potentially wasted money. The bad news was this could mean salted popcorn and no drink if the machine were deemed temporarily out-of-service due to a malfunctioning component.

To the right of the soda machine were stairs to the forbidden balcony. "Forbidden" was an appropriate descriptor because access never seemed permitted. At the bottom of the stairs, a five-foot high, flat wooden caricature of an usher held a sign advising everyone that the balcony was closed...apparently forever. While too meek to ask why, my suspicion was that the management did not want teenagers up there, individuals who might be less interested in the movie and more disposed toward necking, smoking, or raining debris onto those below. Being routinely denied this experience in my youth is the reason that "sitting in a theater balcony somewhere" is now on my bucket list.

Once laden with all the desired refreshments and denied access to the balcony, the only decision left was where to go down one of the two sloping aisles and sit in the left, right, or center section. The theater was supposed to have a seating capacity of 1250, but the only time I ever saw it filled was at the commencement for our 210-member Class of 1965. The disastrous high school fire of 1963 had forced the next four consecutive graduating classes out of the building. Since this need for an alternative site preceded the era when outdoor ceremonies came into vogue, the theater fortunately offered a suitable and nearby venue.

Recalling Saturday afternoons at the movies, my recollection is that we saw a few trailers, sometimes a cartoon or two plus the feature film for fifty cents. A mere pittance by today's inflated prices, the cost of such entertainment fit nicely into the $2.50/week earnings from my paper route. Sometimes the bargain was even greater, when two different movies were shown back-to-back, giving rise to the term "double feature." As if that was not a fair return on an investment, it was also possible to see a movie again and again. For, once the first set of shows ended, they were recycled continuously until the day's run ended late in the evening, and no one was forced to leave after the first round. If the movie was shown six times over an afternoon and evening, it was possible to get in early and watch all the screenings for the one initial ticket price.

To maintain a presence and thereby curtail any rowdy behavior that a darkened theater might engender, ushers with flashlights made routine sweeps up and down the aisles. On occasion, a perpetrator of some anti-social act was identified, corralled, and escorted out. If done early in the show, observing the swift retribution that befell one of their unlucky peers was enough to keep any other potential miscreants in line.

The remaining feature of the old building was its stage, which allowed a variety of performances to be held. In addition to my own graduation ceremony, live performances by country music's virtuosos Hank Williams, Jr., Elton Britt, and Marvin Rainwater drew me to the Capitol on several occasions. In its early days, the theater housed vaudeville shows, and in later years, talent contests and Xmas parties.

Didn't get any better than John Wayne... but the 2nd feature... umm, maybe not so? (Source: Herkimer Evening Telegram)

There were even two instances when I was also required to appear on stage. One was to receive my diploma at commencement in 1965, and the other the other was when my ticket stub was pulled from a bowl in a drawing for a free pass to a show. That piece of blue paper is still in my possession. Being too valuable to use for admittance to just any movie, it remained in my dresser drawer waiting for just the right flick to come along...until there was no longer a theater at which to use it. What had seemed to be a priceless possession eventually morphed into one that was worthless!

But nothing lasts forever. More and more teens were getting cars, so walking downtown to the theater no longer became a chic destination for a date. Cable television arrived in the early '60's. Suddenly there many more reasons to get out the tv trays and stay in for the evening. Beset by dwindling attendance, the end for the Capitol Theater came in 1966, when the projector, the popcorn machine, and the marquee were all tuned off for the last time.

Still waiting for just the right movie to use my courtesy pass...
and, oh yes, for the theater to reopen! Wonder if they will
hassle me about the indication that it was "Issued to: Child?"
(Source: Author's Safety Deposit Box)

A WAR HERO COMES TO TOWN:
GENERAL DOUGLAS MACARTHUR VISITS ILION

W hen it came to name recognition in 1951, one individual who ranked near the top on any list of well-known personalities was five-star General of the Army Douglas MacArthur. A bona fide hero of World War II to many of his countrymen and the mastermind of a brilliant counterstroke in the Korean War, his prominence on the American scene loomed large. So much so that for a time that he even flirted with a run for the presidency on the 1952 Republican ticket. However, when the nod went to Dwight Eisenhower, General MacArthur turned to other irons that he had in the fire.

On August 1, 1952, MacArthur accepted a position as chairman of the board for the Remington Rand Corporation, receiving a salary of $100,000. After an unsuccessful attempt to first bring him on-board in 1949 and then again in 1951, the company's board of directors finally got their man two years later. While remaining in the army on an unassigned basis, MacArthur said that he was "...still entirely available for military assignments, though I do not anticipate any."[1] While some may have seen a conflict between the general serving simultaneously in this combined public/private capacity, the United States Army did not. In fact, a spokesman went on to say that "there was no limit on a five-star officer drawing income from two sources, providing they are not two government sources."[2]

Furthermore, MacArthur avowed that he no longer had any personal political aspirations, nor would he be actively campaigning for any other candidate in the upcoming presidential race. At the New York City luncheon, during which his hiring by the 227-million-dollar-a-year corporation was announced, the old warrior expressed his feelings about entering the world of private sector work: "It is particularly agreeable on this late date of my life, I can pass from a profession of destruction to another of construction—to build rather than destroy. I think it is a gift of God to let an old soldier end this way."[3]

General Douglas MacArthur
(Source: Library of Congress)

At the age of seventy-two, General MacArthur indicated that he would now also begin the life of a commuter, continuing to live with his wife in their Waldorf Astoria apartment in New York City and working at Remington Rand's headquarters building in Norwalk, Connecticut. Then to fulfill his commitment to the army, he would maintain an office In Manhattan, staffed by his on-going military aide.

With August 1 as the starting date of his tenure with Remington Rand, General MacArthur wasted little time in familiarizing himself with the sprawling operations of the large international company with which he was now affiliated. Its demographic profile alone was impressive, "...[employing] 36,000 persons in 22 American plants and 23 factories in 15 foreign countries, manufacturing typewriters, calculating machines, electronic computers, and other office equipment."[4]

However, only so much information could be gleaned from reading reports, studying organizational charts, and meeting with company executives. To obtain a more complete picture of the widespread industrial complex that comprised the holdings of Remington Rand, Inc., MacArthur decided to get in some on-sight inspections. Therefore, only three-and-and-a-half months into his first and what would prove to be his only civilian job, he decided to visit the company's facilities in Ilion. Such inspection tours of the plant were not uncommon for company executives. General Leslie Groves, once head of the Manhattan Project that developed the atomic bomb, had in recent years made two calls at the factory in Ilion, functioning, like MacArthur, in his new capacity as an official in the Remington Rand managerial hierarchy.

The date chosen for MacArthur's arrival was Tuesday, November 11, 1952, which by coincidence was also Armistice Day. The general and his entourage were scheduled to leave for their return trip to New York City that same evening. Due to the immense star-power of this famous visitor, Ilionites could not claim the general's time solely to themselves. While the focal point of his appearance in the Mohawk Valley was clearly the hometown plant, other area residents also wanted a chance to see to see the living legend in the flesh. As a result, activities for what amounted to a whirlwind tour were scheduled in both Herkimer and Mohawk as well.

Evidence that General MacArthur's presence was not going to pass unnoticed was the crowd that greeted his arrival at Union Station in Utica. Alighting from a private railroad car attached to the New York Central Railroad's *Advanced Empire State Express*, the general encountered an estimated 500 well-wishers waiting to see him. Though MacArthur's visit was in a civilian capacity, his persona as a military figure of immense stature was an ever-present, inescapable aspect of his life. To salute him as an army officer, representatives of Herkimer American Legion post—led by country chairman John Bergin—and the color guard from Mohawk's Crowley-Barnum Post 25 was drawn up at attention and met him as he stepped down from the train.

After an official welcome was extended by Utica mayor Boyd Golder, General MacArthur offered a few words to those who had turned out to see him. In a brief oration, he recalled that his unit in World War I was the 42nd Division, one comprised largely of New York troops among whom were quite likely some from the central part of the Empire State. After expressing sorrow that all could not return, he said that "we cannot forget that many of them died making what men from the beginning of time have yearned for, eternal peace. With God's help, we will see it through to a successful end."[5]

After his remarks, a police cruiser whisked the visiting dignitaries off to Ilion to begin their busy schedule. Conspicuous among those traveling with MacArthur were James H. Rand, president of Remington Rand, and General Courtney Whitney, former wartime aide to MacArthur and now also a company official. Led by a state police car, the eight-vehicle motorcade entered the village from the west along Main Street, eventually turning left onto Central Avenue. Though several of the cars were adorned with fluttering flags conspicuously attached to the right and left front fenders, MacArthur's arrival was without undue fanfare. According to a report in the *Telegram*, "No sirens sounded, no crowd collected on the street, as the time of his arrival in the village was not definite."[6]

Once in Ilion, General MacArthur and his entourage were taken on a tour of the company's Ilion plants. Following this inspection, he was driven to Herkimer, where he visited Remington Rand facilities located there too. Then MacArthur was the guest of honor at a late afternoon reception held at the village's Prospect Hotel, where industrial, education, political, and business officials got to rub elbows with the famous old soldier. But altogether too soon for the attendees, the general's party had to depart for its next event—an Armistice Day parade in Mohawk.

This event was scheduled to kick-off at 6:30 p.m. Sponsored by the Herkimer County Veterans of Foreign Wars, General MacArthur was extended the honor of leading the marchers, while he traveled in an open car as its grand marshal. Upon his arrival in Mohawk, he was greeted by its mayor, Lynn Corman, who presented him with a gift from the local Martin Automatic Fishing Reel Company. Parade organizers were very conscious of his tight schedule, for he was expected at a dinner in Ilion at 7:05 p.m. Therefore, the general's car quickly assumed its place at the head of the procession.

Once the line of march began to move, he remained in this forward position slotted in behind a state police car, until he reached the reviewing stand. There he, Courtney Whitney, and James Rand assumed positions on the platform. They remained there as seven bands and contingents from forty-three organizations of marchers passed before them. Aware of MacArthur's need to attend a dinner in Ilion, parade officials did their utmost to keep the line moving. Their attempt at maintaining precision over such a fluid event was not lost on the general, who was quoted as remarking that "this is the first legion parade I ever saw that started on time."[7]

When the parade ended, three minutes early to boot, General MacArthur was immediately whisked off to the venue for his speaking engagement in Ilion. Fortunately, his movement from Ilion to Herkimer, Herkimer to Mohawk, and finally Mohawk to Ilion during the day was facilitated by the proximity of the three villages. This allowed him the luxury of being able to attend so many different functions in such a tightly scheduled visit.

The final stop for MacArthur was the dinner of Remington Rand's 25-year club. Held in the factory's cafeteria in the Clark Street plant, the fete was an annual event, one at which employees who had reached the quarter-century of service plateau at the company's Ilion and Herkimer plants were awarded wristwatches, along with congratulatory handshakes from President Rand and General MacArthur.

The main speaker that night was James H. Rand. In hindsight, perhaps it had been better if he had not spoken at all. Unfortunately, in his remarks, Mr. Rand rhapsodized on the bright future for his company and the village of Ilion, going so far as to "forecast a vast expansion program for the local plants."[8] He went on to say that "we are already placing the production of some of our new electronics equipment in Ilion, and as the capacity of Ilion to absorb this new production increases, this expansion will continue."[9] His prediction for Ilion's glowing industrial future was further embellished by the company's vice-president in charge of production and procurement, B. B. Bond who added that "Ilion will become the center of production of the new electronic computer which is a basic item in the company's expansion plans."[10]

MacArthur seen on his inspection tour of the Remington plant in Ilion next to company president James Rand. (Source: Author's Collection)

For any Ilionite hearing these prognostications from the mouths of the very men who could make them happen, the future of the village looked very rosy indeed on that fall night in 1952. The headline in Utica paper the next day trumpeted the good news far and wide: "Ilion to Become Great Electronics Center."[11] But the business world is comprised of many moving parts. Deals often not even contemplated one week and are suddenly made in the next. Some occur that often have unforeseen, long-term effects. While none of the attendees hearing James Rand speak at that dinner would have in the optimism of the moment believed otherwise, within the next twenty years Remington Rand would be gone from Ilion. But none of the machinations that resulted in empty factories, relocated and unemployed workers, and a severe blow to the local economy were in the wind that night. The whole evening was an all-around, feel-good occasion.

After the honorees received their gifts, the man-of-hour was next up. General MacArthur was introduced by President Rand: "Tonight we are proud to welcome a member of the 50-Year Club, 50 years in service to the United States of America, Inc."[12] While he may have been the main attraction, the general was not scheduled as the primary speaker. That honor went to Mr. Rand. Though the company president brought some very good news, the audience certainly expected to hear from the general too. However, MacArthur's take was apparently different. Thinking that his role was solely a secondary one on this occasion, he had not anticipated having to speak at all. Nevertheless, as a good soldier, he was prepared for the unexpected. He opened with a nod to the purpose of the dinner and his position as chairman of the board, offering that "I hope you will all be here 25 years from now to watch me join the Remington Rand 25-year club."[13]

Then the general produced the following verse from his wallet, sharing with his rapt audience the knowledge that he had read its lines every day for the past twenty-five years in times of war and peace:

"Youth is not a time of life—it is a state of mind. It is not a matter of ripe cheeks, red lips, or supple knees; it is a temper of the will, a quality of the imagination, a vigor of the emotions; it is a freshness of the deep spring of life. Youth means a temperamental predominance of courage over timidity, of the appetite for adventure over the love of ease. This often exists in a man over fifty more than a boy of twenty.

Nobody grows old merely by living a number of years; we grow old only by deserting our ideals. Tears wrinkle the skin, but to give up enthusiasm wrinkles the soul.

Worry, doubt, self-distrust, fear, and despair—these are the long, long tears that bow the head and turn the growing spirit back to dust.

Whether seventy or sixteen, there is in every being's heart the love of wonder, the sweet amazement at the stars and the star like things and thoughts, the undaunted challenge of events, the unfailing, childlike appetite for what is next, and the joy in the game of life.

You are as young as your faith and as old as your doubt; as young as your self-confidence, as old as your fear; as young as your hope, as old as your despair."[14]

— FROM 'YOUTH'—AUTHOR UNKNOWN

General MacArthur concluded his brief, extemporaneous speech by telling those gathered before him to "live every day of your life as though you were going to live forever and a merciful God will bless and preserve you."[15] Then, just prior to his departure to catch a late train out of Utica, the general had the opportunity to speak with several of World War II veterans in attendance. Among them were two Ilion men who had served valiantly with him in the Philippines. These hometown heroes were Jack Fischer and Jack Cheesebrough, courageous survivors of the Bataan "Death March" in 1942. Their brief reunion was featured in a photograph with their former commander on the front page of the next day's *Observer-Dispatch*.

As students in tenth grade World History at IHS in 1962, we were often reminded of these two local veterans by our teacher, Miss Barbara Schwartz, who had taught both men and reverently called them "my boys." She also had a two-and-a-half-foot, bronze-colored statue of a soldier placed on filing cabinet in her room, standing defiantly with fists clenched and captioned across the bottom with the words: "Defeated but Not Conquered." She said that the sculpture served to remind her of her two former students who had left Ilion as young men in 1941 and returned in 1945 as veterans and heroes.

Another unique individual was also introduced to the general that night. His name was Orville Young. He was labeled as a "veteran" too, but one in a non-military capacity. Mr. Young, then all of ninety years old, had been an employee of the Remington Rand for sixty-five years.

For over three decades he had refused to retire, until finally in 1952 infirmities made it too difficult to continue at his job. In recognition of his loyalty and dedication to the company, James Rand placed Mr. Young permanently on the payroll.

Upon leaving the festivities in Ilion, MacArthur and his entourage made their way back to Utica. Waiting there once again was its mayor and a small coterie of well-wishers. With a parting handshake, Mayor Golder said that he hoped, as Macarthur had done in the Philippines, that the general would "return" to Utica also. MacArthur avowed that he would. But with the eventual downturn in Remington Rand's fortunes in Ilion and a gradual deterioration in the general's health, followed by his death in 1964, he never had the occasion to come back to the Mohawk Valley.

So that one shining day in 1952 stands alone as a special moment for those who participated in it, a time when one of World War II's legendary figures came for a visit and left many who saw and heard him with the memory of a lifetime.

General MacArthur (on the left) oversees the Japanese surrender on board the USS *Missouri*. (Source: Library of Congress)

AIRPLANE SPOTTING:

EYES ON THE SKIES

While what may seem like a rather primitive approach when compared to the sophisticated measures in place today, the early years of the Cold War saw a substantial cadre of everyday citizens donating their time in defense of our nation. Beginning in 1950 and continuing until 1959, a key component in America's shield against a surprise air attack by enemy bombers—most likely Russian—consisted of a network of civilian spotters. Under the aegis of the Civil Defense Agency, some 200,000 volunteers were initially enrolled in the program. From pre-teens to octogenarians, these patriotic citizens were officially members of what was called the "Ground Observer Corps."

The base commitment for an observer was for a two-hour tour of duty. At an important post like Ilion's—situated as it was on an approach to the Strategic Air Command's airfield at Griffiss Air Force Base in Rome—volunteers were required to fill an imposing 24/7/365 schedule. At a rate of twelve slots per day, a total of 4380 openings needed to be filled over the course of a year. While the cause was certainly noble, getting enough patriotic souls to continuously man the local station was not a slam dunk. For example, the shifts from midnight to eight in the depths of winter were understandably not the most desirable, calling for hardy individuals with open schedules the next day, so that being awake in the wee hours was not an inconvenience.

In 1952, the master plan was expanded to the point that would eventually include over 800,000 individuals serving in various capacities. With the Korean War in full swing, the aggressive nature of the Red Menace was very clearly in evidence, presenting a threat with which to be reckoned. The knowledge that the Russians possessed a

potent force that consisted of intercontinental bombers, guided missiles, and long-range, snorkel-fitted submarines—all with capabilities permitting them to reach targets in the United States—were scary thoughts, further compounded by the Communists' development of a powerful hydrogen bomb in 1953.

In those early years of growing animosities, America's technological defenses against an air raid were spotty at best. Though radar had existed since World War II, a coordinated, interlocking early warning system of sufficient quality

Bikini Island nuclear testing raised awareness of the apocalyptic fate which the world faced. (Source: Library of Congress)

and reliability was still largely in its developmental stages. Of particular concern, according to Lt. Col. Edgar N. Hamlin, Herkimer County's Civil Defense director, was that existing radar was of "...no service in spotting planes flying lower than 5,000 feet, and it is in spotting these planes that civilian spotters can be of inestimable service."[1] So, until an adequate, fully-functioning electronic screen was in place, the decision was made to employ observers with their eyes focused skyward.

The idea to create such a force was not new. In fact, the Cold War spotter force was the second generation of such a strategy. For, during World War II, a similar Ground Observer Corps had been established.

Concentrated along both coasts, this program was geared to protect the country from air attacks by German and Japanese forces. The same concerns—to some extent hysteria if you will—that motivated patriotic citizens to sign on in the 1940s also provided the impetus for their willingness to participate again in the 1950s.

In the reconstituted version, the focus shifted from a north/south alignment of coastal observation posts to an east/west configuration in a northern arc that stretched from Maine to Washington. The difference in repositioning the lookouts' attention was the new reality that a Russian air attack would most likely come over the North Pole, this route being the shortest distance by which to strike the United States from the USSR. Eventually christened "Operation Skywatch," a rotation of observers would in time man hundreds of stations across the country. Since no one knew when an air strike might occur—with Pearl Harbor being the case-in-point of which the spotters were well-aware—the plan called for someone to be on duty at each watch site continuously—every day, all year. Preferably, when possible, a team of two manned a post.

THE WHITE HOUSE
WASHINGTON

June 8, 1954.

TO EACH GROUND OBSERVER CORPS VOLUNTEER:

Last summer I addressed a statement to you expressing my conviction that citizen volunteer plane-spotters play an extremely important role in our national defense. This is still true. I could not possibly over-emphasize the importance I attach to the formation of an efficient and devoted ground observer corps.

Already some 350,000 of you are contributing your time and effort in observation posts and filter centers. But as you well know, the job calls for almost twice that number.

I hope, therefore, that greater numbers of our fellow citizens will join you in the GOC. I salute you for your patience, your perseverance, your patriotism, and I hope that this letter may help you convince others that the GOC needs them too.

Dwight D Eisenhower

Eventually the President joined in with the recruiting process.
(Source: Author's Collection)

With a strategy in place, the next step was enlisting a cadre of spotters. Advertising was conducted in a variety of ways. Nationally, public service announcements were made, often at times of peak radio listening hours in order to reach as wide an audience as possible. Typical of these mass appeals was one aired on September 20, 1952, during the intermission between acts one and two of the popular western "Gunsmoke." In a solemn tone of voice, one in keeping with the serious nature of the subject at hand, the speaker called for patriotic Americans to step forward: "You personally can help to make sure America has an impregnable fence against invaders along all its borders by volunteering as a ground observer to watch the skies for unidentified planes. Men and women from teenagers on up, write or phone your nearest civil defense center."[2]

One of the early local efforts in this regard occurred in the spring of 1953. Sponsored by state and local civil defense authorities, a recruitment meeting was held at the Municipal Building in Ilion. Its impetus was the urgent, immediate need for volunteers. As the centerpiece of the presentation, a movie titled "One Bomb" was shown. Narrated by then well-known radio and television commentator and celebrity Edward R. Morrow, the film "traced a B-29 bomber which takes off from England and approaches the United States. The plane never goes above 1,000 feet and is at 500 feet for most of the flight, thereby avoiding the radar screen."[3] The implication was clear. If one of our own aircraft could perform this clandestine flight, so also could one belonging to the Russians.

By virtue of public entreaties such as this, loyal Americans began stepping forward. Typical among them was Roger Bennett, my grandfather. Retiring from Remington Arms in 1954, he was an ideal candidate for the task, one that helped him fill-in his now wide-open day with a personally meaningful undertaking while at the same time serving his country. That he allowed me to accompany him was a very heady experience for an adolescent boy. Being just old enough to grasp that we were engaged in serious business gave a real sense of importance to our assigned mission. Having experienced duck-and-cover drills in school at this time further served to confirm that an enemy attack was indeed a credible concern, imparting an even greater since of urgency to our spotting assignment.

Regarding Ilion's participation in "Operation Skywatch," the structure that ultimately functioned as the local observers' perch was in Russell Park, at the Park Avenue end on the west side of the lane opposite the water tank, a reservoir that was not there in the 1950s. Just as the roadway starts downhill and curves out of the park, there is a small plateau on the left. This is where the watchtower once stood. As the highest elevation in Russell Park, this location offered a commanding view of the Mohawk Valley and especially the skies above it.

For those not aware of its historical importance, the site is rather unobtrusive today. Yet the spot can easily be found and accessed, though a visitor needs to realize the trees that presently fill the hillside before it were not there when the spotters' post was active. The view then was unobstructed. A look around the property now will reveal telltale evidence of its former occupancy: the top of a drainpipe, part of an electrical conduit, and two cement foundational pylons. However, the most noticeable vestige that currently remains onsite is a flagpole, though a bit difficult to pick out now. For after almost seventy years, nature has reclaimed so much of the hillock with tall trees and brush. Many times, as darkness set in at the end of his shift, my grandfather lowered "Old Glory" from that very staff and handed it to me to stow away in the tower. Perhaps, in an unintended way, that flagpole is a rusting monument to a different era when the Cold War it was real, and Ilionites…while still at home…were nevertheless in the front lines of a national defense initiative.

As for what the facility provided for spotters, the small building was quite elegant compared to those in some places, where volunteers made do with such sites as ramshackle huts and open rooftops. Prior to the construction of this more centrally-placed, easily-accessible post, local spotters manned a site that was situated "on the Robertson farm near Miller's Gulf Road, between Getmans Corners and Dennison Corners."[4] The station there was rather unique: one of the familiar orange-and black buses formerly the property of the Central Coach Lines. Being perched high up on the Vickerman Hill area along the Mohawk Valley's southern rim, the lookout afforded an unobstructed, panoramic view in all directions.

Approached by a dirt road, the bus clearly stood out in its treeless, hilltop location. Were it not for its remoteness, which prevented some would-be workers from ever getting there, the bus was an ingenious choice as a ready-made roost by officials of the Town of German Flatts. Modifications that were needed—such as a foundation, toilet, sink, table, and telephone line—were installed at cost by volunteers. Since it was a bus, plenty of seating already existed. For an eight-year old boy, the experience of packing a lunch, riding to this isolated site, hanging out in a converted bus, and assisting my grandfather with an important duty had an unmistakable aura of mystery and adventure that was quite appealing. But the bus, though functional, was intended only as a temporary stop-gap measure, serving to get the aircraft observation program up and running as quickly as possible and buying time until a more suitable, permanent location could be found.

While almost two-and-a-half years elapsed before it became operational, that new site was eventually found. Nestled in among the pines that grew nearby in Ilion's Russell Park, a small wooden tower was built in a pleasant, almost camp-like setting. Painted white with green trim even gave it a neat and tidy Adirondack look. Though just around the corner from Highland Avenue, Maple Place, Arlington Avenue, and the Remington Arms complex, the location still seemed rustic and secluded. But the hope was, "with the tower moved closer to the valley towns, that the ranks of volunteer spotters would be swelled by those who were unable to go back in the hills in previous years for the two-hour tours of duty."[5] Also significant in relation to its purpose, "the new post had an unlimited view of the valley in both directions for several miles."[6]

To a pre-teen like me, the edifice itself appeared, in the nomenclature of the times, as "quite cool." It was two-stories in height. The bottom floor had a toilet, a sink, a table, and a refrigerator —the living quarters if you will. Its entrance was on the south side, and a small window was a feature placed high on the adjacent east wall. But it was on the second level where the place became functional. Here the real work was done.

The spotters' tower in Russell Park. (Source: Joe Smith Collection)

The upper floor, accessed by means of a steep interior stairway, amounted to a square cabin. Each side was fitted with a large plate glass window, maybe 3' by 4'. During inclement weather, the spotter could see in all directions from inside and perform his duties accordingly. However, the neatest feature of this observation post was the outside walkway that extended all around the second floor. With its three-foot wide flooring and metal-pipe safety railings, the catwalk provided outside viewing to all points of the compass, and, unlike the interior, also facilitated hearing any planes passing in the vicinity on a cloudy or overcast day. Just as had been the case with outfitting the bus, the construction of the Ilion tower was accomplished with volunteer labor and donated materials.

All totaled, an outlay of just under $500 was spent to get the building up and running. So limited were the funds and tight the budget that a last-minute appeal went out for the donation of one last piece of important equipment: an electric clock. The local director of the Ground Observation Corps, Edward C. Rhodes, was the energetic individual who had almost single-handedly brought the project to fruition. In these days in which we live, known for generous governmental appropriations and grants for a wide variety of projects, it begs credulity to think that a key component of our national security hinged largely on the generosity of the country's citizenry, be it in the form of dollars, labor, or a timepiece.

The ominous black book that aided spotters in identifying planes that were sighted flying past their observation posts. (Source: Author's Collection)

In the eyes of an imaginative youth, the tower had a cursory resemblance to the blockhouses of the Revolutionary era, defensive structures built around the Mohawk Valley to protect setters from enemy raids. In essence, the mission was the same, only now the malevolent intruders would come out of the sky and not the woods. Perhaps 10' by 10' at its base, this modern-day lookout had four sides that almost imperceptibly sloped up ten-to-twelve feet to the catwalk level. Then the housing on the upper floor rose another six-and-half feet and was crowned by a slanted roof that increased the total height of the structure another foot on its north-facing high end. From its base to the peak of the roof, the whole observation post was perhaps seventeen to twenty feet in height.

Inside the second level was a comfortable work area where the limited but important equipment was located. A desk and a chair were the primary pieces of furniture. The heavy, wooden office-style seat was on wheels—a curious contraption we did not have at home. Then, on top of the big desk lay the heart of the system: a phone line that went to the regional filter center in Syracuse. A large pair of binoculars was also kept handy. However, the most attractive item to me was a black, leather-bound booklet, 8" by 12" in size. In it was page after page of airplane photographs and silhouettes. Among them were Russian, American, British, and Canadian bombers and fighters, plus a variety of civilian aircraft. The presence of this ominous little guide, more than any other feature of the observation post, drove home the serious nature of what we were doing there. If anyone was at all uncertain with regard to the importance of the duty with which we spotters were entrusted, the chilling introduction in the Aircraft Recognition for the Ground Observer booklet offered a sobering rationale: "We are in a dangerous position...the awful truth is that for the first time in our history, a potential enemy has the power to make sudden, devastating attacks on any part of Canada or the United States...the broad seas which protected us in the past have been canceled out by the fast, long-range aircraft...a single aircraft carrying an atomic bomb can now wipe out an entire city."[7]

The new Ilion facility officially became active at 5 p.m. on August 30, 1954. While some finishing touches were still needed, the intent was to have them completed before cold weather arrived. In the eyes of those who helped with construction, the building was "the most comfortable and well-equipped post in the area."[8]

While an identifying hat or jacket would have imparted a nice touch of visible authority, the fact that we were protecting our country was nevertheless a very rewarding experience for a young boy. Being able to do this in concert with my beloved grandfather only served to make the assignment all the better. While this cannot be corroborated with any certainty, it makes sense to me that we fulfilled our service hours between 1952 and 1958, as we first first put in some time at the old bus site before moving to the new Ilion facility. This occurred more frequently after 1954, for by then, granddad had retired after forty-four years as an employee of Remington Arms. Furthermore, he was at the Ilion tower only from May to October. In the winter, as a snowbird, performed the same volunteer mission on Anna Maria Island off the west coast of Florida.

Identifying windshield decal issued to GOC volunteers. (Source: Author's Collection)

The observation post there was situated on the beach, with the structure looking somewhat like a lifeguard station, but with the same 360-degree elevated walkway found in Ilion. My presence, of course, had been limited to only the summer months in New York, when school was out. In family lore, that spotter's tower is forever linked to the birth of my brother Kevin on July 16, 1956; for it was on that date —as my sister Nancy, my grandfather, and I were returning home from our two-hour tour of duty in the park— that our next-door neighbor, Irene Adams, rushed out with the glad tidings about the new addition to the family. So that was why my mom was gone that morning, why dad did not go to work, and how it was that my female sibling got to intrude on what to me was thought of as the masculine world of the spotter's tower!

Since we were involved in a serious mission while at our post, no one ever stopped by to chit-chit. For most of the two-hour shift, our eyes and ears were turned skyward. In the event a plane was spotted, there was a prepared form upon which we were expected to record vital data. This information consisted of "the number of aircraft observed, the type and altitude, direction in which it was going, and the approximate distance of the aircraft from the spotter's post."[9] If our contact was visual, we tried to identify the plane using the black book. Once the data was entered, a call was immediately made on our version of a hotline to the regional filter center. The first call sign used was "This is Quebec Papa 5 0."[10] At that point, our job was done. If the filter center could not make contact and determine the nature of the aircraft, then the matter was handed over to the air force, which in turn could scramble fighters to intercept and eyeball the unknown intruder to determine whether the plane was friend or foe.

Occasionally, a specific plane was sent out to test the alertness of the spotters and the accuracy of their reports. In one instance, the designated aircraft was an American bomber, a B-29. We spotted the subject and reported it as such. While the black book was double-checked to assure the proper identification, my years of Revell and Monogram model airplane construction made the recognition of this special overflight a no brainer.

As an example of the system in action, a celebrated, high-profile incident occurred on November 23, 1952. On that date, Secretary of State Dean Acheson was returning from Canada to New York aboard a DC-6, an aircraft that happened to be President Truman's personal plane named the "Independence," a humbler precursor to the Air Force I model that transports our nation's chief executive nowadays. Surprisingly, given the import of the passenger and the plane, no flight plan had been filed. So, when fourteen-year-old Robert Hutchinson observed the aircraft flying low over Newcomb, New York, which is in the heart of the Adirondacks, he immediately called the filter center in Albany. Since no record existed of an airplane scheduled to be flying at this time in the vicinity of Hutchinson's spotter post, the air force was contacted. In short order, two fighter planes were scrambled to intercept the supposed intruder. However, as the jets approached the propellered craft, "the pilots took one look at the word 'Independence' lettered on the side and headed for home."[11]

Making these reports were common practices among spotters. For example, during one week in the summer of 1952, the observation post on Vickerman Hill called in "the passing of 293 planes, either four-motor or jet types."[12] However, though the Ground Observer Corps clearly served the nation well, the program was never intended to be a permanent solution. Initiated as only a stop-gap measure, everyone involved knew that the time would come when their services would no longer be needed. Finally, after several years of dedicated participation in America's air defense system, that day came. On January 1, 1958, the legions of airplane spotters would be ordered to stand down, retired from active service and moved to what the military called "ready reserve."[13]

This status change came primarily as the result of technological advances in detection devices made by contractors working in concert with the defense department. Specifically, the Distant Early Warning Line, or DEW Line, of radar installations across northern Canada was completed in the summer of 1957. In a public statement, "air force officials now feel that this air surveillance system has progressed to the point that adequate warning will be given in the event of an enemy air attack."[14] Calling the existence of "Operation Skywatch" a "powerful deterrent to enemy aggression," the air force did not completely cut ties with its spotters.[15] Instead, the understanding was that volunteers would continue to receive periodic training, and, if an national emergency ever arose, they would be called back to duty.

At the conclusion of the program, certificates of appreciation were awarded to the volunteer spotters, starting at 100 hours of service and progressing upward. One gentleman, by the name of Leo Barnes, had logged an impressive 2,500 hours. Service pins were also given, with a bar or bars hanging underneath, denoting 100, 500, or more hours of time spent watching for an invading enemy.

A small lapel pin like this was given to each member of the Ground Observer Corps. (Source: Author's Collection)

But the kind of individuals who make such personal sacrifices do not seek nor need public recognition. Much in the tradition of militiamen who turned out during the Revolutionary War-era or the air raid wardens of more recent World War II vintage, these spotters performed the same kind of selfless service. Also, like their patriotic forebears, when the job was done, they quietly returned home. Most of those spotters are gone now, as are their posts. But in Ilion, at least a flagpole still stands on a little knoll in a village park, marking the place where a cadre of Cold War-volunteers did their part on the home front to help preserve our freedom.

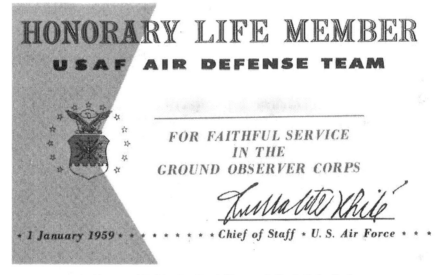

Honorary Life Member Card. (Source: Author's Collection)

🦋 24 🦋

AN OLD-TIME CHRISTMAS:

THE HOLIDAY IN THE '50S

The experience of growing up in Ilion during the decade of the 1950s holds many cherished remembrances for those of us who were children in that era. Among these fond recollections, perhaps none were any more special than those that accompanied and defined the Christmas season. While the displays and events rarely reached the spectacular proportions to which we are now accustomed to seeing, their tasteful, low-key tributes to the season nevertheless set a tone that helped put villagers in a holiday mood. Remembering those days, Ilionite Harold Whittemore wrote in his sentimental journey back in time, called Christmas Memories, of the warm feeling that gradually enveloped everyone in the days following Thanksgiving: "...holly wreaths blossomed overnight on front doors. Colored lights blinked friendly messages, we were humming seasonal songs and Christmas carols and secretly welcoming the soft carpet of white that blanketed the land."[1]

The public observance of Christmas In Ilion was by no means a new phenomenon that arrived in the mid-twentieth century history of the village. Records indicate that the village's first communal Christmas tree made its appearance in 1916, situated grandly atop the mid-town bank building from which it could be easily viewed from multiple directions. Beginning in 1925 and continuing for many years, the Ilion Chamber of Commerce coordinated a program that encouraged the downtown merchants' to decorate their store windows with seasonal exhibits, and, then on an appointed night—December 8 in 1927—all were lighted at the same time. So popular was this event that the *Fort Plain Standard* carried an announcement, noting that "thousands were attracted to Ilion's business section to view the displays on the evening of the Christmas opening."[2] In 1937, a village-wide Christmas door-decorating contest was conducted for the first time. On December 22, 1945, marking the 22nd year for his highly-anticipated, pre-Christmas Eve arrival, "Santa Claus came to Ilion...to help cheer the lives of 260 underprivileged children of this village at a Christmas party sponsored by village organizations and paid for by the clubs and public."[3] That same year marked the return of outdoor lighting around the village for the holidays, welcoming back a tradition that the war and blackout restrictions had interrupted.

In the 1950s, one of first signs that the yuletide season was upon us was hard to miss. Usually right around Thanksgiving, village crews began stringing illuminated garlands on wires above the streets in the downtown area. Though they were not turned on immediately, the appearance of these strands of greenery were a welcomed indication that Christmas was coming. These overhead decorations were "strung from the Ilion Lumber Co. [east] to the Ilion Loan Association [just before the Arms' buildings] on Main Street, up Otsego St., over First Street and [north] down Union and Morgan Sts."[4]

In 1952, Monday, December 1, was designated as the night for switching on the village's Christmas lights. Seven years later, the run-up to Christmas in 1959 was especially memorable; for, in mid-November, just as the seasonal festooning was being hung, a Norman Rockwell scene unfolded, as "the strings of green against the white from the season's first snow reminded residents the Christmas period was near at hand."[5] These decorations consisted of two long strands of garland, interspersed with colored lights and extending to the right and left from a lighted wreath placed in the center of a support wire. All-in-all, perhaps fifteen to twenty of these seasonal displays were suspended overhead for many years through the downtown area. Simple, yet noticeable, their warm glow greeted residents and travelers to the village in the spirit of season. Riding back on the bus from Utica, after a Christmas day visit to my grandparents' house one of the heartwarming sights in Ilion that greeted us were those overhead decorations, announcing that we were at last home again. In an interesting example of the wheel going full circle, the Ilion's downtown decorations for Christmas 2019 once more featured a sight that warmed the hearts of baby boomers—lighted garlands with a wreath at their centers strung across overhead wires!

Overhead Christmas lights hung by village crews can be seen above Main Street. The "Hershey's Ice Cream" sign marks the site of Powers News. Grant's is on the opposite side of the street. The bank clock just behind the light pole serves as a marker for the old corner of Otsego and Main Streets. Union Street is a turn off Main on the lower right, and Central Ave is a left at the corner just beyond the awning of Powers News and then the storefront of Thompson's Gift Shop. (Source: Ilion Free Public Library)

Another seasonal display to which Ilionites once eagerly looked forward were large, hand-painted panels that graced the upper half of part of the Municipal Building's frontage. Located there was a large, hand-rendered mural which was probably about six-feet high by twenty-feet wide. In 1950, a contest was sponsored by the Ilion Light

Department and the Village Board to have a new scene created for display during the upcoming Christmas celebration. According to a local newspaper article, the design selected "deviates from past paintings and depicts with an English town during the Yule season instead of the customary Biblical scenes and choir boys."[6]

The façade of the Municipal Building was a "must visit" sight each Xmas to view its handcrafted murals and hear carols in the air. (Source: The Ilion Sentinel)

What made these pieces of art particularly endearing was their creation by Ilion High School students. In the 1950 rendering, Jean Parks was the talented young lady in charge who had the assistance of other students in transferring her small sketch to the oversized version that hung on the village hall. Featuring an evening sky over snow-covered terrain, the scene was heavy in blue and white. Various colors to liven the appearance of the village were introduced into the picture through the peoples' clothing and their homes. Each year, the mural on the Municipal Building became a "must-see" site. Beheld on a snowy evening served to impart a captivating, almost 3-D quality to the panel. Adding to the Christmas spirit, the holiday music was played for a couple of hours late in the afternoon and again in the early evening from 7 to 8 p.m.

Going a block to the west along First Street and then turning left onto West brought into view another perennial Christmas display, though in this instance one more in keeping with the spirituality of the season. There, along the sidewalk in front of Annunciation Church, was an impressive nativity scene. The figures included were probably ¾ scale, which made them appear lifelike. Placed in a modified stable structure, hay strewn around its floor, and the infant

Jesus laying in the manger—all contributed to the realistic look imparted to this traditional tableau which lay at the very heart of the Christian celebration of Christmas. An added touch in a similar vein was found over the main entrance to Annunciation School, where smaller nativity was mounted, featuring figurines about twenty-inches in height.

But any recounting of the outdoor public displays attuned to the holiday season would be incomplete without taking note of a large red box located in the small park that once existed across from the fire station on Central Ave. This important receptacle served as the repository for children's letters to Santa Claus. When bringing their offspring down to deposit the all-important letters, parents were reminded to be sure that a return address was included on the envelope; otherwise they might not know what their youngsters had requested for Christmas if the child's list could not surreptitiously be returned to them. Set out on December 1, its contents were picked up about two weeks later by no less than old St. Nicholas himself. Customarily, he made his appearance atop the red brick firehouse where he was given sacks containing the vital correspondence. While awaiting his arrival, which at one time was by helicopter, the hundreds of children assembled below sang Christmas carols. Upon his appearance, old St. Nick spoke a few brief words over a PA system, while candy was distributed to the youngsters.

Decorations of the '50s...simple yet beautiful. (Source: Library of Congress)

Cardboard decorations were quite common in the '50s, as many were left over from the lean war years. (Source: Author's Collection)

Among the other heralds of holiday season's arrival were the proliferation of lots around town where various entrepreneurs offered Christmas trees for sale. Evergreens of various kinds and sizes were available at different locations around town: Cormia's greenhouse on upper South Fifth Avenue; Champagne's grocery on the corner of Second Street and South Third Avenue; Ilion Hardware on Otsego Street and Venema's on lower Prospect Ave. Prices were reasonable, starting as low as a $1.00 in some places. Loblaw's market offered two-foot trees, available in natural green or spay-painted silver and attached to a round red stand. Tinsel and glass balls were common decorative items for the trees. Some families liked to string popcorn and cranberries and then loop the long strands circuitously around the tree.

As for lighting, some homes had older versions which featured conical bulbs that tapered for two inches to a blunt point. Newer models had a pudgier bulb that had a more pleasing look with the added advantage of being wired in a parallel circuit, so one light could be out and not shut down the whole entire string—a happenstance that then precipitated the aggravating experience of trying to figure out which bulb had burned out on the older style of strands mounted in series fashion. Perhaps the most expensive and captivating style of Xmas tree-lighting consisted of four-inch tubes filled with a colored liquid, appearing like candles. When attached over a bulb, the substance in the tube heated up and eventually began to bubble.

In those bygone times, outdoor decorating had achieved neither the popularity nor the proliferation that it has today. Far fewer lights and many more wreaths were the standards to which most folks adhered. However, to perk up interest in exterior projects around the village, in 1952 *The Ilion Sentinel* began sponsoring a home "Door Decorating Contest." This new seasonal promotion was intended to "...renew interest in Christmas lighting."[7] As an incentive to generate as much participation as possible, a plan was devised to offer one 1st place prize for each of the three communities of Frankfort, Ilion, and Mohawk, along with a couple of Grand Prizes.

For many of those living in the village, another Christmas imperative along with decorating was shopping for gifts. Mail-order was limited, with the catalog houses like Wards and Sears being among the more popular suppliers. The arrival of the Ward's special Christmas edition usually precipitated a tug-of-war between my sister and me over who got to study it first. Online-ordering, of course, did not yet exist, and utilizing parcel post required enough lead time to assure a pre-Christmas delivery. A one-time trip to Utica—by bus for our family—to shop at Genesee Street's array of retailers such as Woolworth's, Kresge's, and the Boston Store was a highly-anticipated excursion. Herkimer was also a desirable destination due to the presence of Montgomery Ward's and Munger's—with the latter department store offering the extra double feature of Santa Claus and a large Lionel train layout upstairs.

But at some point, most villagers probably made it to downtown Ilion on multiple occasions, where many specialty shops and several larger stores had much to offer for those people on their lists. For many shoppers, the commencement of their holiday gift-buying began with the arrival of their "Christmas Club" checks. To promote saving and insure having ready cash available, patrons would open one of these seasonal accounts at their local bank. Each week, usually at the same time that a paycheck was cashed, a pre-determined amount was earmarked for a Christmas Club payment, submitted to the cashier along with a deposit slip taken from the individual's personal payment booklet. At some point in mid-November, Christmas Club checks were mailed out, along with the encouragement to start a new one immediately for the next year. In 1958, the First National Bank in Herkimer trumpeted that it "had mailed Christmas Club checks totaling $208,658.75 to 2257 forward-looking happy customers..."[8]

While this service is still offered by some banking institutions, the practice in general has gone out of favor. But at one time, many grateful people were thankful that they had enrolled in such a plan. With family budgets tight, the on-going struggle to make ends meet on a weekly basis did not allow much wiggle room to factor in the seasonal burden of buying Christmas gifts. Credit cards in limited numbers did not start arriving on the scene until the end of the decade, and, while putting items "on layaway" at a local store and making payments on an installment plan helped, the extra expenses incurred at holiday time nevertheless called for chiseling a little money out of finite funds each week, "robbing Peter to pay Paul" as the adage went. However, those with the foresight to set up Christmas clubs breathed a little easier when the holiday shopping rush began.

To accommodate the working public as well as allow moms to slip out alone while dad watched the kids, virtually all stores in the run-up to Christmas stayed open until nine o'clock; however, due to the combination of blue laws and social mores, these same establishments were prevented from being open on Sundays. For the 1952 season, *The*

Herkimer Telegram announced that the Ilion Businessmen's Association had decided that "stores in Ilion will remain open evenings beginning December 12."[9] For shoppers, Freeman's on Otsego Street offered women's coats for $29.95—a seasonal discount of 35%. Huyck's on E. Clark Street offered "A Christmas Gift for the Whole Family," albeit the well-oiled family, when it suggested making a purchase from its in-stock models of Feather Craft aluminum boats and Evinrude outboard motors.[10]

Other items available to discriminating shoppers in town were touted by the Best Appliances and Furniture Store, located on the corner of Main and Morgan Streets, where "New 1960 Appliances for Christmas! The Appreciated Gift!" could be purchased.[11] In the two downtown blocks created west from Morgan to Otsego along Main Street, then south along Otsego one block to First Street, and east along First Street back to Morgan were located most of the retail businesses in Ilion. Therein could be found Enjem's Variety Store, Niles' Music Store, Bonn's Sporting Goods, Buckminster's Jewelers, Roach's Liquors, Warner's Men's Shop, the National Auto, Thompson's Gift Shop, and W. T. Grant's "5 and 10 Cent" store to name but a few of the places frequented by in-town Christmas shoppers.

In walking these streets one snowy pre-Christmas night with my dad, we had the pleasurable experience of running into one of Santa's "helpers." Probably sponsored by local merchants, his job was to wander the business district and spread seasonal good will. Being about 13 years old by then, the facts behind St. Nicholas were no longer a mystery to me. Yet, when the jolly old pseudo-Santa greeted the two of us with a warm "Hi Joe, Hi Joe," a different kind of amazement struck me. How did he know who we were? After the two adults batted the breeze for a few minutes, we parted company. The jolly old elf went on his way to spread more Christmas cheer, while we continued window shopping. A few steps along, dad asked if I knew who that was. After my negative reply, he said: "That was your social studies teacher—Mr. Manion!" Another Christmas mystery solved… and what wonderful typecasting. For if anyone had an outgoing demeanor, twinkling eyes, and upbeat spirit to portray Santa Claus, that person was Martin Manion—all of which can be readily affirmed by those of us fortunate enough to have experienced his unique pedagogical skills as a social studies teacher or been greeted by him when he moonlighted as the holiday superhero.

Along with the obvious absence of online shopping in the 1950s, also missing were emails and text messages. With telephone communication still its relative infancy, the post office was required to step up each year, stand tall, and handle the deluge of packages and flood of first-class mail—at three cents a letter or card—which the holidays generated. Weeks before Christmas, local postal officials began their annual pleas for people to mail early. For public consumption on November 20, 1952, Ilion's then postmaster Thomas Morris issued a statement, assuring villagers that his workers were ready for the anticipated deluge of mail: "The Christmas season is officially underway. Here at the post office we have a tremendous job to do. Naturally, our main concern is the delivery of all gift packages and Christmas cards by December 25."[12]

When possible, part-timers were hired. In the early '50s, the extra help received $1.26 an hour. In 1952, for example, twenty-nine temporary workers were enlisted to help process what became the then record of "275,000 greeting cards."[13] In years when an insufficient number of takers came forth, the regular staff often was called upon to shoulder the burden and work overtime. As the days wound down ever closer to the 25 of December, the post office extended its window hours until 7 p.m. To expedite home distribution during the weeks preceding December 24, a morning and an afternoon delivery of mail was quite common in the Ilion of that era. Every effort was made to get all possible pieces of first-class mail dispersed by closing time on Christmas Eve. Even then, as a final holiday gesture, the postmaster made it known that "all gifts and special delivery mail will be delivered Christmas Day."[14]

As December 25 approached, the tempo of holiday-related activities picked up. Virtually every organization in town sponsored some sort of observance or pitched-in on behalf of children. As noted by *The Evening Telegram*, "in churches in Ilion, youngsters presented traditional plays and programs prior to the parties featuring refreshments and exchange of gifts."[15] Fraternal organizations such the Moose, Elks, VFW, and the American Legion all held seasonal gatherings for the children of their members. The Police Benevolent Association traditionally threw a party for community's younger set at the Capitol Theater, where a movie was shown, and candy and oranges distributed.

Perhaps the last of the lead-in events to the big day occurred early on Christmas Eve. This highly anticipated event in our house was the arrival of a Kiwanian, clad in the garb of Santa Claus' helper, at the front door. What triggered this drop-in was turning on the porch light and placing a folded newspaper in the front window. We got a big "Ho-Ho-Ho," an encouragement to get to bed early, and candy. While the sugary delight was a Planter's Peanut Bar that we detested, the visit was nevertheless an always eagerly anticipated ritual. Furthermore, it was possible to have a picture taken with jolly old St. Nick, though parents were advised to have a flash camera on-hand and ready. Santa could not tarry, as he many houses and miles to go before he could call it a night.

In 1953, eleven club members volunteered for what must have been a rewarding though arduous assignment. Even starting out at 5:30 p.m., the challenge to these men must have seemed daunting, as Ilion was not a small town by any means. The ever-generous Kiwanians also added a special adjunct to their rounds that night a, thoughtful touch that encompassed another contingent of Santas being sent to the homes of underprivileged children, bearing gifts to insure that these less fortunate young people would not suffer the disappointment of nothing under their trees.

Another pre-Christmas event—a one-timer that occurred around 1953—was a visit by a Coca-Cola representative. How she gained entrance to our house is a mystery to me now because my mother would never answer the door if she perceived that the caller might be a salesman. Maybe the fact that she could see that a woman was doing the knocking made mom put her guard down. At any rate she did, and the outcome was that we were given two promotional trays. Made of metal and slightly more than 10" in width a little over 13" in length with sides that were beveled inward, they were extremely colorful with seasonal scenes around the outside edge Centered in the middle was an attractive, well-groomed lady drinking a coke. While not items

(Source: Author's Collection)

we would likely have purchased at a store, the sturdy, good-sized platters turned out to be quite useful. For instance, one of these trays was always pressed into service if one of my siblings or I was ill, it then served as the conveyance used for delivering us our breakfast, lunch, and dinner. How we were chosen to be the trays' recipients we never asked, nor did we have any idea how extensive the distribution of these promotional gifts was. But, as freebies go, these two items proved welcomed and durable.

While most people agreed that Christmas was for kids, this did not preclude adults from joining in on the merriment. As a result, different organizations found a variety of ways to celebrate the season. For the Ilion Historical Club, its members took the opportunity to have their December meetings focus on themes related to the holidays. One year the topic was "Christmas Carols Around the World," while on another occasion the group had centered its holiday gathering around "Christmas Customs." The Ilion Little Theater Club, DAR, the Odd Fellows and Violet Rebekahs, the Ilion Home Bureau, the various other fraternal clubs, business organizations, and church-affiliated groups around town held Christmas parties for their respective members, sometimes built around covered dish suppers and bazaars and often featuring choral singing.

Because it was a different era, one in which political correctness had yet to weigh in and determine a new appropriateness, the component levels of the school system also all had Christmas observances of varying kinds. For example, an evening program was once held at North Street Elementary School, where the well-attended performance featured choral singing by kindergarteners and several plays by older students. In grade school classrooms in the district, real Christmas trees could be found in a corner and decorations on the walls. Often the windows of the room were also adorned with some additional form of seasonal art. Parties were held just before the holiday recess, and gifts were exchanged among students, the receiver of a particular present being determined by its giver having pulled a recipient's name from a hat.

Joining in, the high school did its part by customarily featuring an evening concert, sometimes with an elementary chorus mixed into a cast that seemed like thousands. One year the program showcased the "Orpheus" Club, the "Eleven Belles," and a 60-member elementary boys' choir. Another highly anticipated seasonal event at the upper level was the senior class' Christmas Ball, customarily held in that era in the school's gym. Themed "Fantasy in Snow" in 1956, the live music was provided by Chuck Paddock, Jr.'s 12-piece band.

It was a time when old-fashioned Christmas carols were sung, including hymns with religious themes. West Hill Elementary had a yearly pageant wherein the proceedings commenced with each grade level marching into the auditorium. As we came in from the hall, went down a flight of stairs, and headed for our seats, each class from youngest to oldest sang a carol or hymn. The difficulty level increased as the students matured, so as sixth graders our selection was "We, Three Kings"—and no one seemed to have a problem with what today would be construed as a politically incorrect carol.

The final observances of the season, appropriately on Christmas Day, was in the hands of the churches. In 1953, for example, the Episcopal Church held a midnight service, followed by two more the following morning, with all featuring choral as well as solo hymns being sung. That same year, the Protestants held a combined service at the Baptist Church, beginning at 11:00 p.m. on Christmas Eve, and then they followed up with individual observances in their own respective churches the next morning.

In summing up the Christmas experience in the 1950s without coming across as overly wedded to nostalgia, those times were different when compared to how the holidays are celebrated today. Not necessarily better or worse, just different as part of a lifestyle that marched to a different drummer than that of modern America. The aura created was one which appeared to be not as commercialized, far less glitzy, comparatively less expensive, and more grounded in the traditional values of family and church.

Harold Whittemore—a very observant, accomplished, and respected local newsman of the era—captured his impression of those bygone days for his readers and himself in a column called "That Magic, Zany Season is Here" when he wrote: "And the Christmas bells will chime, the stores will be brightly-lighted, colorful, and fun to be in...the crowds will push and shove but gently...the traffic will be horrendous...people will shop until they drop...the kids will get so excited they can't sleep...and, suddenly, it will be Christmas Eve and its own special magic and we need it."[16]

What he was describing was a time for many of us when Ilion was the hub of our universe. For all practical purposes, the village that existed in the 1950s was virtually self-sufficient. If an item or service was needed, it was most likely available somewhere around town. With a fine hospital, well-run library, an excellent school system, many retail stores, and plentiful factory jobs, residents in general had little call on a daily basis to go out of town to fulfill their needs. This held true for the Christmas season too. Other than perhaps to visit distant relatives, the celebration of the holidays was done in Ilion. Long before Thomas Kinkaid started producing paintings of cherished but now by-gone times—his much admired "Hometown Christmas" scenes—the people of Ilion were living in them.

25

A MEMORABLE FALL DAY:
WHEN JFK CAME TO TOWN

Sept 29, 1960, was not a normal autumn Thursday in America. With a hotly contested presidential contest in full-swing, newspaper headlines on a daily basis carried the latest updates on the travels, stops, and speeches of opposing politicians. Elective offices were being contested at all levels; however the race that grabbed the most headlines was the one for President of the United States between Richard Nixon and John Kennedy. Having entered the fray only recently, President Eisenhower was now out campaigning vigorously for Nixon, the Republican candidate. This evening would find the beloved Ike in Chicago, where he would address 2000 people gathered in the ballroom of the Conrad Hilton Hotel. Meanwhile, Nixon was boldly carrying the fight onto his opponent's home ground—Boston. Before a huge audience of his own, he delivered what *The New York Times* called "...one of the sharpest political attacks to date on Senator Kennedy."[1]

As for JFK, he was taking his campaign into the central part of New York, a region traditionally a bedrock of support for GOP candidates. An imbedded reporter for *The New York Times*, traveling in the entourage with the then junior senator from Massachusetts on this upstate swing, noted that "Senator Kennedy's crowds were not so large and enthusiastic today as they were in western New York yesterday."[2]

By contrast, urban throngs in both Buffalo and Rochester had welcomed him "with enthusiasm and noise...greater than at any Democratic rallies since the days of Franklin Roosevelt..."[3] Now, on day two of his brief New York State junket, he was riding in a motorcade that would bring him from the capital district west to Syracuse, a driving distance of one-hundred-and-forty-six miles. Along the way, he was scheduled to make speaking stops of varying lengths of time. In retrospect, the underwhelming receptions through the Mohawk Valley reflected exactly why he made the trip— perhaps by seeing and hearing him in person, some voters might be persuaded to break their long-held Republican preferences and cast their ballots for a Democratic candidate.

(Source: Library of Congress)

Just like its counterparts in other parts of the nation, Thursday, September 29, 1960, would not unfold as a typical day in Ilion either. Setting this date apart from the regular rhythms of everyday life in the small upstate village of Ilion in southern Herkimer County was the fact that a bona fide presidential candidate was coming to make a stump speech. This unexpected revelation had been announced six days before in a small blurb inserted in the local newspaper. Equally noteworthy was *The Evening Telegram's* added affirmation that "his speech here will be his only public appearance in Herkimer County on his tour through upstate New York."[4] The decision that finalized plans for the candidate's visit had been made in the evening of September 22, when the county and state Democratic chairmen—Tom Morris and Dan Reardon—met with members of Senator Kennedy's advanced team. The upshot was that Ilion was given the green light to host the campaign stop.

In ongoing jousts among the five small, adjacent enclaves of Little Falls, Herkimer, Mohawk, Ilion, and Frankfort—all compacted within a relatively linear ten-mile stretch—matters of civic pride were of paramount interest. As a result, Kennedy's campaign stop represented a real coup for Ilion, giving its citizenry a major talking point in the game of one-upmanship with their neighboring communities.[5] Adding further import was the rarity of the occasion, for no one could recall a previous presidential candidate ever coming to town. For sure, none have made the stop in the over sixty years since the Kennedy visit.

Located in the upper Mohawk Valley, east of the larger urban cities of Syracuse and Utica and west of the Albany metropolitan area, Ilion was never a customary destination on the itinerary of those seeking national office. County Democratic Party chairman Tom Morris put Kennedy's appearance in its proper perspective when he commented that "it is the first time in Ilion's 100-year history

(Source: Author's Collection)

that a presidential candidate had stopped at its door."[6] But in the 1960 election, where pollsters had the candidates running neck-and-neck, no stone was going to be left unturned by either contender in his quest for every possible vote. The stakes were high, but the reward was greater. Hanging in the balance were New York State's then formidable block of forty-five electoral votes.

What made this occasion so memorable in hindsight was that the visiting politician was John Fitzgerald Kennedy. At the time, he was a young Democratic legislator from the Bay State, one to whom some in the village would in five weeks give their votes; however, a little more than three years later, a tragic assassination moved his growing popular support as president to the level of venerated immortality. For many of those Ilionites who had ignored a light rain to see him, his brief visit was eventually held as that of a cherished memory.

After a luncheon in Canajoharie, Kennedy's motorcade had taken the Thruway west until exiting at Herkimer. By now the time was 2:10 p.m., making the senator already twenty-five minutes late for his speaking engagement in Ilion, where the first elements of a crowd had begun gathering as early as 12:30. Still, the vote-seeking politician in him could not resist a brief, unscheduled stop to shake the hands of the toll takers and maintenance workers present at the Herkimer Thruway exchange. Then, escorted by Mohawk and Ilion police, his motorcade continued west again, traveling along NYS Route 5S until it arrived in Ilion two-and-a-half miles later.

Once in town, the convoy of automobiles proceeded along Main Street, first funneling through the narrow canyon created by the factories of Remington Arms on its left and Sperry Rand on its right, just before the motorcade burst into the downtown shopping area. After passing the National Bank to its left on the corner where Otsego Street (i.e.-Route 51) joined Main Street (i.e.-Route 5S), the six-car and two-bus procession turned sharply right onto Central Ave, moving between the offices of the *Utica Daily Press/Observer-Dispatch* on the eastern side of the street in the Wilcox Block and Dr. Robert Luke's optometry office and Fred Emden's accounting business on the end of the Powers Block to the west. After moving north on Central Avenue for about two-hundred feet, the convoy turned slowly left onto what was then a rather constricted passageway known as West State Street, passing as it did close along the north side of the village's Central Fire Station.[7]

The objective of the Kennedy caravan lay just ahead to its left. There a temporary speaker's stand had been erected, a wooden platform which was located a few hundred feet down the road, in fifteen feet from the south side curbing of West State Street and set up in a large municipal parking lot. As his car slowly approached, JFK was highly visible as he sat perched on top of his chauffeur-driven auto's trunk, his feet resting on the back seat of a light-colored, big-finned Cadillac convertible. Just as folks had seen on news footage about his

Kennedy motorcade arrives in Ilion. (Source: Sweeney Family Home Movie)

visits to other towns and cities, JFK cheerfully waved to the first elements of the crowd on the sides of West State Street, which led to the platform constructed in the parking lot on his left behind the Central Fire Station.

Given the narrowness of the street, people standing along the edge of road were within six feet of the presidential hopeful, giving them an up-close look at the candidate. Considering the extensive proportions to which security measures for candidates, much less presidents, have evolved in recent years, Kennedy's protection that day was in evidence, though the resources brought to bear were of state and local origins. A sheriff's car and state police cruisers had been inserted into the motorcade, accompanied by a vehicle filled with "security men."[8] All members of the Ilion Police and Fire Departments had been pressed into service. Any days-off were cancelled. Contingents of the village's volunteer police and firemen were also pressed into service for this momentous occasion. According to the IPD's chief Maurice Goldin, an additional precaution was taken "by interspersing reliable persons, in plain clothes among the crowd in case of any disorderly conduct on the part of hecklers, drunks, or fanatics."[9] However, since the crowd proved well-behaved, no incidents occurred that tested the tight security.

Yet, considering the tragedy that the future held in store for John Kennedy, it is amazing in hindsight the proximity to the candidate which spectators were allowed. While he was speaking, people were closely packed on three sides of platform. Some were so close...often only a few feet away...that they could easily have reached out and touched him. Since the "Campaign of 1960" was conducted in the last days of innocence for America, extending protection to candidates for the high office was not considered a necessity. The assassination of Robert Kennedy in 1968 changed that line of thinking virtually overnight. Reacting to the shock and horror of RFK's death, Congress authorized Secret Service protection for major candidates running for the Presidency and Vice-Presidency of the United States. However, in 1960, federal involvement in the protection of presidential office-seekers was non-existent for challengers. The onus for handling the situation, as it existed in Ilion, fell squarely on the shoulders of local authorities. That the whole affair was handled so well was a tribute to the efficiency and diligence of the Ilion Police Department, the village's volunteer force, and state troopers.

John Kennedy earnestly delivering his campaign speech in Ilion. (Source: Author's Collection)

For a county that was traditionally a Republican bastion—going for Eisenhower in '52 and '56—the turnout was indeed impressive. While Republican governor Nelson Rockefeller—a supporter of Richard Nixon—had generously decreed that "state employees may take time off to see and hear Democratic presidential candidate Sen. John F. Kennedy when he speaks on the Capitol steps," he was extending an opportunity that most private sector businesses did not match.[10] As a result, the mid-afternoon timing of the event precluded many local workers from attending. The best some of those wage earners in the first shift at the Remington plants could do was to watch from factory windows on both sides of Main Street, getting a fleeting glimpse of the candidate's motorcade traveling along the two-lane canyon created by four-story, block-long brick buildings on both sides of East Main Street.

Another individual whose work commitment prevented his attendance was Jim Garnsey. A long-time Democrat and later five-term Ilion mayor of Ilion, on the day of the Kennedy visit Mr. Garnsey was a phone company employee working at an out-of-town job site. "Of course, I would have liked to have been at the rally," he offered, "but no way was I going to get the afternoon off."[11] In spite of the absence of Mr. Garnsey and many others like him, folks who also had to stay at their jobs, the crowd's size was nevertheless noteworthy.

Even with so many who were unable to attend due to work obligations, the headcount was still impressive. In her assessment of the assembled mass, reporter Mary Edwards offered an estimate that "...between two and three thousand cheered the candidate as his car drove up to the platform."[12] Ilion's chief of police Maurice Goldin ventured an even more substantial estimate that saw the crowd as numbering between "...3000 and 4000."[13] However, regardless of the actual tally, few would dispute that the throng which did gather constituted an impressive turnout, especially for a Democratic candidate.

Among the waiting spectators was Jean Spamin Putch, who had served as a family chauffeur. "My mother was a life-long Democrat," Mrs. Putch shared, "and this was an opportunity that she did not want to miss."[14] In addition to the retirees, housewives, and businessmen in the crowd, its numbers were boosted by a sizable contingent of students from the Ilion Jr.-Sr. High School, pupils who were excused at 12:55 "...upon a written request from their parents."[15] From the standpoint of their partaking in a live civics lesson, as well as a having front row seat to history-in-the-making, Ilion's wise, distinguished Superintendent George Purple deserved kudos for allowing these students the opportunity to attend and be a part of a current events experience.

༂༂༂

FOUR MONTHS LATER, in Room 120 of the high school's old D-wing, social studies teacher Martin Manion—possessing the same philosophy of exposing students to on-going historical events as Mr. Purple—had a television console set up in his classroom. Those willing to forego their lunches had the chance to observe the inauguration of John Fitzgerald Kennedy as the 35th President of the United States. For some of us, impressionable though generally apolitical youth that we were, watching the inauguration brought the wheel full circle.[16] Many had seen him on September 26 in the first of what became a series of four televised debates. Then he was in Ilion just three days later. Now he was on television again at 12:00 noon on January 20, 1961, the result of having achieved electoral success in part due to that very debate we had watched at home and the stump speeches like the one that we had heard downtown.

༂༂༂

WALKING from the campaign car to the speaker's dais, Senator Kennedy appeared as many would thereafter always remember him— "well-tanned, flashing his well-known smile while shaking hands with people near the platform."[17] As he moved through the crowd which pressed close around him, he reached out to many of the nearby well-wishers, including several women positioned at the entrance to the speaker's stand. After the candidate had passed by, one of the more rabid fans among this feminine group was heard to exclaim: "I'm never going to wash this hand until that glorious man is elected!"[18] As he made his way slowly from the car to the podium, JFK was accompanied by a small contingent of law enforcement officers. One of these men, guarding the candidate's back, was a proud fellow Irish-Irish and long-time village resident, then Patrolman Alfred Seymour of the Ilion Police Department.

As he was making his way to the specially-constructed platform, Kennedy's catchy campaign song blared over the PA system. Some folks still recall hearing the unmistakable sound of Frank Sinatra crooning the adapted version of his 1959 hit "High Hopes." Substituting for its original words, Sinatra—an ardent Democrat—and his lyricist Sammy Cahn rewrote the lyrics in support of JFK's presidential bid. Totaling twenty-six lines, the first six of the memorable tune were:

"Everyone is voting for Jack
Cause he's got what the others lack
Everyone wants to back—Jack
Jack is on the right track.
'Cause he's got high hopes
He's got high hopes..."[19]

Upon reaching the speaker's platform, the candidate was greeted by the Hon. Jack Manley, Ilion's mayor and master-of-ceremonies. After several dignitaries were introduced, the youthful senator from Massachusetts stepped up to the microphone. By virtue of a fortuitous change in the weather—wrought by Divine intervention, the luck of the Irish, or a meteorological anomaly—the rain had stopped when Kennedy reached the platform's steps and held off until he departed. On that wet, dreary September day, he did not speak for long—perhaps all of fifteen minutes tops. Looking out upon a sea of upturned faces...mine included...he spoke with what seemed an odd accent, for full-blooded Bostonians did not find their way into the world of a thirteen-year old Ilionite very often. His occasional punctuation of the air with his hand was a distinctive mannerism that we would come to expect whenever he addressed an assemblage after his election.

The canned message that he delivered was certainly intended to appeal to his audience. For central New Yorkers of both parties, jobs were a topic of acute interest, and Kennedy readily took the incumbent Republicans—which included his opponent Vice-President Nixon—to task for not doing more to achieve full employment. To address this problem, "he pledged 'aggressive efforts to stimulate jobs' if he was elected."[20] Also included in his brief commentary, the candidate touched on other subjects of fiscally-related interest: the concept of financing medical care for the aged through Social Security; advancing the hourly wage rate to $1.25; and increasing federal aid to schools.

When he had finished his prepared remarks, Senator Kennedy had agreed to take three questions at random from the crowd. The first query addressed a consistent Cold War concern: "Would you make any changes in our missile program?"[21] This was followed by a question that unknowingly foreshadowed what would become one of President Kennedy's biggest headaches: "How would you cope with the problem in Cuba?"[22] Finally, in more of a policy statement than an inquiry, a spectator said: "Any action we do take should be taken through the Organization of American States. We should not carry out a unilateral action unless driven to it by direct military intervention."[23]

Since the third person never actually posed a question, a fourth individual got to ask it: "Do think after last week Nixon will show up for the next debate?"[24] In this instance, the gentleman was referencing Richard Nixon's poor performance and haggard looks in the first of four scheduled debates. Kennedy's diplomatic response was: "I am sure we will both be there."[25]

What he had verbalized in his brief Ilion address was not unlike the message that he had articulated to other crowds during what would prove to be a long day, one that started in Albany at 8:20 in the morning in the city's venerable Dewitt Clinton Hotel. Fortified by a breakfast consisting of a "large orange juice, two four-minute boiled eggs, broiled bacon, dry toast with butter and jelly on the side and a large coffee," he was ready to face a grueling schedule, one that would see him cover approximately one-hundred-and-seventy miles from the Capital District on the Hudson River, up through the Mohawk Valley, and then west to the central region of the state on Onondaga Lake.[26]

Leaving the state capital, his motorcade first went eight miles north and turned east to nearby Troy. Then the procession backtracked westward, going to Schenectady, Amsterdam, and Canajoharie before arriving in Ilion. From there, the Kennedy entourage continued west to Utica, Rome and Syracuse. Traveling with JFK were two well-known Democrats: former governor of the Empire State and career diplomat Averill Harriman; and the incumbent mayor of New York City Robert Wagner. Representing the senator's extensive extended family on the current barnstorming tour was sister-in-law Ethel Kennedy, later to be a public figure in her own right as the wife of the senator's brother Bobby.

Through the day, it is worth noting that Mr. Kennedy was not feeling in tip-top shape. After having been examined by a local Rochester physician on September 28, he was taking a prescribed medication to combat a head cold, a condition that contributed to a hoarse tenor in his voice which became more noticeable as the day progressed. However, with the general election looming in little less than six weeks, time was of the essence. Under the weather or not, he had to persevere and get his message across at every opportunity.

For all the hype and anticipation of his campaign stop, Kennedy's time in Ilion proved somewhat disappointing—not for the lack of star-power by the charismatic senator, but rather in the brevity of his visit. However, that was the understood nature of these whirlwind tours. Once conducted off the back platforms of railroad coaches, those former whistle-stop visits had been modernized with airplanes, automobiles, buses, and cars supplanting the iron horse as the preferred modes of transportation. As was the case in Ilion, motorcades not only offered far greater mobility in reaching places and people removed from the railroad's right-of-way, but they also forged a much more personal experience between the candidate and spectators than the use of trains allowed. Because of the physical proximity permitted, a small child could be lifted to present the smiling candidate with a bouquet of three orange mums, and the late Jerry Walsh, an Ilion High School freshman at the time, was able to distinctly recall "Sen. Kennedy's smile and the image of him waving, leaving the village in an open-air convertible…"[27]

Not surprising to those fans who knew of the New Englander's personal idiosyncrasies, Kennedy did not wear a hat, an article of clothing that would have afforded excellent protection for a man with a head cold; however, the candidate's long-standing aversion to such coverage precluded his donning a fedora. Consequently, his shock of thick brown hair was becoming wetter by the minute, until the convertible's top was eventually raised for the ten-mile ride to Utica and his campaign rally in the city's Memorial Auditorium. Though eschewing a hat, the senator had finally taken to wearing a buttoned-up, light-colored trench coat, as a shield from the rain for the ailing candidate. At least from the neck down, he was protected from the elements.

The candidate delivers his speech in Ilion before a large crowd in the downtown parking near the local landmark of the Best Garage. (Source: Ilion Free Public Library)

From Utica, Senator Kennedy would conclude his day with a

formal address in Syracuse. After speaking there that evening, he was scheduled for a quick visit home to Hyannis Port. "His grueling 15-hour schedule carried him 500 miles by airplane and motorcade into six cities between the Niagara Frontier and Albany," noted reporter Mary Edwards, "[and] the strain of campaign speech-making began to show as Kennedy's voice grew raspy as the day wore on."[28] Considering his physical discomfort, was JFK's venture into a Republican stronghold worth the effort? In assessing the value of his two-day foray deep into the Empire State, *The New York Times* suggested that "he carried with him the assurance that, even if he fails to carry New York, he has given Democratic morale up-state a tremendous lift."[29]

As the candidate winged his way home that night, via a flight path to the east that took him through the skies above places that he had just visited only hours before, the local nightly news broadcasts recapped the day, as many of those Ilionites who heard him were now doing in their minds. While his stopover passed in what seemed like an instant, the after-effects of that handful of minutes lasted a lifetime for many who were there that day. Reporter Ernie Sitts captured the feeling that engulfed a number of us when he wrote: "All told, it was a good show. And hundreds of county school children, dismissed for the event on their parents' consent, went home happy that they had seen and heard, personally, a presidential candidate."[30]

Evidence of what became an enduring connection, forged in those fleeting moments, was provided by the late Joseph Short, a long-time village resident who was an eighth grader in the fall of 1960. Thirty-three years later, his memory of that singular event was still vivid. "He wore a yellow tie. I was trying to get close to shake his hand. He was tanned. And with that yellow tie, he stood out," Mr. Short recalled regarding the candidate's appearance.[31] He added that "you are looking for heroes as a kid. He represented youth. He gleamed."[32]

Then, in a more somber tone, Mr. Short, referencing President Kennedy's untimely passing, shared the lasting memory of the tragic assassination by simply saying: "I still have not gotten over it."[33] Forty-six at the time of the interview, Joe echoed the feelings still carried by many other village residents who had been touched by the charisma, vitality, and promise personally conveyed in JFK's few moments among them. Such was the impression that Senator Kennedy made by his visit, election victory, and 1000-day presidency that it was not unusual to find his portrait hanging somewhere in homes and offices around town. These pictures, originally framed as an honor to a man their owners admired, soon took on the aura of shrines to the memory of a departed leader.

Kevin Hall, who left Ilion in his early teens but took fond memories of the village with him, remembers that his grandparents had a pair of pictures hanging on their living room wall. Being devout Catholics, one was understandably of their savior Jesus Christ. Since they were also committed Democrats, the other portrait was a photograph of their deceased president John F. Kennedy.

Beginning in the late '60s and continuing into the '70s, the village of Ilion underwent a period of transition in which an extensive urban renewal project drastically changed the physical face of the community. With the removal of many buildings dating back to the previous century and the closing and re-routing of various streets, the site of Kennedy's speech was so altered that it became difficult to envision in a contemporary context. For example, parts of Main Street were eliminated. West State Street has ceased to exist entirely. The alignment of upper Central Avenue was reconstituted into a sweeping curve, while the configuration of the old municipal parking lot was revamped. Only the Central Fire Station remains in its original location from that day in September of 1960 to serve as reference point.

In effort to preserve the memory of that special day for future generations, a marker was placed by a former mayor as near to the location as possible where he remembered the speaker's stand had stood. Etched into the granite slab was the following inscription: "Near this place on 9 29 60, JOHN FITZGERALD KENNEDY spoke to the people of Ilion during a campaign rally."[34] Fittingly, on June 4, 1993, as the stone was unveiled amidst the memories that flooded back, Joseph Short was present, representing a living connection along with the mayor back to that day when John Kennedy came to town, the village was afforded a window into a historic presidential campaign, and many townsfolk became imbued with the sense of promise offered by JFK and his New Frontier.

For those of us who were there, the thrill of that day will never fade. Beyond that which exists in our minds' eyes, many still have a tangible reminder that, yes, we were really in the crowd the day John Kennedy came to Ilion. In a dresser drawer or on a bookshelf, a few little metal pinbacks rest—campaign buttons once scooped from a basket offered by a Kennedy worker. These symbols of support appreciated in five weeks from badges simply touting an aspirant for the nation's highest office to that of substantiating the memory of having seen someone in person who became a President of the United States. Then, in just over three years, the pins attained an intrinsic, priceless value to many who had them. For, after only three years in office, the man who had once stood before us was gone. His untimely passing meant that he would never return to Ilion, but the pins and the memories have remained as parts of a bright and shining moment when a current in national history swept through our town.

The inauguration of John Fitzgerald Kennedy on January 20, 1961. (Source: Library of Congress)

26

URBAN RENEWAL:

THE VILLAGE GETS A FACELIFT

Hindsight is always 20/20. As an example, for an event of significant national import such as the decision to drop the atomic bomb on Hiroshima, the whys and what ifs surrounding this historic event have in the decades since formed the basis of on-going debates.

In a similar vein but much closer to home, such retrospection comes into play when the topic of Ilion's urban renewal project of the 1960's and 1970's becomes the subject. While this complex undertaking was completed almost a half-century ago, the subject still generates passionate reactions today—particularly among generations yet unborn at the time. The concept of "urban renewal"—as it applies to Ilion—refers specifically to an extensive construction project that witnessed parts of the village undergoing a thorough structural tear-down followed by rebuilding or "rehabilitation," as the process was called. By no means does the removal of a few blocks of buildings and rerouting a road equate in magnitude to the disaster of blowing up a city and killing tens of thousands of people in one fell swoop, which two of the culminating events of World War II did. Here, the comparison is one of contrasting apples to oranges. But that is not to say that the horror and revulsion that modern-day revisionists harbor at two Japanese city's misfortunes does not have a counterpart in the dissatisfaction and disappointment that recent generations of Ilionites have felt about the radically altered appearance of their village. In this sense, the juxtaposition is then more akin to apples to apples.

However, like the dropping of atomic bombs from beneath a pair of B-29s in 1945, the current revulsion is often against a picture clouded by the passage of time that contemporary opinions about the use of atomic bombs—and Ilion's urban renewal—are commonly assessed. Looking at the after-effects in either case, devoid of any reappraisal of what factors went into decision-making in the first place, can make for a skewed view when applying today's perceptions to realities that existed over a half-century or more ago. Regarding Ilion, not knowing what the situation was in the 1960s, when urban renewal planning first gained support and traction not only in Ilion but across the country, overlooks not only the prevailing thought processes of that era, but also the ongoing plight of downtowns everywhere in the last fifty years.

Many in recent generations have frequently expressed disappointment at having missed out on the idyllic life in a small-town American village that Ilion once epitomized. Yes, for those of us who lived there in 1950's, the concept of those years being filled with "happy days" is not at all that farfetched. While it is family, friends, and institutions that helped form the bedrock upon which the memories that are held so dear were built, the physical village itself certainly provided the pleasing backdrop within which our daily lives were played out.

Going "downtown" to some or "overtown" to others meant entering a different world than that which characterized our residential neighborhoods. In the business district, stores existed in tightly packed rows. Large picture windows offered displays of the goods available inside. The vehicular traffic was heavy, and the sidewalks bustled with pedestrian activity. At night, the area was awash in brightly colored lights.

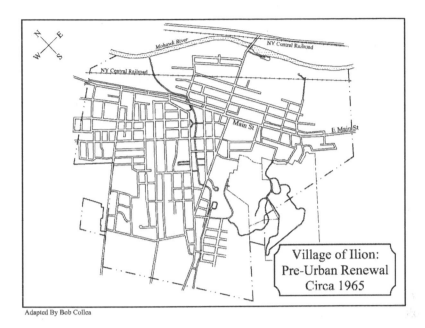

Village of Ilion:
Pre-Urban Renewal
Circa 1965

Adapted By Bob Collea

In its heyday, Ilion was a self-sufficient community, a place where groceries, dry goods, hardware, medications, lumber, toys, and clothes were available somewhere within what was a compact labyrinth of streets. The professional services of doctors, dentists, and lawyers could also be found there, often housed on the second floor over the retail establishments. Residents safety and security were protected by effective and efficient fire and police departments, also located on the fringe of that same downtown are. A highly regarded school system and competently staffed hospital offered vital professional services. Churches of various denominations met the spiritual needs of villagers. Along with restaurants, gas stations, and car dealerships, most of the requirements Ilionites had for daily living could be fulfilled by a trip to the village's central core or the areas immediately bounding it. In the pursuit of their basic needs, shoppers rarely had to leave town.

On the surface, the status quo appeared to be humming along just fine. Most residents seemed content with the appearance and functioning of their village as it existed in the 1950s. However, factors existed locally that sooner or later were going to require attention. One was aging of the downtown buildings. Many of the blocks dated back to at least the turn-of-the-century and beyond in some cases, and they were becoming of questionable, if not obviously deteriorating condition. Maben's Opera House on First Street represented a good case-in-point. Constructed in 1874, the building had long-since ceased to contain a viable business. Pigeons roosted in the upper floor. Windows were broken, and the roof leaked. By 1960, the venerable old building—once the entertainment hub of not just Ilion but the entire Mohawk Valley—was now nothing more than a gigantic eyesore as well as a safety hazard. Stripped of any valuable furnishings by previous owners, collectors, and vandals, the grand old dame stood in shame, dying a little more each day, defenseless against the slow, insidious ravages of time and the elements, and no longer valued by the town that once reveled in the glories of her stage.

In a similar vein, other aspects of the downtown area were also slowly falling into disrepair. The W. T. Grant store in the Morgan Block on the southeast corner of Main and Union Streets was another example. A three-story, flat-topped brick structure, its roof leaked like a sieve, so much so that barrels were spotted around its attic to catch the intrusion of rain and snow that were slowing eating away at the structural integrity of the building. Farther west on Main, this time at its southeast corner with Morgan Street, was another three-story building in the Cosman Block and known as "Best Supply Company" or more commonly referenced simply as "the hardware store." This building was an equally antiquated structure too. The enterprise had been there a long time. In its shellacked wooden floors, soaked with spillages of paint and turpentine, the danger of fire lurked. In an era when sprinkler systems were not mandated, the potential for a serious conflagration was a concern. Eventually, the building was in fact destroyed in a raging inferno, though not until ticketed for urban renewal demolition. By then, its loss did not matter, though it served to point out the susceptibility of many of these old buildings to quickly become enveloped in flames.

A different problem that plagued the downtown area to an increasing extent was a lack of readily available parking in reasonable proximity to the stores patrons wished to frequent. Granted a large, municipally-owned lot existed to the west behind the fire station and south of West State Street; however, though accessibility to Main Street's stores was only a short walk, leaving a car in this location meant a hike to the shops on Otsego, First, and Union Streets. Carrying any bags or packages only served to make the walk even more difficult and exhausting for some people.

Along with these local concerns that would only fester and worsen as time passed if unaddressed, several national trends were in their incipient stages of growth—all harbingers of changes that would in time adversely impact downtowns not only in Ilion but others across the country too. With or without any urban renewal, they would have affected the local community at some point between the 1960s and the present. One of these emerging cultural trends was the increased mobility that increasing numbers of Americans were starting to enjoy compliments of the automobile. Industry statistics bear out this shift, for these "freedom machines" now allowed people to range far beyond their normal boundaries to shop, eat, or attend a movie at more distant venues. "In 1960, Americans owned 61,571,390 passenger cars or about one car for every three people," but "in 1990, Americans owned 133,700,496 passenger cars, or little more than one car for every two people."[1]

Another development that blossomed concurrently with the proliferation of automobiles was that of shopping centers. Usually consisting of several stores with outside entrances strung together, these strip malls became extremely desirable destinations, especially during the holiday season. One that became a popular, almost Mecca-like objective for Mohawk Valley residents was the New Hartford Shopping Center, first opened in 1957. However, the downside of this attractive plaza for local retailers was that every dollar spent there was a dollar no longer spent at a business in Frankfort, Mohawk, Herkimer, or Ilion. While only a few people would have been prescient enough to foresee the profound effect that these and later incantations of retail outlets—such as sprawling indoor malls and big box stores—would have on consumers' shopping habits, the reality existed—again with or without urban renewal's intervention—that significant change was in the wind. The status quo, no matter how dearly some might have wanted to hold on to it, was going to be affected by forces that were both inevitable and unyielding.

For Ilion, the wheels that led to its urban renewal project were first set in motion in 1962. At that time, the Ilion Chamber of Commerce and a few interested citizens independently made proposals to the village board, suggesting that consideration should be given to a rehabbing of the downtown area. At the time, federal funding was available through loans and grants to facilitate the rehabilitation of crumbling parts of inner cities. While to some Ilion seemed slightly outside the profile of the severely-blighted urban areas intended for this improvement program, the village nevertheless was able to qualify for assistance at both the state and federal levels.

In 1964, the Ilion Urban Renewal Agency was created to conduct and coordinate the gathering of information and, if the initiative ultimately bore fruit, to then take the lead in managing the program on behalf of the village. Later that same year, "five advisory boards in the Village voted unanimously to apply for federal funds for a feasibility study to determine if urban renewal was desirable for the village."[2] Important to note at this juncture was that growing interest for rehabilitation was not driven by any one individual, but instead found backing across a widening base of community leadership.

It was in these preliminary stages between 1964 and 1967 that a figure of $125,000—representing at the time the village's share of the proposed urban renewal project—made the rounds. Though based upon inaccurate calculations, this misstep still served to put a reasonable number before the public, particularly considering the much higher revised numbers that came later. However, to some skeptical taxpayers it seemed like a bait-and-switch: getting them on board using the lower figure and then rolling out the larger number later.

Comprised of both elected and appointed members, the various advisory entities were not sown with crackpots, naysayers, and obstructionists, but instead their ranks were populated with many leading citizens, people who were progressive-minded thinkers and gave their time in the best interests of the community. The combined support of these groups—the Village Board, Planning Board, Board of Appeals, Citizens Action Committee, and the Urban Renewal Agency —provided a powerful approval too for the decision to continue with the process of further investigation. Moving forward, much of the early work in carrying the ball was efficiently and effectively done by the Planning Commission, under the leadership of Albert Theuerkauf. According to a report in *The Evening Telegram*, over time "a plan was developed at commission meetings and resulted in an application and eventual approval of the huge project."[3]

In hindsight, if any glaring gap existed at this point in a program that was gathering steam, the fact that the commitment had yet to have widespread involvement of the general public, much less received its stamp of approval, stamp of approval, led to insufficient understanding and support by some members of the community. In time, this oversight became the project's Achilles' heel. The disenchantment and opposition that would come was not so much grounded in the notion that urban renewal was inherently a bad idea in some form, but rather in the contention that too few appeared to be making monumental decisions without asking the many who would ultimately be affected as to what they thought. In a project that was to have such a profound and lasting effect on the community, the greater the numbers of its informed supporters were, the better the chance of disarming and minimizing opposition, much less continuing down a road from which no return was possible.

As momentum continued to build into 1966, the next step was to obtain funding for a feasibility study. Working with the Housing and Home Finance Agency (HHFA), the Planning Commission did some leg work for the Urban Renewal Agency, obtaining clarification on how the funding outlays worked before the village signed any contractual agreement. As this introductory phase came to be understood, the village would receive a $144,470 grant from the

HHFA with which to conduct a feasibility survey. The federal authorities also earmarked the rest of their potential share of the project, slightly more than $2,000,000, for use if and when the village qualified to go-ahead. However, if after the survey results were reviewed and the village board decided to proceed no further with an urban renewal project, then the preliminary cost would be borne by the federal government. If the opposite were true, the survey cost would be included in the overall budget.

At this juncture, the first inkling of any organized opposition to the project arose, when an *ad hoc* voters' committee requested that the village board hold a referendum. The purpose of the desired poll seemed like a timely and reasonable appeal: to determine where taxpayers stood with respect to moving forward with the project. However, the mayor of Ilion, John Morris, informed the group that no referendum would be held, at least not at this time. His rationale was that "in the event that no large sums of money will be required for an urban renewal program, the village board will not have a referendum."[4] He added: "However, if a bond issue was necessary to carry out the urban renewal project, a public referendum will be called on the bond issue, which will in essence be a vote on urban renewal."[5]

Another factor that may have influenced the mayor and certainly supported his position was the reality that Ilion was a charter village. This meant that the board had the power to act without being required to hold a referendum. Legally the mayor and trustees were working within the boundaries of their proper authority to forego this step at that time. But in the eyes of some constituents, the matter was open to conjecture as to whether—solid ground or not—this was the optimum political position to have taken, regardless of its legality.

Shortly after the mayor's statement, Ilion's share was revealed to be around $400,000. Mayor Morris may have correctly calculated that coming up with an amount in this neighborhood was not going to prove as difficult as some might thought. With the village providing a cash sum, donating village property, and taking on the separate construction of the parking area, he may have felt that the village's share could be lowered, making its monetary contribution smaller and more fiscally manageable. Very astute with regard to financial matters, the incumbent mayor may have had insights into how this could successfully play out. However, when an unexpected wave of severe inflation hit the country in the late 1960's, dollar figures for the project more than doubled. By then, Jim Garnsey was mayor. He eventually had to wrestle with raising a local share that had now ballooned to the vicinity of $800,000.

Amid these external developments, local efforts continued to move forward. Once promise of federal funding for the study had been obtained, a consulting firm out of Buffalo was hired to make four determinations: (1) what were the structural conditions of the buildings situated in the target area; (2) how many business owners might potentially be displaced; (3) how could they be relocated for both the short and long-terms; and (3) what was the marketability and reuse of the designated area going to look like.

The section identified for rehabilitation was designated as "Central Plaza Project Area #1."[6] Included in the target zone were "113 buildings...95 businesses, 5 private clubs, and 10 professional people."[7] Bounded on the east by Otsego Street, on the south by First Street, on the west by West Street, and the north by Clark Street, 19.5 acres of prime downtown property were encompassed in the proposed plan. Of note, the projection included an expansion in available parking in the main shopping district to from 250 to 535 spots...with an added bonus being the elimination of the much-despised meters.

After the feasibility report was submitted by consultants from City Planning Associates-East in 1967, representing a document three years in the making, the estimated price tag that followed for completing the project came in at $3,468,645. In accordance with the regulations in place, the cost would be borne by three different entities. The federal government's share would be 70%, the state's 15%, and the village's the remaining 15%. For Ilion, its local obligation at that point was $433,581. However, New York State— through its Department of Housing and Urban Renewal—did not commit to shouldering its 1/8 share until 1970. Though village officials operated under the belief that it would eventually do so, Ilion was for a time technically on the hook for ¼ of the urban renewal cost. This amounted to over $850,000, a figure that represented almost a seven-fold increase above the original late-'60s estimate.

Now that the project had some facts and figures that could be shared with taxpayers, the planning commission and later the village board each held a public hearing in the spring of 1968. At the second of these presentations, fifteen people were in attendance. A month after the April hearing, the village board entered into a Cooperation Agreement with the federal government, thereby committing Ilion to the project. The legality of this action—which some viewed as unilateral since the taxpayers were not given the opportunity to vote on the matter—was again completely permissible according to the village charter. This foundational document delegated the power to take such actions to the governing board, with the only stipulation being that a public hearing was required before such any legislative action could be taken. At the time of agreement, the total cost of the project was still expected to come in at $3,468,645.

While this expenditure may not seem exorbitant by today's standards, a time when billions are bandied about to complete some construction projects and the federal debt is in the multiple trillions, adjusted for inflation the price tag for the 1967 undertaking is $26,778,982 in 2019 dollars. If the project were being done now with the same regulations in place as they were five decades ago, Ilion's share would be about $3,400,000. Interestingly, a figure that would have all but paid for the entire project fifty years ago!

Unfortunately, not long after these preliminary numbers were released, an inflationary spiral hit the United States. In addition to a rise in the everyday prices that Americans had to pay for goods and services, a proportionate increase in the projected cost of Ilion's urban renewal project also occurred...and it was substantial because construction industry was one of the areas hardest hit by the economic spike. So steep were cost increases that the original $3,500,000 tab shot up to $7,200,000, making the village's share now over $800,000.

Concurrent with the announcement of this unexpected cost

adjustment, a new administration took over the reins of Ilion's government. Had it not been for the disastrous turn-of-events on the fiscal front, the Ilion Village Board as constituted following the spring election of 1971—with Mr. Garnsey as mayor—would have enjoyed relatively easy going with respect to the project. All contracts had been signed. Each of three participating governmental entities was on-board with paying its original share, and verbal assurances had been obtained that the increases would also be covered, as both federal and state officials had confirmed that their respective agencies "had never turned down a request by a community which requested additional state funds because of an increase in the net project cost."[8] Work at the site was progressing nicely, with almost half the buildings scheduled for demolition already down.

Then, virtually overnight, it became gut-check time. While the new administration was getting itself up to speed on the project as rapidly as possible, three realities quickly became evident. One was the significant shortfall in funding caused by the cost increases. Another was that the village—unlike the federal and state governments—had no significant pot of contingency funds with which to meet unexpected developments, particularly those of such a substantial nature. Finally, as an editorial in *The Herkimer Telegram* pointed out, the public needed to keep in mind that "...the present board that has been handed this situation."[9] Not surprisingly, Mayor Garnsey later recalled that these months comprised "...a very stressful time in village history."[10]

At the crux of the problem, as it stood in the spring of 1971, was a very simple yet equally difficult question that had to be answered soon: what was to be the source of the village's one-eighth share of the project's expenses? Since the inception of the plan in 1962, four mayoral administrations had come and gone over nine intervening years. No bond issues had been sought, nor had any other concrete source been established to produce the local funding. As Trustee Harold Riddell pointed out in a letter-to-the-editor in January of 1972, "to date the state has contributed $394,503, [but] the village has not yet contributed any part of its one-eighth share. However, it has not been imperative that they do so until now."[11]

The game-changer was the substantial amount of money that now constituted the village's share. Understandably, the new administration was very reluctant to unilaterally encumber taxpayers with a bond issue to generate the requisite funding. With time of the essence as the demolition work was ongoing, a solution was needed sooner than later. Finally, in the fall of 1971, a plan of action was devised that offered peace of mind to the village fathers, as well as the taxpayers if they were so inclined to accept it.

At their November 9 meeting, the board took a major step and decided to bond for $900,000, but with the window left open for the public to weigh in through what was known as a "permissive" referendum. This strategy allowed that "if anyone in the village wanted to have a public vote on the referendum, they would have to present petitions with a specified number of signatures (463) to the village clerk within 39 days."[12] In less than a month, the village clerk received petitions signed by over 600 people. With the clock ticking, a vote on the proposed bond issue was scheduled for January 27, 1972.

Knowing that the petitions' submission clearly indicated some level of opposition, possibly intermixed with confusion regarding the project, the board opted to take its case the people. In a joint statement intended to chart a course for the next few weeks, the board members said that "...we intend to have several open hearings on the bond issue, and we will do our best to get the all of facts to the public."[13] In all, a series of five public information sessions were held. Additionally, several meetings were conducted with local civic and service organizations. The board had a two-fold purpose for this communications blitz. One was to review the history of the whole urban renewal project, and the other was to allow attendees to question village officials regarding what the results would look like.

The intersection of Main and Otsego Streets, facing northwest. Only the bank remains intact of all the structures in the picture. Ye Olde Medicine Shoppe and adjacent parking lot is now located about where the rubble is piled in the lower righthand corner of the photograph. (Source: Ilion Free Public Library)

When the day of decision finally arrived on the fourth Thursday in January of 1972, the sitting village board—in office for only nine months—could rightfully feel pride and satisfaction for having taken the appropriate steps to put the matter before and in the hands of the public. Regardless of the outcome, these gentlemen had done right by their constituents. Perhaps this attempt at obtaining the public's validation should have occurred much sooner in the long process, but at this point any perceived past miscalculations were beyond revisitation—all were now water under the bridge. Regardless of the results, it was going to be a momentous day. In the words of *The Evening Telegram's* editorial on the eve of the vote: "The Village of Ilion is facing one of the most important decisions in its history tomorrow."[14] The paper went on to cast its support by stating that "... it is our opinion that the best interests of the village and its residents would be served by voting "yes" on the $900,000 bond referendum."[15]

Come Thursday morning, village officials had done all that they could. The outcome was now in the hands of the people. However, as is often the case with local elections, concern centered on what the turnout of eligible voters would be like. Often the numbers who do not cast a ballot indirectly represent more of a deciding factor than those who do. Knowing that residents were historically very phlegmatic when it comes to exercising their suffrage rights, both the supporters and the opponents of the question at hand had good reason for harboring reservations about the turnout. Percentages of under 50% were the norm, with numbers dipping into the 20% to 30% range not uncommon for votes on school budgets, village boards, and bond issues. One of the long-standing ironies in America has been, while voting is a right in a democracy, so also is not voting.

With the Municipal Building serving as the only polling place, five machines were made available to expedite the registering an opinion. Doors were open from 12:00 p.m. until 9:00 p.m. Despite worries that people might not be inclined to take the opportunity to express their opinion, a steady stream of voters throughout the day dispelled that concern. Confirmed by the next day's paper, the "2317 total vote ranks among the largest turnouts at a major village election event."[16] But as gratifying as those figures were, it was the headline of the front-page article that heralded the news which mattered most: "UR wins 1,797 to 520: Resounding "Yes" By Ilion Voters."[17] With "4,462 voters" on its registration rolls, the turnout amounted to over 50% of those eligible to cast a ballot.[18] Looking at the same numbers in a different way, 520 opposed out a possible 4462 ballots that could have been cast meant that only 14% of the eligible voters went on record as being against the bond issue.

Though the outcome had specifically been to approve borrowing the necessary funding, the favorable vote had also been an acknowledgement that the urban renewal project should be seen through to its completion. A jubilant Mayor Garnsey, speaking for most of his fellow townsmen who had chosen to support the bond issue, said that "this was doing it the right way. It was hard work, but now we know the people are behind our project. I know it will go easier from now on, and we will see progress in Ilion."[19]

Jim Garnsey left office in March of 1981, following a decade of dedicated governmental service to his hometown. Over the course of those ten years, Ilion's urban renewal project was completed. For his tenure as mayor, he deserves tremendous credit for helping the village successfully navigate the turbulent waters of the urban renewal crisis. Though he was the glue that held this effort together, the mayor has always been quick to point out that the contributions of others were essential to the positive outcome. He lauded the efforts of Trustee Harold Riddell as particularly indispensable and indefatigable throughout the process. Though separated by differing party affiliations, the two men had nevertheless bonded to promote a united front for the benefit of the village.

Ever the team player, Mr. Garnsey was quick to praise many of his contemporaries, men whose contributions helped to move the project forward to a successful conclusion during his time in office. Among the individuals that he cited in addition to Trustee Buck Riddell were his fellow board members Jim Spellman and Bob Reynolds and the urban renewal office's staffers Don Hall, Ben Stubley, and Manny Laura.

Three more years would elapse before the last act in the lengthy urban renewal saga finally transpired. Then, in 1984, Ilion's new mayor, David Wickersham, travelled to Albany with a delegation of local officials where they were to receive the final installment of funds from the state. "Now we no longer have urban renewal over our heads," Mayor Wickersham said, "We can put urban renewal to one side. We have completely closed out our obligations. This was our last step."[20] After a span of nineteen years across the administrations of six mayors, the end of a prolonged, trying, and sometimes acrimonious journey had been reached.

Yet, for those aging residents whose lives spanned the before and after years of urban renewal, forgive us for shedding a tear over what was lost. When faces of old friends can no longer be seen, we carry their memories in our hearts and minds for the rest of our lives. For us, the village of Ilion—pre-urban renewal—was one of those old friends. No matter what the issue, there will always be those among us who long for the "good old days"—whatever personal mental

images and satisfaction those yearnings may conjure up. Picnicking in
Russell Park instead of eating in a booth at a fast food restaurant...
walking to a neighborhood school like West Hill or North Street
Elementary in lieu of riding a bus to a more distant building...seeing
two movies at the Capitol Theater for fifty cents rather than viewing
one at the mall for twenty times the cost of admission.

To those too young to have experienced a walk downtown a half-
century ago through the small but welcoming web of streets, yes you
did miss something special. In its pre-urban renewal days, Ilion was a
quaint, old village...but mindfully one that was aging more with each
succeeding year. Just like many of us who still mourn its passing, the
countenance of the Ilion, circa 1959 and sans the intervening urban
renewal, would not have looked the same today anyway. The aging
process can be just as devastating and disfiguring on structures of
bricks and mortar as it is on bodies of flesh and bone.

Unfortunately, nostalgia often has a way of clouding rational
judgment. Was life in Ilion "back in the day" better than life today?
How much of that perceived satisfaction was the result of the
existence of a few streets and several rows of buildings? A little, some,
or a lot? The answer depends upon your individual perspective as
much as anything. Consider giving up your computers, cell phones,
microwaves, flat-screen televisions, Netflix, and snowblowers among
other innovations before responding. The effect that the emergence of
large malls, big box stores, and online ordering has had on our
shopping habits and preferences should probably be reflected upon
before answering too. Then the loss of jobs due to large factories,
chain stores, and small businesses closing or relocating, along with a
steady decline in the village's population, cannot be discounted.
Which more adversely affected Ilion—the loss of Remington Rand or
urban renewal?

Nor can the rise and fall of the business cycle be discounted. W. T.
Grant, the National Auto, and the A & P are all gone—not just in Ilion
but everywhere. Loblaw's and the P & C, whose properties were not
touched by urban renewal, also shuttered their doors long ago. In the
post-urban renewal era, Fay's and the Grand Union can be counted as

having failed despite having good locations. Locally-run pharmacies have given way to much larger enterprises than sell much more than medicinally-oriented products. Would the highly-successful "Home Service"—an early form of convenience store—have withstood the competition from the current genre of those businesses, such as Stewart's and Fast Trac, which are establishments with the added attraction of selling gas, backed by the resources of larger corporations, and featuring easy in-and-out locations? Without doubt, these variables would have to be weighed before any judgment is honestly rendered on the success or failure of urban renewal.

Like the nostalgic world that Thomas Kinkade evoked in so many of his paintings, Ilion of the pre-urban renewal days brings similar images to mind for both those home-towners who experienced them and many other latter-day residents who wished they had. But those flights of fantasy eventually had to come to grips with the realities that came to exist between then and now.

Suffice to say, even without urban renewal, Ilion would have appeared differently today. Fifty more years of disintegration and depreciation would have affected the appearance and value of numerous building in the central core, structures that by now would in many instances be at least one-hundred years old, if not more in some instances. Competition from malls would likely have precipitated the closing of many small, specialty businesses that once served the town, with empty storefronts following in their wake. The already tight parking problem would have been exacerbated by a further proliferation of cars, with no way to increase the number of downtown spaces. The eventual loss of Remington Rand and other manufacturing facilities would diminish the local availability of good-paying jobs and disposable incomes. While much of this could not have been foreseen with any certainty by the advocates of urban renewal, Ilion was perhaps better served by remodeling for a future in a changing world than trying to maintain an outmoded past set in an era that was already starting to vanish. While having an antique on a shelf to admire and enjoy can be satisfying, it is a an entirely different proposition to live and work in one.

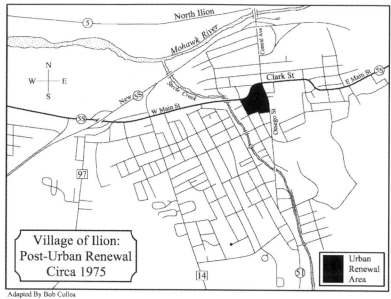

Adapted By Bob Collea

27

THE SELLING OF MAIN STREET:

IT MADE PERFECT SENSE AT THE TIME

Across the United States, communities of differing sizes— 7644 of them altogether—share the name "Main Street."[1] Almost without exception, this principal thoroughfare in most instances cuts through the heart of a city or village, often making it the primary route of entrance and exit from the town. Contrary to what might have been the popular belief, up until 1967 Ilion was not one of those communities, for it technically possessed no Main Street. A look at Polk's Herkimer, Mohawk, Ilion, and Frankfort Directory for 1959 will confirm this.[2] Instead, at its intersection with Central Avenue in mid-downtown, East Main immediately transitioned into West Main. Conjoined, the two were known to the state as part of "Route 5S—the "S" signifying the highway's location south of the Mohawk River and thus not to be confused with Route 5 on the waterway's northern side. Nevertheless, in the parlance of the times, residents usually referenced the stretch of roadway between Hoefler and West Streets as being "Main Street," with East and West Main attaching at the opposite ends.

For approximately a two-mile stretch, these three contiguous segments combined to bring locals and travelers into, across, and out of Ilion from either its eastern or western approach. Like the limbs of a tree, a score of generally shorter roads led north and south off the East/Main/West Main Street chain into the residential areas where

further branching occurred. On either side of this narrow corridor were the town's business districts: the two-by three-block core to the south where downtown's retail, professional, and service stores and offices were primarily situated; and, to a lesser extent, a number of retail and service offerings lay to the north for two blocks and west for one. At the north-eastern end of Main is the location of the Remington Arms complex, while to the south in the village's heyday were located several industrial facilities, the buildings belonging to the Remington Typewriter Company being the most notable.

At quitting time, the canyon-like road between the Arms' and Typewriter's buildings was a hive of activity. (Source: Remington Centennial Souvenir)

Considering how vital an artery this roadway through Ilion had become over the course of two-and-a-half centuries—virtually since the community came into existence—the notion that a portion of this route could be eliminated would have seemed a preposterous idea to Ilionites of bygone generations. Yet, that is exactly what happened just over fifty years ago.

While East and West Main remain largely intact, they are no longer directly connected and function as the main traffic artery through the village. The little that is left now of old Main Street amounts to nothing but a one-hundred-foot section that is effectively a dead-end. This remnant of the road that still exists is a portion that was once the right-hand turn off Otsego Street, where it intersected in a T with Main. Its south side still appears as it did before the street's closure, featuring as it does several storefronts. The opposite side, which once was also home to numerous businesses, is now a parking lot. Where the beginnings of the Arms and old Typewriter buildings exist—on the

right and left sides of Main Street directly to the east of the few
remaining stores and the parking lot—is blocked by fencing and a
gate, installed once Remington took control of Main Street from that
point to Hoefler Avenue.

The portion of Main Street that was sold to Remington Arms begins in a line
from the white-globed lamp on the right across to the east end of the low,
light-colored building on the left just beyond the second hanging black sign. At
the far end, Hoefler Avenue marks the eastern end of the Arms' owner-ship of
Main Street. Otsego Street is the turn located at the lower right. (Source: Ilion
Free Public Library)

While several generations of Ilionites have grown up knowing no
other downtown street configuration than that which currently exists,
the time once was when the entrance to Ilion from the east was both a
unique and impressive experience. Once past the Hoefler Avenue
intersection, cars proceeding west on Main Street moved through
what resembled a manmade canyon. On the north or righthand side,
the four-story brick factory, which was originally the home of
Remington Typewriter, ran almost the whole length of the street to its
intersection with Otsego, coming up short only at that handful of

storefronts that extended from the last stretch of the building west to the corner with Central Avenue. With the factory constructed only the width of the curb and sidewalk from the road, the appearance created was imposing.

On a traveler's south or left side, another industrial site located there ran the same distance and stopped just shy of Otsego Street with a more abbreviated row of storefronts than was the case on the northside. While at each end could be found sections of four-story factory buildings—this time belonging to Remington Arms—the wall of brick on this portion was broken up by a large parking lot, sealed off by a high, green iron fence. About seven-feet high, its thin evenly-spaced bars resembled long, green lances, topped with what appeared as spear-like points.

Here also could be found an extra-wide gate to permit the entrance and exit of freight trucks and workers' cars. In the back reaches of this large expanse of open space could be seen other supplemental buildings sited at the base of Armory Hill, the powerhouse being one of the more prominent structures. So large was the gun company's array of buildings—inspiring some to liken it to "a city within a city" —the whole of it "could not be completely viewed from this low-level perspective along Main Street."[3]

Adding to this unusual introduction to the village were the sights sounds of manufacturing in progress: the steady hum and whir of machinery, occasional bangs and clanks from certain processes, and the screech of saws cutting wood. Hissing steam came out of various apertures, and a heavy column of smoke wafted skyward from a giant stack. Overhead, five enclosed passageways over Main Street connected the two sets of buildings. This route not only offered an up-close glimpse of an industrial site, but also served as constant reminder that a pair of business enterprises constituted the heart-and-soul of the community, putting it on the map and providing jobs for hundreds of workers—at times in its history over thousands—and the reason for the town's existence.

Once their automobiles had successfully negotiated this narrow, 600-foot-long passageway, travelers were immediately introduced to the primary business district of the village. Bursting forth as if from a chute, the hustle and bustle that once characterized downtowns everywhere lay before visitors. Neon signs, hanging signs, varied stores, parking meters, traffic lights, a taxi stand, a bus stop, and painted crosswalks all announced that the epicenter of the village had been reached. Transiting the whole of Main Street—from Hoefler Avenue to West Street—once constituted a half-mile through the vibrant heart of the village.

Today, however, that impressive introduction to Ilion is a vista that now exists only in old photographs, vintage postcards, and aging minds. As of 1967, ownership of 95% of Main Street was transferred to Remington Arms. While the once highly-travelled passageway is still visible from either end, only trucks delivering raw materials and hauling away finished projects navigate its asphalt surface...and generally only via the eastern gate at that. When the Arms' second shift ended on the evening of June 7, 1967, their cars were among the last to make the familiar journey out of the parking lot and down the Main Street corridor, for the dawn of the next day witnessed the erection of temporary barriers. Subsequently, in more permanent fashion with a gate and chain-link fence at each portal, the passageway was closed forever to local traffic. As time marches on, the how and why this historic phenomenon occurred falls deeper into the past, making the rationale for this action foggier and less clearly understood.

As sometimes can happen with historical events, looking at them outside of and beyond the context of the times in which they occurred can make past actions seem unnecessary, short-sighted, and even irresponsible. This distorted view holds true for the decision by the village fathers to turn over most of Main Street to Remington Arms. To best understand why such an unusual transaction came to fruition, a larger event—urban renewal—which was taking place at the same time needs to be considered.

Two aspects of that extensive community revitalization project had a direct bearing on the future importance of the eastern end of Main Street. In the first and most radical change of all, the portion of this thoroughfare east from Otsego to its intersection with West Street would cease to exist, reconfigured into a large pedestrian mall comprised of an entirely new set of buildings and parking lots. The second adjustment came with the rerouting of the entrance and exit to the village, shifting it one block south to Clark Street. Sweeping curves at each end took drivers off East and West Main Streets from where they once connected with old Main and looped them south to Clark. This new connection now served as the primary route across town for vehicular traffic.

In the end, these changes in the network of streets comprising Ilion's downtown sector—in addition to giving the village a whole new look and feel—left the remaining portion of Main Street with but an almost vestigial purpose. Once part of a major community lifeline, the stretch that remained was at best a shortcut for the residents living in the eastern part of town; however, with the possibility of traffic lights needed at both ends, taking this route might not necessarily have been the quickest way to go crosstown. After factoring in the obligatory maintenance costs of plowing, sweeping, repaving, and policing this stretch, letting go of this last remaining remnant of Main Street was not such a far-fetched idea.

The possibility of selling the property to the Arms first surfaced in 1967, At the time, the New York State Department of Transportation had approved the changes that would encompass the two curves attaching both East and West Main respectively to Clark Street. Also included in the alterations in Ilion's street grids was an s-curve at the end of Otsego Street in order to effect a juncture with Central Avenue. The NYSDOT held jurisdiction in these two instances because the two roads involved were state highways—Otsego Street/Central Avenue being Route 51 and the new East Main/Clark/West Main combination now a realigned Route 5S. Once consent was forthcoming from Albany, the days of what would be left of Main Street as the village's primary thoroughfare were numbered, though no overtures to consummate a land transfer would materialize for several years.

According to Jim Garnsey, the mayor of Ilion at the time, the wheels finally started turning in earnest in 1970. At that time, he received a call from the plant manager of the Arms, addressing the possibility of Remington's acquisition of the property. Given the vital importance of the company to the economy of not only the village but central New York as well, Ilion authorities have understandably had a reoccurring history of being both sensitive and accommodating to the company's needs, so the land transfer under consideration was very much in line with this long-held philosophy.

Once a transfer was reached in principal, checking off the requisite details followed in a logical progression. An appraisal came first, followed by an agreed upon selling price of $13,000. In the spring of 1971, "the village conducted the necessary public hearing regarding the possibility of closing off the street in anticipation of the sale."[4] In December of the same year, the board of trustees agreed to the sale and gave the go-ahead to village attorney Jack Manley to draw up the appropriate paperwork.

Once the purchase was consummated, the Arms moved quickly to close off the passageway. Eventually its Main Street guardhouse was relocated so as to cover this new entryway onto the property. (Source: Ilion Free Public Library)

Finally, on March 14, 1972, the transaction was completed when Mayor Garnsey—duly authorized by the village board—signed a contract with Remington Arms. Not wanting to waste any time, villagers were notified by Remington that the closure of the street was imminent. The shutdown followed very quickly. Company workers set up temporary barriers on Tuesday, April 4, 1972. Soon the installation of more permanent metal fencing followed. However, effective as of 9:00 a.m. that first Tuesday of the month, the venerable old street— once the gateway to the town—was no longer an accessible thoroughfare. In addressing what amounted to a dramatic alteration in a long-standing traffic pattern, village engineer Ed Snow conceded that "there may be a few problems at first, but that happens whenever there is change."[5] However, he was also quick to point out that "people will soon get used to the fact that the block will be closed , and we expect no major problems."[6] Mr. Snow's conjecture proved accurate, as no significant hiccups or pushbacks have occurred over the almost half-century since the road's closure. Several generations have since grown up, not knowing any other route through the community than that which currently exists.

Over the course of several months, while waiting for the legal consummation of the land transfer, the Arms' hierarchy had moved forward on other related fronts. The most significant step which they had taken to date had been the purchase of several properties formerly owned by Remington Rand. One was Plant 3, directly across Main Street from the Arms' complex along the north side of Main Street. The plan was to use this now empty facility for storage, thereby freeing up space in the company's existing buildings for enhanced production purposes. By acquiring the abandoned portion of Main Street, possession of the road now placed Plant 3 contiguous with existing Arms' property. While no immediate plans were contemplated for any expansion of manufacturing processes across the street, Tom Pratt, service superintendent for the company, did indicate that Plant 3 would "be renovated, including sprucing up the outside of the building with new windowsills and other work."[7]

Also acquired in the same transaction was UNIVAC's former Plant 1 factory and foundry, another elongated, four-story brick building. This structure ran parallel to Plant 3, though unattached and several hundred feet to the south along the south side of Clark Street. The new owners intended to demolish this structure, pave and landscape the property, and use it as parking lot.

As one last improvement project on this parcel, a bit of face-lifting was scheduled for the area directly behind the Plant 3. On that location existed Ilion's only remaining section of the Erie Canal. For years, it had been kept as a reserve source of water in the event of a factory fire. No longer considered a necessity, the Arms served notice that it intended to fill in the couple hundred feet of the old canal bed which it had just acquired.

However, missing in the anticipation that the Arms' acquisitions could lead to increased production...if not jobs too...was its subtle, unintended, and unavoidable impact on the heritage of the village. Gone forever would be the last local vestige of the "Grand Canal," a transportation innovation in its day that contributed to Ilion's early growth. Also removed from use was a dramatic entranceway that had served the village since the early 1800s, impressively showcasing for visitors the village's industrial prosperity. No longer would the thump of tires be felt over partially covered trolley tracks on Main Street, evoking mental images and pleasant thoughts of another quaint aspect of bygone times.

Sometimes change in the name of progress confronts decision-makers with choices, options that in the end were not really those of selecting among equal alternatives. Since fifty years later Remington Arms is still in Ilion, few would argue that selling an incomplete street, filling in an unneeded ditch, or tearing down an empty building were small sacrifices to pay to help the region's largest employer continue to prosper...and by so doing, keeping the village a viable place to work and live. However, possessing such positive hindsight does not preclude room in our hearts for pangs of nostalgia for what was lost.

28

POWERS NEWS STORE:

READ ALL ABOUT IT

Almost every village of any consequence has an establishment, usually one of long-standing with a central location, that is known to all and serves as a hub of community activity. The case can be made that in Ilion, from the 1940s on into the 1970s, Powers News Store was just such a focal point. The store, before it was closed in 1983, had a lineage going back over one-hundred years. Originally known as "Jepson's News Room," the enterprise was located on the south side of Main Street next to Osgood's Hotel, currently the site of the Berkshire Bank. Then, in 1908. William J. Powers bought the business. He operated the store for many years, until selling the operation to L. Bentley Williams in 1933. Mr. Williams ran the newsstand until 1947, when the going concern was sold to Merle Moore and his wife Mildred.

Mr. Powers eventually purchased property on the opposite side of Main Street and several doors to the west of its intersection with Central Avenue. The building that housed his store's permanent home was known as the Powers/Thompson Block, with the newsstand's address being 8-10 West Main Street. Making access easy for customers was the existence of two doors. The primary entrance was directly off the village's central thoroughfare. One step up from the sidewalk, the entry was set back maybe five feet, so that a small, angled alcove funneled customers into a wide door was created. Over the store's two large windows and across the entrance niche could be found a large green awning, which in its "down" position protruded out over the sidewalk and offered shade from the summer sun. Typical of several other establishments along Main Street, the awning was operated by a hand-cranked system. The proprietor, on opening for business each day, used a log pole with a gear system at one end. He would insert that mechanism into a receptacle high up at one end of the retracted sunshade and crank away at the handle end—shaped like that of an old-fashioned hand auger—slowly lowering the canopy in the morning and then at the close of the day's business raising the covering back up.

Powers had a second means of entrance/egress that came off the large municipal parking lot that ran behind the building. Nothing fancy and narrower than its counterpart in front, this door was brown, wooden, and had a pane of glass covering most of its upper third. It also had the unusual feature of being hinged in such a way that it swung on a pivot, so that it was pushed open regardless of whether a customer was leaving or entering the store. The parking lot extended from the back of the current Central Fire Station west to West Street and north to West State Street. Using the firehouse as a point of orientation, the back side of the Thompson block and secondary door to the newsroom would have been ten-feet or so west on the left of the station and maybe fifteen feet to its south—roughly along the line of the wooden fence that now separates the eatery from the firehouse property.

Inside of the store, Harold Whittemore—long-time local newspaperman in Ilion known to his many friends as "Whit"—took note in one of his "Lifestyle" columns of a sign above that back door: "Jimmy Rand's Back Door." This name was appropriate because so Remington Rand employees came through the front door, bought a paper or cigarettes, went out the back door, and returned to work at nearby Plants 1 or 2.[1] The reference to "Jimmy Rand" was, of course, to man who was the president of the company, James Rand.

With the Coca-Cola sign hanging over its entrance, Powers News occupied a prime location on Main street in downtown Ilion. Just below the Arms and Typewriter factories, the store saw considerable foot traffic over the course of the day. Being a stop for Central Coach buses, with a nearby taxi stand another plus, further increased the flow of customers. (Source: Ilion Free Public Library)

Powers was first and foremost a source of printed materials. Newspapers, periodicals, and paperback books formed its traditional mainstays, just as its name proclaimed. But being a precursor to the modern convenience store, the newsstand vended a wider variety of goods than just paper products. Not an overly spacious place in which to maneuver, the store was tightly packed with its shelves, counters, and tables overflowing with merchandise sitting atop its creaking wooden floors. To maximize its available wares, some items even dangled from overhead racks. Aisles were difficult to negotiate, especially when other customers were heading in the opposite direction from you. Other than candy and ice cream treats, grab-and-go food items were not as readily available as they are today in convenience stores. Tobacco products, however, ranked high among the non-print articles that sold well, with cigars, pipes, and various smoking-related accessories also being steady sellers. There was also a well-stocked stationary/office supply section that purveyed such articles as black and white postcards of Ilion on a rotating iron display wheel, high-quality writing and typing paper, notecards, poster board, envelopes of differing sizes, corner hinges for mounting pictures in photo albums, pencils, pens, bottled ink, glue, and packets of colored paper.

In addition to the eclectic variety of goods that it offered, Powers served as a destination for weary travelers or the jumping off point to those heading off on an out-of-town adventure. In the early days, they rode the trolleys whose tracks ran east and west along Main Street. Beginning in 1930, a new mode of transportation became available— buses running on the Central Coach Lines between Utica and Little Falls. Potential riders could buy a ticket in the store and then wait out in front, under the awning, in the summer. During cold or inclement weather, standing inside behind one of the big store windows offered a clear view of the arriving orange, black, and white transports. In fact, the existence of the buses' schedule is what determined a 5:30 a.m. opening time for the store, done in order to accommodate those who rode the 5:38 passing through town.

One aspect of Powers News that Mr. Whittemore greatly appreciated and took pains to point out in his reminiscence of the store was the sense of humor displayed by its employees from the top down. He described Merle Moore as a quiet and reserved man, but still one who was "magnificent with his dry sense of humor at the most unexpected times."[2] He mentioned Eddie Sullivan, Miles Hammond, and Bob Sampson—all behind-the-counter guys with Mr. Moore—as being fast-on-their-feet with a timely quip. Perhaps a prominently displayed sign provided a silent but revealing window into the whimsical approach to life practiced by those who worked at Powers: "The Wonder Store: You wonder if we have it, and we wonder where it is."[3]

Along with the smiles and laughter, regular customers enjoyed the fact, like the "Cheers" bar of Boston and tv fame, that Powers News was a friendly kind of place where you were recognized. Along with the demise of mom and pop groceries, those days are largely gone now. Corporate ownership has replaced local, family-owned outlets. A part-time work force that comes and goes with frequency often has no interest much less the time on the job to remember who you are. "Powers News was fun place," remembered one Ilion woman, "a place where they always knew your first name...and everything else about you too...and you didn't mind."[4]

The Moore's had a nice run at the prime location on Main Street. But all of that changed in 1973. Urban renewal in Ilion took out the core of old buildings in the downtown area. Among these was Thompson Block of which Powers News was a major tenant. Forced to shutter their doors or move, co-proprietors Merle and Mildred decided to take up residence in the new downtown plaza. Located on the south side of the chain of attached stores, Powers News occupied the space now filled by Franco's Pizzeria. With the Great American below it and Fay's Mall in front, the location was not unattractive. However, for shoppers using the parking lot adjacent to and behind the post office to access Fay's, their path would not necessarily have taken them past Powers' new location.

Another downer for the newsstand happened when Central Coach Lines added a fleet of new and larger buses. Since it was no longer possible for these bigger vehicles to swing in front of Powers, the Oasis Laundromat across the parking lot, West Street, and situated in a more accessible locale became the new station. Not surprising, Powers lost revenue. Nevertheless, the Moore's ran the store together until Mr. Moore's passing in 1980. In failing health herself, Mrs. Moore kept the store going until 1983, when she decided that it was time to close the business.

After the store had shuttered forever at 6 p.m. on Sunday evening, March 13, 1983, a fitting epitaph was penned for the *Observer-Dispatch* by Harold Whittemore: "But Powers, to a generation before me, to my generation, and a generation after me, was something special. A brightly-lit haven on a stormy winter night, a gigantic rumor mill, and a theater for some of the great local comedians...who worked there.... but the village will survive...Lifestyles and habits will go on, but it will never be quite the same without Powers News."[5]

That change is inevitable, few would disagree. The idea that change is easily accepted, however, represents a horse of a different color. For those who come after the alterations have been in place for a while, they may hear about what they missed, but never get to experience it. Those who suffer the greatest pangs of disappointment and sense of loss the members of the bridge generation. Those of us whose parents once took him to Warner's Men's Store for his first suit and who plied the aisles of Grant's looking for affordable Christmas presents, bought baseball cards in one penny and nickel packs at Klippel's, picked up a bag of newspapers for delivery from *Observer-Dispatch* office...and purchased the latest pro football magazines at Powers News are destined to spend the rest of our lives with our bodies inexorably planted in the 2000s...and our minds often drifting back to the unforgettable middle years of the preceding century... otherwise known as "the good old days" of our baby-boomer generations youth.

29

BOOTS DAY:

HOMETOWN MAJOR LEAGUER

One of the glories of youth is that we are imbued with vivid imaginations and unfettered dreams. No matter how outlandish, our callow minds are able to perceive achieving a goal that some would see as a reach beyond our grasps. As we grow older, roads taken and not taken often lead us to unintended destinations—not necessarily those about which we once fantasized. Unfortunately, for a many people, hopes of the past often become unfilled aspirations in the future.

Try as we might, the cards do not fall as we had envisioned. Each year thousands of boys come to the abrupt realization that their skill set in baseball is not of high school or college, much less big-league, caliber. However, for one Ilionite—Charles Frederick "Boots" Day— this would not be the case. His childhood ambition to become a major league baseball player was a goal from which he never wavered.

After moving easily through Little League and Babe Ruth levels of competition, a stellar high school career followed which saw him amass a record of 17-1 as a pitcher. After his graduation in 1965, Boots spent the following summer keeping his skills finely tuned by playing for Koehler's Grill in the highly-competitive games of the Utica (NY) MUNY League to stay sharp, biding his time until his

First year in organized baseball.
(Source: Boots' Scrapbook)

eighteenth birthday arrived on August 31. Then he could legally sign to play professional baseball. Nevertheless the summer's experience proved worthwhile. Performing in the roles, of pitcher, first baseman, and centerfielder on a championship team, he was duly rewarded for the exemplary caliber of his play by being named the league's MVP.

For Boots, the first benchmark in the climb up his professional career ladder finally came that fall. The memorable date was September 12, 1965. Twelve days after his birthday, he signed a contract with the St. Louis Cardinals' organization. As an undrafted, amateur free agent, he did not have much bargaining leverage. By his own admission, "the bonus I received wasn't much, and I didn't care about the money."[1] Not surprisingly, he added: "I just wanted to play."[2] The dream was still alive...and he received 400 bucks a month, which Boots confessed was "like a million dollars to me."[3]

The Cardinals sent him immediately to St. Petersburg to learn the ropes and play a bit in the Florida Instructional League. When spring came, he was off to South Carolina as member of the team's affiliate in the Western Carolina League. Between 1965 and 1969, his ascent to the big leagues was one marked by steady, measured progress, moving as he did from A ball in Rock Hill to AA in Little Rock and the cusp of the bigs at the AAA-level in Tulsa. Playing in Oklahoma for the Oilers meant that Boots was now just one rung below joining the parent club in St. Louis.

After five years of progressing through the minors, Boots' long-awaited arrival at the top came in 1969, when received a call-up from the St. Louis Cardinals in mid-June of 1969. In the same vein as Ebby Calvin "Nuke" Laloosh of "Bull Dunham" fame, the twenty-two-year-old centerfielder had his dream within reach—he was going to "The Show!"

Though his debut on June 15 was only as a pinch-runner, the inauspicious circumstances did not matter to him. Standing on second base, he had arrived. As low-lying on the field as the bag was, the little canvas bump located at twelve o'clock on the diamond represented the conquering of a metaphorical mountain for Boots. He had finally attained the highest level of his chosen profession. He was participating finally in a major league baseball contest! However, after an eleven-game trial, he was sent back to Tulsa for more seasoning.

Then, during the off-season, he was unexpectedly dispatched to the Chicago Cubs. Boots received the news while playing winter ball in Venezuela, where he was part of a team comprised of American professionals and local youngsters. His reaction to the trade was to say that he was "very happy" about being sent to Chicago.[4] In this sense he was in somewhat of a minority, for many players do not react so positively to news about such a radical, life-altering change. "The conflicting feelings of being wanted by your new team, but not wanted by your old one sometimes put given individuals on an emotional rollercoaster."[5] But Boots has always been for the most

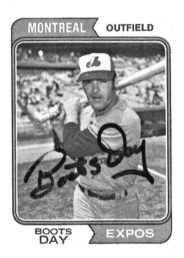

His autographed 1974 Card. (Source: Topps trading card used courtesy of The Topps Company, Inc.)

part a positive, the "glass-is-half-full" kind a guy. He understood that at its bottom-line baseball was a business, so like it or not he would report to the Cubs and show them that they had acquired a quality player. He did this successfully, making the Opening Day roster on his new team. Still this accomplishment was ultimately rewarded in a rather unexpected manner, as he was abruptly shipped to the Montreal Expos eight games into the 1970 season. While being traded twice in a five-month span is a bit unusual, Boots thrived with his new team north of the border, ultimately playing there for five seasons.

With his career closely followed at home—the local paper carried his picture and current stats daily on the sports page—his fans wanted him to know that they were pulling for him. The result was a birthday telegram. Received by Boots on August 31, the wire was signed with over 1000 names. The celebratory message was sent in care of Bob VanHorne, a member of the Expos broadcast team, who took the message down to Boots. At the time, the birthday boy was about to take his pre-game swings in the batting cage. The announcer later recalled that "Boots was really proud of the telegram, so much so that he took it to the dugout after batting practice to show the other players."[6]

At the close of his first full season with the Expos in 1971—one which saw Boots finish with a robust .283 average—the people of his hometown were eager to recognize his singular accomplishment. To do so, they chose to by honor him with a "Welcome Home Boots" weekend on October 7-10. The festivities began with the county legislature officially proclaiming, "Boots Day Weekend," followed by the Village of Ilion giving him the key to the town and making him "Honorary Mayor" for a day. The schedule for the three days was packed with an instructional clinic for young ballplayers, two banquets, a golf tournament, and a reception. For his many fans and admirers, the various events provided several opportunities to interact not just with any major leaguer...but rather their own hometown major leaguer. In response to this overwhelming display of local esteem and admiration, Boots spoke from the heart when said: "This is the proudest moment of my life, and I want to thank each and every one of you who made this weekend come true."[7]

A follow-up event the next season provided an equally memorable occasion for Boots and his local fans. August 5, 1972, a Saturday, was designated by the Expos as "Boots Day Day" at Jarry Park. Descending upon the city for the Expos' game against the defending World Champion Pittsburgh Pirates were over 1000 people from the Mohawk Valley. Six busloads and countless automobiles brought them north of the border to cheer on their native son. Included in the recognition that day, Little League players from Ilion and Mohawk were afforded the opportunity to march around the field before the game, along with the Ilion Firemen's Band. Boots was honored in a pre-game ceremony, during which time he was presented with a gift from his local admirers. After the game, "a Hospitality Room [was] open to all area fans at the Windsor Hotel in downtown Montreal."[8] Along with Boots there to greet people, members of the Expos management and the team also made appearances.

Boots went on to play major league baseball for six years. He had hoped that his time competing at sport's highest level would have lasted longer, but his career passed in what he later said seemed like "a snap of a finger."[9] Nevertheless, his half-dozen seasons in the majors is on the high side of the "5.6 year average for players" and in the process qualified him for a pension, which was locked in after four years.[10]

During his playing days, Boots professed that he preferred having a bat in his hands rather than a glove on one of them. As he phrased it, "I loved to hit."[11] Together he and his favorite 33-ounce, 35-inch sized Adirondack stick had many memorable moments while members of the Expos. Among some of his notable accomplishments, Boots had: 16 sacrifice bunts in 1972; 13 pinch-hits in 1973, with one being a homer in the bottom of the tenth inning to clinch the victory for his friend and pitcher Steve Renko; and two difficult catches and three runs batted in to support teammate Bill Stoneman's no-hitter in 1972.

Even though Boots favored the offensive side of the game, he made a name for himself as a defensive standout. Blessed with speed and quickness, he patrolled centerfield in a most-capable manner. Bob Prince—the astute, award-winning "Voice of the Pirates" for twenty-eight years—extolled this sometimes overlooked aspect of Boots' game when he said: "He's one of the few centerfielders who can consistently take away hits or rob batters of extra-base hits that they really earned."[12] Often times Boots, in fearless pursuit of a fly ball, would collide with an outfield wall, on one occasion to the extent that he wound up unconscious. But, as a reporter observed, "that's Boots Day's way."[13]

Playing hard was the only way Boots approached the game, as he is shown doing in this full-tilt slide safely into home against the Cubs. (Source: *The Montreal Gazette*)

After being released in the spring of 1975, Boots caught on with the Detroit Tigers organization. He played five more years for its affiliate at Evansville, Indiana, hoping to resurrect his career. Then, in 1980 at the age of thirty-three, his playing days ended. In so doing, the first two stages of his baseball life were complete. The first phase had been getting to the point where at 18 he had signed a pro contract, while the second stage consisted of his playing career—four years in the minors on the way up, five plus years at the top, and then five more trying to make it back. When he was asked what made him make the decision to move from a role as a player to that of coaching, Boots gave a candid assessment of his prospects in achieving a call-up at the age of thirty-three when he said: "I knew that he wasn't going anywhere," meaning back to the majors.[14]

However, unlike most of his teammates and competitors, after his playing days were over Boots was not ready to leave the game that he loved. The next phase began forty years ago, when Boots began his journey through baseball's non-playing, support periphery. Over the intervening four decades, he has filled roles as a scout, coach, and manager. The reason that there is no fourth stage is because Boots has yet to retire. Currently, he is serving as the bench/first base coach for Evansville Otters. Based in Indiana with the Frontier League, 2021 marked his ninth year with the team...and represents not only his fifty-fifth participating professionally in some baseball capacity, but also stands as the same number of one-year contracts that he has inked! To put those annual signings in perspective, the managerial career of Walter Alston with the Los Angeles Dodgers has been much-heralded for his having signed twenty-three one-year contracts—a benchmark that Boots surpassed over thirty years ago!

So what exactly is a bench coach? Boots described his role as that of "assisting the manager by being his eyes."[15] In this capacity, one of his important duties is the proper positioning of the defense. Depending upon a given batter's known tendencies as well as the count, outfielders are frequently moved in or out or to the right or left. Boots also shared with me that he still enjoys pitching batting practice and hitting fungoes. Not bad for a septuagenarian.

Since the Frontier League once had a rule that its players cannot be over twenty-seven, the dugout was often full of young men to whom Boots can serve as both a coach and father-figure, for he is old enough for all of them to be his offspring. Much like another character from "Bull Durham—the inimitable "Crash" Davis—Boots brings to the dugout the cachet of not only having played in the majors, but also the sagacity that comes with having spent over a half-century in the game. Rather than rue the passage of time and the slow erosion of his once finely-honed skills, Boots has accepted where he is in life and his beloved sport today. In his official capacity as bench coach and de facto role as hitting instructor, he serves as a teacher for the younger players. In return for imparting his accumulated knowledge, he gets eternal youth in his mind's eye. As he put it, "the game keeps me young."[16] That being said, Boots knows that Father Time is waiting somewhere not far down the road ahead. The day is approaching when he will take off a baseball uniform for the last time. He recently said that he would probably return for a fifty-fifth year, if "they will have me," and then hang up his spikes.[17] They did...and he did.

Then, now that the final page of the long third phase of his career is finally written, what will be said of the prolonged time spent in and around the game by this man, one that led a writer to identify him as a "baseball lifer"?[18] While Boots Day's playing career is neatly accounted for in *Baseball Reference*, statistics do not begin to tell the depth and breadth of his story nor the meaning of his life and career to others.[19]

As a player with the Expos, he was always very approachable by the fans. When contingents from Ilion frequently made the four-and-a-half-hour trip to see him play, Boots would meet them in the hotel lobby, answer their questions, and in general welcome and orient his fans to the city. At the park, he would gladly pose for pictures and graciously sign autographs. Already a highly popular hometown hero, Boots also became a fan favorite among Montrealers. It was observed, when he was introduced over the public address system at the park, that "his name when announced excited the youngsters who responded with yells and applause."[20]

In addition to the many fans that these public gestures of good will made for the young outfielder, Larry Chaisson, then public relations director for team, was another individual who was very appreciative of Boots positive attitude and conduct. He noted that "Boots is a model type of ballplayer who has always cooperated, and when we call on him to make public appearances, he always cheerfully agreed."[21] For Boots, ever humble and grateful to be where he was, the looking-glass aspect of being in the public's eye was to him all a part of living the dream which he readily accepted. Unlike some athletes and entertainers who often have oversized egos commensurate with their success, Boots kept both feet on the ground and his head out of the clouds. To gather information for an article about Boots during his heydays with the Expos, a local Mohawk Valley newspaper once sent a reporter to Montreal. One of the questions that the inquiring scribe posed was: "Has success spoiled "Boots" Day?" From speaking with team personnel, fans, and employees at the Windsor Hotel where Boots stayed, journalist Dick Frosch concluded that "the answer would have to a positive NO!"[22] To those in Ilion who knew Boots, this assessment came as a reaffirmation, not a surprise.

Even to this day, when Jarry Park, the Expos, and his playing days are warm but distant memories, Boots still retains his cordiality with fans. He frequently receives requests for his autograph on cards and photographs, to which he is pleased to respond. On a recent talk show interview, a caller asked Boots, if he came down to Evansville, would the coach sign a baseball for the man. Ever polite and accommodating, Boots' response was completely in character: "Yes, I would love to sign the ball if you made the drive, no problem, as many as you would like."[23]

With respect to those cherished pieces of cardboard— "bubblegum cards" as they were called—they served as a kind of validation for a player, affirming for all to see that, yes, he had finally made the big time. Boots said that it "felt pretty good" when he first saw his picture on the yearly Topps product and shared that he still possesses all of his. When asked how the portraits were taken during his playing days, he said that the league handled the sessions. Usually they occurred when teams in each league cycled through New York City to play the Mets or Yankees, which is also where Topps' headquarters is located. Unlike graduation or wedding pictures wherein the subject(s) gets to pour over multiple shots and select those most-favored, Topps—not the player—made the decision with regard to which pose would be printed.

Another admirable aspect of his baseball career is the degree to which it demonstrates his enduring love of the game, a passion that has never left him even after more than fifty years of growing old around ballparks. "Sure," some would say, "what's not to like about being a major league ballplayer?" But, as easy as that question may be to answer, what explains Boots' still being in a dugout so many years after that career ended? In a country where many American workers are dissatisfied employees, finding an individual who is not disaffected is somewhat of a rarity these days. Boots, however, has long seen the world through a different lens. He would readily agree with an adage which prophesizes: "Find a job that you like, and you will never work a day in your life." In a world where a Gallup Poll found that an astounding "...85% of the people hate their jobs," Boots has proven to be a refreshing anomaly.[24]

First and foremost, his is a success story about a boy from a small town who had dream, one of which he never relinquished. By exhibiting steadfast determination, perseverance, and diligence, Boots stayed the course until he achieved his goal. Though one of the knocks against him was his comparatively small stature, he never let that conception serve as a roadblock or excuse. Little guys everywhere can take heart from his experience. The same fans who appreciated and rooted for diminutive players like Nellie Fox and Luis Aparicio who preceded Boots, Fred Patek and Joe Morgan who were his contemporaries, and modern-day players like Jose Alteuve and Dustin Pedroia would have seen the same character and attitude personified by the Ilion native. For all of them, the true measure was not the size of the dog in the fight, but the size of the fight in the dog. While serving as an inspiration for others is not a posture that is usually planned, the benefits derived can be as incalculable as they were unexpected.

Bart Shelley was a man who loomed large in Boots' life. First, as the principal of the grammar school which he attended—West Hill Elementary—and later as the scout who signed Boots to his contract with the Cardinals. Mr. Shelley used to attend most of our Babe Ruth games. He lived only a block north of the South Fifth Avenue ballfield. He would bring his folding chair and set up under a tree down along the foul line in right field. From that vantage point, it is likely that he saw every game in which Boots played for his three years in that league along with those of his varsity career, which gave the astute scout as good an idea of what Boots could do as anyone had.

In addition to his roles in education and sports, Mr. Shelley also earned the rank of "Colonel" in the United States Air Force Reserves. One area where all his backgrounds coalesced in this man of strong principles and commanding presence was in the value that he placed on character. In a small town like Ilion, what this well-known, esteemed, and respected individual thought of you mattered— immensely. When Boots was but eighteen, Mr. Shelley had this to say about him: "Youngsters can learn a great lesson from studying Boots and his habits, on and off the field. He has always displayed a desire, a devotion, and a dedication to hard work and high ideals."[25]

As a talented youngster of seven, Boots got special permission to play Little League a year earlier than the established bylaws permitted. He was that good even then. Now, sixty-seven years later, that little boy who loved baseball so much that he slept with his glove under his pillow has become a sagacious elder statesman of the game, steeped in the life and lore of baseball as he experienced it across a wide spectrum of time, geography, and competition. While he no longer sleeps with his mitt, he has retained the spirit that the practice embodied—an abiding love for the sport. Well-nigh past being a prospect and long-since settled in as an old pro, he has joyfully embraced what has amounted to almost a pre-ordained destiny, one that he would never have traded for the world. Starting out as baseball enthusiast, he saw that proclivity evolve into a career and, by so doing, engaged in one that never necessitated that he report to work in an office or factory—only having to "go to the park." While growing old in a baseball uniform may not appeal to everyone, it has clearly suited Boots, and, as result, it is with pride and satisfaction that he humbly accepts the reverence and respect that accompanies the sobriquet of being known as a "baseball lifer."

One of the indicators of achieving success: being asked to autograph a baseball. *Author's note: Boots retired at the end of the 2021 season. (Source: Author's Collection)

30

PAINT NIGHT:

GRADUATES LEAVE THEIR MARK

I n Ilion, "Paint Night" is a tradition of long-standing, one that can be traced back one hundred years to at least the end of World War I. When interviewed in 1991, by *Herkimer Evening Telegram* reporter John McGraw, Ilionite Doris King said: "I can still see those numbers—'1918' and '1919'—on that concrete wall opposite the Masonic Temple."[1] Since Ms. King used the word "tradition" to describe the event in which she participated, the conclusion which could logically be drawn was that its origin preceded the Class of 1918 by some years, pushing it somewhat closer to the turn-of-the-century.[2]

Held on the Thursday evening prior to graduation, the event allowed that seniors should artistically affix their names to a choice piece of cement or asphalt, usually the sidewalk leading up to the graduate's residence or a nearby, hard-surfaced driveway. Sometimes the property had other planes available. Across from my parent's house on South Third Avenue, the lucky student who lived there—Richard Hall, Class of 1953—had a two-foot high and ten-foot long retaining wall along the sidewalk upon which to print his name. Being six-years old at the time, awakening one June morning to see that "Dick 1953" in green paint had appeared across the way was a mystery, until my mother Ruth Bennett Collea—IHS Class of '38—explained the significance of this graphic art. In the vein that Grauman's Chinese Theater and the "Hollywood Walk of Fame" enshrined famous people, pavement paintings were a local way that graduating seniors announced for the world to see that a successful student lived nearby.

As for Dick Hall, the class valedictorian certainly had a primo palette. Due to its vertically, the wall had the effect of being a billboard, so for the next several decades we were reminded daily of the young man and his year of departure from high school. Also noteworthy, considering the problems arising in later years, the barrier on which he wrote his name was on family-owned property and not a public roadway or bridge.

The Otsego Street wall. (Source: Author's Collection)

Given the varied talents of the individuals involved, the renderings—usually made with whatever house paint and brush dad happened to have in the cellar or garage—were sometimes very attractive, with multiple colors and blocked letters and numbers. Great care was exercised by some in producing this simple form of folk art. Usually the grad's first name and class year constituted the entire creation. Dick Hall's effort, while standing the test of time, was not particularly attractive, as it was rendered in monochromatic, one-foot high scrawl of forest green. But unquestionably, it served its purpose—long and well.

But somewhere between Dick Hall's artistry and the late '80s, the wheels started coming off this quaint little tradition. Mies Van Der Rohe, a renowned architect of the 20th century, was considered a minimalist in his approach to building styles, once saying that "less is more." However, in marked contrast, Ilion seniors started embracing a

To some folk art...to others vandalism. (Source: Author's Collection)

philosophy that was just the opposite when paint night rolled around. If decorating several sidewalk blocks in front of one's own house was deemed as a good idea, then expanding the practice to other parts of town and surfaces seemed like an even better one. Since neither the school district nor the village condoned or discouraged the event, paint night consequently had no official rules or parameters, just a basic tradition that students extended over time.

Over the course of 70+ decades, this very novel and seemingly harmless activity gradually broadened in scope. Friends began going over to their classmates' houses and adding their monikers to any available space, which often encompassed the street in front of the graduate's house. This became an early form of computer "likes." Popular students had a significant number of signees in the proximity of their property. Others who may have lived farther out from the village core or were less a part of the in-crowd had fewer and sometimes no added names. At some point, the would-be artists— some townsfolk not too enamored with the tradition called them "vandals"—starting casting about town for additional canvases. Each year seemed to inspire the current crop of graduates in trying to outdo their predecessors by finding more places to apply their brushes.

According to Mrs. King, the "wall" was the premier public go-to place upon which to apply painted names. Beginning at the Benedict Avenue corner and continuing north along the east side of Otsego Street for maybe 100 feet is a retaining wall. Perhaps three feet high, this barrier was intended to hold back slippage and erosion off the embankment above it. Each year, the newly inscribed names would remain displayed there for a while, and then village crews would paint over them with a light color. By covering this latest batch of signees, two results were achieved. First, the wall, seen as defaced and unsightly to some, was neutralized as a perceived eyesore, but, on the other side of the coin, the clean surface was now ready for the next graduating class to autograph.

While a tendency exists to blame many societal ills on the unrestrained, anti-authoritarian youth of today, the adage that "kids will be kids" is a transcendent observation that is most applicable to the evolution of paint night. For as early as 1937, problems had developed with the by then firmly imbedded custom, leading to a report in the local paper that the Ilion Board of Education was considering instituting a ban on paint night. If passed, the death knell would have sounded for this rather unique and much anticipated rite of passage. Overzealous students had prompted residents' complaints about too much of a good thing gone bad. In addition to the public outcry, school authorities had their own issues, one which led to "several members of the class being ordered Monday to remove red letters painted on the side of the high school building."[3] While many of these teens would in few short years become contributing members of the "Greatest Generation," some may still have had some growing up to do.

But this little pre-World War II episode was soon forgotten. Unfettered by any specific guidelines, painters continued broadening their quest to leave their mark on the village. Warren Schulz, author of Ilion—The Town That Remington Built and himself an IHS graduate, commented in 1977 on the evolution of this local practice, writing that "an interesting tradition...was the painting of graduates' names on their home sidewalks, [but] unfortunately the custom has gotten out of hand in recent years."[4]

What had started out as a brief few minutes of relatively confined painting in the early 1900s had become a much bigger operation by the 1980s. The rule of thumb for selecting appropriate surfaces expanded into an open-ended quest to find suitable surfaces anywhere and everywhere. Front sidewalks, driveways, and the wall became but minimal starting points. From there, the entire community became a massive canvas. Roadways, not just in front of a graduate's house, but all over the village became fair game. Two of the most prodigious accomplishments of this genre were painting down the highly traveled Second Street hill and the long, winding approach to the high school via Phillip's Street. These two endeavors took a lot of time, the coordinated efforts of multiple participants, and a fair amount of paint.

Another element that abetted this expansion in terms of size and scope was the lack of any curfew, other than that which a given individual's parents might specify. This came to mean that what started out as "paint night" often wrapped around into "paint morning." Students were known to be on the streets until the wee hours. After participating in a long night of such artistic revelry, undoubtedly more than one participant did not answer the bell for school that day.

When the erstwhile Van Goghs and O'Keefes had finally stowed away their brushes and cans, the result was that the seniors had literally painted the town. Unfettered by a rules or regulations, enterprising students had understandably let their imaginations and inhibitions run wild. But for many residents, the pendulum had finally swung out too far. Not only had all roads become fair game, but telephone poles, lamp posts, and street signs were sometimes inscribed with names and dates. Occasionally, a giant blotch of color existed where a can was inadvertently spilled. Footprints appeared here and there where newly applied paint had been accidentally trod upon by artists. Random drips and drabs were common.

In the late 1980s, a new round of complaints started coming into the school and village offices. Some of the most-irate calls were from people who drove to work early in the morning before the paint had dried. Many had splatters of color tossed up by their cars' tires onto the lower portions of their vehicles. Some, who did not have a graduate, objected strenuously to having the immediate vicinity of their property being included in the random wave of creative artistry that had seemingly run amuck. Still others felt that what had just occurred all around the village was nothing less than organized, condoned vandalism. Of special concern to everyone were the racial epithets, obscenities, and personal attacks that were expressed in a few of the writings on school property.

Along with input from the public, Ilion police chief Lloyd Wadsworth voiced concerns which the village board also took under advisement. The chief noted that "there had been arrests in the past where students refused to leave businesses, while there have been several 'close calls' between vehicles and students on hills, where visibility is restricted"—even more of a possibility after dark.[5] The situation was quickly becoming one that was going to require governmental intervention.

The school board was the first to act. In May of 1990, an unequivocal prohibition on painting anywhere on school grounds was promulgated. Though the district had security guards of its own, the Ilion Police Department was also requested to help monitor school property. Later that spring, the village board followed suit, though not to the extent of implementing an all-out ban. Attempting to mitigate the excesses of "Paint Night," without abolishing a popular tradition, a curfew was set at which time painting was to cease, and road inscriptions were ordered to stay within three feet of the curb and off main thoroughfares.

However, these limited parameters did not prove strong enough, so in 1991 the village board readdressed the issue. The result was a compromise. Painting was now permitted between 10 o'clock and 2 o'clock, which was a concession to students. In return, all art work was restricted to the graduate's home sidewalk or driveway or, with the owner's permission, the property of another individual. While still not satisfied with the curtailment of what had in the past been a highly anticipated night of unfettered fun and camaraderie, to their credit the seniors over the next few years nevertheless adhered to the new constraints. As time has passed, what was at the time a significant change has become the accepted norm.

As often happens when a major alteration or curtailment in a past practice is instituted, the initial pushback comes immediately following the change, usually by those who had expected to be operating under the old set of rules. Since historically for paint night no previous limitations existed, not surprisingly any reining in of excesses would be viewed as undesirable and stifling. However, as time goes by, the changes become ancient history, and those who were not around in the good old days only know the current status is as it applies to them.

For all of angst that the governmental restrictions promulgated in the early 1990s caused seniors—decrying the destruction of a long-standing activity was a common rallying refrain—the reality was just the opposite. Instead of the wide-ranging, all-night social event that it had morphed into over the years, the more personal, low-key experience was reaffirmed. By curbing the excesses that threatened the continued existence of "Paint Night," not only was the tradition preserved, but it was also brought back more in line with the acceptable format and boundaries that had existed at the time of its inception.

After the last set of changes were made, the mayor challenged the seniors to set the proper tone. They were advised that "it is not often that you have the ability to have a tradition in your hands to maintain."[6] By virtue of their overwhelmingly positive compliance, a bump in the road was weathered without incident. Heading into its second century, "Paint Night" continues as a tradition grounded more in keeping with the past than ever before.

Far less intrusive to the village as a whole, seniors now confine their painting to their own property, allowing a tradition of over hundred years to continue in a modified but acceptable format. (Source: Author's Collection)

31

HOT DOGS IN ILION:

HE HAD THE MEAT

Want a cheeseburger? Not too difficult to find with so many fast-food outlets so readily available. But, if you craved a hotdog—straight up, laced with mustard, or garnished with various fixings—going to the ballpark of your choice was one sure way, unless of course you happened to live in Ilion. Then you would have had the option of going downtown to the Central Plaza parking lot. There, rain or shine, five days a week from May to September a purveyor of wieners would have been found in the person of Norm Thomas—aka "the hot dog man."

Over four decades—from 1977 to 2017—he regularly plied his trade. Norm opened for business at eleven in the morning and closed-up shop at three in the afternoon. He proudly recalled that he "never missed a day," with his honest rationale being that with a family he "needed the money."[1] By keeping his equipment in the garage behind Jerry Walsh's First Street barber shop, Norm only had to push his cart a short distance to his favorite spot in front of what was originally called "Fay's Mall."

No jingly music or flashing lights were necessary to call attention to his whereabouts, nor did he pay for any advertising in the media. Word of mouth was all he needed, and, over the years, he counted several generations of the same family as customers, as fathers brought their children and then later their grandchildren. With his ubiquitous patio-style umbrella and two-wheeled silver cart, Norm was never hard to find. Unlike many of his brick and mortar neighbors, he had no prescribed uniform nor fancy duds, wearing by his own admission whatever he pulled out of the closet on any given day.

A native of Rome, New York, Norm's connection to Ilion began when he became an employee of Remington Arms. Then chance and a whim changed his life forever. It seems that he and his family were in Fort Plain one day. While there, they came upon a vender selling hot dogs from a cart—a little metal wagon that quickly caught Norm's eye, along with the unique form of entrepreneurship that such an enterprise offered.

In short order, Norm found a distributor for the type of cart that he would need. Before long, Ilion had a resident hot dog vender. As a testament to the adage that "they don't make things like they used to," Norm used that same cart for most of his forty years in business. Over the decades, not unexpectedly, his propane-heated unit suffered breakdowns. But with no repairman readily available, the task of staying open for business became, as Norm said, a "fix-it yourself" proposition."[2] Umbrellas were another matter, however, and over the years he had to replace his signature protective canopy on several occasions.

With respect to the bill of fare, the choices Norm offered were hot dogs, rolls, condiments, soft drinks, and snacks. Among his more popular garnishes were spicy onions, sauerkraut, and chili, but the one which he called "the mess"—which amounted to a dog with everything on it—was the most requested topping of all. About the only change of significance over time came with removal of New England-style buns from the menu, as they had gotten increasingly more expensive. When asked if he had ever thought of expanding to a bigger cart or larger menu, he responded that he liked it best as a manageable one-man operation. Keeping the menu simple also held the overhead down and kept the product fresh from frequent turnover.

Being a small operation, the cost of doing business was relatively controllable. Since Norm was his only employee, wages per se were not an issue. A limited selection kept spoilage and unsold items to a minimum. A vender's permit was required from the village each year, and, while there was no charge for this authorization, he did have to pass a yearly, unannounced state health department inspection, which had its own requirements: a fee and photograph of the cart in its established location.

Norm Thomas and his ubiquitous cart. (Source: Mrs. Joan Thomas)

Like many folks who enjoy their life's chosen work, Norm eagerly looked forward to setting up shop each day. But experiencing enjoyable employment comes with a long-term downside: the passage of time often occurs more quickly than realized. Beginning with the spring of 2018, the old cart and the older man can no longer be found in downtown Ilion. They were now in retirement. Once he began to feel physically less able to handle his daily routine, Norm knew that the time had come to call it quits. But he readily admits that giving up the job has had a decided consequence. "I miss meeting people and talking to them," he said.[3] Like many retirees, the abrupt passage from being active with a daily sense of purpose to the isolation of no longer having a place to go or tasks to perform on a regular basis was disconcerting.

On the other side of the coin, in losing its venerable hot dog man, Ilion has seen the passing of a village institution. Like the milkman, the "Greeks" restaurant, Marian the "flag lady," and the Lighthouse Miniature Golf Course, Norm Thomas has now joined an esteemed company of beloved village icons. He, too, will now become the revered subject of many nostalgic digressions about people and places, the topic of conversations that begin: "Do you remember...?"

32

FROM INCINERATION TO THE BAG SYSTEM:

A BUNCH OF GARBAGE

Once upon a time, the human inhabitants of the earth did not concern themselves with the damage which they were inflicting on their planet. Through a combination of ignorance and negligence, Ilion was as guilty as the next community in violating the environment. One of the worst instances involved the process once used to eliminate garbage.

First, the Ilion Municipal Dump was sited between the Mohawk River and residential streets in the southeastern part of town, little more than a half mile from the heart of the main shopping district. The spot consisted of two open-air dumps. One was comprised of raw organic material and combustible wastes that were destined to be burned in the incinerator, while the second pile consisted of non-burnable trash. Piling up garbage, even for a short turnaround-time before burning it, created several problems. One was the presence of rodents, rats that sometimes were known to leave the dump and made their way north and west into inhabited parts of town. Another was polluted leachate, created when rains caused a contaminated run-off that found its way into the ground water as well as the Mohawk River. Then, there was the unavoidable odor which wafted up into the air, riding wind currents in different directions.

Along with the festering mound of refuse, a partner in fomenting environmental damage was the adjacent incinerator. Easily identified by its tall stack, this facility spewed toxic emissions into the atmosphere from the burning garbage that was processed in its furnace. Using a conveyor belt, the waste was dumped on a hearth. As the refuse was burned, its ashes fell through a grating and into a pit below. While the residue still had to be disposed of, its volume per cubic yard was considerably far less than that of the same measure of unburned raw garbage and trash. Burying the material in a nearby landfill, begun in the 1970s, was a relatively inexpensive proposition at the time, compared to the budget-straining costs that would come later.

When the dump was eventually closed, the incinerator still held the potential as a saving grace to the garbage problem. However, having been built in 1937 as a Depression-era PWA project, the furnace's efficiency had gradually decreased over time. On top of that, state regulations had become more stringent, particularly regarding clean air standards which underscored the outmoded nature of this vintage equipment. Acceptable in its day, the antiquated incinerator was by the decade of the 1970s seriously in need of an upgrade if the village intended to continue operating the plant.

Then, when the incinerator was finally shut down in 1971, the local, in-house options were gone. Succeeding village budgets were perforce obligated to include a substantial line item to cover the cost of burying garbage in the area landfill. However, village officials were not ready yet to give up. If the incinerator could be sufficiently modernized to comply with the New York State Department of Environmental Conservation's regulations, then Ilion could once again burn its garbage. Not only would this reduce landfill costs, but also open the door to processing refuse from neighboring communities for a fee. This concept created the tantalizing possibility that Ilion could turn a profit on the operation of its incinerator, or at worst the added income generated from taking in and burning its neighbors' combustibles could be used to defray or maybe even cover its own landfill fees.

Not a lot to like about Ilion's former village dump—much too near to residential
areas, too close in proximity to the Barge Canal/Mohawk River waterways, and
in the lower left an outdated Incinerator. (Source: Ilion Free Public Library)

Once the dump and then the incinerator were shut down, all
collected refuse was then transported to what was known as the GFIM
(i.e.-German Flatts, Ilion, Mohawk) landfill on Mortz Road outside of
Mohawk. After being picked up by Ilion's DPW, no interim off-loading
or secondary handling occurred. The village trucks went directly to the
landfill, which amounted to a twenty-four-mile round trip. Even with
the low mpg of the packers—which were never intended for long-
distance, over-the-road hauling—and the $3.00 per cubic yard for
deposited garbage charged by the landfill, the cost to the village for
disposing its refuse in this manner was initially deemed manageable.

But the anticipation of increases in this service could not be
discounted. Sure enough, by 1980, that charge was up to $62,000 per
annum. In a related matter, since village trucks had to make the round
trip to the disposal site, expenditures for the vehicles' gas, tires, and

maintenance also had to be factored into cost projections. For the 1985-1986 fiscal year, landfill expenses had risen to the astounding, almost astronomical amount of "$204,905 in garbage collection costs."[1]

As the decade of the '70s passed, thoughts of bringing the incinerator back on-line were seriously entertained. In and of themselves, these burners were not unilaterally verboten by state regulations; however, there was a catch. They needed to meet certain emissions standards, which a device over forty years old was not likely to do. With the expectation of getting the incinerator up to the proper state codes, Ilion officials became involved in back-and-forth discussions with the state between 1981 and 1986.

In 1981, hopes soared when Ilion was issued a permit to operate its incinerator. Over the next five years, Ilion officials' pursuit of the proper upgrades that would suit state regulations became like a horse chasing a carrot on a stick—held so close that the vegetable could almost be touched, but just far enough away that it remained forever unreachable. Unfortunately, while Ilion was trying to get its old incinerator—of the "open hearth" variety—up and running, the laws were changing faster. By 1986, not only was Ilion's permit about to run out, without ever getting an opportunity to be used except for an experimental run, but open-hearth furnaces were now also banned.

This meant that a whole new system would have to be installed if the village still wished to stay in the incinerator business. Alan Staring, a very knowledgeable and progressively-minded village administrator, had been dealing with the whole garbage disposal matter for years. In his words, the state's pulling the rug out from under the village's good-faith efforts to get its burn facility up and running left local officials "...upset and angry."[2] The Department of Environmental Conservation, not to leave the village high and dry, offered an alternative plan: Ilion could build a new plant, but it would be limited to the burning of paper and cardboard.

Yet, even with those limited parameters, Mr. Staring estimated that these two categories of refuse alone "take up 60% of what we take to the landfill."[3] If Ilion was allowed to burn these two items, then the benefits realized would be two-fold: the village's landfill costs would be more than halved; and the life of the landfill would be extended proportionally. The stumbling block to all of this was funding a state-of-the-art incinerator. According to Staring's calculations "a new incinerator for Ilion would cost at least $400,000 plus a new roof and about $16,000 to $30,000 worth of smokestack work. Not to mention the purchase of scrubber and electrostatic machinery to clean the smoke and air of particles and pollutants."[4]

Given the choice of floating a substantial bond issue or moving on to other solutions, the decision was made to see if further options existed. To cut down the flow of solid waste, which in turn would reduce landfill costs, community-wide recycling came to forefront as a partial solution. As easy as it seems at face value, recycling was not an overnight panacea. But fortunately for the village, Mr. Staring was again on top of this situation too, having done substantial research and investigation into what was necessary to have a viable recycling program. He discovered that a successful recovery effort involved many differing component parts: "...collection equipment, storage, transportation, prices, manpower, education, participation, markets, separation...have to be covered."[5]

Then, amid the disheartening incinerator debate with the DEC and the closure of the GFIM landfill, the new destination for Ilion's garbage—the Mohawk Valley Sanitary Landfill in the Town of Frankfort—doubled its tipping fees "from $5 per cu. yd to $10 a cu. yd."[6] The situation was rapidly becoming fiscally acute. As framed by Antoine Clark, the astute managing editor at the time for *The Evening Telegram*, the problem was that "escalating landfill tipping fees have caused costs of garbage disposal to skyrocket, leaving Ilion with some tough budget decisions."[7]

*　　　＊＊＊*

AS IS OFTEN the case with the cost of doing business, expenditures in general have the disheartening tendency to rise. Consumers encounter this every time they go grocery shopping, when the price of a given item increases or the size of the can or box decreases so that the price can remain the same. Shoppers then have the choice to buy the product at its new cost, accept the reduced size, buy a similar but different one, or go without. Other alternatives would be to seek a pay raise or add a part-time job, thereby increasing their income and not letting price escalations from necessarily deterring them from making a preferred choice.

In essence, governmental entities face the same problems, though in different configurations. For the village of Ilion, these considerations came in the form of employees' wages, insurance coverage, facilities upkeep, equipment maintenance...and landfill tipping fees. To provide the requisite funding to carry out citizens' expectations regarding services, the primary means is through taxation. If the cost of conducting village operations increases, then more revenue is needed. As the village cannot have a bake sale or sell enough "I Love Ilion" bumper stickers to make up the difference, the board is left as its primary source of gaining additional funds the pockets of residents. The other alternative, reducing services, is of course also a possible way to lower expenses. But in the final analysis any cuts in police, fire, and dpw services—which usually represent the largest costs in a municipal budget—are very difficult and often controversial decisions.

THE BUDGET STRAITS to which Mr. Clark was referring was the conundrum with which the village board was faced in 1987: raise taxes to cover cost increases or scale back services. While an unpopular choice with the public in either case, the matter was not even that easy. For making any decisions on a new budget much more difficult was the fact that increases in the assessment rates over several years had inched the village ever closer to its constitutional tax limit. The troubling situation that now faced elected officials was a need for the intake of greater revenue without the ability to increase the levy much higher. In this worst-case scenario, cutting back on services was looming as the only viable option. If the crisis did not hit for the upcoming fiscal year, a day of reckoning was not far in the future.

As it turned out, the storm was weathered on that occasion without a need for deep cuts, much less an austerity budget. But with the potential for a worse version of the same predicament likely to arise soon, discussions had to begin immediately to address the matter before it was too late. Fortunately for the village, the late Alan Staring was serving as village administrator. To his credit and the community's benefit, Mr. Staring had over the years already been giving thought to the garbage collection vis-à-vis the rising cost of tipping fees at the landfill. In fact, "to his credit," as lauded by an editorial in *The Evening Telegram*, "he has done much of what has been accomplished in Ilion on his own...he has a lot of things that could occupy his time besides a recycling program..."[8] Starting with paper products in 1986, Mr. Staring eventually broadened the program to include glass and metals.

The success of the recycling program in Ilion was evident in reduction of wastes taken to the landfill. Five years after its introduction, the data for 1993's recycling efforts was showing a marked increase in separated trash, while garbage loads to the landfill decreased proportionally. "Prior to recycling's advent," reported a local paper, "Ilion was taking an average of 25 tons a month to a landfill, now it's only an average of 15 tons of garbage, [with] 10 tons of recyclable material [removed]."[9]

No question that this was a positive step, one that benefitted both the environment and taxpayers. However, recycling was not intended as a stand-alone program. Mr. Staring, working closely with the DPW's superintendent Jim Rowland and village treasurer Gale Hatch, also devised another cost-effective plan known as the "bag system." With two sizes of plastic bags available, residents could tailor their refuse needs accordingly and save money in the process. As an adjunct to this approach to garbage collection, Mr. Staring had also arranged for residents, who so chose, to purchase trash compactors, the use of which could reduce their need to purchase bags as often and over time save the village and them money by having to send a smaller volume of waste to be buried.

The operative concept behind the bag system was not complicated. Essentially the total cost of disposal—which collectively included landfill tipping fees, sanitation workers' pay, gasoline, and equipment maintenance and replacement—was calculated. This figure was then divided by a projection for the number of bags that would be needed and at what cost they had to be sold to achieve the disposal figure. In its initial stages, some degree of educated guesswork was required to balance the numbers. But the kinks were successfully worked out, and over time the collection/recycling programs had a two-fold impact—one fiscal and one environmental. By helping the village budget stay below its constitutional tax limit and residents reduce their share of the waste stream, money was being saved. By recycling, villagers were making their contribution to saving the earth.

Another more subtle argument in promoting the bag system was that this approach allowed the cost of disposal to be done without making any money. As the mayor at the time confirmed, "on the subject of accruing a profit from this service, that is not its intent. It is set up to be a break-even proposition."[10] This approach contrasted with the other alternative, which was to allow a private waste hauler to contract with the village, thereby taking over garbage collection and disposal. Since these businesses had to turn a profit, the prevailing thinking was that the village could perform the same service cheaper, and, while costs would inevitably go up over the years in both the public and private sectors, the village would still be able to keep them lower than an enterprise in business to turn a profit.

Fast forward to 2019, over thirty years after their implementation, recycling and the bag system are no longer innovations, they have instead been accepted and assimilated into the everyday lives of the people. In Ilion, a generation has been born and grown to adulthood not knowing any other means of disposal. Just like few of us baby boomers from the '50s remain who recall not only that there used to be an "ash truck"—a vehicle into which metal tubs containing the residue from coal furnaces was dumped, after first being laboriously hauled upstairs and outside—but also the long-gone service when sanitation workers brought garbage cans and ash tubs out to the curb and later returned them back behind residents' houses once the containers were emptied, the time will come, too, when no one remembers how refuse was collected before 1987.

Yet, however, mundane the history of garbage collection may seem, Ilionites should never lose sight of the fact their community was a leader in both recycling and the bag system. After their inception and proven worth, communities across the country and even Canada contacted the village to learn more about the program. Some, such as the Province of Quebec, even sent representatives to the village to study the operation first hand. Alan Staring was in demand as a conference speaker. While Ilion is far better known for its production of guns and typewriters, saying that has a unique history in the collection of garbage is not just talking trash!

DOWN THROUGH THE YEARS

The Remingtons at Ilion will build another addition to their sewing machine works.

— ROME SENTINEL – JUNE 18, 1874

Frequent brawls and knockdowns occur along First Street and Union Streets. Where is the policeman?

— ILION CITIZEN – APRIL 2, 1880

The Mount Kisco Weekly says that it is reported from a reliable source that the Ilion Armory of Ilion, N.Y., is negotiating for the Empire Sewing Machine Works, near Katonah, and in the event of a purchase, move a portion of their works there.

— THE PEEKSKILL DEMOCRAT – JANUARY 8, 1881

John Schimdt, president of the village, is our official representative at the nation's capital for the inauguration ceremonies for President Garfield.

— ILION CITIZEN – JUNE 3, 1881

The Remington Arms works in Ilion is working full-time in all departments, adding more men almost daily to its force.

— THE SYRACUSE COURIER – DECEMBER 23, 1883

The Ilion Citizen leaves all other papers in the rear by having all of its type set by machinery, and its press run by the aid of electricity.

— CANAJOHARIE COURIER – SEPTEMBER 30, 1884

Part of the Agricultural Works are working until 9 p. m. on making electric air brakes to be placed on passenger cars of the Central and West Shore Railroads. Mr. J. F. Carpenter is the inventor.

— ILION CITIZEN – OCTOBER 7, 1887

The Ilion Citizen and the Herkimer Citizen have both enlarged to eight pages. Typographically and editorially they are bright and clean and give evidence of the prosperity that is attending the efforts of their publishers.

— THE ROMAN CITIZEN – JANUARY 13. 1888

Has Ilion a game warden? If so, he had better keep an eye on Steele's Creek Sundays. Open violation of the law is becoming very annoying to law-abiding people. In these good democratic times there is plenty of time to do all necessary fishing on weekdays.

— ILION CITIZEN – JULY 20, 1894

The "Spinsters," the new organization of Ilion Wheelwomen, had their first club run Wednesday evening.

— ILION CITIZEN – APRIL 30, 1896

The attendance at the Arbor Day exercises of the Ilion public school this morning was the largest ever seen at the opera house on a similar occasion, over 1,100 being present. The exercises were very interesting and frequently applauded.

— UTICA DAILY PRESS – MAY 6, 1898

On an upstate campaign swing in his bid to be elected Governor of New State, Theodore Roosevelt was scheduled to leave Utica at 9:30 a.m., his next destination was a brief stop in Ilion before heading eastward down the Mohawk Valley to Albany.

— BUFFALO EVENING NEWS – OCTOBER 21, 1898

It is a common occurrence for a resident of Ilion, when traveling, to have strangers to this section of the country question the statement that Ilion with a population of 5,000 employs 2,000 men. At the same ratio employment of male labor to population, as compared to other cities, with its factories giving employment to 2,000 men should have fully 10,000 population.

— THE ILION SENTINEL – APRIL 21, 1901

Ilion having a population of over 5,000 voters will be required to register in person before they can vote. Registration days are October 12, 13, 18, and 19, and all residents of the village or town must go to the place of registration in person and register their names in order to vote at the next election.

— ILION CITIZEN – AUGUST 16, 1901

Gov. Odell was on his canal trip through Ilion, going west, between 6 and 6:30 p.m., Tuesday. With him was a party of state officials and friends. The company is traveling in two steam launches, the "George W. Aldridge" and the "State Inspector." The time of the arrival of the party became noised about and quite a crowd gathered on the dock and saluted his excellency who stood in the bow of one of the boats and returned the compliment by lifting his hat.

— THE ILION CITIZEN – SEPTEMBER 6, 1901

The annual parade of the Ilion Fire Department, which took place on Saturday last and which attracted more than 6000 visitors to the typewriter town, may be the means for bringing to this town the Tri-County Convention...The companies wore their new uniforms of flaming red shirts, black trousers and helmets. The steamer, hook and ladder apparatus, and hose carts were nearly hidden beneath the decorations of flowers and bunting.

— SYRACUSE EVENING-HERALD – OCTOBER 5, 1901

The saloon keepers of this village have been busy for the past few days renewing their licenses for this year. There are in the neighborhood of 20 saloons in town...

— UTICA OBSERVER-DISPATCH – APRIL 29, 1902

An unprecedented boom is on in Ilion, and over 100 new buildings are already contracted for, in addition to those now in the course of erection. The armory is being rushed with orders...the company has so many orders to fill that they will in all probability run overtime for some time to come. The typewriter works are behind in orders to the number of nearly three thousand machines..."

— THE OTSEGO FARMER – MAY 21, 1902

Paid Advertisement: Ilion Dental Rooms, 3 First Street, Ilion, NY - Best set of teeth, $3.00. We guarantee a perfect fit. Teeth extracted free and without pain. Open Evenings. Dr. F. A. Olmstead

— ILION CITIZEN – AUGUST 1, 1902

The bandwagon which was conveying the Ilion baseball team to Suburban Park, was struck at the Broad Street crossing in Lestershire [near Binghamton] by Erie train No. 2. The driver was instantly killed, and six others were injured, one seriously. Both horses were instantly killed…The Ilion team will be able to play tomorrow.

— ROCHESTER DEMOCRAT-HERALD – JULY 31, 1902

The Ilion Military Band will give another open-air concert on Main Street opposite the lift bridge tomorrow evening. The one given last week was to have been the last but owing to requests and the pleasant weather it was decided to have one more.

— UTICA HERALD-DISPATCH – SEPTEMBER 4, 1903

The water in Steele's Creek is flowing in a large quantity, and with a roaring noise like a large cataract, not equaled by any freshet this year. It has rained continuously in this vicinity for nearly 35 hours. The river flats are overflowed, the lower end of River Street being underwater.

— UTICA HERALD-DISPATCH – OCTOBER 10, 1903

A horse attached to a cutter occupied by three young people became frightened at one of the big interurban cars on East Main Street, near Hoefler Avenue yesterday afternoon and ran away. The cutter was overturned, and the occupants thrown out. The horse started up Main Street at a fast clip, and in front of the Bank Block a gentleman who was waiting to board the trolley car ran in front of the animal and captured him. Not much damage was done.

— UTICA HERALD-DISPATCH – JANUARY 2. 1903

The Big Fires of Frankfort defeated the Ilion All-Stars in a game of basketball at Harter's gymnasium Saturday afternoon by a score of 10 to 5.

— SYRACUSE EVENING HERALD – JANUARY 26, 1904

The most successful celebration and convention held by the Tri-county Firemen's Association during its existence of thirteen years was held at Ilion Thursday and Friday of last week. Ilion is noted for doing well whatever it undertakes and it is fair to say that no other village or city in the three counties, where the convention has been previously held, managed the affair so well and where hospitality was so generously dispensed as at the village made famous by the manufacture of typewriters and firearms.

— ILION CITIZEN – JULY 11, 1907

One of the delivery horses belonging to H. B. Chandler, the groceryman, ran away this morning. The driver was in a house on Otsego Street, and the animal was frightened and ran over Otsego and Morgan Streets to Main Street and finally turned into a driveway in the rear of the post office. While coming down Morgan Street, the rig collided with the carriage belonging to Dr. Warner. Only slight damage resulted.

— UTICA HERALD DISPATCH – DECEMBER 15, 1910

"Disgrace!" Collier's [i.e. – nationally-published magazine] says in referring to Ilion School problem ...according to the report made by its superintendent of schools to Collier's, there are but 1,767 seats to accommodate 2,000 students or a shortage of 233 seats.

— UTICA OBSERVER-DISPATCH – SEPTEMBER 9, 1923

War contracts which have been obtained by the Remington Arms and Ammunition Company are expected to result in a big business boom in Ilion, and some believe the size of the village will be doubled as a result of the construction of a $1,000,000 plant in which to carry out the contract. Upon the reported terms agreed upon by one of the warring nations of Europe—reportedly Great Britain—the plant must have an output of 1,500 army rifles per day...

— SOUTH NEW BERLIN BEE – DECEMBER 19, 1914

With the rapid increase in the population of Ilion, the need for an increase in the police force becomes more apparent every day. With a population of over 10,000, Ilion has only five policemen including the chief. In all places of any size it is estimated that there should be one policeman for every 1,000 inhabitants. Ilion has one for every 2,000.

— THE OTSEGO FARMER – JUNE 16, 1916

Reduced fares New York Central Lines – Albany...$1.90 (from No. Ilion) Round trip going every Sunday and holiday to September 4, inclusive. Return limit same day.

— ILION CITIZEN – JUNE 16, 1916

The issues of the state campaign will be placed before the voters of Ilion Monday noon [October 23] when Governor Whitman and Hon. William Calder, nominee for United States Senator from this state, will expand the doctrines and advocate political desires for which the Republican party stands…Will deliver speeches from Bridge Square.

The Democratic candidate for Governor will speak at corner of First and Morgan Streets…Hon. Samuel Seabury…will address an open-air meeting Friday evening Oct. 20 at the Temple corner at 6:30 p. m.

— ILION CITIZEN – OCTOBER 19, 1916

Commencing Thursday, a war tax of one cent on every ten and fraction thereof must be collected on every theater ticket. Motion picture theaters come under this ruling.

— ILION CITIZEN – NOVEMBER 1, 1917

Many an Ilion motorist is sprouting a few more gray hairs after riding down Second Street or along Otsego Street any evening or on weekends and desperately trying to guess what madly pedaling bicyclists will do next. We suppose parents are just as worried and the police are doing what the can. But it is of no avail. The younger generation seems to think that the streets were made for bicycles and a blast of the horn is usually only a signal for the rider to dart one way or the other or stop in the middle of the street and give motorist a dirty look. Ilion has had fatal bicycle accidents and will certainly have more unless the young men—and women—currently riding the two wheelers exercise a little more judgement and concern…

— THE ILION SENTINEL – APRIL 28, 1918

The plans for the "Take in a Roomer and Boarder" campaign inaugurated by the Remington Arms-Union Metallic Cartridge Company were successfully launched. Twenty-five employees of the company have been designated to canvass the town...It is hoped to call on every house in Ilion and ascertain how many rooms there are to rent and how many boarders and roomers can be accommodated. It is the intention of Remington Arms to take on a number of additional help in the coming weeks, and it is necessary for the people of Ilion to cooperate in order that these men may have room and board.

— UTICA HERALD-DISPATCH – JUNE 7, 1918

Saturday afternoon at Hunt's field will take place one of the most interesting football games ever staged in Ilion between two rival high school teams. The opponents are Ilion and Fort Plain high schools. The students, with several new songs and yells, will attend. Notwithstanding the weather conditions, a large crowd is expected, and all enthusiasts are invited. As both Ilion and Fort Plain are fast teams, an excellent game is promised.

— UTICA DAILY PRESS – NOVEMBER 23, 1918

That there is a desire for Sunday movies in this village [Ilion] was made very plain yesterday afternoon and evening. In the afternoon both theaters were filled and, in the evening, never was there such a throng waiting to get into the Opera House. There were two shows at this theater. Both times the house was crowded to capacity and many were turned away...Charlie Chaplin in the new and popular play "On Guard" was the feature picture. Chaplin was a scream in this production.

— UTICA HERALD-DISPATCH – DECEMBER 16, 1918

About the first of the month, at 64 Railroad Street [i.e. Central Avenue], a new store dealing in infants' and children's wear, will be opened by Mrs. A. G. Fish of this village. This store will be a new departure for Ilion. Mrs. Fish is currently in Boston and then will go to New York. She will remain away for about three weeks while purchasing goods preparatory to the opening.

— UTICA HERALD-DISPATCH – MARCH 20, 1919

The New York State Railways made a concession in the matter of the increase in trolley fares among the valley places. The noon round trip between Frankfort and Ilion, Ilion and Mohawk, and Mohawk and Herkimer has been lowered from seven to six cents.

— UTICA HERALD-DISPATCH – JANUARY 28, 1920

Need a taxi in Ilion? Dial 444, and VanAtten's seven-passenger car will be at your service.

— UTICA MORNING TELEGRAM – MARCH 17, 1921

Today we received some news relative to a radio club which was organized in Ilion. This club was organized last October and has grown so rapidly and fast that the members have arranged to hold a fair and convention the latter part of the month. Why? Because Ilion has gone wild over radio.

— NEW YORK EVENING MAIL – APRIL 1, 1922

The Remington Cash Register Company, Inc., has just brought out another new cash register, model "C."

— UTICA DAILY PRESS – AUGUST 11, 1922

Ilion is blessed with four industrial plants that would do credit to many cities several times its size and which support not only Ilion but its sister villages from an industrial and business standpoint. Those industries are the Remington Typewriter Works, Remington Arms plant, Library Bureau, together with the A. N. Russell & Sons, Co., the Sterling Mills, all in fine condition with a fine outlook for 1924.

— RICHFIELD SPRINGS MERCURY – MARCH 13, 1924

Former governor and president. Colonel Theodore Roosevelt, on a speaking tour, took time out to visit a patient in the Ilion hospital. John Aversa, a local farmer, had been anxiously waiting to hear Mr. Roosevelt speak, but, just before the appointed day, Mr. Aversa had injured himself dynamiting stumps on his property. Colonel Roosevelt kindly obliged his admirer with the unexpected visit.

— THE YONKERS STATESMAN – OCTOBER 22, 1924

The park commissioners announce that they wish to ascertain the names of parties who have been using the canal as a dumping ground...That portion of the canal west of Weisbecker Hill to the Junction is planned for use for skating purposes, and the glass and sheet metal which has been recently dumped in the canal is a menace to the safety of children who may wish to skate.

— UTICA DAILY PRESS – DECEMBER 10, 1924

Semi-pro hockey will make its debut in Ilion within the next two weeks, according to an announcement yesterday by the Remington Rand Plant 1 Athletic Association. Officers of the association stated that the work of completing two skating rinks on Typewriter Park was under way.

— UTICA DAILY PRESS – DECEMBER 15, 1927

Fireworks were in order at 9:30 Wednesday night on Main Street... a trolley wire broke and coming in contact with the metal frame of the Smith and Robinson campaign banner caused a short circuit, causing heavy flashes. The banner caught fire but was quickly taken down with very little damage done to it. Trolley service was held up on the westbound tracks for a short time while temporary repairs were made...

— UTICA DAILY PRESS – SEPTEMBER 20, 1928

A campaign to sell people who work in Ilion, but who live elsewhere, the idea of living in Ilion will soon be undertaken by the Ilion Chamber of Commerce as a major activity for 1929.

— THE OTSEGO FARMER – FEBRUARY 1, 1929

J. G. Prindle, principal of Ilion High School, has received a handsome silver-mounted basketball on a green bakelite base, to be awarded to the winners of this season's championship in the Central New York Basketball League. The trophy was presented by the Alumni Association of Rensselaer Polytechnic Institute of Troy. The teams competing for the trophy are Frankfort, Ilion, Mohawk, Herkimer, Little Falls, Fort Plain, and Utica Free Academy.

— UTICA DAILY PRESS – JANUARY 26, 1931

Arriving aboard the executive yacht Inspector II, Governor Franklin Roosevelt, his wife Eleanor, and other state officials transferred at the Ilion dock on the Barge Canal to waiting automobiles, which would then take his excellency on his second annual tour of New York's hospitals

— ALBANY TIMES-UNION – AUGUST 5, 1931

A supposed gun battle proves to be a mock affair...the mystery of the night ride of racketeers through the residential part of Ilion late last night seems to be solved. The story that seems to solve the affair is that some of Ilion's younger set attended a dance at Columbia Springs in the Ilion Gorge last night and decided upon putting on a mock battle. Two cars, a coupe and a roadster, were involved and the racing and the shooting as described were real, but instead bullets blank cartridges were used.

— UTICA DAILY PRESS – AUGUST 11, 1931

Ilion will welcome tomorrow afternoon Mrs. Franklin D. Roosevelt, wife of Governor Roosevelt, who will address the Parent-Teacher Association of the Parochial School at its October meeting to be held in the auditorium of the school at 3 p.m....Mrs. Roosevelt, who is both a mother and teacher will speak on Social Guidance." An invitation has been extended to other parent-teacher associations and the people of Ilion to attend.

— UTICA DAILY PRESS – OCTOBER 13, 1931

An electric storm struck the Mohawk Valley just before 7 o'clock Friday night of last week with terrific force...Between Mohawk and Ilion, many cars were stalled due to wet ignitions. Ilion fared the best of any of the three villages. There being very few flooded streets.

— THE OTSEGO FARMER – JULY 7, 1933

Four youthful robbers, all masked and carrying weapons, raided the Ilion Hotel here early today, but their hold-up netted them considerably less than $50.

— THE SARATOGIAN – FEBRUARY 17, 1934

More than 35,000 letters were put through the cancelling machine yesterday at the Ilion Post Office yesterday to climax the busiest day since 1929...More than 35 employees were kept busy throughout the day, but despite their efforts the mail became slightly congested in the early evening, and the men were forced to work several hours overtime last night.

— UTICA DAILY PRESS – DECEMBER 22, 1936

The first group of regular mailmen in Ilion—four in number—made their rounds on bicycles, wore gray helmets similar to those worn by London's Bobbies, and blew a whistle to let patrons know that a letter or catalog had been delivered.

— THE ILION SENTINEL – JANUARY 7, 1937

Ilionites are reading more than ever, according to the November report of Mrs. Luella Griswald, librarian here. Books circulated last month totaled 8176, of which 5624 were adult and 2652 juvenile.

— THE ILION SENTINEL – DECEMBER 9, 1937

The new municipal skating rink was opened Thursday night...Joseph Ana, superintendent of the street department, and Earle P. Watkin, superintendent of schools, allowed skaters on the rink at the rear of the high school building after inspecting the ice Thursday night.

— UTICA DAILY PRESS – DECEMBER 30, 1938

In 1889, Walter Stilson wore the first police uniform to be seen on the streets of Ilion

— THE ILION SENTINEL – NOVEMBER 19, 1941

The sub-zero weather of the past few days has made it possible for Charles Wheelock, of Upper Otsego Street to start the harvesting of some 40,000 tons of natural ice from his five-acre pond at the extreme southern end of the village.

— THE ILION SENTINEL – FEBRUARY 5, 1942

150 residents of the Village of Ilion have volunteered to be Air Raid Wardens and must complete an intensive training course before being certified to perform their duties.

— THE ILION SENTINEL – MARCH 5, 1942

The Post Office and the Central New York Power Corporation building's basements and the old Catholic church have been offered as air raid shelters the Ilion War Council has been informed. The preparation of luminous signs to direct persons to those centers is one problem air raid wardens are considering.

— UTICA OBSERVER-DISPATCH – AUGUST 9, 1942

The designation of a home in each block for school children to assemble in during an air raid test or alarm was decided upon at the annual fall meeting of the Central Council Parent-Teachers Association, held Monday afternoon....Each home will be marked with a red, white, and blue victory sticker, or similar mark, and the children will know that sign.

— THE ILION SENTINEL – SEPTEMBER 17, 1942

Decades ago, on the sports' page of local newspapers, players who engaged in the revolutionary indoor game invented by Dr. James Naismith at Springfield in 1890 were referenced as "basketeers!"

— THE ILION SENTINEL – FEBRUARY 4, 1943

Last year Ilion boys and girls turned 860 pounds of "grease" in the annual Halloween Fat Salvage Contest...This year the contest started earlier, and indications are that the youngsters are doing a very thorough job of canvassing. Consequently, the committee is hoping for a thousand pounds.

— THE ILION SENTINEL – OCTOBER 21, 1943

Over the quota by half. That is the result of the Sixth War Loan in Ilion...Total bond sales amounted $1,210, 622.75...Individual sales $449,945.75 and corporate $760,677.

— THE ILION SENTINEL – JANUARY 4, 1945, P. 1

It is time to make postwar plans now! ...Let us take our own community as an example. At the close of the war some 1400 or more of Ilion's young men will return to their homes. Ilion's job is to be able to have jobs ready for these men when they return.

— THE ILION SENTINEL – JANUARY 4, 1945

Speeding motorists with be shown no leniency when brought to Ilion court, according to acting chief Silas Mott of the Ilion Police Department, as a campaign is being launched during the week of to curb all speeders in East Main street, on Route 5-S...Ilion has two motorcycle patrolmen, one on days and the other on night duty. It is planned to schedule regular patrol of the area during both day and night hours to eliminate the speeding condition.

— SYRACUSE HERALD-JOURNAL – SEPTEMBER 10, 1945

The official opening of Ilion's Victory Loan drive took place yesterday at the Remington Rand Plant 1 cafeteria, as three wounded veterans of World War II told plant employees to continue to invest in Victory Bonds.

— SYRACUSE HERALD-JOURNAL – NOVEMBER 1, 1945

WANTED —Boy over 16 for work in diner. Apply Mickey's Diner. Main St., Ilion.

— THE EVENING TELEGRAM – JANUARY 8, 1946

Everybody loves a parade, but what's a parade without a band? And what is a band without uniforms? The newly organized civic band is getting all-ready for our next parade—but they have nothing to wear. (Well, I really mean uniforms.) They have a director...They have over twenty musicians...but no uniforms...Tentative plans are being made by the Fireman to hold a turkey dinner to raise funds for uniforms. It is hoped that there will be lots of interest and a large turnout.

— THE ILION SENTINEL – JANUARY 17, 1946

The New York State Education Department had recently recommended the employment of a dental hygienist which the Ilion system has now actively engaged.

— THE EVENING TELEGRAM – DECEMBER 18, 1946

It is expected that within the next few years more than 300,000 stores will handle frozen foods as compared to the 50,000 at present.

— THE EVENING TELEGRAM – FEBRUARY 3, 1947

Town and village crews Ilion, Mohawk, Frankfort are today battling the heaviest snowfall of winter which has closed Ilion schools, crippled transportation service, and disrupted electric power lines in each of the three communities. Village and town plows have been operating almost continuously for the better part of 24 hours keeping village roads passable.

— THE EVENING TELEGRAM – MARCH 3, 1947

Remington-Rand has abandoned attempts to operate three strike-bound plants at Ilion and one at Elmira. Company officials turned the keys over to municipal authorities yesterday for protective custody of the three Ilion plants.

— THE AUBURN CITIZEN-ADVERTISER – JULY 17, 1947

The multicolored Christmas lights with their gay holiday wreaths which were lighted in the Ilion business section that this week brightened not only the business streets but also the hearts of many a village resident. It just doesn't seem like Christmas until the lights go up and the holiday wreaths and the trees do up. There's a soft spot in our hearts, too, for the scores of Ilion residents who decorate their homes with Christmas lights.

— THE ILION SENTINEL – DECEMBER 18, 1947

Ilion's reputation as a Republican town has apparently attracted national attention. Elliot Roosevelt brought the house down last night when he referred to this fact at a labor rally last night at the Mohawk Armory. "When I told my mother I was coming to Ilion tonight, she was horrified," Roosevelt told the crowd with a grin." Why you can't go up there, Elliot," she returned, "they didn't even have a Democrat who voted in the last election."

— THE ILION SENTINEL – FEBRUARY 5, 1948

Important steps in a planned campaign to improve parking and traffic congestion in Ilion's streets, especially the business section, are being taken by the Village Board. ...One of the most important will be making First Street a one-way street wet from Otsego Street to Morgan Street with parking allowed on both sides and certain loading zones designated along these two blocks.

— THE ILION SENTINEL – JUNE 3, 1948

The day is not too distant when all of Ilion's residential streets will be as brilliantly lighted as the business section...The installation of the lights through the village won't be overnight. It takes time and money, but the commissions have a long-range program for installing them first on the important streets and intersections and eventually on all streets.

— ILION CITIZEN – JULY 29, 1948

Ilion businessmen were in conference with Old Man Winter last night, for all that is needed to insure success tomorrow of Economy Day is good weather. Local merchants have gone "all-out" in this first post-holiday sale to offer special bargains for valley shoppers, and downtown streets are expected to be crowded throughout the day and tomorrow night. Sales will start at 9 a.m. and will continue through tomorrow evening with virtually every store planning to remain open to accommodate shoppers after working hours.

— THE ILION SENTINEL – FEBRUARY 24, 1949

Nearly 1000 children marched in a Halloween parade in Ilion last night, with prizes being awarded for the outstanding costumes.

— THE EVENING TELEGRAM – NOVEMBER 1, 1949

More than 2,100 music-lovers attended the first summer band concert of the season at Ilion's Russell Park last night, and another capacity crowd is expected for the second program next Wednesday night.

— THE ILION SENTINEL – JULY 13. 1950

Mrs. [Harry] Truman's gift [was] the top item for sale at Ilion's Episcopal Church bazaar...the package from Mrs. Truman contained an etching of the White House.

— UTICA OBSERVER-DISPATCH – DECEMBER 8, 1950

Signed petitions, totaling 1,068 names who were against the installation of parking meters, failed to sway the village board last night and the meters will be installed approximately July 1.

— THE EVENING TELEGRAM – APRIL 18, 1951

The Ilion Cut-Rate Market, where "BUDGET MINDED HOUSEWIVES WILL GRAB AT THESE SPECIALS," offered "Well-Trimmed Sirloin steaks @ $.89/lb., Porterhouse for $.95, and Ground Beef @ $.69."

— THE ILION SENTINEL – JULY 12, 1951

A "Bicycle Ordinance, " comprised of 14 Sections, for the Village of Ilion stated in Section 5 that "the Chief of Police for the Village of Ilion is hereby authorized, upon application of the owner of each bicycle, to issue to each owner a registration card and a metallic registration plate, which registration plate shall bear the name and address of the bicycle owner, a registration number which shall correspond to the number on the registration plate...

— THE ILION SENTINEL – JULY 19, 1951

More than 200 workers will canvass the village tomorrow between 7 and 8 p. m. for signatures to the Freedom Scroll and donations for the Crusade for Freedom. Residents of the village interested in furthering the cause of spreading freedom throughout the world are asked to leave a light shining from a window or on the front porch.

— THE EVENING TELEGRAM – OCTOBER 8, 1951

A bit of Hollywood will be transplanted to Ilion next Saturday afternoon when a quartet of famous actors will appear here in connection with a nation-wide "Movietown" campaign...it is known that a group including Greer Garson, Victor Jory, Audrey Trotter, and Sterling Hayden, is scheduled to be in Ilion next Tuesday afternoon at 4:15. The village is erecting a platform in front of the Municipal Building, and it is here that the stars will be greeted by the local welcoming Committee.

— THE ILION SENTINEL – APRIL 17, 1952

The Little Theater Club has been invited to put on a play at the State Fair in Syracuse on Tuesday, September 8 at 5 p.m. Mrs. Lloyd Elston will direct a scene from "Midsummer Night's Dream."

— THE SENTINEL NEWSPAPERS – SEPTEMBER 1, 1953

Parents of Ilion boys and girls were asked today by the Police Department to warn their children against pre-Halloween pranks that damage property. Police said residents of West Hill are incensed over several pranks so far this week. In a section where several new homes are just being built windows were broken by thrown stones sometime Monday night. The homes were on Hall Street.

— THE ILION SENTINEL – OCTOBER 1, 1953

Traffic violators in Ilion will now face stiffer penalties, the Police Department announced today, pointing out fines have been raised from $3 to $5 in an effort to reduce carelessness. The new fine, already in force is levied for drivers arrested while passing red lights or driving through stop signs.

— THE EVENING TELEGRAM – JULY 24, 1954

Valley men given golden opportunity to join needed Husbands Protective Association, a national organization which understands the plight of the married man and attempts to make the going for him much easier.

— THE SENTINEL NEWSPAPERS – NOVEMBER 22, 1954

School health officials and parents were still seeing spots before their eyes this week—and the odds are the spots will be around for a few more weeks. The spots are measles and chicken pox, and Ilion is literally loaded. The official count last night was 362 cases…of this number, more than 300 children were out in the five grade schools.

— THE ILION SENTINEL – JANUARY 6, 1955

Ceremony marks Arms ten millionth sporting gun…the gun is a premier grade Sportsman-58 autoloading shotgun and sold inlaid and delicately engraved and in marked contrast to the first muzzle-loading flintlock produced by hand by Eliphalet Remington on a farm forge 141 years ago.

— THE EVENING TELEGRAM – MAY 20, 1957

Details of Gov. Nelson Rockefeller's reelection campaign swing through Valley communities were announced today...Rockefeller will...proceed in a motorcade eastward over Route 5-S, traveling slowly through the main streets of Frankfort and Ilion to the Remington Arms plant...he will be conducted on a 45-minute tour of the plant...From 10:35 to 11, he will make a sidewalk tour of the Ilion business district.

— THE EVENING TELEGRAM – SEPTEMBER 24, 1962

About 250 youths, one of the biggest crowds of her summer, turned out last night for a dance sponsored by the Ilion Youth Center, Otsego Street. The boys and girls danced from 8 to 11 p.m. to music by The Manhattans.

— THE EVENING TELEGRAM – AUGUST 23, 1963

A review of the new rules and regulations governing the police department will be made by the Village Board and Chief Maurice Goldin at a meeting last night. The new regulations...are the first major changes in the department's law in more than 40 years. The last regulations were adopted in 1920.

— THE EVENING TELEGRAM – NOVEMBER 10, 1964

Union Street in Ilion in 1885 was a dirt thoroughfare with plank sidewalks...The street in later years boasted ten saloons and was dubbed "Saloon Alley" or "Saloon Belt."

— THE EVENING TELEGRAM – JUNE 11, 1966

On January 2, 1968, the Best Garage, for years open 24 hours a day, seven days a week, clothes doors permanently in the path of urban renewal.

— THE EVENING TELEGRAM – JANUARY 2, 1968

Two professional exterminator companies have been hired to control a sudden problem of rats invading the residential area near the Ilion dump...three reasons given for this migration were that the rodents' food source was cut off by a fire, earth being used to cover the dump, and the closing of the area for the depositing of refuse.

— THE EVENING TELEGRAM – JULY 23, 1971

Construction begins on Ye Old Dog House in Ilion on June 5, 1971.

— THE EVENING TELEGRAM – JANUARY 1, 1972

UNIVAC's Plant 2 on Spruce St., where more than 6,000 people once worked, but which is now virtually shut down, has been sold...With the sale of Plant 2, Sperry Rand is virtually out of Ilion. The Remington Arms Company purchased Plant 3 on East Main Street in January and will complete the purchase of Plant 1 on Clark St. in June and will use them for possible expansion.

— UTICA OBSERVER-DISPATCH – MARCH 3, 1973

Although state law permits teachers to administer corporal punishment in restraining and correcting pupils, most area schools resort to this form only as a last resort or not at all...The Ilion Central School is another area school following the state policy with no written school policy in existence, according to James Dunn, superintendent.

— THE EVENING TELEGRAM – DECEMBER 6, 1973

Ilion Board to vote on cable tv rate hike...Teleprompter is seeking an amendment to its Ilion village franchise seeking an increasing of its monthly service rate from $5 to $6.95 and the monthly rate for additional services from $1 to $1.50.

— THE EVENING TELEGRAM – JUNE 11, 1974

There was no idle banter, no chuckles, no greeting of friends and neighbors at Powers News Room in Ilion last Sunday morning. No talk of weather or the New York Yankees or last night's high school basketball game. "Here we go again," said the glum faced as regular customers came in. "How do we say it in a different way?" They were telling their customers that at 6 on Sunday evening Powers News would close its doors for the last time.

— UTICA OBSERVER-DISPATCH – MARCH 16, 1983

Getting millions of people [i.e. – New Yorkers] to separate their garbage for recycling obviously won't be easy. But don't tell that to Ilion's administrator, Allen Staring, who is forging ahead with a fledgling village program...Starting in early December, Staring asked Ilion residents to participate in a trial separation of paper products...Soon the village enterprise will move into high-gear with residents being asked to separate glass and metals, too.

— UTICA OBSERVER-DISPATCH – JANUARY 14, 1987

ACKNOWLEDGMENTS

One of the more enjoyable aspects of writing about local history is that an author usually does not have to travel far in search of resources, in particular the human kind because they are often found just around the corner or down the street. So, it was fortunate for me that the Ilion Free Public Library was located but three blocks away, a storehouse bursting with a treasure trove of primary source materials related to the village's history. But, if this repository proved a gold mine of information, then one of its curators had to be considered an absolute gem.

That individual was Jean Putch—IHS Class of '54. Not only was she a master of the library's "Ilion Room" and its holdings, able and eager to help me unlock its secrets, but she was also a lifelong resident of the village which made her a valuable resource unto herself. As a result, I looked forward to my visits to the library, timed for Wednesday afternoons when her shift ran from 1 o'clock to 5 o'clock. I went each time with a couple of topics about which I wanted to gather information. With Jean's help, I usually left with more than I anticipated finding. In addition, I also departed with valuable pieces of uncatalogued information, for we also talked about what each remembered regarding the town. Sometimes they were personal vignettes of a shared experience. On other occasions, because we grew up in different eras, the recollection was about a place, a person, or an event about which one or the other of us was unfamiliar.

Now in the opposite direction from the library, four blocks southwest of my home, can be found another prized asset of the community, one who like Jean is also a lifelong inhabitant of Ilion. In this instance, the gentleman was the Hon. James Garnsey—IHS Class of '49. A five-term mayor of Ilion, Jim possessed a fountain of information on village history, either because he lived it or made it. Like Jean, he was more than willing to share his memories of a place which he recalled from many different perspectives, among them those being a student, employee, resident, parent, coach, and elected official. Part of Jim's enduring charm is that he is never at a loss for words, many of them fashioned into colorful stories that he remembers about a long-ago event or an individual whom he knew. It was my good fortune to spend several afternoons interviewing him about his thoughts, opinions, and recollections on topics from Ilion's past. Like the time spent with Jean, these sessions were both enjoyable and informative experiences.

I am deeply indebted to Jean Putch and Jim Garnsey and wish to thank them for the time and knowledge which they so willingly shared with me. In their own unassuming ways, they are representative of the Ilion in which I grew up—a close-knit, nurturing community where someone was always willing to help another person out, a town comprised of many civic-minded individuals willing to step forward and shoulder responsibilities for the good of all. Among these volunteers could be found Little League coaches, Girl Scout den mothers, PTA committee members, civil defense workers, church bazaar organizers, and parade coordinators. These Samaritans engaged in such acts of kindness not with the expectation of personal gain or reward, but rather because extending such unselfish assistance to a neighbor or the village was the norm in life "back in the day."

While I did not spend the same amount of time with him as I did Mrs. Putch, her replacement when she retired was a young man named Michael Disotelle. Like his predecessor, he too was most helpful. Mike has become quite well-versed in Ilion's history, knowledge which he shares with the public in many ways. One of his popular efforts has been "Throwback Thursday," when each week he posts old photographs of Ilion on the library's Facebook page. Recently, in monumental achievement, he has digitized almost one-hundred years of Ilion High School yearbooks, a real boon to former graduates.

For the most part, those people who played parts in the formative years of my life are all gone now. But during the first twelve years of my existence, the world I inhabited encompassed the block created by South Third Ave, Grove Street, South Fourth Ave, and Second Street— five houses or buildings on its northern and southern ends and about sixteen to eighteen homes on the longer western and eastern sides— around fifty structures altogether.

On the northern boundary of "my block," Jordan's Pharmacy and Woody's Grocery were located close together on the corner of Second Street and South Third Avenue. Champagne's Market was on the opposite, northeastern corner of South Third. Across Second to the west and easily accessible were Klippel's variety store and West Hill Elementary School. While both of those stores and the school were "across the street," they were nevertheless integral parts of the extended neighborhood,

Heading a block south led to Grove Street, where my grandfather Bennett's house along with those of the Jones', Runge's, and Jensen's were located; then, proceeding west around the corner to South Fourth Avenue's east side resided the Nasons and the O'Connells. Across the street from them lived the Walkers, Kerrs and Colburns, facing the block but not actually on it.

At the Grove Street end of South Third, one up from the corner was number 88, our house, inhabited by Joe, Ruth, Nancy, Kevin, and Harold—respectively my dad, mom, sister, brother, and uncle—on our right were the Adams and to the left were the Kerrs, Rapenskis, and Snyders, while across from us resided the Schalpes, the Halls, and the Joneses. The latter three—again not on our block—but by their proximity and friendliness still a part of the neighborhood.

Though predominantly a blue-collar area, a few professionals and businessmen could be found in the mix. Three of the women were elderly, but in my days none from any of the other families with children—ten in number—had mothers who worked outside of the home.

My world, for its first eleven years, constituted a finite existence in a warm, safe, and nurturing neighborhood, one from which no family ever moved. Fences did not exist, nor did most folks lock their doors. While none of these neighbors necessarily made any overt, specific contributions to my personal history in the same vein as my parents or grandfather did, they all subtly had an impact on me during my formative years. Without their collective influences as caring families, good friends, watchful neighbors, and role models, the individual writing this book would be of an entirely different character today, as would the perspectives and impressions which formed the bedrock of thoughts and values that went into creating this written history.

Two other groups which should be thanked profusely are those of the teachers, administrators, and support staff at West Hill School between 1952 and 1959 and those at the Ilion Junior-Senior High School from 1959 to 1965. Collectively they provided me with a quality education, instilled self-confidence in a shy boy, and most significantly engendered a career goal from which I never wavered. Having been so impressed by their devotion to a chosen calling that to join their professional ranks as an educator myself became an objective imbedded in me at a young age, giving me a purpose and direction in life that proudly carried me through a forty-seven year career.

As has been the case with my two previous books, family members also contributed to the successful completion of this effort too. My daughter-in-law Laurena did a fabulous job with the formatting, along with teaching me the value of using "Dropbox" as a safe repository. Then my son Bob contributed his usual map-drawing and picture-retouching skills to round out the finished product.

While my hand may have written this book, it was held and guided by many others along the way.

END NOTES

INTRODUCTION

1. www.brainyquotes.com
2. Bruce Springsteen, "Your Hometown." Columbia Records, 1995, Track on "Born in the USA" album

1. EARLY SETTLEMENT:

1. H. Paul Draheim, "Indian Land Deed Dated 1722, Before Arrival," *Evening Telegram*, May 15, 1976, p. 4
2. "Only Roots Remain Now of Legendary Ilion Elm," *Utica Observer-Dispatch*, July, 1923
3. Nelson Greene, *History of the Mohawk Valley: Gateway to the West*. Chicago: The S. J. Clarke Publishing Co., 1925. p. 511
4. *Evening Telegram*, May 15, 1976, p. 4
5. Ibid., p. 520
6. Ibid
7. "Part Two—The Massacre at Palatine Village, Herkimer, New York," *Legacy*, Herkimer County Historical Society, 2007, p. 2
8. Peter Silver, *Our Savage Neighbors*. New York: W. W. Norton & Company, Inc., 2008, p. 46
9. *Evening Telegram*, October 31, 1981, p. 4
10. *Evening Telegram*, May 15, 1976, p. 4

2. PRESENT AT THE CREATION:

1. *The Ilion Citizen*, August 24, 1916, p. 1

3. THE ERIE CANAL:

1. *Herkimer Evening Telegram*, December 11, 1962, p. 4
2. www.canals.ny.gov/history/history.html
3. Lionel D. Wyld, *Low Bridge! Folklore and the Erie Canal*. Syracuse: Syracuse University Press, 1962, p. 11
4. Peter Bernstein, *Wedding of the Waters: The Erie Canal and the Making of a Great Nation.* New York: W.W. Norton & Co., 2005, p. 311

5. Mildred Baker, *The Erie Canal," Essay in Bound Volume of Ilion Historical Society Papers*, 1951, p. 536

6. Warren Schulz, Ilion—The Town That Remington Made. Hicksville: Exposition Press, 1977, p. 128

7. Alden Hatch, *Remington Arms: An American Industry.* New York: Rinehart & Company, Inc., 1956, p. 34

8. Mildred Baker, "The Erie Canal," Essay in Bound Volume of Ilion Historical Society Papers, 1951, p. 536

9. Ernie, Sitts, "Debris-Laden Ditch Vanishing Reminder of Once Busy Canawl," *Utica Observer-Dispatch*, June 6, 1954

10. Ibid.

11. Ibid.

12. Mildred Baker, "The Erie Canal," Bound Volume of Ilion Historical Society Papers, 1951, p. 536

13. Ibid.

14. Mary Edwards, "The Glamour of the Erie Canal Lives in the Past," *Utica Observer-Dispatch*, January 27, 1963, p. 28

15. Emily Denton, "Relics of Old Canal Lingered Long After," *Herkimer Evening Telegram*, April 16, 1981

16. Ibid.

17. *Utica Observer-Dispatch*, January 31, 1934

18. Ibid.

19. Ibid.

20. Margaret Hall, "The History of Ilion," Paper presented to the Ilion Historical Club, 1948, currently in possession of the Ilion Free Public Library

4. LET US CALL OUR VILLAGE ILION:

1. William R. Farrell, *Classical Place Names in New York State: Origins, Histories, and Meanings.* Jamesville: The Grove Press, 2002, p. 1

2. *Ilion Citizen*, September 18, 1919, p. 1

3. *Utica Daily Press*, "Choosing a Name for Ilion," Loose-leaf Volume of Historical Essays, Ilion Public Library

5. THE OCTAGON HOUSE:

1. "Octagon House Memento of Days of Progress Among Ilion Pioneers," *Utica Observer-Dispatch*, October 3, 1948

2. *The Ilion Sentinel*, August 13, 1857, p. 2

3. Ibid.

4. *A Drive Through the Architectural History of Ilion-Mohawk-Herkimer Villages*, 1960, p. 18

5. Ibid.

6. THE PASSING OF LINCOLN'S FUNERAL TRAIN:

1. John C. Power, *Abraham Lincoln: His Life, Public Services, Death and Great Funeral.* Chicago: H. W. Rokker, 1889, pp. 115-116

7. MANSION ON THE HILL:

1. Mary Ellen Leonard, "Remington's Famous Mansion," *The Upstate Monthly*, August 1942, p. 19
2. Alden Hatch, *Remington Arms, an American History.* New York: Rinehart & Company, Inc., 1956, p. 146
3. K.D. Kirkland, *America's Premier Gunmakers: Remington.* East Bridgewater, MA: World Publishing Group, Inc., 2014, p. 34
4. George Layman, *The Military Remington Rolling Block Rifle (Expanded Edition).* Prescott: Wolfe Publishing Company, 1992, p. 3
5. Ibid. p. 144
6. Leonard, p. 19
7. Ibid.
8. C. Vance Haynes, Jr, *General Custer and his Sporting Rifles.* Tucson Westernlore Press, 1995, p. 50
9. Ibid.
10. Ibid.
11. Hatch, p. 149
12. *Utica Observer-Dispatch*, February 22, 1928, p. 11
13. The conservatory was a greenhouse, while the formal parlor was also known as the drawing room.
14. Leonard, p. 19
15. Ibid.
16. Hatch, p. 149
17. *Utica Observer-Dispatch*, September 30, 1920, p. 16
18. *Utica Observer Dispatch*, March 9, 1928, p. 20
19. *Fort Plain Standard*, April 3, 1928, p. 4
20. Ibid.
21. *Utica Observer-Dispatch*, April 12, 1928, p. 32
22. *Utica Daily Press*, April 1, 1928, p. 20
23. *Utica Observer-Dispatch*, February 22, 1928, p. 11

8. MABEN'S OPERA HOUSE

1. John Zavinski, "19th Century Opera House Gave Small Town High Culture," *Life & Times*, December 2010, p. 22
2. Ibid.
3. *Utica Morning Herald*, April 16, 1878, p. 2
4. Ibid.

5. H. Paul Draheim, "Ghosts and Phantoms at the Opera House," *Utica Daily Press*, September 22, 1984, p. 4

6. Ibid.

7. Ilion 1852-1952, *Ilion: Ilion Centennial Commission*, 1952, p. 51

8. *Ilion Citizen*, August 25, 1882, p. 2

9. United States Department of Labor

10. www.careertrend.com/salaries-in-the-1880s

11. *Ilion Citizen*, October 7, 1881, p. 4

12. *Ilion Citizen*, February 28, 1882, p. 2

13. *Ilion Citizen*, August 19, 1881, p. 2

14. "Curtain's About to be Rung Down on Maben's Opera House in Ilion," *Utica Observer-Dispatch*, September 7, 1946, p. 7C

15. *Ilion Citizen*, October 1, 1893, p. 5

16. *Utica Morning Herald and Gazette*, January 29, 1883, p. 2

17. *The Ilion Citizen*, January 5, 1883, p. 2

18. Ibid.

19. Ibid.

20. George Hardin and Frank Willard, *The History of Herkimer County*. Syracuse: D. Mason & Co., Pubishers,1893, p. 171

21. History of Herkimer County, p. 231

22. *Ilion Citizen*, October24 , 1912, p. 1

23. Draheim, p. 4

24. Ilion 1852-1952, Ilion: Ilion Centennial Committee, 1952

25. Ibid.

26. "Curtain's About to be Rung Down on Maben's Opera House in Ilion," *Utica Observer-Dispatch*, September 7, 1946, p. 7C

27. *Ilion Sentinel*, June 1954, p. 6

9. THE SPANISH BALL:

1. George Layman, The Military Remington Rolling Block Rifle (Extended Edition). Prescott: Wolfe Publishing Company, 1992, p. xvi

2. H. Paul Draheim, Ghosts and Phantoms at the Opera House." *Herkimer Evening Telegram*, September 22, 1984, p. 4

3. "Brilliant Reception by the Gentlemen of Ilion for the Spanish Ordinance Commission," *Utica Morning Herald*, December 19, 1874, p. 2

4. Draheim, p. 4

5. Draheim, p. 4.

6. Margaret Hall, "The History of Ilion," Ilion: Bound volume of papers by the Ilion Historical Club, 1948, Ilion Free Public Library

7. Ibid.

8. *Utica Observer-Dispatch*, August 7, 1949, p. 9

9. *Herkimer Democrat*, December 19, 1874, p. 1

10. Draheim, p. 4

11. "Brilliant Reception by the Gentlemen of Ilion for the Spanish Ordinance Commission," *Utica Morning Herald*. December 19, 1874, p. 2

10. FRUIT OF THEIR LABORS:

1. *The Utica Daily Observer*, June 21, 1889
2. "Ilion Strawberries," A brief recollection written by Katherine Osterhout Cameron, "Strawberry Growing" file, Ilion Free Public Library, Ilion, NY, p. 2
3. Ibid.
4. *The Glens Falls Morning Star*, June 29, 1893
5. *The Utica Sunday Tribune*, June 24, 1894
6. *The Canajoharie Courier*, June 30, 1899
7. *Richfield Springs Mercury*, June 18, 1932, p. 8
8. *Ilion Citizen*, June 18, 1906, p.6
9. Cameron, p. 1
10. *The Utica Daily Observer*, June 21, 1889
11. Cameron, p. 3
12. *The Utica Daily Observer*, June 21, 1889
13. Cameron, p. 3
14. *Fulton County Republican*, June 15, 1904
15. Cameron, p. 1

11. CHRISTOPHER LATHAM SHOLES:

1. *The Laurenceton Examiner*, February 16, 1924, p. 8
2. *The Little Falls Journal and Courier*, July 24, 1923, p. 1
3. *Brandon Daily Sun*, June 25, 1923, p. 3
4. *Rome Daily Standard*, September 11, 1923, p. 4
5. *Buffalo Evening News*, November 1, 1923, p. 23
6. *Scientific American*, December 15, 1888, p. 375
7. *A Brief History of the Typewriter.* New York: Remington Rand, 1961
8. *Harrisonburg (VA) Daily News-Record*, June 30, 1973 , p. 6
9. Monument inscription in Forest Hill Cemetery, Milwaukee, Wisconsin
10. *Newburyport Daily News*, June 15, 1923, p. 10
11. *The Philadelphia Inquirer*, July 7, 1931, p. 10
12. Ibid.
13. Ibid.
14. *Scientific American*, December 15, 1888, p. 375
15. Ibid.
16. Ibid.

12. BOBBING:

1. "Bobsledding Down Ilion's West Hill was Great Winter Sport in the Old Days," *The Ilion Sentinel*, January 26, 1950
2. *Utica Observer-Dispatch*, January 13, 1957
3. Ibid.
4. Ibid.

5. John Hutchins, *The Narrow Way.* Utica: T. J. Griffiths, Printer, 1891, p. 472
6. *Utica Observer-Dispatch*, January 13, 1957
7. Evidence indicates that John Street, south off Second Street near its bottom, may also have been used for runs. However, the length of the grade is only about a fifth that of West Hill. It may be that this side route was a Victorian version of a bunny or beginner's slope.
8. Ibid., p. 471
9. "Social History of Ilion," Margaret Hall, paper presented before the Ilion Historical Club, 1948, Bound Collection, Ilion Free Public Library
10. Ella Dimmock, Ilion History Collection, Vol. 12, p. 113
11. "Social History of Ilion," Margaret Hall, paper presented before the Ilion Historical Club, 1948, Bound Collection, Ilion Free Public Library
12. Ella Dimock, Ilion History Collection, Vol. 12, p. 113
13. Ibid.
14. *The Ilion Sentinel*, February 26, 1950, p. 4
15. Aileen Carney, "Who was on the Red Cloud Crew: Asked the Ilion Sentinel January 26, 1950?" www.ilionalumni.com
16. *The Ilion Citizen*, May 7, 1883, p. 4
17. *The Ilion Citizen*, February 22, 1884, p. 2
18. Ibid.
19. *Utica Weekly Herald and Gazette and Courier*, February 19, 1884, p. 4
20. *The Ilion Citizen*, February 22, 1884, p. 2
21. *Utica Weekly Herald and Gazette and Courier*, February 19, 1884, p.
22. *The Ilion Citizen*, February 29, 1884, p. 2
23. Ibid.

13. DRILLING FOR OIL:

1. *Utica Observer-Dispatch*, July 8, 1961
2. *The Otsego Farmer*, February 25, 1921, p. 1
3. Ibid.
4. Ibid.
5. "50 Awesome Quotes on Risk Taking," www.huffpost.com

14. THE SILENT SENTINEL:

1. Cara Giamo, "Those Mass-Produced Civil War Statues Were Meant to Stand Forever." *Atlas Obscura Newsletter*, August, 2017
2. Chris Carola, "Silent Sentinels Still on Guard in North, South." *The Valley News*, April 19, 2015, p. B7
3. Ibid.
4. *Herkimer Citizen*, May 7, 1905.
5. Carola, p. 57
6. *Herkimer Citizen*, May 7, 1905
7. *Ilion Citizen*, May 31, 1906, p. 1
8. Giamo

9. Ibid.
10. Philo Scrapbook, Ilion Free Public Library, p. 10
11. The official designation of Memorial Day as the last Monday in May took place at the federal level in 1968, with all 50 States eventually following suit over the next few years.
12. Ernie Sitts, "He Started Lonely Vigil 54 Years Ago." *The Evening Telegram*, May 28, 1960, p. 9
13. *Ilion Citizen*, May 31, 1906, p. 1
14. Ibid.
15. *Herkimer Citizen*, May 7, 1905
16. *Ilion Citizen*, May 31, 1906, p. 4
17. Sitts, p. 9

15. HATS-OFF TO REMINGTON ARMS:

1. *Ilion Citizen*, August 31, 1916, p. 1
2. Ibid.
3. *Ilion Citizen*, March 2, 1916, p. 4
4. Ibid.
5. *Utica Daily Press*, September 18, 1915, p. 15
6. *The Syracuse Herald*, January 7, 1916, p. 24
7. *Utica Daily Press*, September 15, 1915, p. 15
8. *Utica Herald Dispatch*, August 29, 1016, p. 7
9. Ibid.
10. *Utica Daily Press*, August 29, 1916, p. 4
11. *Ilion Citizen*, August 31, 1916, p. 5
12. Ibid.
13. *Ilion Citizen*, July 27, 1916, p. 4
14. *Ilion Citizen*, August 24, 1916, p. 1
15. *Utica Herald-Dispatch, August 29, 1916, p. 7*
16. *Bismarck Daily Tribune*, September 1, 1916, p. 2
17. *The Bridgeport Evening Farmer*, August 31, 1916, p. 12
18. *Cumberland Evening Times*, July 27, 1933, p. 9
19. *WSSA Newsletter*, Jan-April 2018, p. 2
20. *The New York Telegram*, July 9, 1916
21. "Remington Centennial," Booklet published by the Remington Society
22. *Ilion Citizen*, August 24, 1961, p. 1
23. *The Bridgeport Evening Farmer*, November 19, 1916, p. 6
24. *Ilion Citizen*, July 27, 1916, p. 1
25. *The Otsego Farmer*, September 1, 1916, p. 1
26. *Elyria Chronicle Telegram*, January 21, 2013, p.3
27. *The New York Evening Post*, August 25, 1916, p. 15
28. *Utica Herald-Dispatch*, August 21, 1916, p. 3
29. *The Ilion Citizen*, August 24, 1916, p. 1
30. Ibid.
31. *Ilion Citizen*, August 27, 1916, p. 5
32. *Ilion Citizen*, August 31, 1916, p. 1

33. *The Utica Observer*, August 31, 1916, p. 1
34. Ibid.
35. Ibid.
36. "Remington Centennial Historical Souvenir Programme"
37. *The Utica Observer*, August 31, 1916, p. 1
38. Ibid.
39. *Ilion Citizen*, August 24, 1916, p. 1
40. In the hundred-plus years since the dedication, two significant changes have occurred: (1) although seven chapters of the United States Daughters of 1812 still exist in New York today, the Ilion chapter is no longer one of them; and (2) due to a widening of the highway in recent years, the plaque-bearing boulder had to be relocated to the opposite side of the road and, in order to be read, placed facing in the opposite or wrong direction.
41. *Utica Herald-Dispatch*, August 29, 1916, p. 7
42. Ibid.
43. *Utica Herald-Dispatch*, Wednesday, August 30, 1916, p. 3
44. Ibid.

16. THE CENTENARY CONTINUES:

1. *Utica Herald-Dispatch*, August 30, 1916, p. 3
2. *Ilion Citizen*, September 5, 1916, p. 1
3. *Utica Herald-Dispatch*, August 30, 1916, p. 3
4. *Utica Daily Press*, August 29, 1916
5. Ibid
6. Ibid.
7. *The Little Falls Journal and Courier*, September 5, 1916, p. 1
8. *Ilion Citizen*, August 31, 1916, p. 4
9. *Utica Daily Press*, August 31, 1916, p. 3
10. Ibid.
11. Ibid.
12. *Utica Herald-Dispatch*, August 31, 1916, p. 3
13. *The Utica Observer*, August 31, 1916, p. 10
14. Ibid.
15. Ibid.
16. *Utica Daily Press*, September 1, 1916, p. 8
17. *The Utica Observer*, August 31, 1916, p. 10
18. Ibid.
19. Ibid.
20. *Utica Herald-Dispatch*, June 14, 1920, p. 17
21. *Ilion Citizen*, August 24, 1916, p. 7
22. Ibid.
23. *Utica Daily Press*, September 1, 1916, p. 8
24. *Ilion Citizen*, August 29, 1916, p. 1
25. *The Utica Herald Tribune*, August 20, 1916, p. 6
26. Ibid.
27. *Richfield Springs Mercury*, July 17, 1916

28. *The Utica Observer*, August 30, 1916, p. 10
29. *The Syracuse Herald*, August 27, 1916, p. 17
30. *Ilion Citizen*, September 7, 1916, p. 5
31. *The Little Falls Journal and Courier*, September 5, 1916, p. 1
32. *Utica Daily Press*, September 1, 1916, p. 3

17. SAMUEL RUSSELL'S LEGACY:

1. *Utica Observer Dispatch*, August 8, 1949
2. Ibid.
3. *The Evening Telegram*, July 13, 1950, p. 2
4. *The Sentinel*, March 13, 1952, p. 7
5. *The Sentinel*, September 10, 1942, p. 3

18. THE REMINGTON TYPEWRITER COMPANY:

1. Richard Snow, "Christopher Latham Sholes: The Seventy-sixth Inventor of the Typewriter," *American Heritage*, August/September 1972, Volume 33, Issue 5
2. *Journal and Courier*, July 21, 1923, p. 1
3. Ibid.
4. *Utica Observer-Dispatch*, September 9, 1923, p. 1
5. *Utica Observer-Dispatch*, September 11, 1923, p. 4
6. *Utica Observer-Dispatch*, August 14, 1923, p. 4
7. *Little Falls Journal & Courier*, September 18, 1923, p. 1
8. *Utica Observer-Dispatch*, September 12, 1923, p. 1
9. Ibid.
10. Ibid.
11. *The Watertown Daily Standard*, September 17, 1923, p. 7
12. *Utica Observer-Dispatch*, September 12, 1923, p. 7
13. Ibid.
14. *Amsterdam Evening Recorder*, September 13, 1923, p. 14
15. Ibid.
16. Ibid.
17. *Buffalo Evening News*, November 1, 1923, p.23
18. Ibid.
19. *Beacon Daily Herald*, September 29, 1923, p. 8
20. Ibid.
21. Ibid.
22. Ibid.
23. *Utica Observer-Dispatch*, September 12, 1923, p. 1
24. *Amsterdam Evening Recorder*, September 13, 1923, p. 14
25. Ibid.
26. Ibid.
27. *Richfield Springs Mercury*, August 23, 1923, p. 3
28. Ibid.
29. *The Murphysboro Daily Independent*, October 1, 1941, p, 5

30. *Utica Observer-Dispatch*, September 12, 1923, p. 1
31. Ibid.
32. Ibid.

19. GINKGO TREES:

1. Peter Del Tredici, "The Ginkgo in America," *Arnoldia*, Volume 41, #4, July, 1981, p. 150
2. "A Bit of Oriental Life: Elements No Threat to the Ilion Grinko (sic) Tree," *Utica Observer-Dispatch*, May 24, 1953
3. Ibid.

20. THE DEMISE OF THE AMERICAN ELM:

1. *Utica Observer-Dispatch*, May 9, 1962, p. 4
2. *Richfield Springs Mercury*, March 13, 1964, p. 6
3. *Otsego Farmer*, March 9, 1934, p. 5
4. *Schenectady Gazette*, June 8, 1934, p. 8
5. *The Waterville Times*, March 31, 1938, p. 6
6. *The Ilion Sentinel*, December 31, 1947, p. 7
7. Ibid.
8. *Richfield Springs Mercury*, April 25, 1957, p.4
9. *Herkimer Evening Telegram*, July 20, 1949, p. 2
10. *Herkimer Evening Telegram*, August 27, 1969, p. 11
11. Ibid
12. Author's interview with Carol Lincoln, December 13, 2018
13. *Utica Observer-Dispatch*, April 29, 1965, p. 19
14. Ibid.
15. *Utica Observer-Dispatch*, June 16, 1979, p. 7
16. *Herkimer Evening Telegram*, October 6, 1967, p. 3
17. *Utica Observer-Dispatch*, September 11, 1975, p. 11
18. *Utica Observer-Dispatch*, August 3, 1974, p. 1
19. *Herkimer Evening Telegram*, May 21, 1981, p. 5

21. A CAPITOL DESTINATION:

1. In its original setting, the theater was not located on the corner, but rather, as I recall, one storefront to the left or south of First Street. Like so many such settings, over the years different business occupied the corner site. One of the last, if not the last, was a variety type of store—sort of a limited precursor to the convenience stores of today. In straightening out First Street during the course of the urban renewal project, a row of store-fronts along the south side of First Street were removed, the effect of which was to "move" the theater to its present corner location.
2. While more often referenced as a "gargoyle," the term "grotesque" is the correct

architectural name for the subset of building adornments used here, as they do not serve as decorative waterspouts to guard against pools from forming that could eventually lead to leaks.

22. A WAR HERO COMES TO TOWN:

1. *Lubbock Morning Avalanche*, August 1, 1952, p. 1
2. *Fairfield Daily Ledger*, July 31, 1952, p. 1
3. *The Humboldt Times*, August 1, 1952, p. 1
4. *The Fairfield Ledger*, July 31, 1952, p. 1
5. *Utica Observer-Dispatch*, November 11, 1952, p. 1
6. *The Evening Telegram*, November 12, 1952, p. 2
7. Ibid.
8. *Utica Observer-Dispatch*, November 12, 1952. P. 1
9. Ibid.
10. Ibid
11. Ibid.
12. Ibid.
13. Ibid.
14. *The Evening Telegram*, November 12, 1952, p. 4
15. Ibid.

23. AIRPLANE SPOTTING:

1. *The Evening Telegram*, March 20, 1953, p. 6
2. CBS, "Gunsmoke," Episode titled: "Drop Dead," Aired on: September 20, 1952
3. *Utica Observer-Dispatch, April 3, 1953*
4. *Utica Observer-Dispatch*, February 19, 1952
5. *Ilion Sentinel*, June 17, 1954
6. *Utica Observer-Dispatch*, August 1, 1954
7. *Aircraft Recognition for the Ground Observer,* AF Manual 355-10, Department of the Air Force, 1955, p. 1
8. *The Ilion Sentinel*, August 30, 1954, p. 1
9. *Utica-Observer Dispatch*, August 1, 1954
10. Ibid.
11. *The Ilion Sentinel*, November 21, 1952, p. 3
12. *The Evening Telegram*, July 29, 1952, p. 3
13. *Syracuse Post-Standard*, December 29, 1957, p. 18
14. Ibid.
15. Ibid.

24. AN OLD-TIME CHRISTMAS:

1. Harold Whittemore, **Christmas Memories**. Holland Patent: Steffen Publishing Co., 1984, p. 22
2. *Fort Plain Standard*, December 1, 1927, p. 1
3. *The Evening Telegram*, December 24, 1946, p. 2
4. *The Ilion Sentinel*, December 6, 1945, p. 1
5. *The Evening Telegram*, November 18, 1959, p. 2
6. *Utica Observer-Dispatch*, December 3, 1950
7. *The Evening Telegram*, December 6, 1952, p. 3
8. *The Evening Telegram*, November 24, 1958, p. 6
9. *The Evening Telegram*, December 1, 1952, p. 6
10. *The Evening Telegram*, December 23, 1959, p. 9
11. *The Evening Telegram*, Monday, December 7, 1959, p. 2
12. *The Sentinel*, November 20, 1952, p. 1
13. *The Evening Telegram*, December 24, 1952, p. 2
14. Ibid.
15. *The Evening Telegram*, December 21, 1953, p. 5
    Chapter 34
16. Harold Whittemore, **Christmas Memories**. Holland Patent: Steffen Publishing Co., 1984, p. 22

25. A MEMORABLE FALL DAY:

1. "250,000 Hail Nixon in Foe's Home City," *The New York Times*, September 30, 1960, p.1
2. "Kennedy Assails Foreign Policies," *The New York Times*, September 30, 1960, p. 17
3. "Kennedy Raises Hopes of Party Leaders," *The New York Times*, September 29, 1960, p.1
4. "Senator Kennedy to Visit Ilion, Plans Brief Talk," *The Evening Telegram*, September 23, 1960, p. 3
5. A mere 12.4 miles west to east separates the villages of Frankfort, Ilion, Mohawk, and Herkimer with the city of Little Falls
6. Agnes Doyle, "Jack's Ilion Visit Is Called a Shot in the Arm," *Utica Observer-Dispatch*, September 30, 1960
7. East State Street still exists, providing access to the Ilion Bowling Alley and connects with Hope Street to its east
8. Ernie Sitts, "Weather Breaks for Jack," *The Evening Telegram*, September 30, 1960, p. 3
9. Doyle
10. "Time Off for Speech," *Albany Times-Union*, September 28, 1960, p. 2
11. Fate later compensated Mr. Garnsey, when in the mid-sixties he was unexpectedly, but ever so gladly, recruited to chauffeur then Senator Robert Kennedy around the Mohawk Valley.
12. Mary Edwards, "Kennedy Gets Hearty Welcome at His Brief Appearance in Ilion." *The Evening Telegram*, September 30, 1960, p. 3

13. Doyle
14. Mrs. Jean Putch, as told to the author on March 17, 2018.
15. "Ilion High School Students to Attend Kennedy Rally," *The Evening Telegram*, September 28, 1960, p. 2
16. A few months later—on May 5, 1961—a television materialized in Mr. Manion's room again, allowing his students to once more view history as it unfolded, this time in the form of Alan Shepard's suborbital flight into space.
17. *The Evening Telegram*, November 23, 1993, p. 3
18. Sitts
19. www.jfklibrary.org
20. Edwards, p. 3
21. Doyle
22. Ibid.
23. Ibid.
24. Ibid.
25. Ibid.
26. Ed Fennell, "Kennedy Is Up at 8:20 A. M., Fresh as a Daisy," *Albany Times-Union*, September 30, 1960, p. 9
27. John McGraw, "JFK's 1960 Campaign Visit Recalled," *The Evening Telegram*, June 4, 1993, p.3
28. Mary Edwards, "Kennedy Gets Hearty Greeting at his Brief Appearance in Ilion," *The Evening Telegram*, September 29, 1960, p. 3
29. "Kennedy Assails Foreign Policies," *The New York Times*, September 30, 1960, p. 17
30. Sitts
31. McGraw, p. 3
32. Ibid.
33. Ibid.
34. Ibid.

26. URBAN RENEWAL:

1. https//.cars.lovetoknow.com/ownership/statistics
2. Dick Frosch, "Highlights of U.R. in Ilion," *The Evening Telegram*, January 25, 1972, p. 3
3. Bob Kelder, "Ilion Gets Final Plaza Payment ," *The Evening Telegram*, June 30, 1981, p. 1
4. Frosch, "Highlights"
5. Ibid.
6. "UR Agency May Name Heads Next Week," *The Evening Telegram*, October 23, 1965, p. 3
7. Ibid.
8. Dick Frosch, "Voting Tomorrow on Ilion Urban Renewal," *The Evening Telegram*, January 26, 1972, p. 3
9. Editorial, *The Evening Telegram*, January 26, 1972, p. 3
10. James Garnsey, Letter to the author, November 20, 2019
11. Harold Riddell, Letter-to-the-Editor, *The Evening Telegram*, January 26, 1972, p. 3
12. Frosh, "Highlights"

13. Ibid.
14. Editorial
15. Ibid.
16. Bob Kelder, "Resounding "Yes" By Ilion Voters," *The Evening Telegram*, January 28, 1972, p. 1
17. Ibid.
18. Dick Frosch, "Urban Renewal Fate Up to Ilion Voters." *The Evening Telegram*, December 9, 1971, p. 3
19. Bob Kelder, "Resounding "Yes" By Ilion Voters," *The Evening Telegram*, January 28, 1972, p. 1
20. Bob Kelder, "Ilion Gets Final Plaza Payment," *The Evening Telegram*, June 30, 1981, p. 1

27. THE SELLING OF MAIN STREET:

1. National League of Cities: www.nlc.org
2. Polk's Herkimer, Mohawk, Ilion, and Frankfort Directory [for] 1959. Boston: R.L. Polk and Co, 1959,.p. 408-411
3. *Herkimer Evening Telegram*, November 1, 1984, p. 4
4. *Herkimer Evening Telegram*, December 14, 1971, p. 1
5. *Herkimer Evening Telegram*, March 29, 1972, p. 1
6. Ibid.
7. *Herkimer Evening Telegram*, May 12, 1972, p. 7

28. POWERS NEWS STORE:

1. Harold Whittemore, "Ilion Loses a Valued Friend," *Utica Observer-Dispatch*, March 16, 1983, p. 11
2. Ibid.
3. Ibid
4. Ibid.
5. Ibid.

29. BOOTS DAY:

1. Don Laible, "Boots Day—50 Years As A Baseball lifer," www.uticaod.com/article/20150927/BLOGS/309279998
2. Ibid.
3. www.44news.nevy.com/evansville-otters-boots-day-going-strong-51st-consecutive-one-year-baseball-contract
4. *The Evening Telegram*, December 6, 1969, p. 6
5. Tom Healey, "What Is It Like to Be Trade?" Marlins' Straily Knows the Feeling, *The Atlanta Journal Constitution*, July 30, 2017
6. Dick Frosch, "Gene Mauch's Greatest Thrill: Steady Improvement by Boots'," *The Evening Telegram*, October 4, 1971, p. 7

7. *The Utica Daily*-Press, October 11, 1971, p. 21
8. "'Boots Day' Day This Sunday: *The Evening Telegram*, August 4, 1972, p. 7
9. *The Evening Telegram*, December 6, 1969, p. 6
10. Sam Roberts, 'Just How Long Does the Average Major League Career Last?" *The New York Times*, July 15, 2007, p. 6
11. Phone interview by author with "Boots" on June 6, 2019, when he was in Joliet on a road trip with the Otters.
12. *The Utica Observer-Dispatch*, July 1, 1972, p, 7
13. Ibid.
14. Phone interview by author with "Boots" on June 6, 2019, when he was in Joliet on a road trip with the Otters.
15. Ibid
16. Laible
17. Phone interview with "Boots" on June 6, 2019 when he was in Joliet on a road trip with the Otters.
18. Laible
19. www.baseball-reference.com
20. Dick Frosch, "Boots Day Asset to PR Chief," *The Evening Telegram*, October 6, 1971, p. 13
21. Ibid.
22. Ibid.
23. www.reddit.com
24. www.returntonow.net/2017/09/22/85-people-hate-jobs-gallup-poll-says/
25. Frosch, October 6

30. PAINT NIGHT:

1. John McGraw, "Woman Remembers Senior Paint Night as Far Back as 1918." *Herkimer Evening Telegram*, June 21, 1991, p. 3 The Evening Telegram,
2. Ibid.
3. *The Ilion Sentinel*, June 24, 1937, p. 1
4. Warren Schulz, Ilion—*The Town That Remington Built*. Hicksville, Exposition Press, Inc., 1977, p.166
5. John McGraw, "Ilion Board Limits Paint Night to Private Property, Sets Curfew," Herkimer Evening Telegram, June 17, 1991, p. 1
6. John McGraw, "Modified Ilion Paint Night Set For Second Year in a Row," May 6, 1991, p. 3

31. HOT DOGS IN ILION:

1. Phone interview by author with Norm Thomas, June 4, 2018
2. Ibid.
3. Ibid.

32. FROM INCINERATION TO THE BAG SYSTEM:

1. *The Evening Telegram*, January 11. 1986, p. 3
2. *The Evening Telegram*, May 11, 1987, p. 4
3. *The Evening Telegram*, September 16, 1986, p. 1
4. *The Evening Telegram*, May 11, 1987, p. 4
5. *Landfill Costs Will Double*, October 10, 1987
6. Bob Kelder, "Landfill Costs Will Double,"
7. Antoine Clark, "Ilion Facing Garbage Crisis, Special Meeting Set on Issue." *Evening Telegram*, April 11, 1987, p. 1
8. *Evening Telegram*, February 9, 1987, p. 4
9. John McGraw, "Ilion Reports That Recycling is on the Rise." *Evening Telegram*, January 11, 1993, p. 3
10. Letter to the Editor, *Evening Telegram*, August 25, 1992, p. 4

BIBLIOGRAPHY

NEWSPAPERS

Albany Daily Advertiser
Albany Times-Union
Amsterdam Evening Recorder and Daily Democrat
Amsterdam Journal Recorder
Beacon Daily Herald
Bismarck Daily Tribune
Booneville Herald
Brandon (Ont.) Daily Sun
Bridgeport Evening Farmer
Brooklyn Daily Eagle
Buffalo Courier
Buffalo Evening Times
Canandaigua Daily Messenger
Canajoharie Courier
Cumberland Evening Times
Daily Albany Argus
Elyria Chronicle Telegram

Fairfield Daily Ledger
Fort Plain Standard
Fulton County Republican
Glens Falls Daily Times
Glens Falls Morning Star
Herkimer Democrat
Herkimer Evening Telegram
Ilion Citizen
Kerrville (TX) Morning Sun
Kingston (Jamaica) Daily Gleaner
Little Falls Journal & Courier
Lockport Daily Journal
Lubbock Morning Avalanche
Mt. Vernon Argus
Oswego Palladium-Times
Oswego Times & Express
Otsego Farmer
Richfield Springs Mercury
Rome Daily Sentinel
Syracuse Herald
Syracuse Post-Standard
The Canajoharie Radii
The Chillicothe Constitution-Tribune
The Daily Graphic
The Groton Journal and Courier
The Homer Republican
The Humboldt Times
The Ilion News
The Ilion Sentinel
The Livonia Gazette
The Mancelona Herald
The Murphysboro Daily Independent
The New York Evening Post
The New York Times
The New York World Gazette

The Peoples' Friend
The Philadelphia Inquirer
The Sabbath Recorder
The Sporting News
The St. Johnsville Enterprise
The Troy Daily Times
The Utica Daily Observer
The Waterloo Observer
The Watertown Daily Standard
The Watertown Times
Utica Daily Press
Utica Daily Tribune
Utica Herald-Dispatch
Utica Morning Herald
Utica Observer-Dispatch
Utica Saturday Globe
Utica Sentinel and Gazette
Utica Weekly Herald and Gazette and Courier
Walton Advertiser
Warren Republican
Wyndham Journal

PAMPHLETS

A Drive Through to the Architectural History of Ilion-Mohawk-Herkimer Villages, 1960

A Brief History of the Typewriter, New York City, Remington Rand, 1961

Ilion: 1852-1952. Ilion: Ilion Centennial Committee, 1952

Ilion, New York Sesquicentennial Celebration 1852-2002, Ilion: Ilion Sesquicentennial Committee, 2002

Souvenir Book of Ilion of the Anniversary of Ilion Lodge No. 400 of
the Independent Order of Odd Fellows, Ilion, 1924

PERIODICALS

Carola, Chris, "Silent Sentinels Still on Guard North, South." *The
Valley News*, April 19, 2015

Del Tredici, Peter, "The Gingko in America," *Arnoldia*, Volume 1, #4,
July 1984

Giamo, Cara, "Those Mass-Produced Civil War Monuments Were
Meant to Last Forever," *Atlas Obscura*, August 25, 2017

Leonard, Mary Ellen, "Remington's Famous Mansion," *The Upstate
Monthly*, August 1942

"Remington Typewriter," *Scientific American*, Vol. LIX, No. 24,
December 15, 1888

Snow, Richard, "Christopher Sholes: The Seventy-sixth Inventor of the
Typewriter, August/September 1982, Volume 33, Issue 5

Zavinski, John, "19th Century Opera Houses Gave Small Towns High
Culture." *Life & Times*, December 2010, p. 22

PRIMARY SOURCES

Cameron, Katherine Osterhout, "Ilion Strawberries," Essay, Ilion Free
Public Library, Ilion, NY

Hall Kevin, Ilion: My Childhood, My Memories. Rochester: Self-
Published, 2021

Hutchins, James H., The Narrow Way. Utica: T. J. Griffiths, Printer, 1891

Whittemore, Harold, Christmas Memories. Holland Patent: Steffen Publishing Co., 1984

SECONDARY SOURCES

Bernstein, Peter, Wedding of the Waters: The Erie Canal and the Making of a Great Nation. New York: W. W. Norton & Co., 2005

Farrell, William R., Classical Place Names in New York State: Origins, Histories, & Meanings. Jamesville: The Grove Press, 2007

Greene, Nelson (Ed.), History of the Mohawk Valley.: Gateway to the West Volume II. Chicago: The S. J. Clarke Publishing Company, 1925

Hall, Margaret, "Social History of Ilion," Paper Presented to the Ilion Historical Club, 1948, Ilion Public Library

Hardin, George, The History of Herkimer County, New York. Syracuse: D. Mason & Co., Pub., 1893

Hardin, George A. & Frank H. Willard, History of Herkimer County. Syracuse: D. Mason & Co., Publishers, 1893

Hatch, Alden, Remington Arms. New York: Schuster & Co., 1956

Haynes, Jr., C. Vance, General Custer and his Sporting Rifles. Tucson: Westernlore Press, 1995

Herbert, Edgar, How to Study Local History. Portland: J. Weston Walch, Pub., 1965

Ilion Alumni Website

Kirkland, KD, America's Premier Gunmakers: Remington. East Bridgewater, MA: World Publishing Group, Inc., 2014

Layman, George, The Military Remington Rolling Block Rifle (Expanded Edition). Prescott: Wolfe Publishing Company, 1992

Peterson, Harold, The Remington Historical Treasury of American Guns, New York: Thomas Nelson & Sons, 1966

Polk's Herkimer, Mohawk, Ilion, and Frankfort Directory [for] 1959. Boston: R. L. Polk & Co., 1960

Schulz, Warren, Ilion—The Town Remington Made. Hicksville: Exposition Press, 1977

Silver, Peter, Our Savage Neighbors. New York: W. W. Norton & Company, Inc., 2008

Swarthout, Elwyn, Stable in the Sticks. Ardmore: Dorrance & Company, 1979

Whittemore, Harold E., Christmas Memories. Holland Patent: Steffen Publishing Co., 1984

www.emotions.com

www.thevalleyside.com

Wyld, Lionel D., Low Bridge! Folklore and the Erie Canal. Syracuse: Syracuse University Press, 1962

INTERVIEWS

"Boots" Day, *former Major League baseball player (2)*
James Garnsey, *former Mayor of Ilion (3)*
Kevin Hall, *former Ilion resident*
Tim Parisi, *Ilion Chief of Police*
Jean Putch, *curator of the Ilion Room of the Ilion Public Library (5)*
Bill Remmers, *former Ilion resident*
Joe Smith, *former Ilion resident*
Christine Sweeney, *former Ilion resident*

INDEX

B

Made in the USA
Middletown, DE
13 January 2022